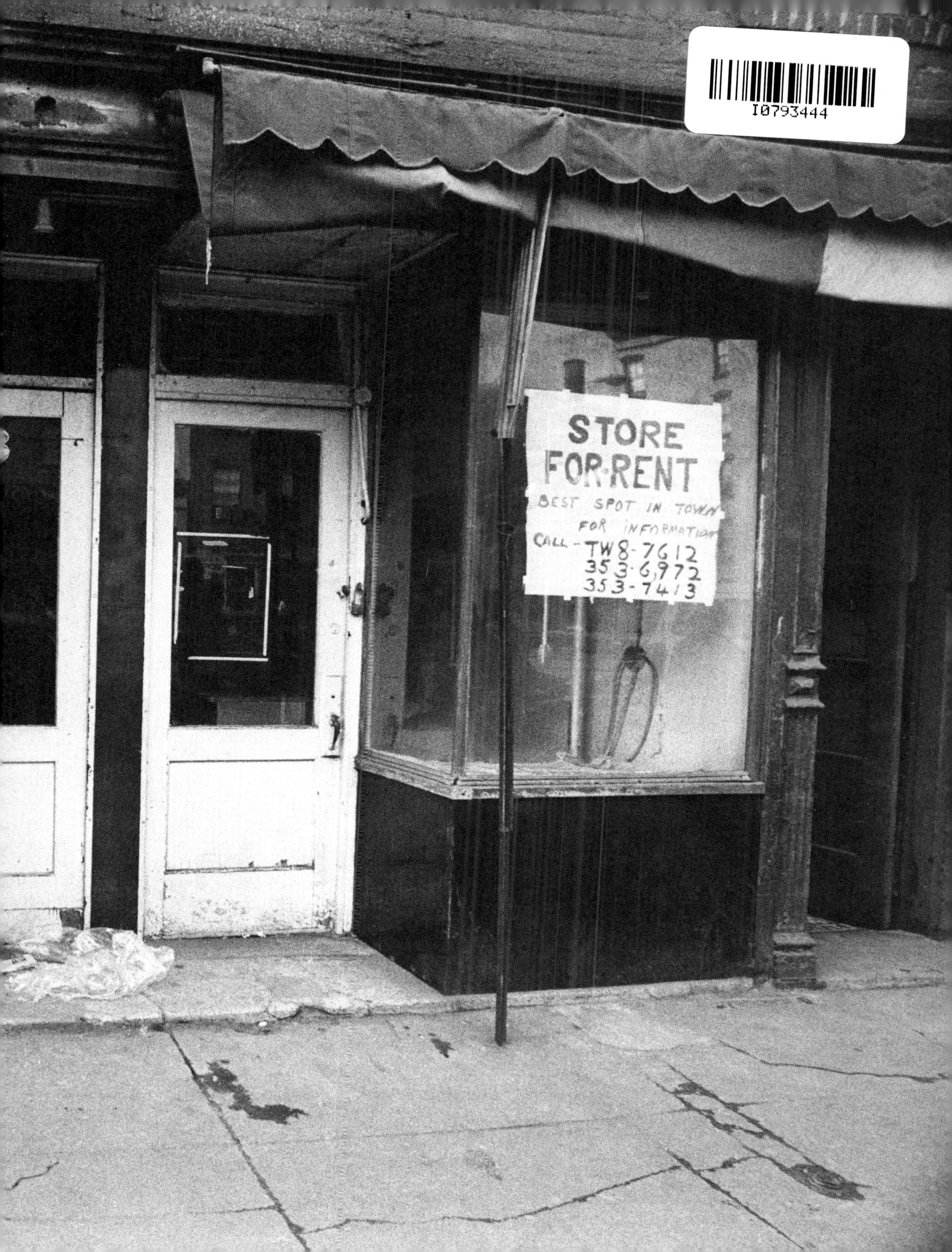
STORE
FOR-RENT
BEST SPOT IN TOWN
FOR INFORMATION
CALL - TW8-7612
353-6,972
353-7413

POINT OF VIEW

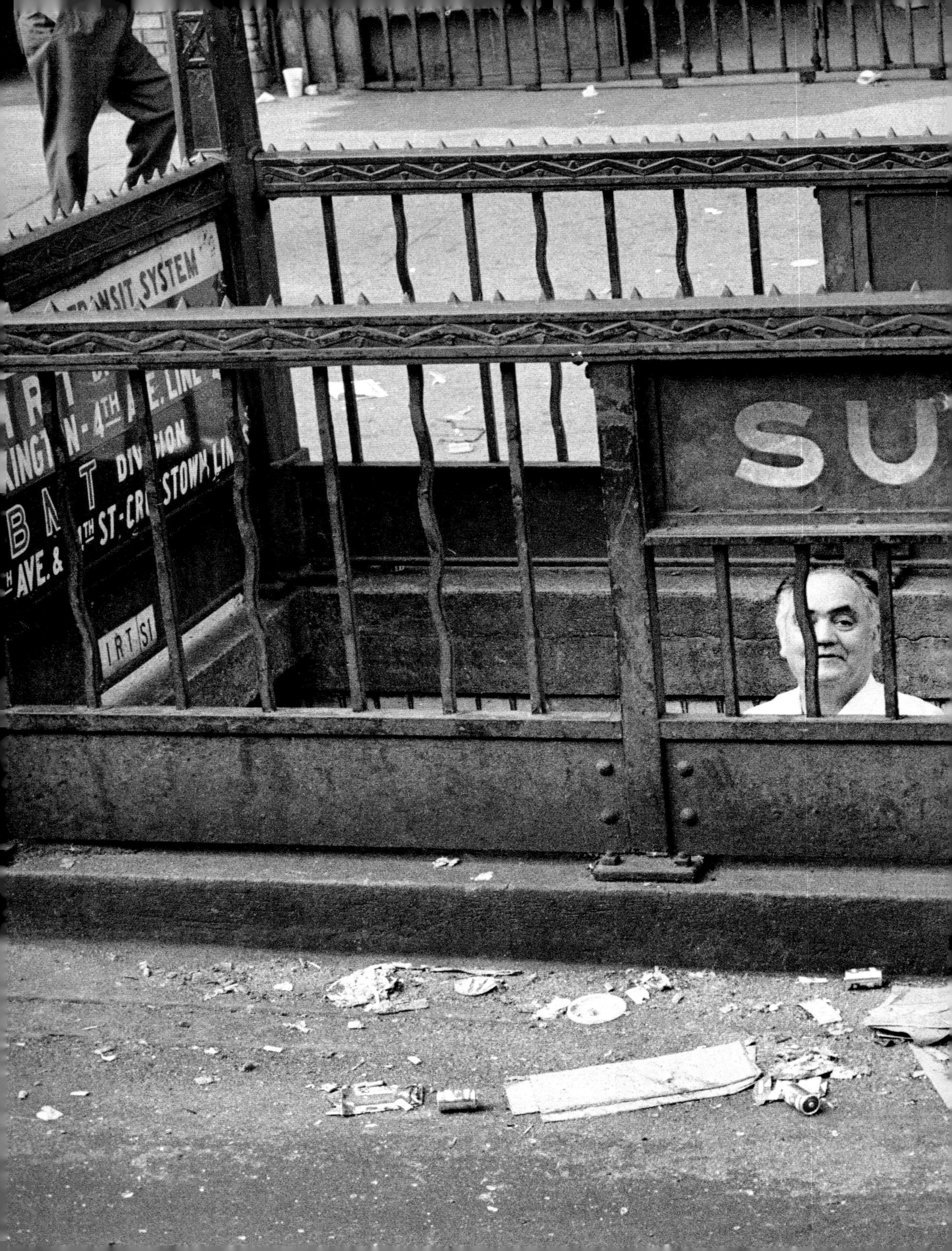
TRANSIT SYSTEM
SU

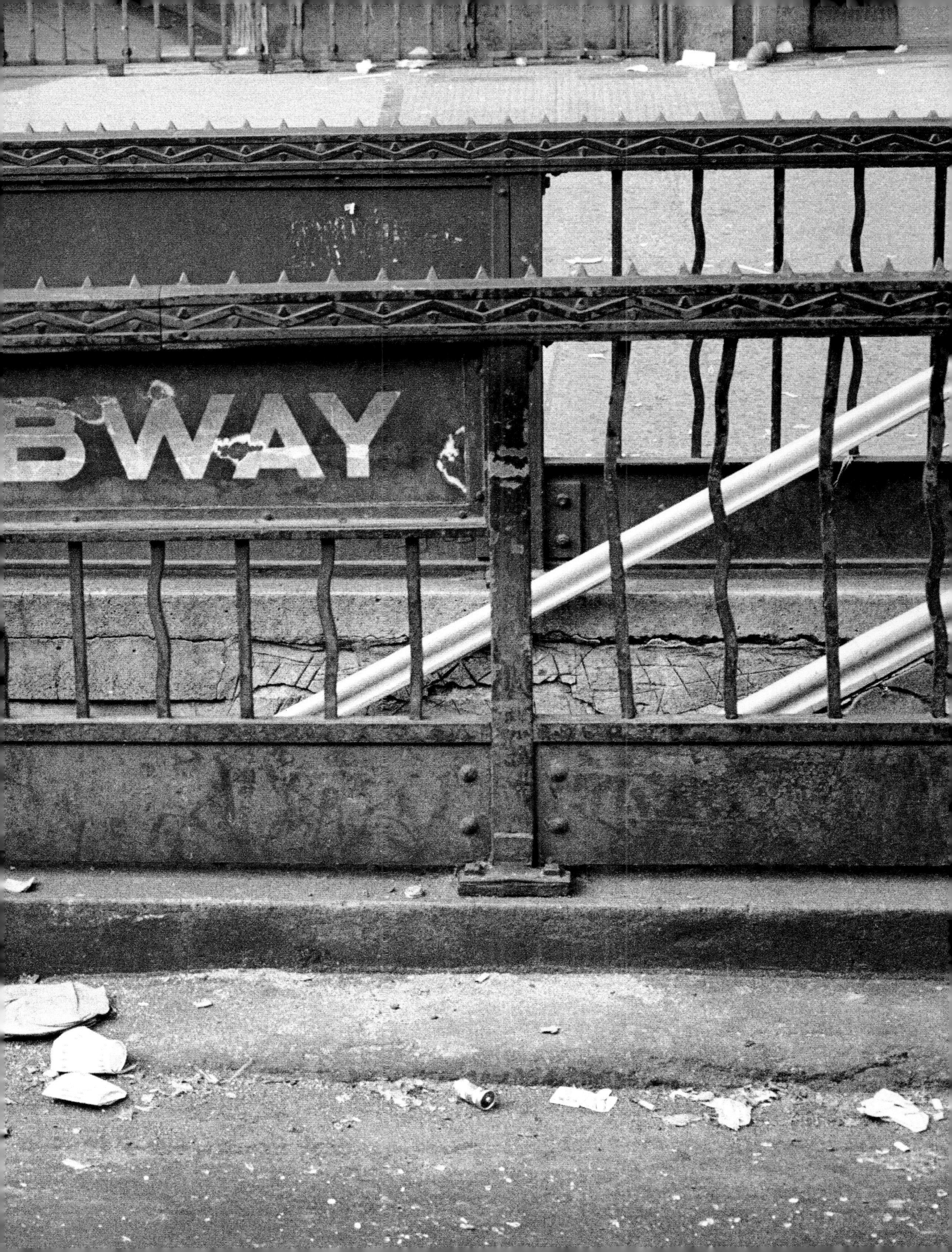
BWAY

BARBARA, AKIRA, AND VALI—
ALL MY LOVE AND THANKS FOR CONNECTING ME TO THE FUTURE

CHRIS STEIN
POINT OF VIEW

ME, NEW YORK CITY, AND THE PUNK SCENE

RIZZOLI
NEW YORK
New York · Paris · London · Milan

First published in the United States of America in 2018 by
Rizzoli International Publications, Inc.
300 Park Avenue South
New York, NY 10010
www.rizzoliusa.com

Design by Jan-Willem Dikkers

ISBN: 978-0-8478-6218-4
Library of Congress Catalog Control Number: 2018949566

2019 2020 2021 2022 / 10 9 8 7 6 5 4 3 2

Printed in China

10 **FOREWORD BY JON RONSON**

14 **INTRODUCTION: THE CITY AND THE CITY BY CHRIS STEIN**

22 SELF-PORTRAITS IN SHEEPSHEAD BAY

43 WOMEN'S HOUSE OF DETENTION

53 THE APARTMENT

64 ERIC EMERSON

70 TREASURE HUNT

75 KIDS ON A STOOP

84 CONEY ISLAND

94 CARE FIRE

113 THE FILLMORE EAST

126 WILLIAM BURROUGHS

139 THE FENCE

162 FANNE FOXE AND DIVINE

171 THE OFFICE

207 **AFTERWORD BY CHRIS STEIN**

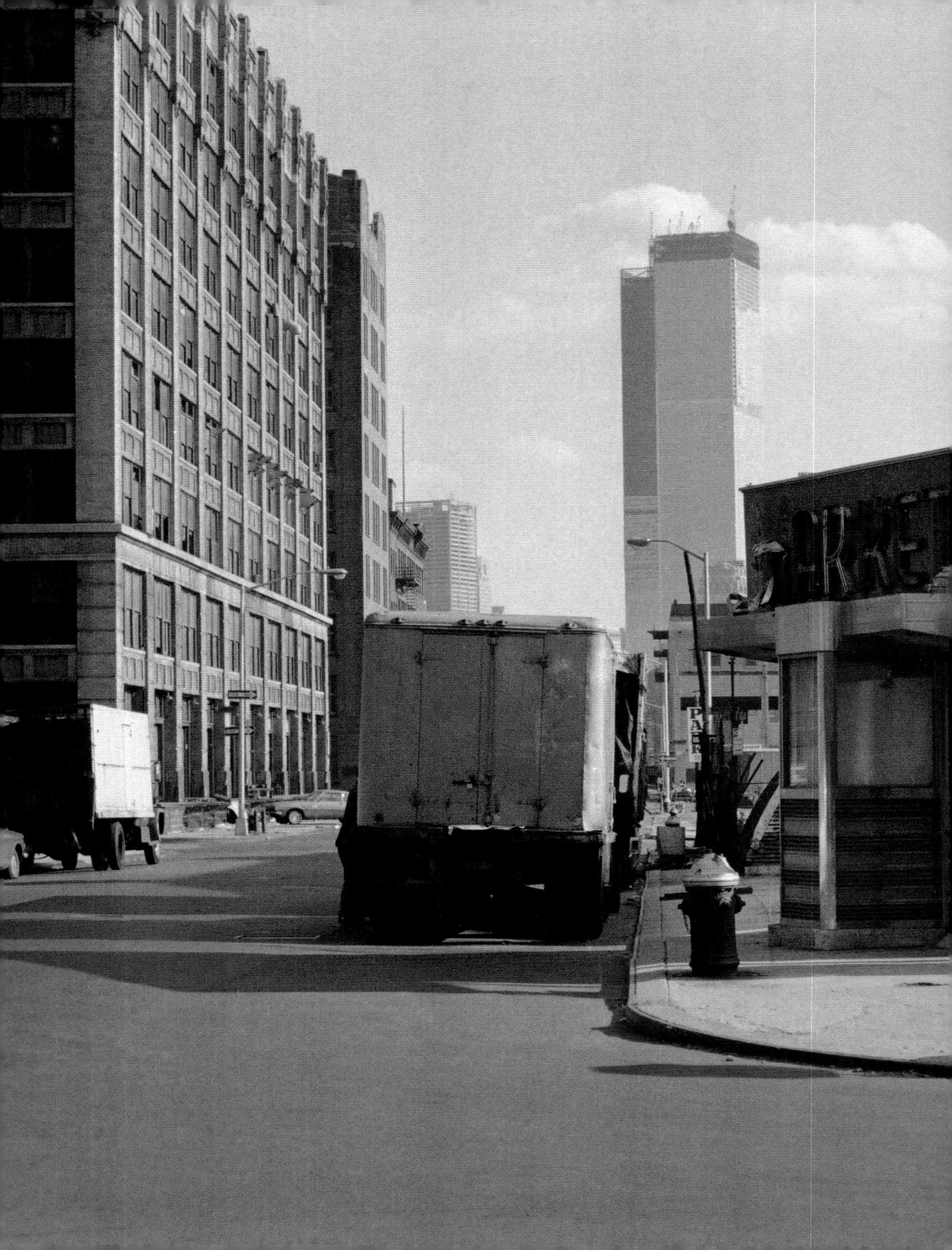

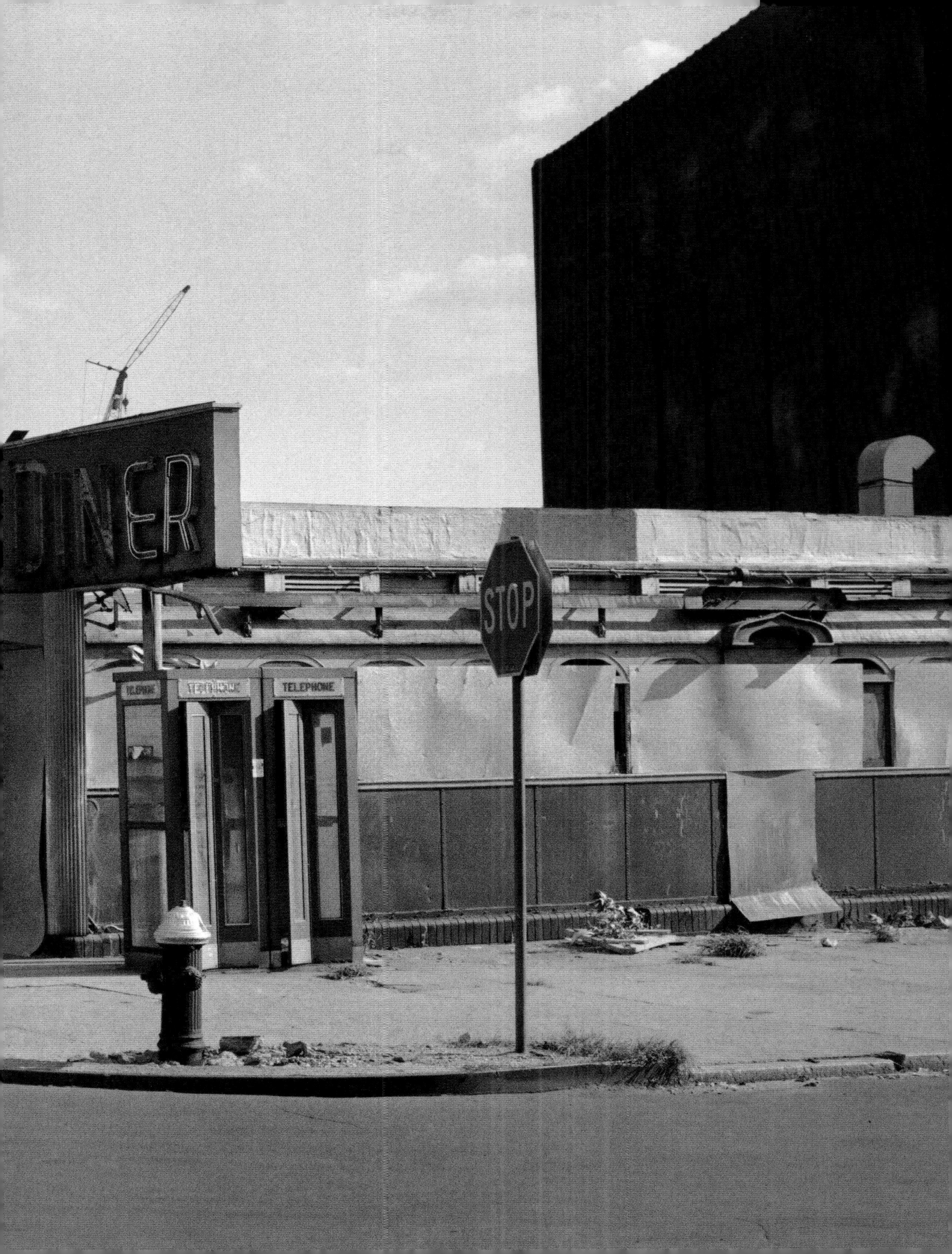
DINER
TELEPHONE
TELEPHONE
STOP

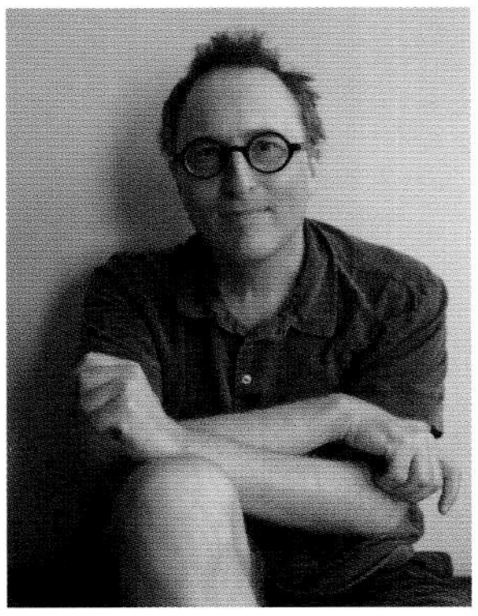

Jon Ronson, present day

FOREWORD BY JON RONSON

I live here now but I missed all this—New York City in the 1970s. The first time I visited was on June 20, 1999. (I can be this specific because I caught a taxi from the airport—the guy overcharged me $50—climbed out in Lower Manhattan, turned the corner, and there was Nelson Mandela. They were giving him a ticker tape parade. The skies rained shredded print-outs.) Giuliani wouldn't be Mayor for three years and so war hadn't yet been declared on homeless people and Times Square peep shows and dirty bookstores and ferrets. Yes, Giuliani outlawed ferrets as part of his mid-1990s eccentricity-purge. He had a radio phone-in show and shortly after his ferret ban, a ferret rights activist telephoned in to confront him about it:

"The excessive concern you have for ferrets is something you should examine with a therapist, not with me," Giuliani yelled at him. "I'm not insulting you. I'm being honest with you. There is something very sad about you. You need help. This excessive concern with little weasels is a sickness. Something has gone wrong with you. Your compulsion about it is a sign of something wrong in your personality."

Ah, my blood is boiling as I transcribe that now. Sure, crime was a bit out of control in New York City back then, but Giuliani's war on idiosyncrasy, on weirdness, on the amazing flotsam and jetsam Chris Stein captures in this wonderful book—the scrappy, fucked-up milieu from which the great music emerged—was heartbreaking.

As Chris Stein took these photographs, I was growing up in Cardiff, Wales. It's funny which memories stick in your head. Here's one: One day, word spread throughout school that Blondie were coming to Cardiff. We couldn't believe it! *Blondie* were coming to *Cardiff*? I was beside myself with excitement. I begged my parents to buy me a ticket. And then the truth emerged: Blondie *weren't* coming to Cardiff. Of course they weren't. It was just a lie spread by a malicious child to fill us with false hope. I guess this memory is so vivid because it was another spur for me to grow up as fast as possible and move somewhere like London or New York City.

Actually, this memory is totally unfair to Cardiff. When I lived there I saw The Specials and Genesis and Dexy's Midnight Runners and plenty of other great bands. Blondie probably *did* play there. I'm sure they did. But Debbie Harry was *so* otherworldly to the eleven-year-old me, so ethereal, it just seemed impossible that *they* would visit *our* town. These people were from another planet. We didn't identify with them. We marveled at them from a distance and wondered, "What goes on inside *their* heads?"

Now that I've read *Point of View* and Chris Stein's other brilliant book of photographs—*Negative: Me, Blondie, and the Advent of Punk*—I feel I can answer that question. The inside of Chris Stein's head is a *very good place.* I've met other people from that amazing era and sadly the same can't be said for them all. Some people hold onto resentments. Grudges are harbored forever. Slights rankle. And, boy, I empathize with that fucked-up perspective: I remain annoyed about affronts meted out to me in the early 1980s.

But not Chris Stein. I think *Point of View* bears testament to his wonderfully positive worldview. This book isn't jam-packed with sadness and fear and violence. This is not *The Warriors.* Well, there's some of that. But there is also amid the rubble a huge amount of happiness and fun and adventure and curiosity and excitement and freedom. A photographer doesn't feel inspired to capture that stuff if it doesn't course through his veins, too.

In this book people are smiling, creating, living their lives. Look at how many of his subjects are smiling! Even those who aren't smiling look basically fine. Well, most of them do. You can tell that even Lester Bangs, evidently hugely uncomfortable on the beach at Coney Island, is secretly having a good time. And at night? Wrestling, very early Blondie in tiny shorts, Andy Warhol on balconies, hanging out with Iggy and Meat Loaf and Bowie and Ray Davies. Chris Stein has really photographed the best people and lived the best life. There are rays of sunlight everywhere.

(My version of this, by the way, was in Manchester, England, in the mid-1980s. Everyone was in a band. Rehearsal spaces were cheap or free because they were located in abandoned warehouses that were dripping with exposed asbestos. The difference is that in Manchester it never stopped raining, which is why our punk groups sounded like Joy Division, whereas New York City's punk groups were sprightlier because they, occasionally at least, got some sun.)

The bands that emerged from the milieu Chris Stein captures so perfectly here created some of the greatest music of our lifetime—Suicide, Blondie, Talking Heads, Lou Reed. It's a great part of the reason why I wanted to spend at least some of my life living here. So we moved here in 2012. We rented a place on the Upper West Side. Shortly after signing the lease, I read a *New York Times* article about a man who hosted 'Influencers' dinners' in my neighborhood. The article described him standing on a table and telling his cheering, applauding guests—socialites, philanthropists—"Thank you for coming to my home and spending my life with me." The reporter described it as the loveliest thing she'd ever seen, but it sounded to me like the scene in *Paths of Glory* where they have to slap the man awake so they can execute him. What had happened to the grime, the great eccentrics, the sketchiness? Where had it gone?

What had happened, of course, was gentrification. I despaired. I was here too late. Rich people heard The Ramones, wanted a piece of it, moved here, the rents skyrocketed, and nobody could afford to be in a band any more. I'd stand in Riverside Park and watch police officers glare suspiciously at everyone. (This was 2012—Mayor Bloomberg's New York—and there had been a resurgence of Giuliani's 'broken windows' policing, war on small-time offenders and nonconformists.) So many cops, so many forms to fill out, fucking health insurance. . .

I took a walk along the Hudson up to the George Washington Bridge. I saw a fisherman and a woman staring out across the water. "There's someone out there swimming," the woman said to me. "Some crazy woman is swimming out there." And then four fire trucks arrived, and two ambulances, and divers in wet suits and a helicopter and three N.Y.P.D. rescue boats—that overabundance of emergency workers that converge in seconds at the site of a crisis in New York City. Sometimes this city feels like a great machine, and all of us cogs within it, like clock parts, beavering away for the greater good, and when something goes wrong the machine corrects itself with discipline and efficiency. The victim—the suicide—was a girl, seventeen, who had hours earlier been caught cheating in school.

I fell out of love with New York after that. I couldn't get that girl's death out of my head. This place was hard and cold and regimented.

And then something happened. Something weird and tiny. But it really cheered me.

I was taking our dogs for a walk, and a woman bent down, I assumed, to stroke them, but instead she yelled in Floppy's face: "You're an *asshole*." About ten minutes later a different passerby told me, "Your dog has *bad energy*."

"You're *wrong*," I didn't yell back. "Floppy has *extraordinary energy*."

The truth is, New York City may be gentrified but it's still fabulously fucked up. You'll still find avant-garde clubs in Bushwick and Bedford-Stuyvesant—clubs which sound just as experimental and unpredictable as CBGB must have been. The other night my son went to a place where the performer was a naked Japanese woman sticking her head into her husband's saxophone while he played it. The scenes captured in Chris Stein's brilliant photographs—they aren't dead. They live on. These are great days.

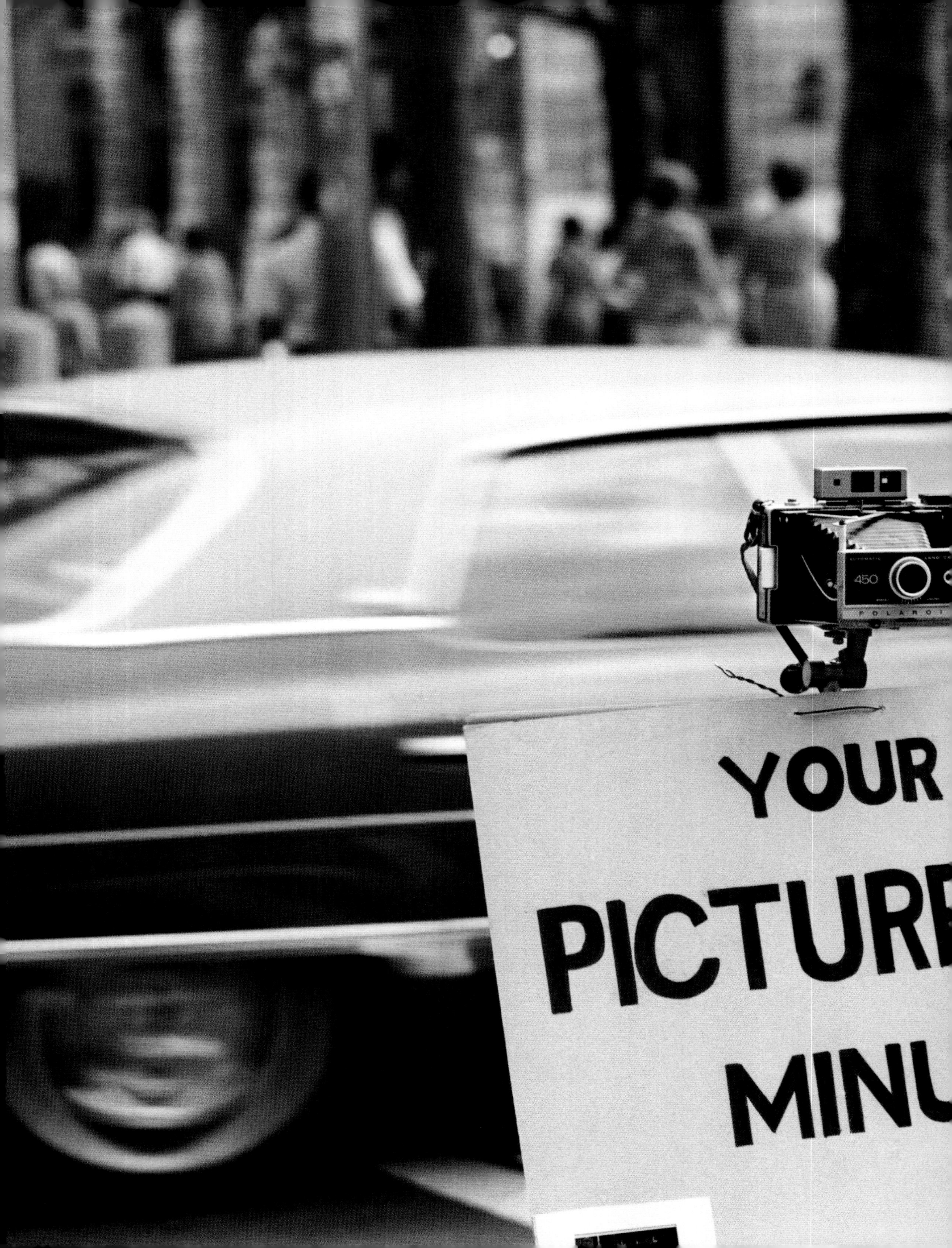
YOUR
PICTURE
MINU
450
POLAROI

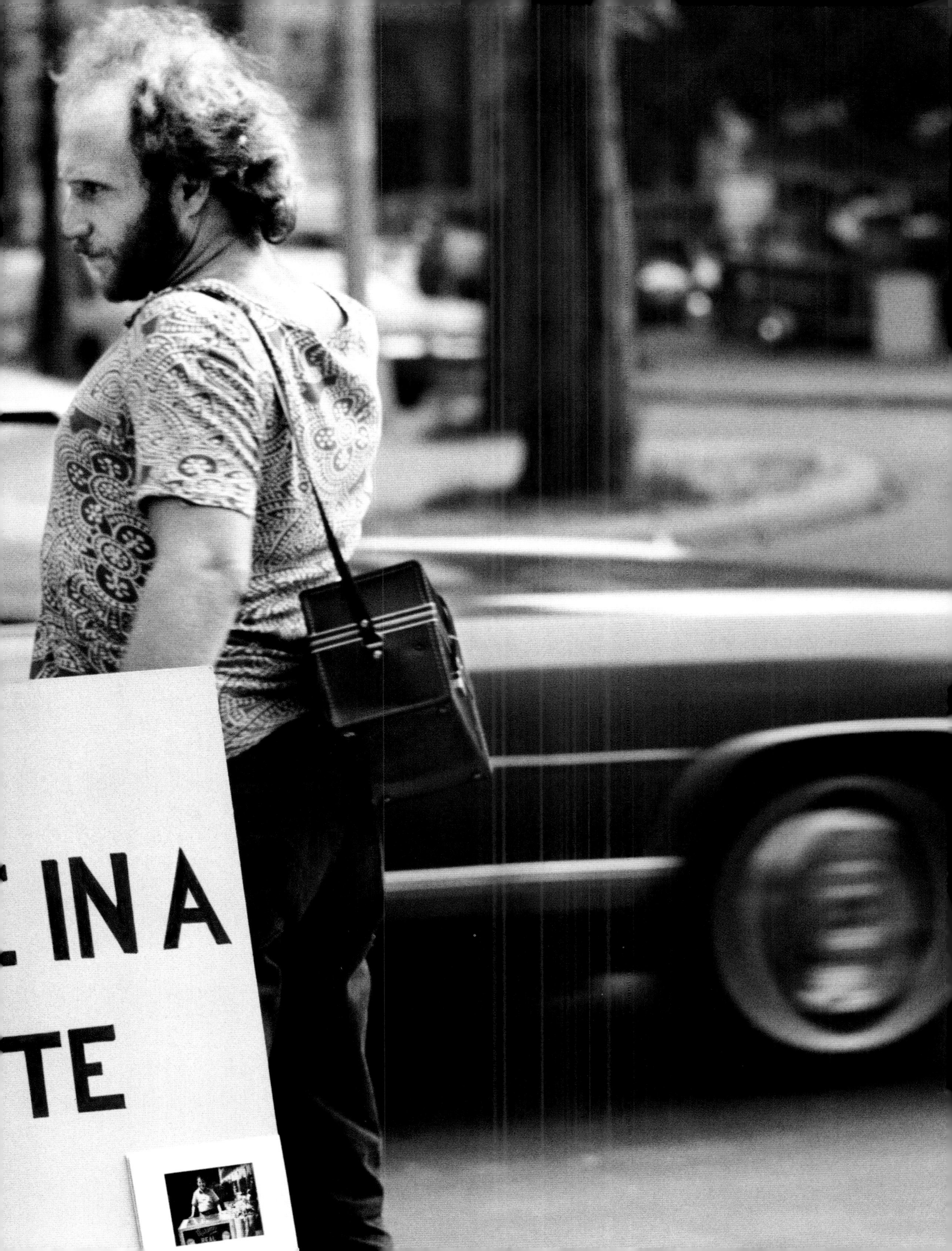
E IN A
TE

THE CITY AND THE CITY

When I was really little, we lived on Coney Island Avenue in Brooklyn, up a flight of stairs over a store. I remember things from this period, the early fifties, the roundish cars and the atmosphere of the neighborhood. Downstairs and around the corner was a TV repair shop run by a Mister Daniels. Stacked with the big wooden TVs that were the norm, Mister Daniels's shop—though a pretty regular type of place—had a unique thing that made it stand out even then. It was filled with cats. Mister Daniels obviously loved cats, and the store was populated with them. I remember being in there on a sunny afternoon and seeing the cats draped over the TV sets and wandering around on the counter next to the big cash register. Think about a Best Buy filled with cats today.

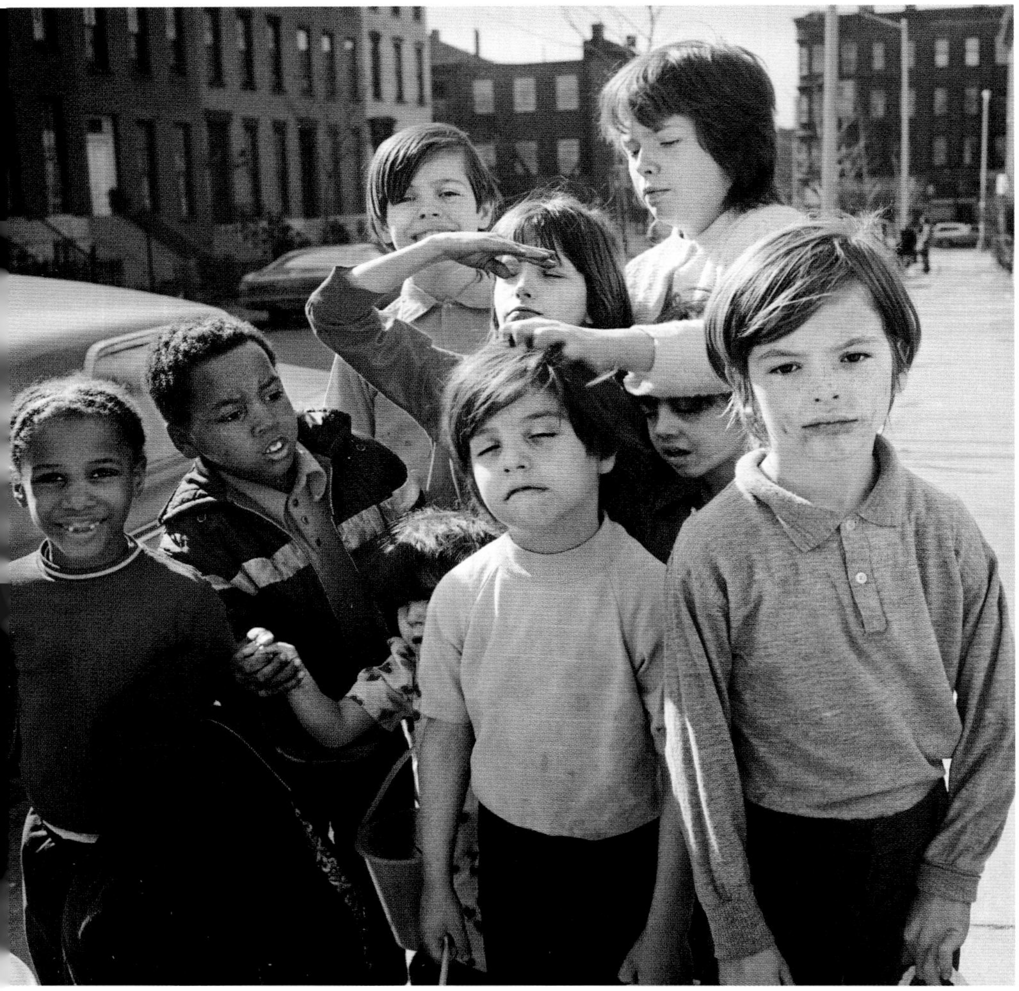

Around 1980, I got a Bearcat police scanner, a portable one. This was a handheld thing that let you listen, but not broadcast, to police, fire, ambulance calls, et cetera. In July 1983 I spent an afternoon listening to the craziness surrounding a free Diana Ross concert in Central Park. The free concert was partially rained out, and various members of the really large crowd lost it and ran around dealing mayhem to nearby people and places. On another muggy summer evening, I accompanied an associate to some downtown drug dealer's tenement apartment. I didn't know the dealer guy, so I waited in the hall listening to my scanner. While I was sitting on the stairs, some other character passed me and went into the same apartment. When my friend finally came out, he was very amused and told me the second person had come in wide eyed and paranoid and announced that "there is a cop sitting in the hall." So, that scanner.

When I moved downtown to Greenwich Street in the mid-to-late eighties, I stumbled onto a new genre of signals coming from the Bearcat: guys on car phones. Now, car phones go way the hell back—the first ones came into play in 1946—but these calls indicated the beginning of normal use. I heard a lot of calls, and after a while I was actively searching for them on the few frequencies that they came through. I noticed that the calls could be divided into several pretty specific categories. One was guys (the calls were exclusively made by men) calling wives and girlfriends and discussing food. This was pretty mundane stuff. A dude would be asking what was for dinner and sometimes if he could bring something back with him. The second more amusing one was guys attempting to impress their dates or girlfriends with the fact that *they had* a car phone. These would play out with the person announcing that they were "in front of your house," or "in my car." I did hear one call that involved a man negotiating with what was presumably a sex worker, attempting to set a price for entertaining his

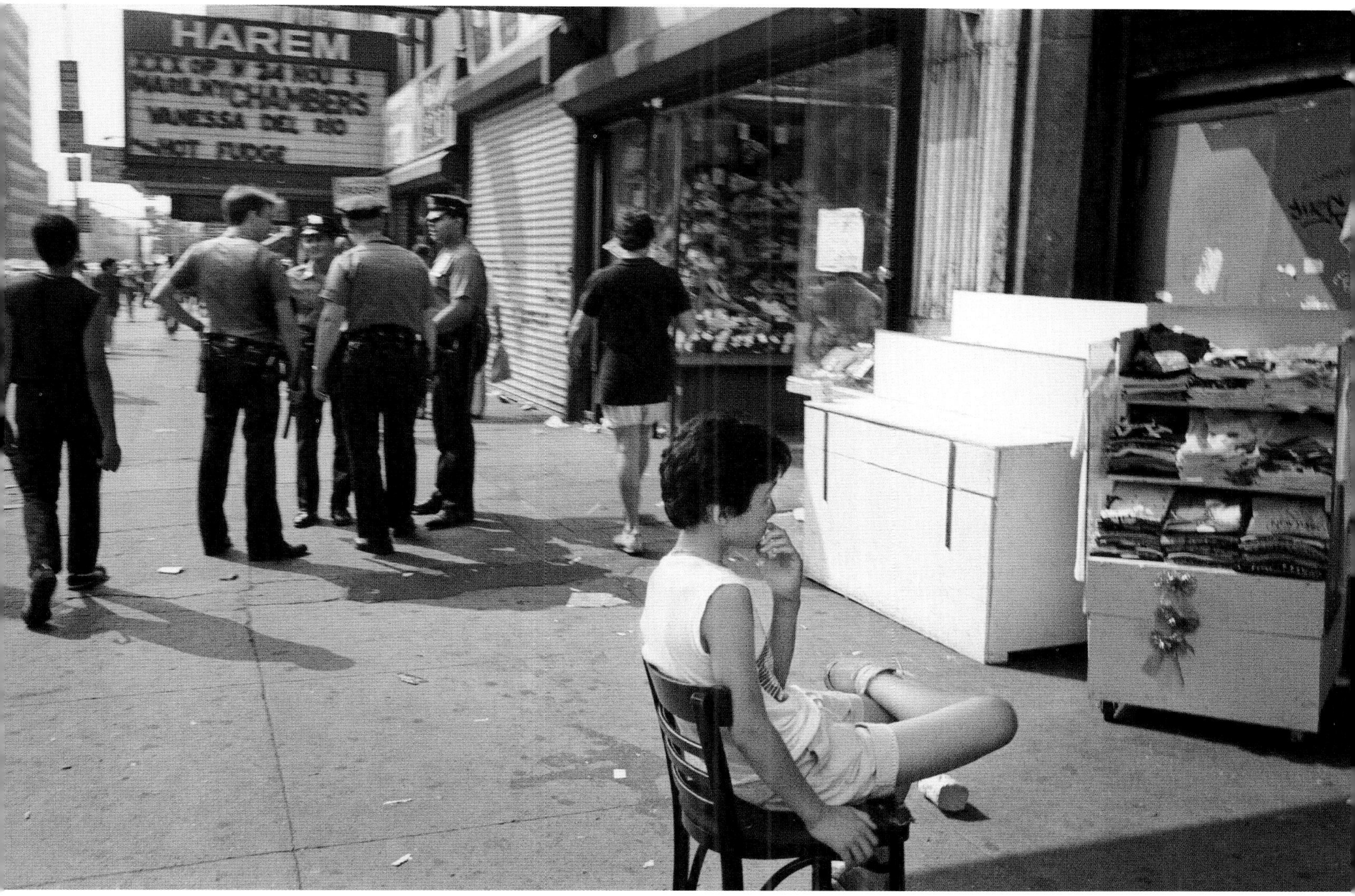
HAREM
VANESSA DEL RIO
HOT FUDGE

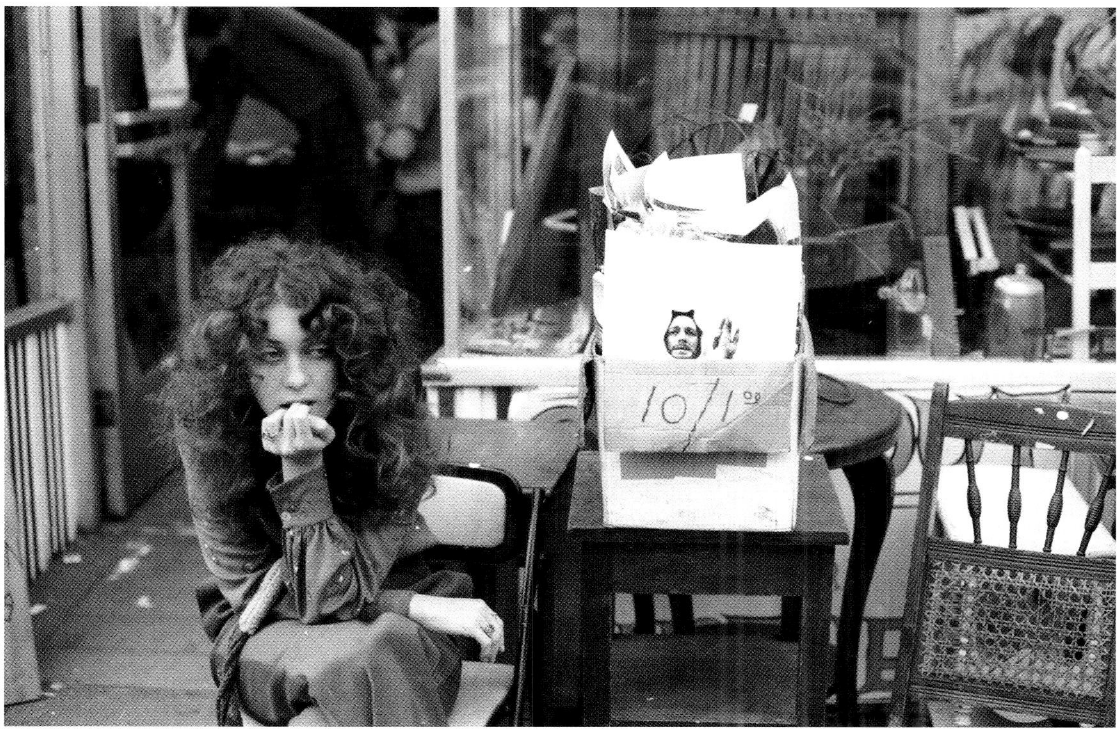

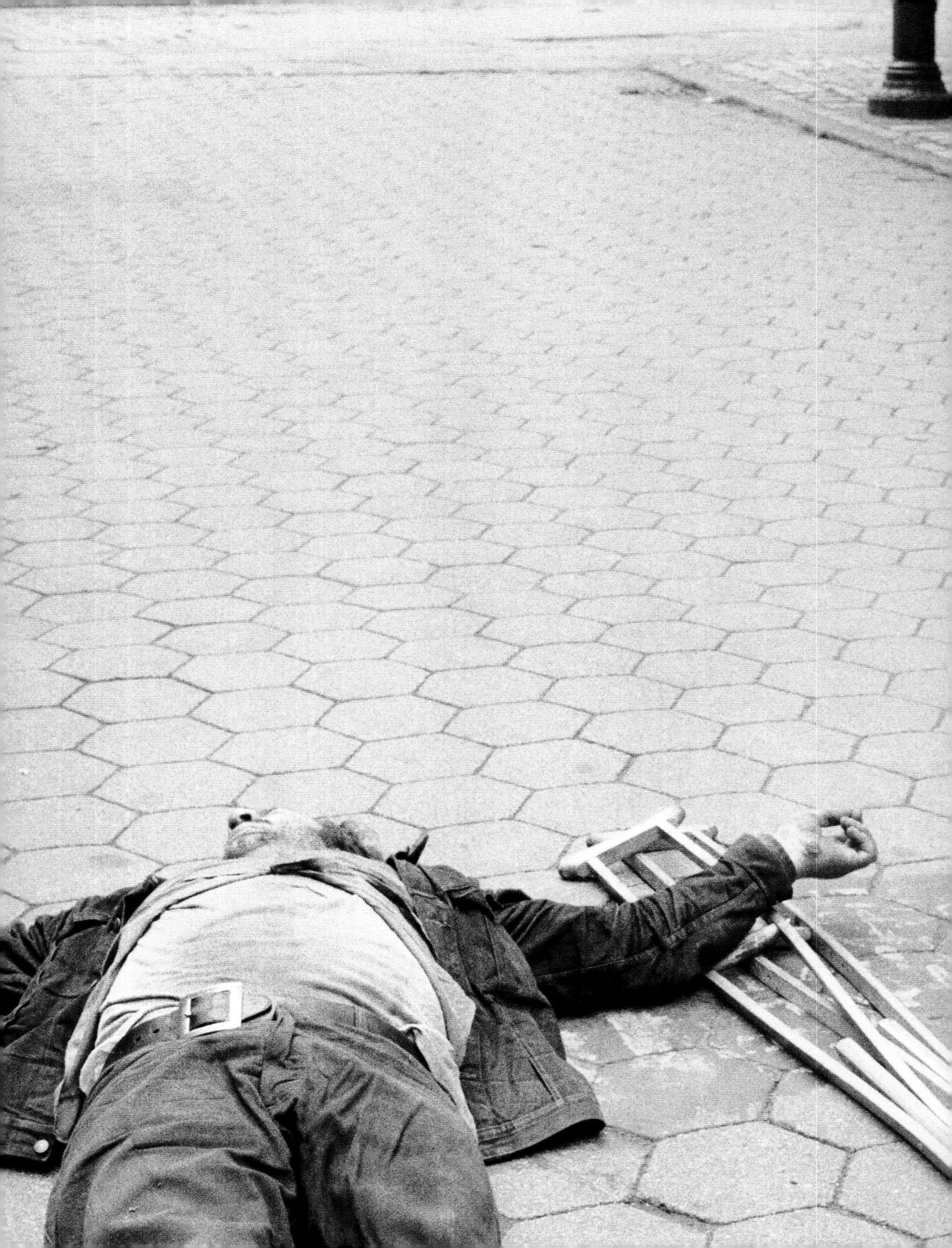

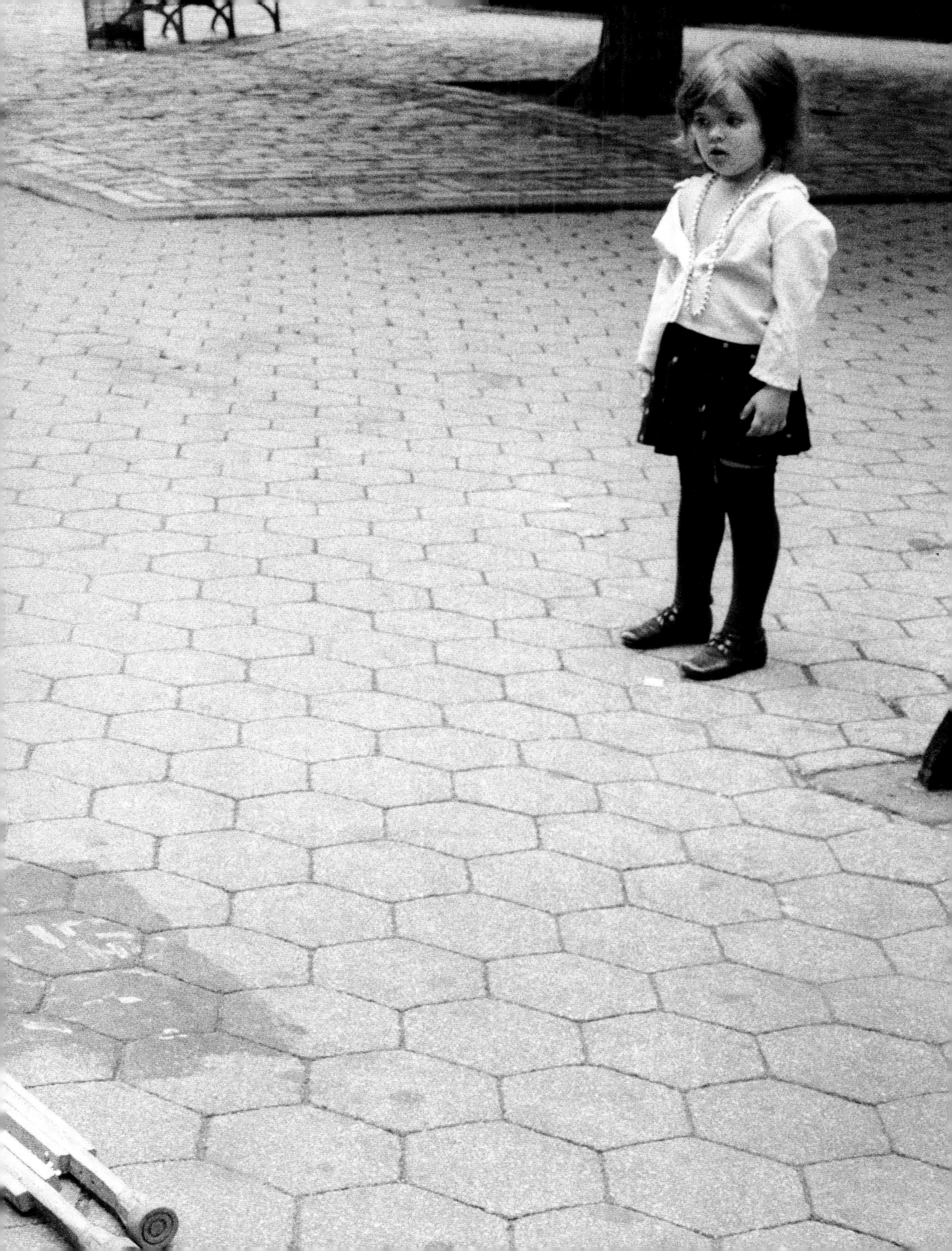

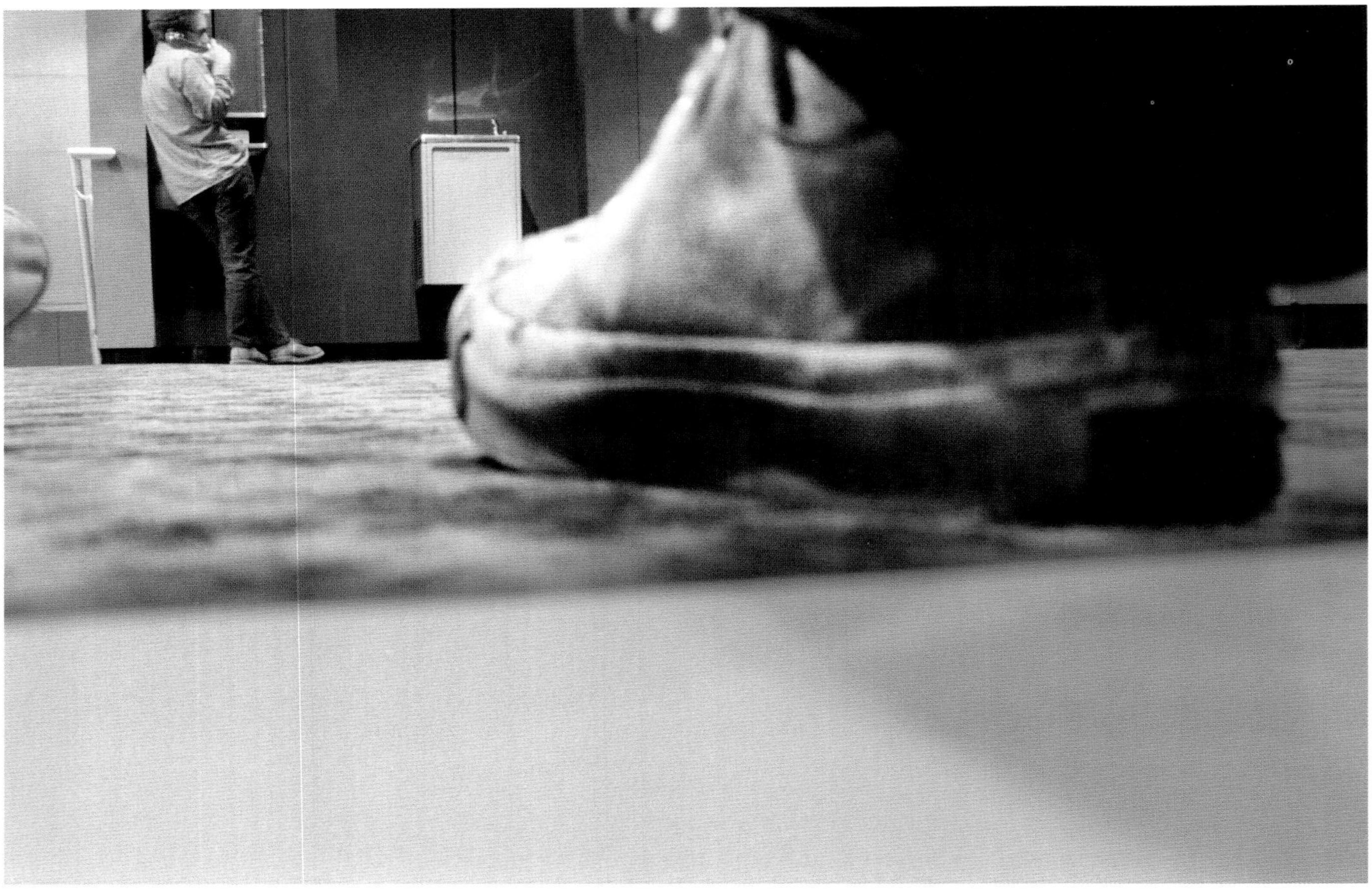

buddies at some future date. But out of the many calls I heard, that was the only one that wasn't in the realm of day-to-day, dull stuff.

Here's the thing, then. Somewhere in there I must have anticipated everybody having a car phone, and maybe even thought about people carrying phones around, but I didn't see it coming. The specific mechanics of the future, our current here and now, were totally alien and in a way unimaginable. I had a computer, too, but the evolution of tech and this era of false hive mind was not anything I could have envisioned. In 1984's *Neuromancer*, William Gibson does a masterful job of calling up the future, but the boring staring-at-phones addiction and selfie culture just isn't something that visionaries, even William, gleaned.

Conversely, there is an exercise I indulge in that involves my sense of nostalgia (that sense has advanced in conjunction with my years). If I time traveled back to New York somewhere between, say, 1900 and 1920, what would I do with myself? Time travel is pointless without being able to retain your existing set of memories, so there I am, and what is it? Find a guitar, a camera, a typewriter? None of it seems like it would resonate; maybe I'd get a job as a bartender. The past is as cloudy as the future.

I'm glad I got to live in a New York that was closer in tone to a hundred years ago than where we are now in the digital age. I remember phone booths. Not the last generation of them, but the old wooden ones that one would see in the lobbies of office buildings and subway stations. Or those chipped gray paint ones with metal seats and little table things that were under the phone where you'd put a notebook or newspaper. When I was a kid, we somehow discovered a weird trick whereby one would take the foil from a cigarette pack, fold it, and stick it into the crack next to the coin box of a pay phone, jiggle it around until it formed a connection and produced a free dial tone. This actually worked on one or two occasions, I can attest.

Tattooing was technically illegal in NYC from 1961 till 1997. I knew tattoo artists, and though some had storefront shops, they would have to work with an 'appointment only' situation.

The city in 1970 was physically similar in many ways, but the atmosphere was extremely different. It was much less crowded. There weren't many tourists. It was darker and there was more magic around. It was the heyday of occult bookstores, and pretty much every little bookshop had an an occult or mystical section. Headshops weren't akin to modern smoke shops, but were often styled with a 'spiritual' bent. I can't figure out the specific location of Timothy Leary's League for Spiritual Discovery storefront on Hudson Street, but I had an amazing trip there one snowy winter day. The league space was all the way west by the West Side highway. Most of the elevated highway was torn down between 1977 and 1982, after it started seriously falling apart in 1973, but while it was still up the area around it reflected the old docks and seaport atmosphere of 'ill repute.' There were very funky, old loft buildings and storefronts in the shadow of this ancient, decrepit, and huge iron structure.

Antique stores, junk stores, and flea markets recycled amazing stuff. In the eighties, some friends who worked regularly at the 26th Street flea market took me uptown where a fellow they knew offered to sell me a pre-Columbian Peruvian mummy. It's mouth was open in an eternal scream. It was great, but was so scary that I didn't think I wanted it around all the time. I still wonder if I should have gone for it.

On one foray into the Lower East Side that I made maybe in 1968 or 1969, I went into a run-down shop that was owned by an elderly couple. The wares were piles of clothing on the dusty floorboards. I found an antique motorcycle jacket that I paid five bucks for. Around 1972 I traded it for a pair of green boots, but in later years came to realize that the jacket must have dated to the fifties or even the forties, and I should have passed on the boots (I did wear them a lot though). During my teenage years, the Lower East Side was still in neighborhood mode before the influx of drugs

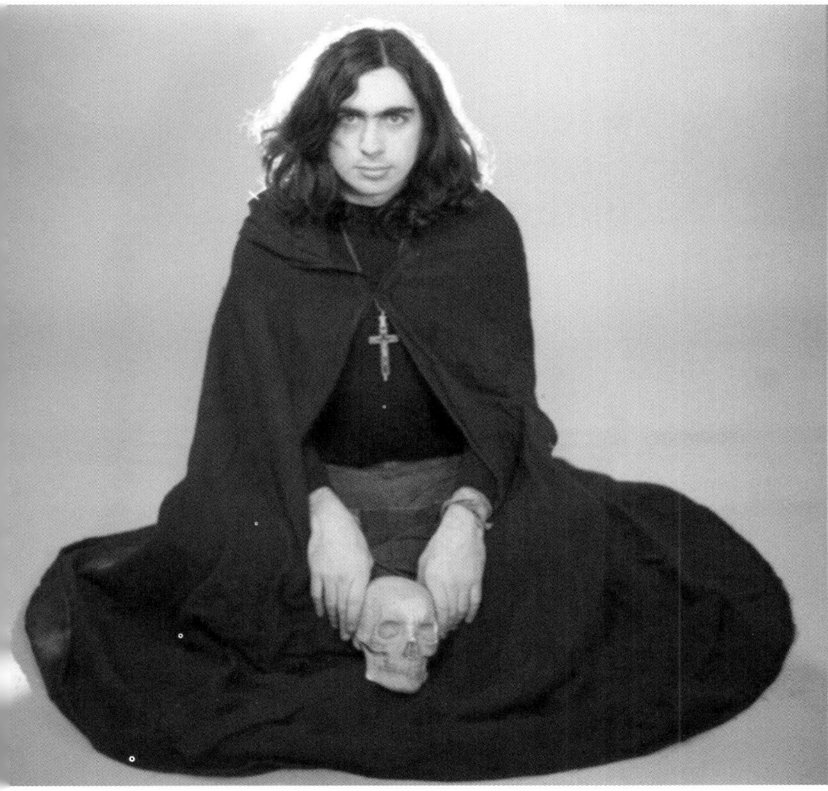

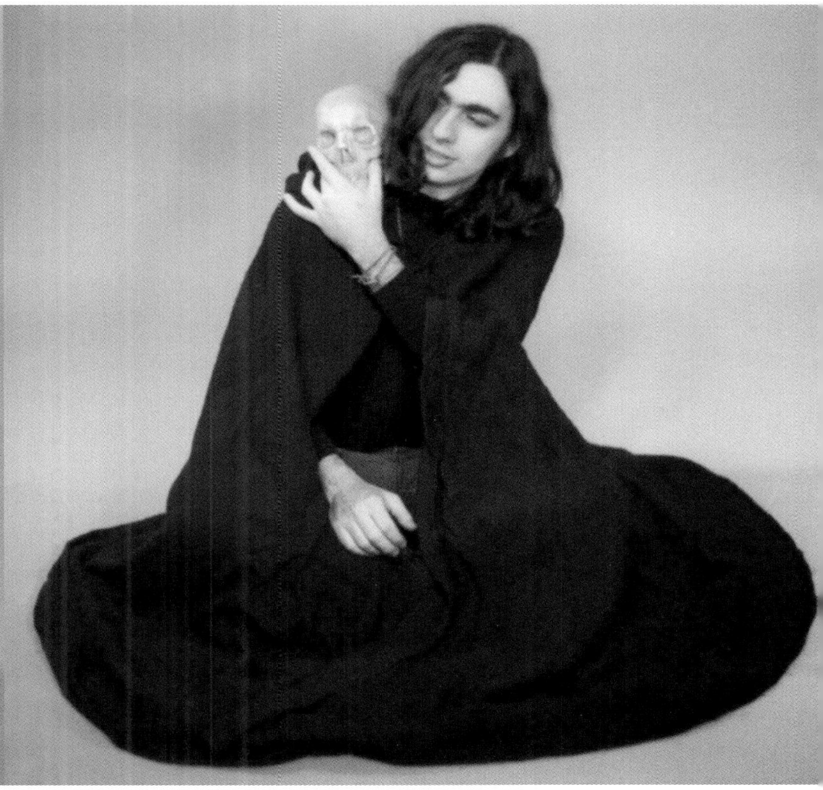

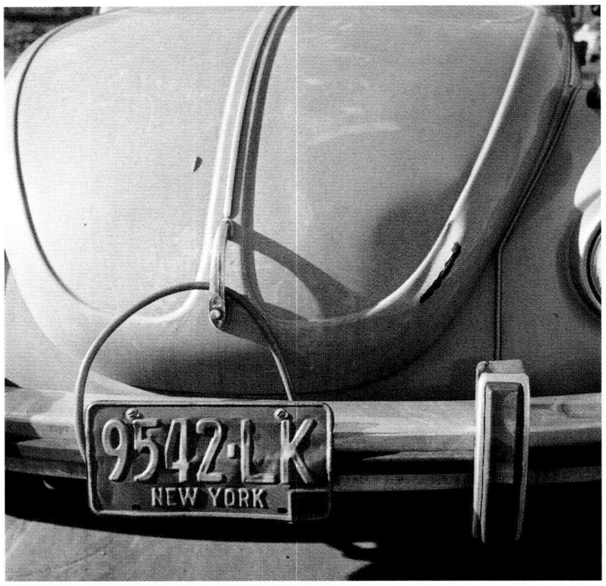

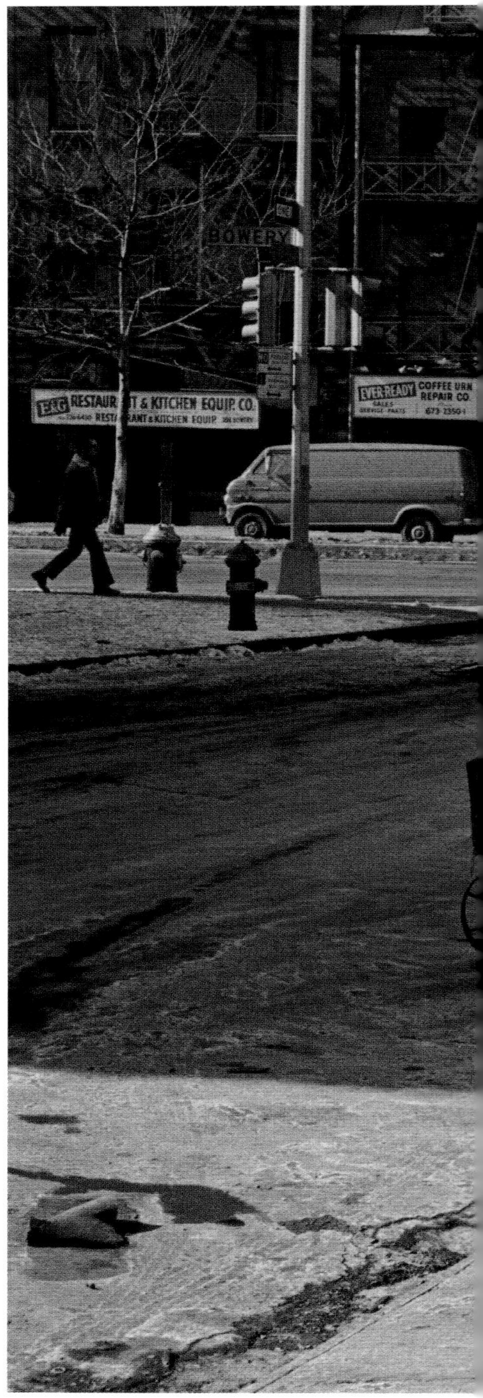

and mayhem that peaked in the eighties. In what must have been around 1967, my friend's older sister rented an LES 'studio' apartment for twenty-four dollars a month.

SoHo particularly drives me crazy. I remember when it was full of trucks and artists and it wasn't a high-end shopping mall. Now it's the antithesis of what it at one time represented. The Meatpacking District has gone through mind-blowing, silicone-injected, very expensive plastic surgery.

Even by the time I was traveling with the band in the mid-seventies, New York had a scary cache. People would want to know about the daily danger and intrigue. At some point everyone I knew would complain about how dirty and grotesque the city was, how they were considering leaving, but nobody left. There's a great Lou Reed monologue about how horrible New York is but how much more uncomfortable he would be anywhere else.

Decay and dissolution were all around; the city was in a state of winding down that was a dramatic contrast to the constant upbuilding that we're in the midst of now. I've always been attracted to old, falling down, dusty stuff. I don't know where this comes from. Maybe everybody has this to some extent and that's why visions of the future are frequently presented as dark and dystopian landscapes laid out next to the clean shiny ones.

Memory is subjective. We live with so many tweaked, photoshopped recollections that we've adjusted during our lives. I'm always reminded of a favorite story by Russian author P. D. Ouspensky, *The Strange Life Of Ivan Osokin*. In a nutshell, the dude lamenting his fouled-up existence goes to a magician and says, "If you let me go back and do my life over again I will fix everything." The magician sends him back and he does everything exactly the same.

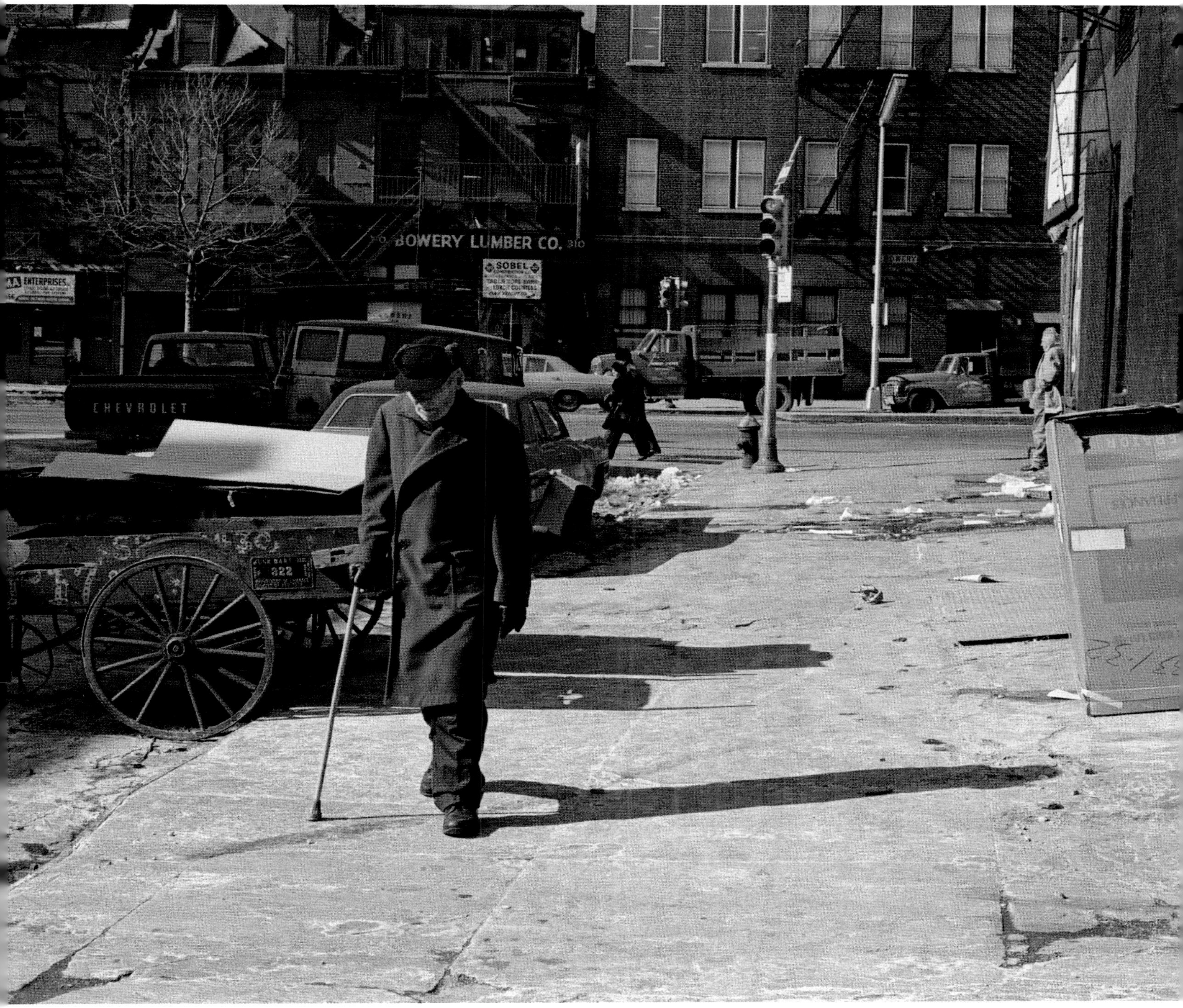

First Street, looking west toward the Bowery, 1969–1970—coincidentally around the corner from where CBGB would be about three years later.

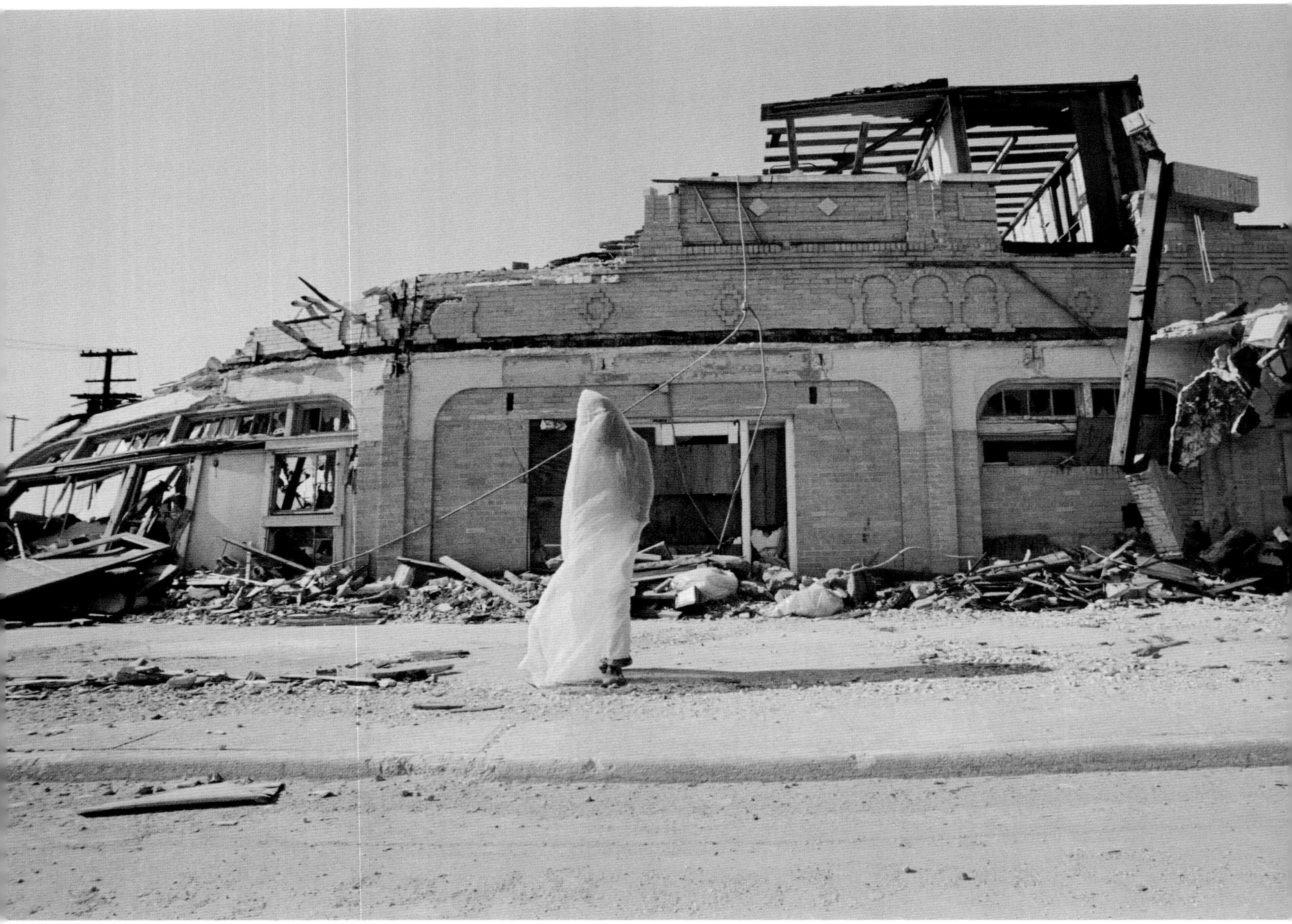

SELF-PORTRAITS IN SHEEPSHEAD BAY, 1969–70

By the time I was staying with a girlfriend out by the beach in Sheepshead Bay, the area that had been the Sheepshead Bay Maritime Service Training Center was a large demolished necropolis. It opened in 1942 and until it closed in 1954 was the largest center of its kind in the US; it could train thirty thousand merchant seamen a year. In 1969 it was a vast crumbling city complete with streets and lots of destroyed buildings. I loved it. I dragged the camera and a tripod out there one bright day and did these shots of me wearing a piece of a parachute and a grass skirt. Kingsborough Community College was already taking hold there, having started in 1963. But most of the place was still devoted to the remains of the base. I had some friends who went to school there, and the sunny seaside location enabled them to grow some pretty passable weed on the grounds.

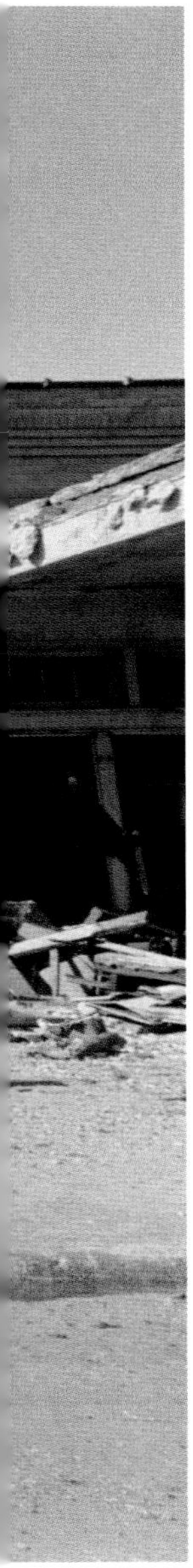

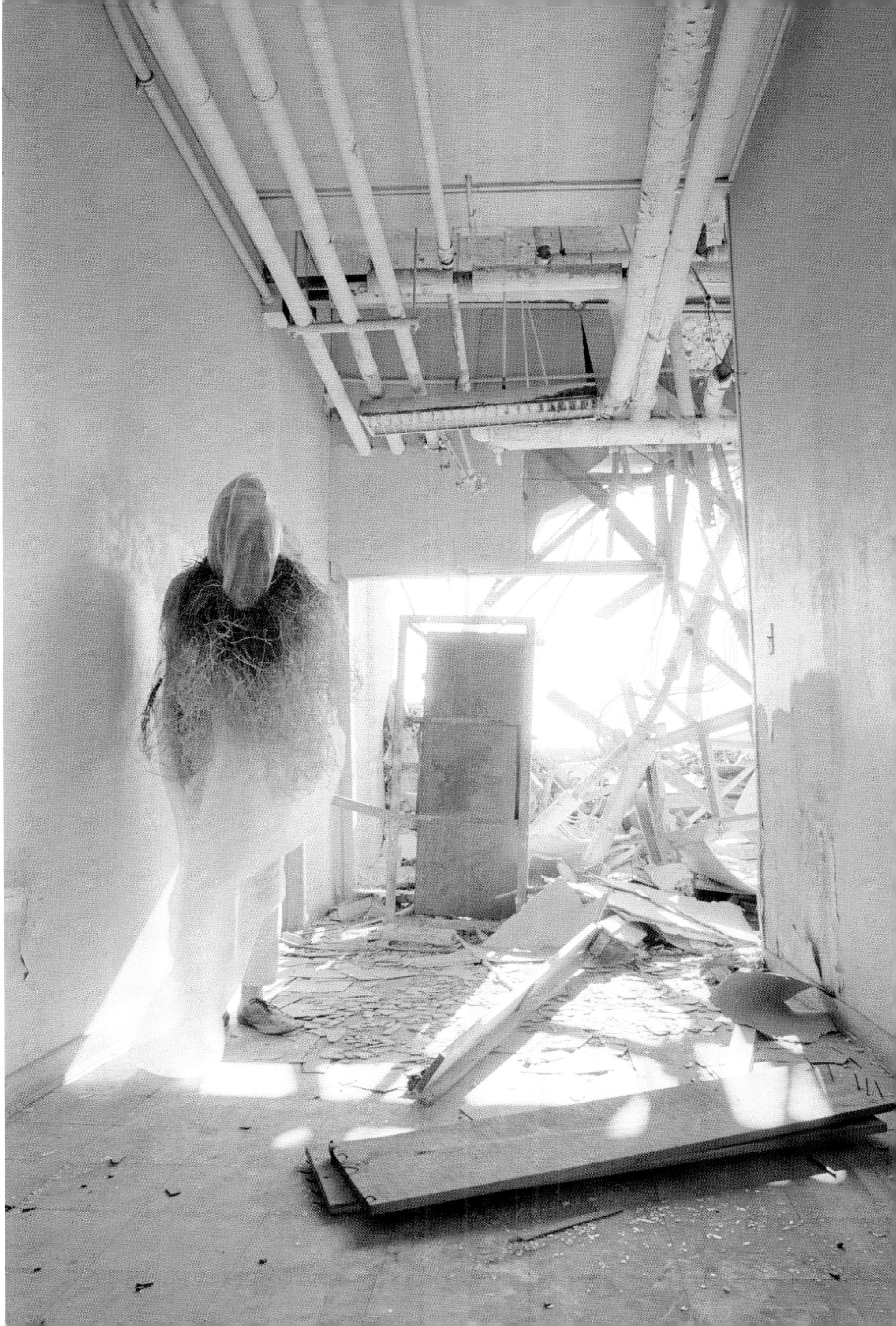

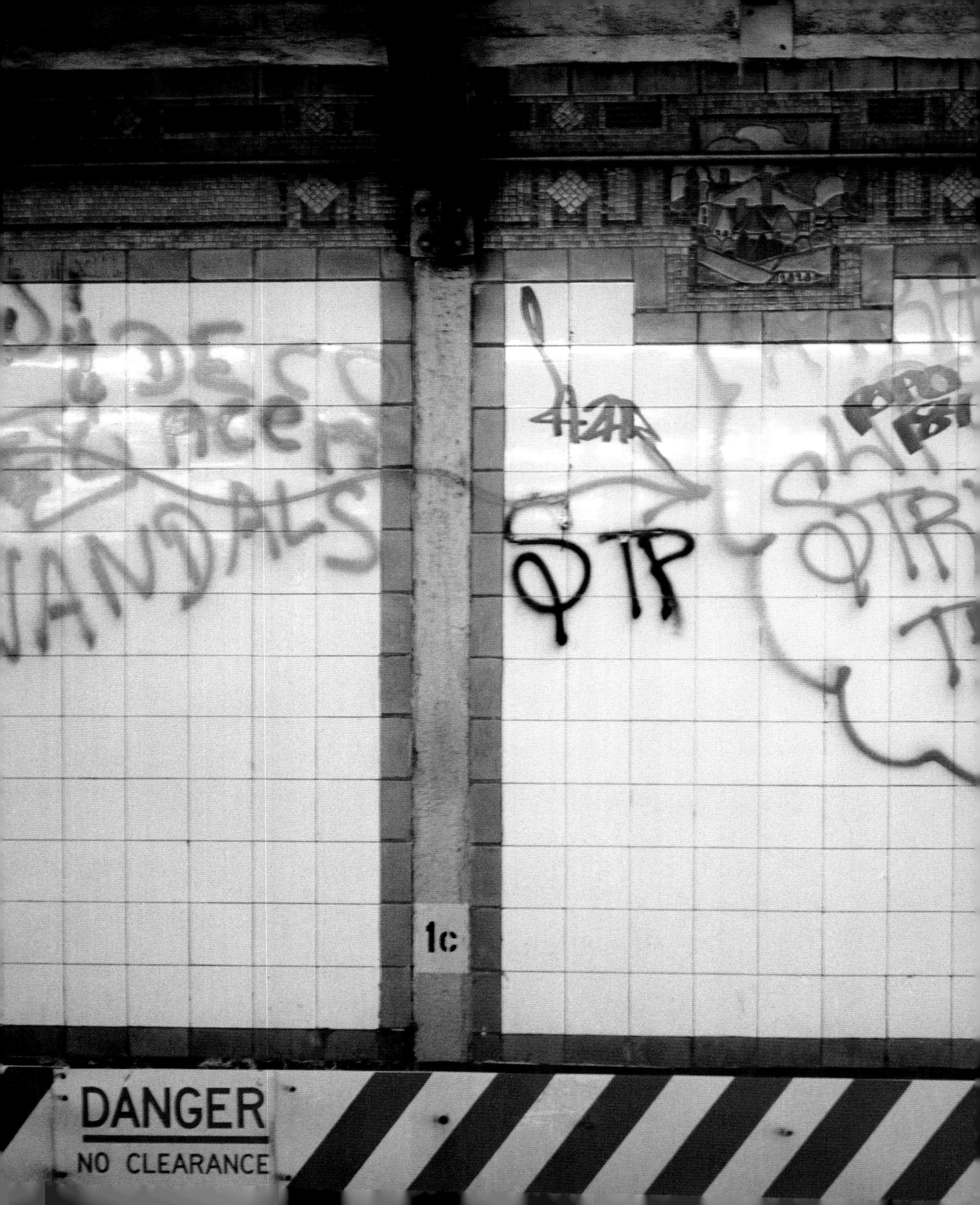
1c
DANGER
NO CLEARANCE

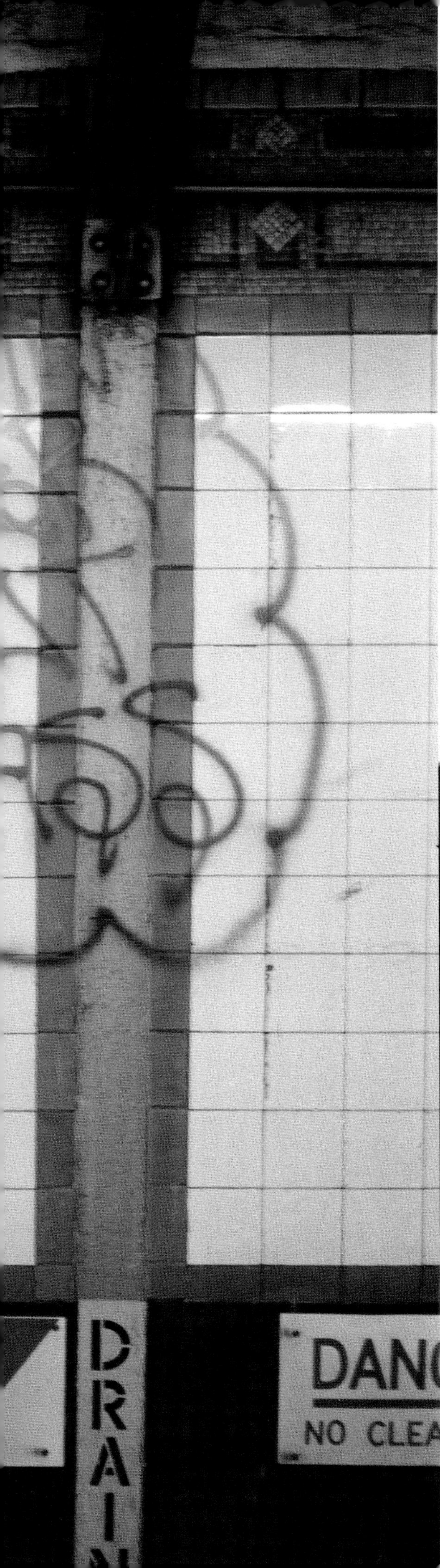

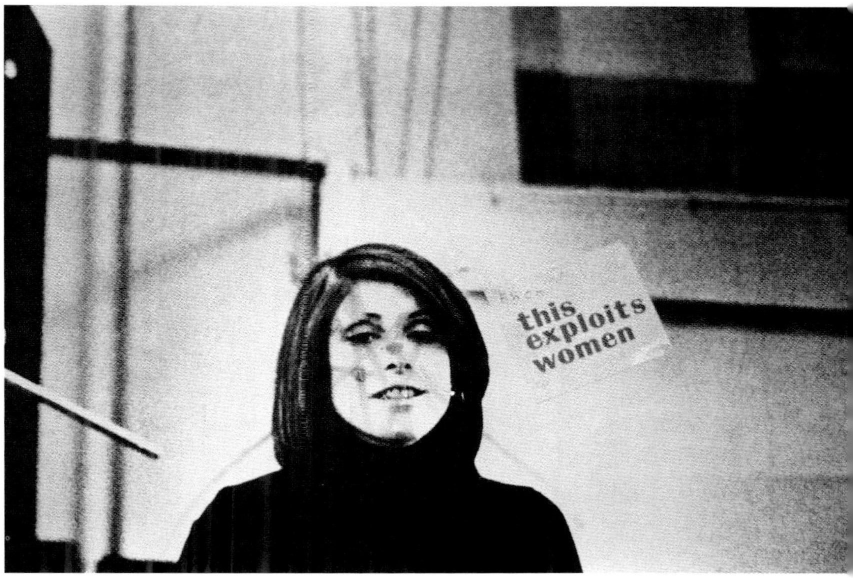

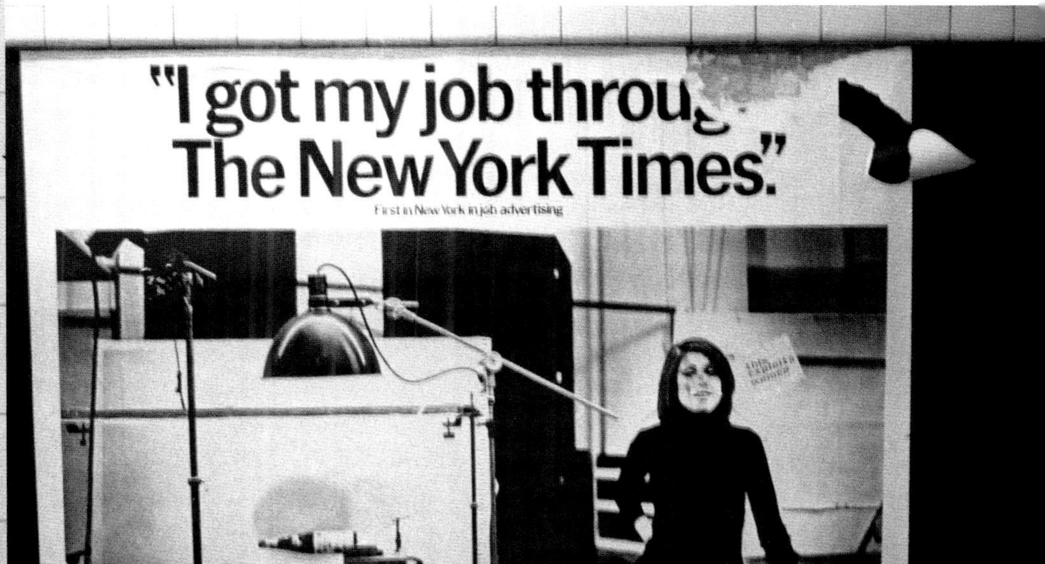

Dennis McGuire was a big influence on my photography. He hung around the Factory with Warhol and even worked briefly for Diane Arbus. He shot these images for the "I got my job through The New York Times" campaign.

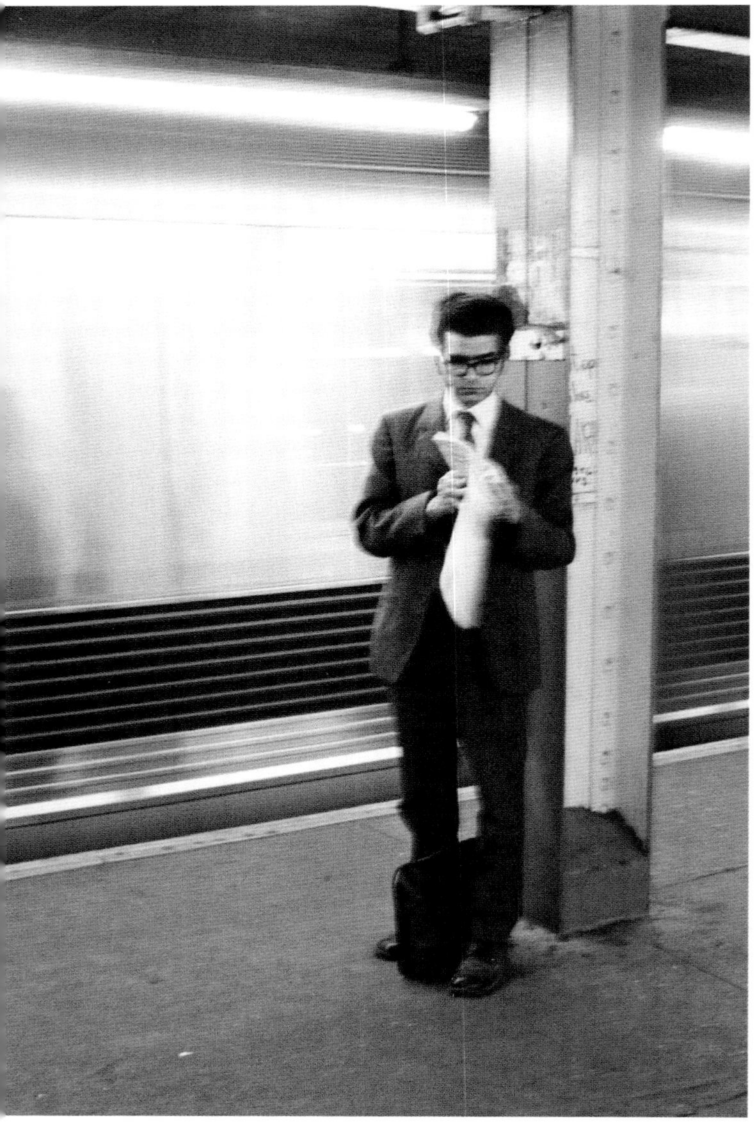

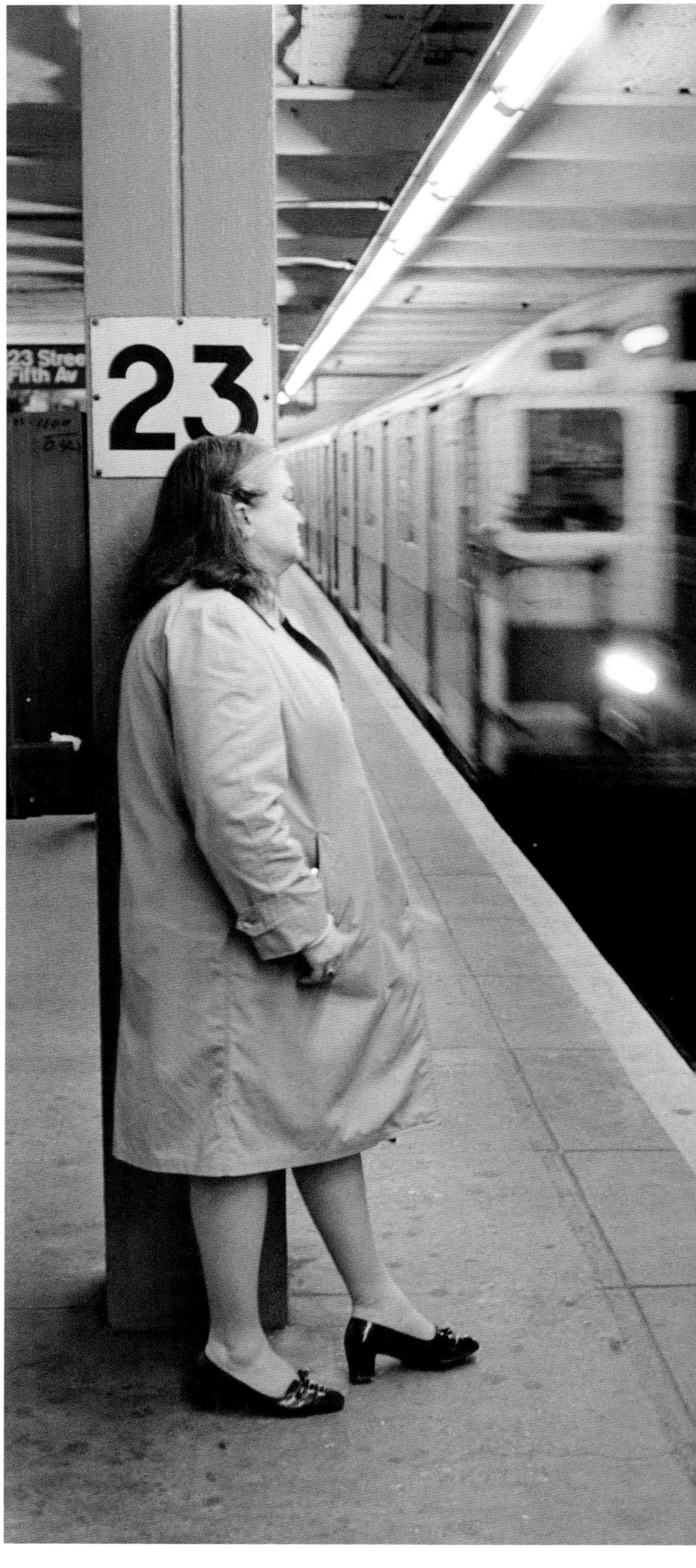
23
Fifth Av

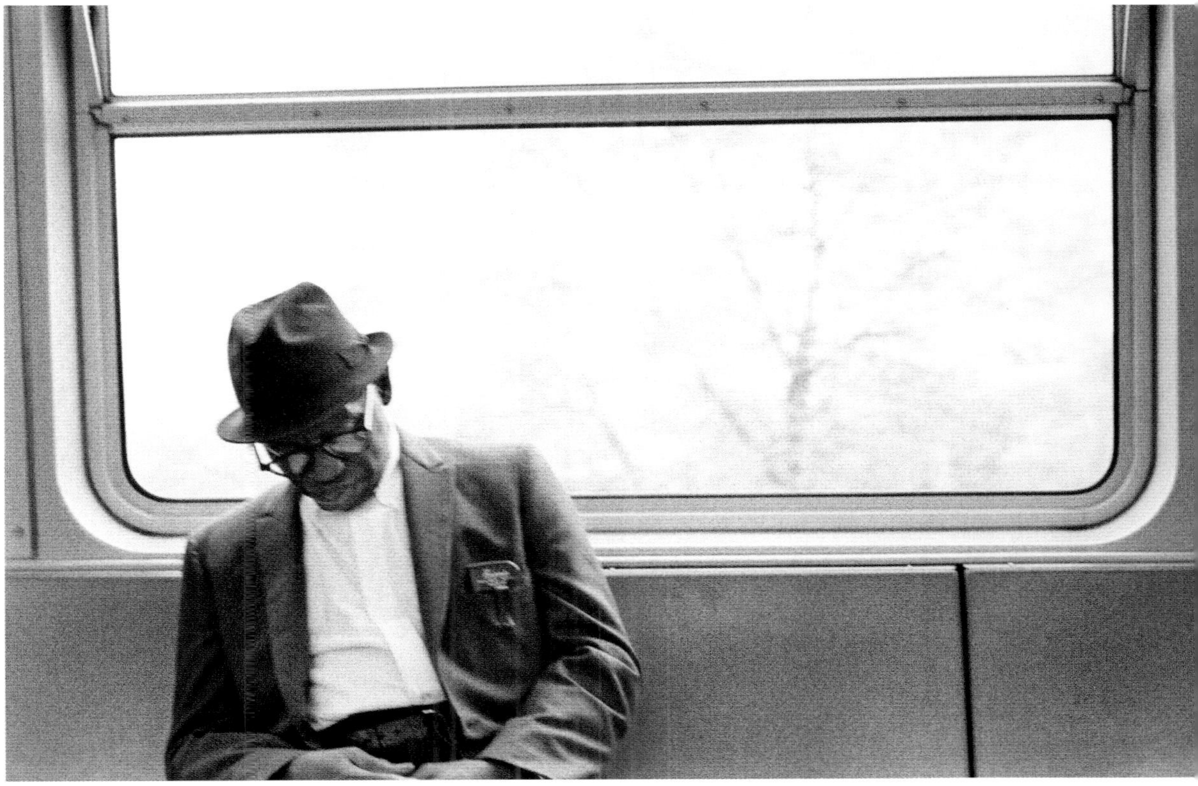

Commuters and [following pages] Debbie on the subway, 1973–74.

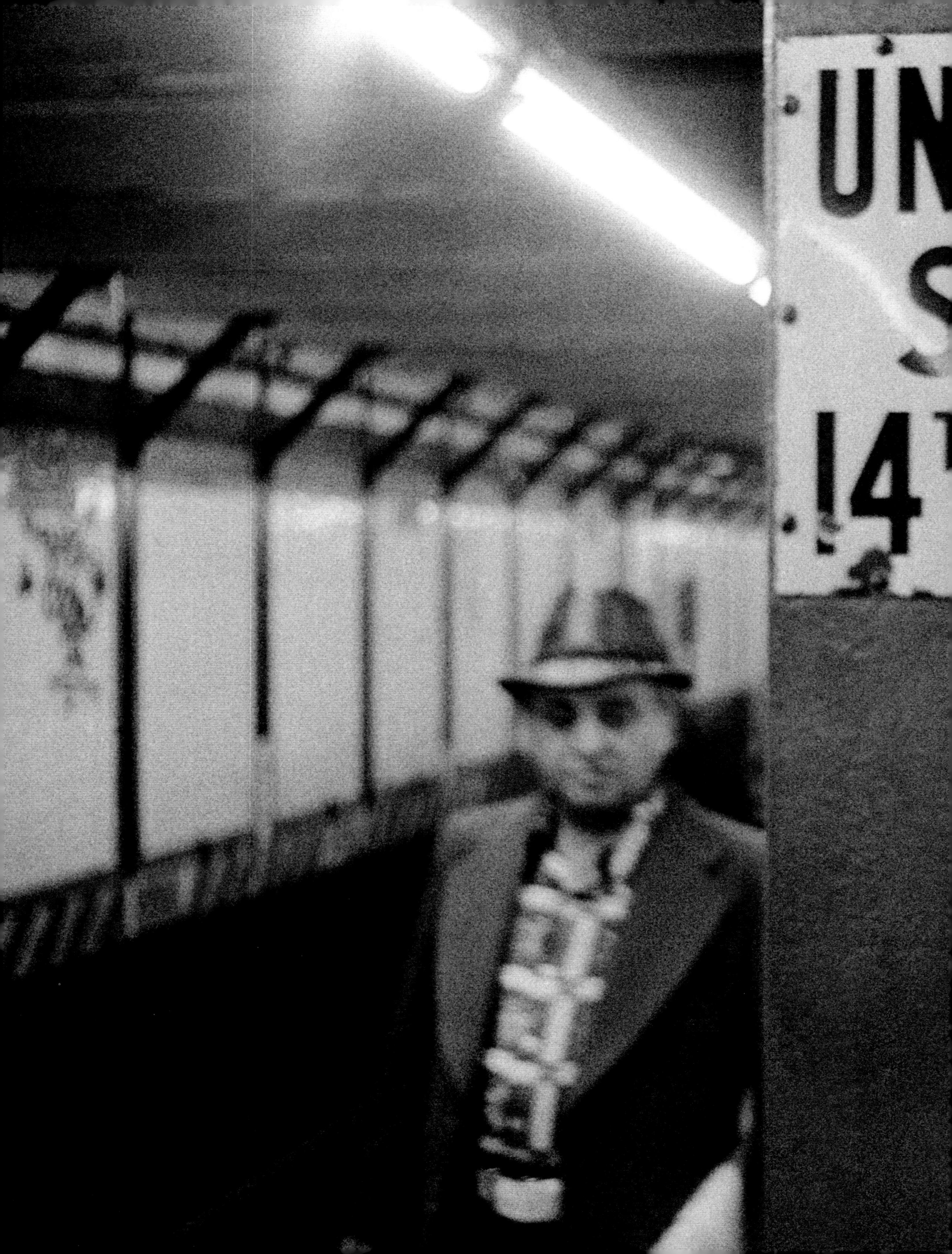

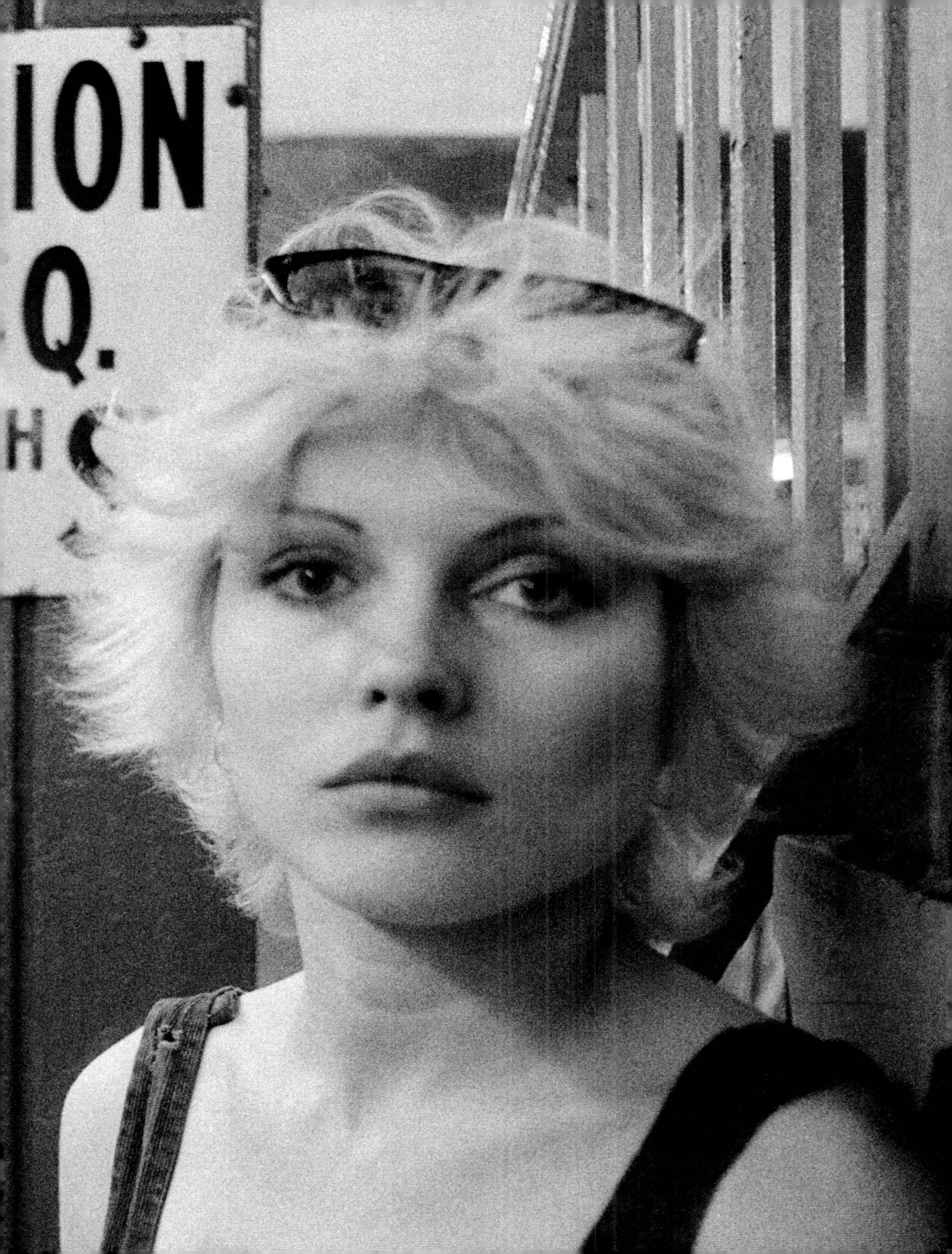
ION
Q.

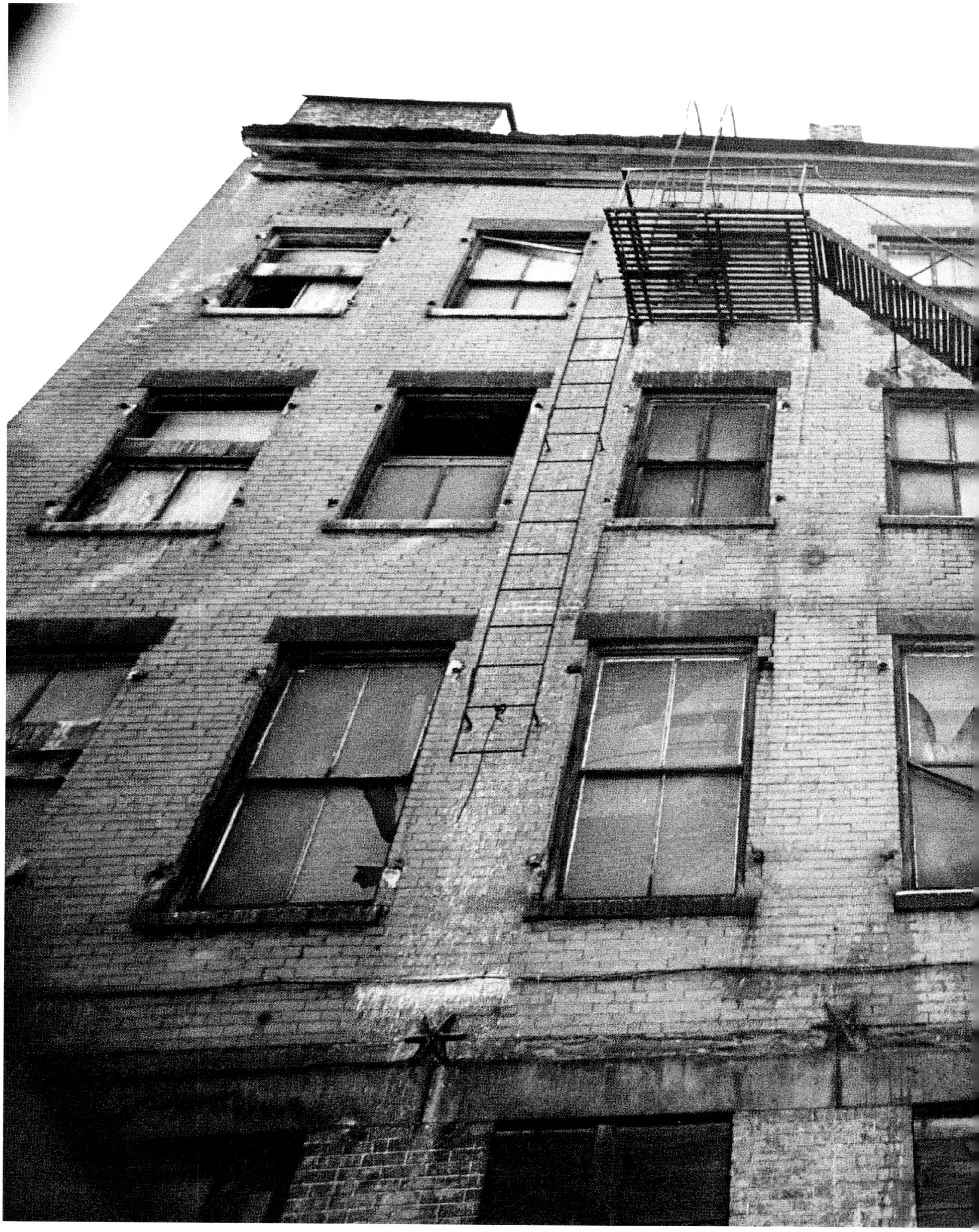

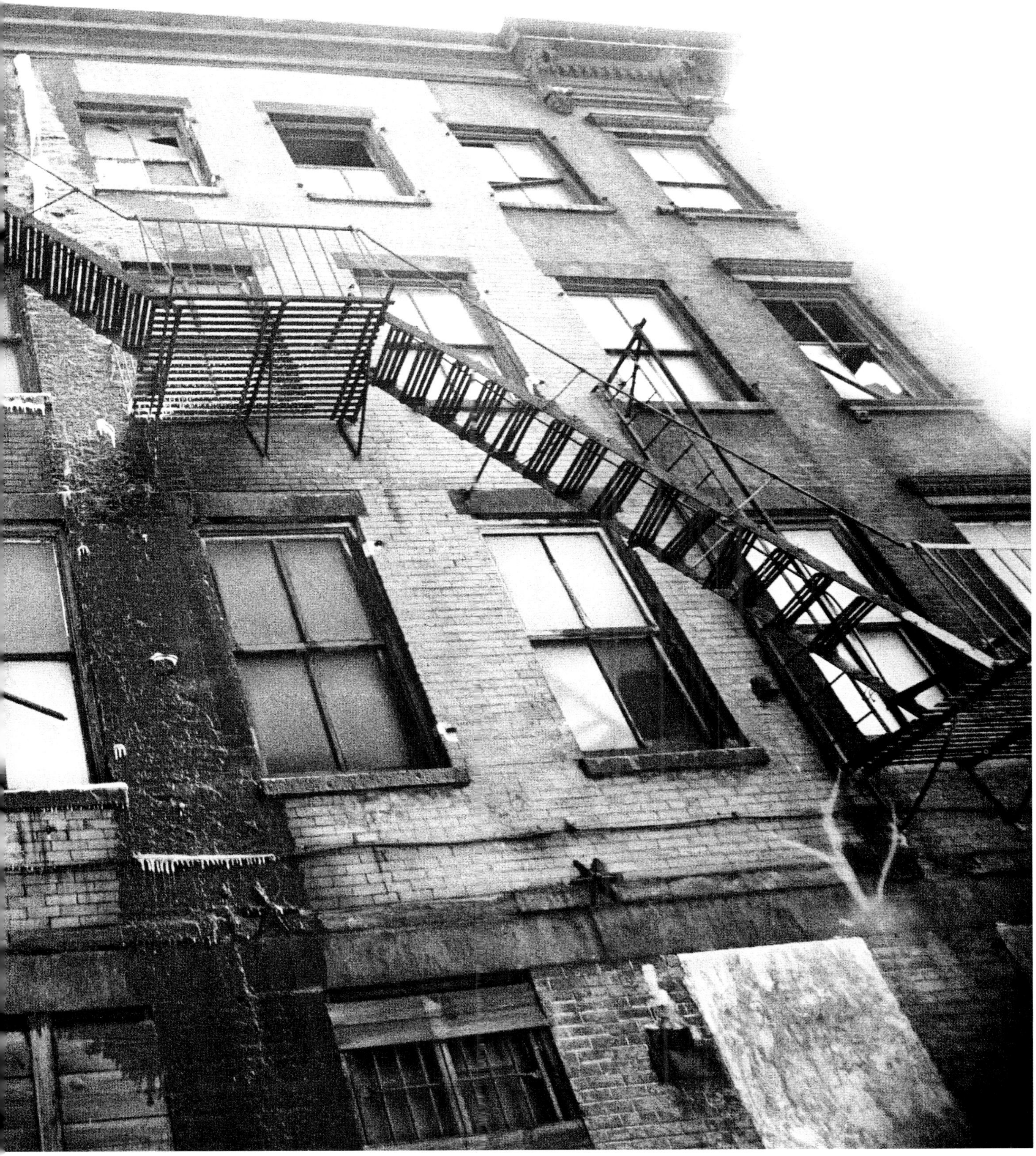

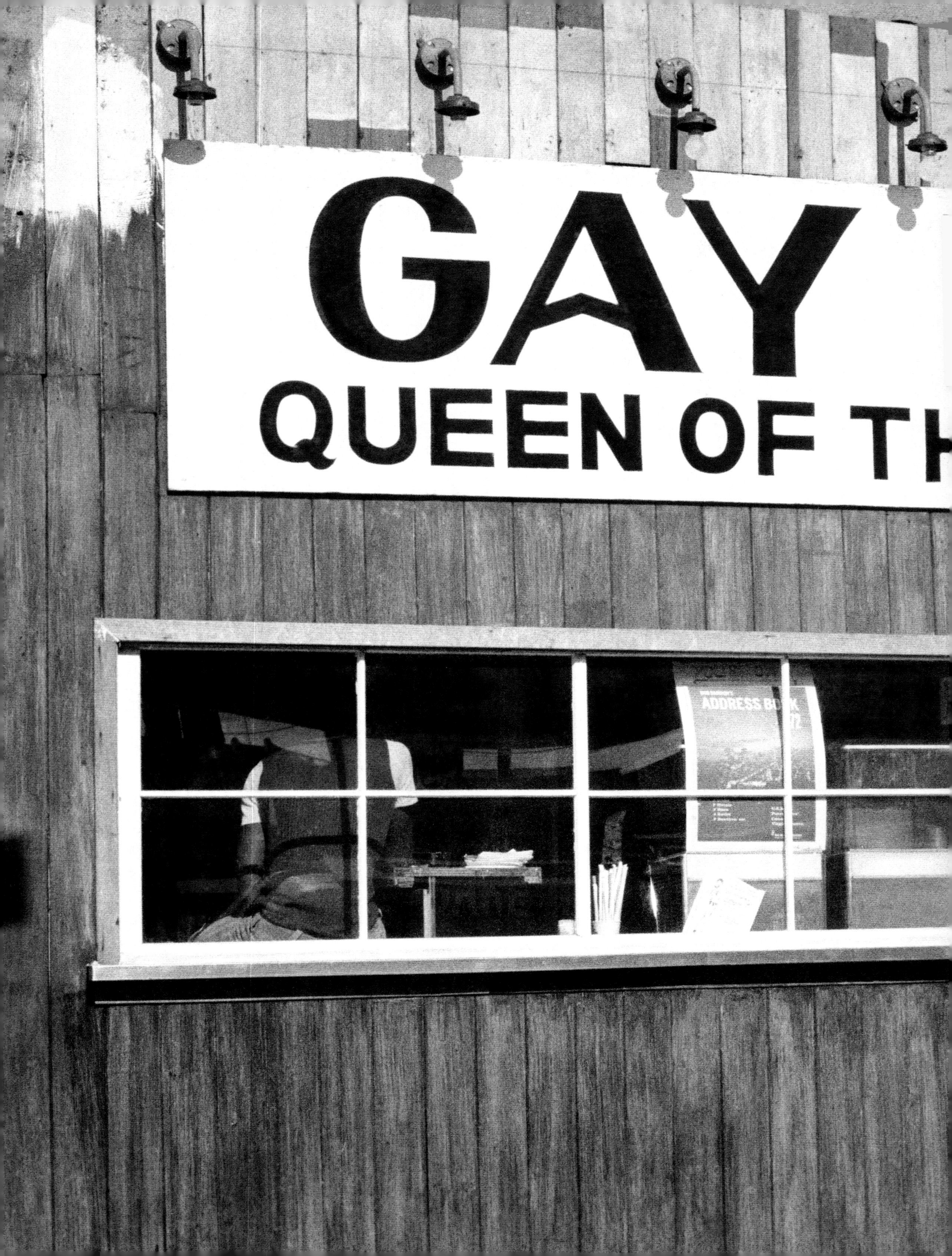
GAY
QUEEN OF TH

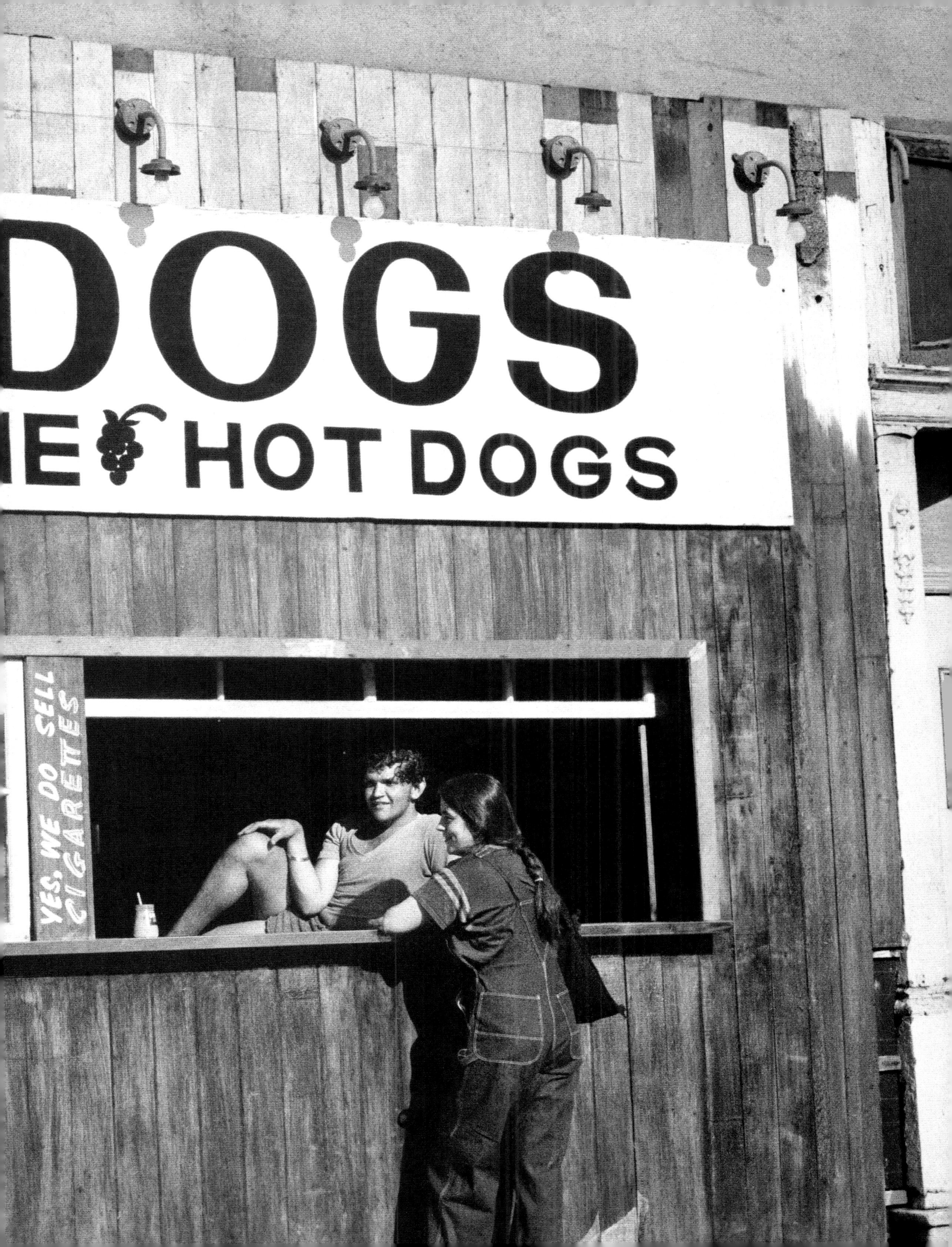
DOGS
IE HOT DOGS
YES, WE DO SELL
CIGARETTES

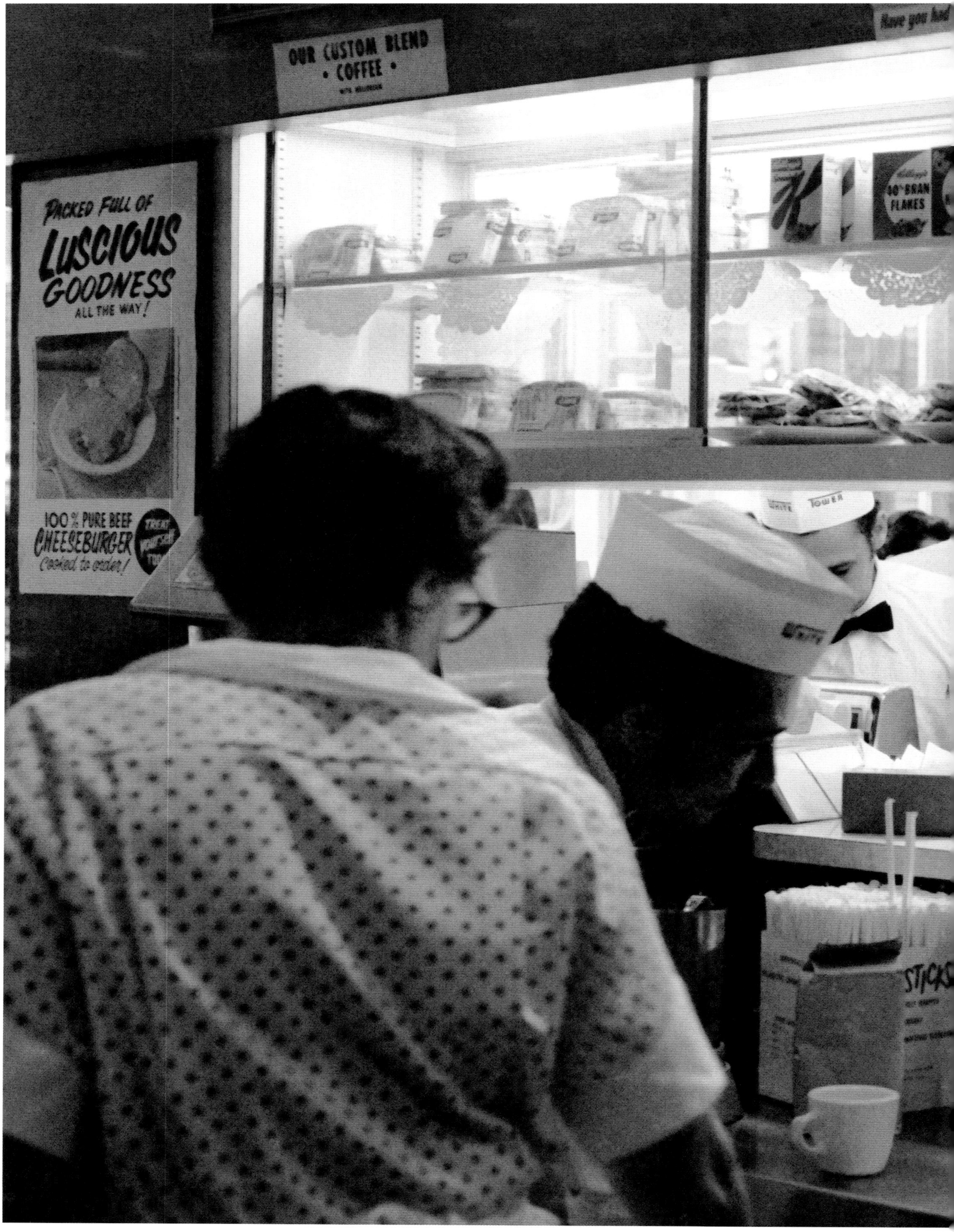
OUR CUSTOM BLEND
• COFFEE •
PACKED FULL OF
LUSCIOUS
GOODNESS
ALL THE WAY!
100% PURE BEEF
CHEESEBURGER
Cooked to order!
40% BRAN
FLAKES
WHITE TOWER

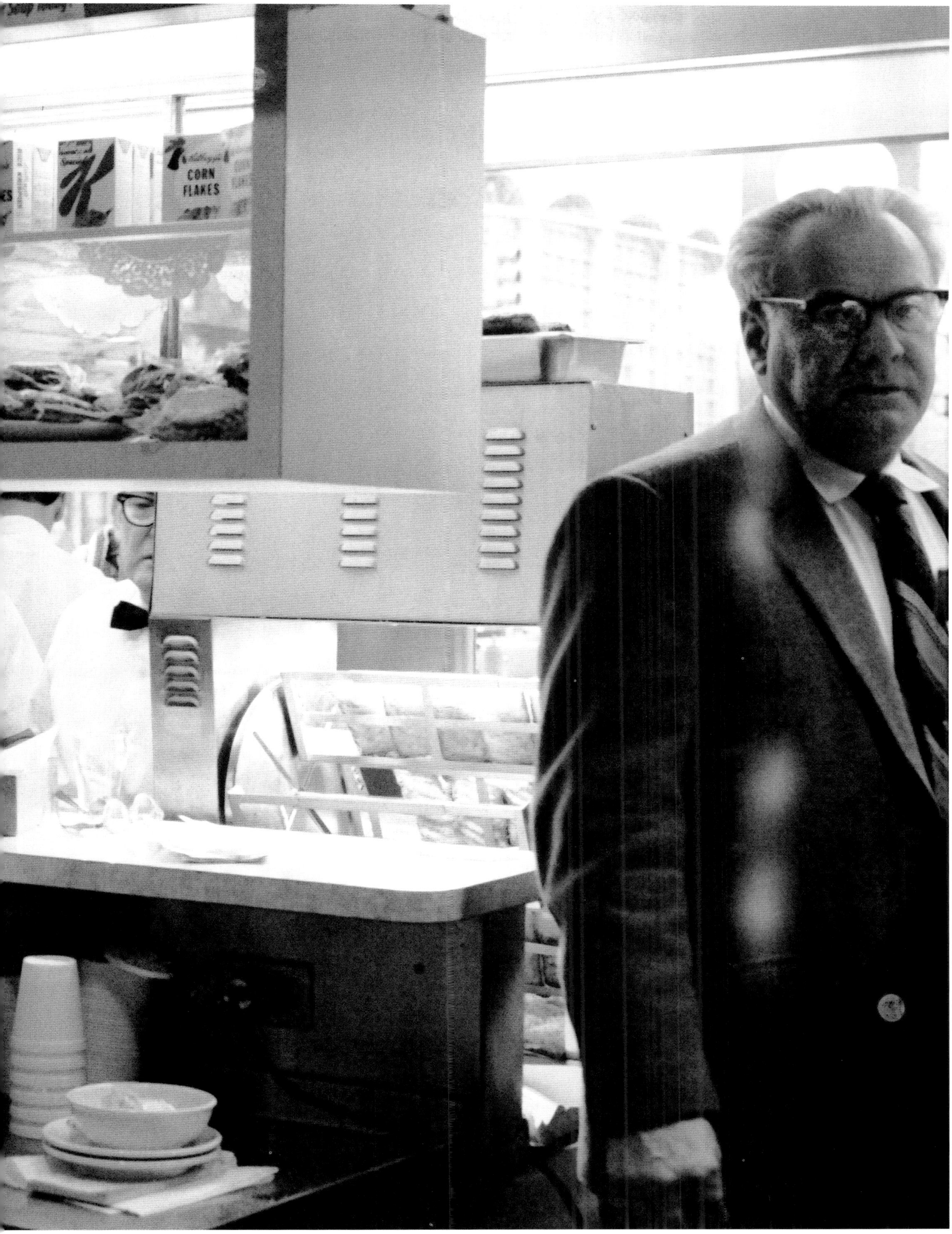
CORN
FLAKES

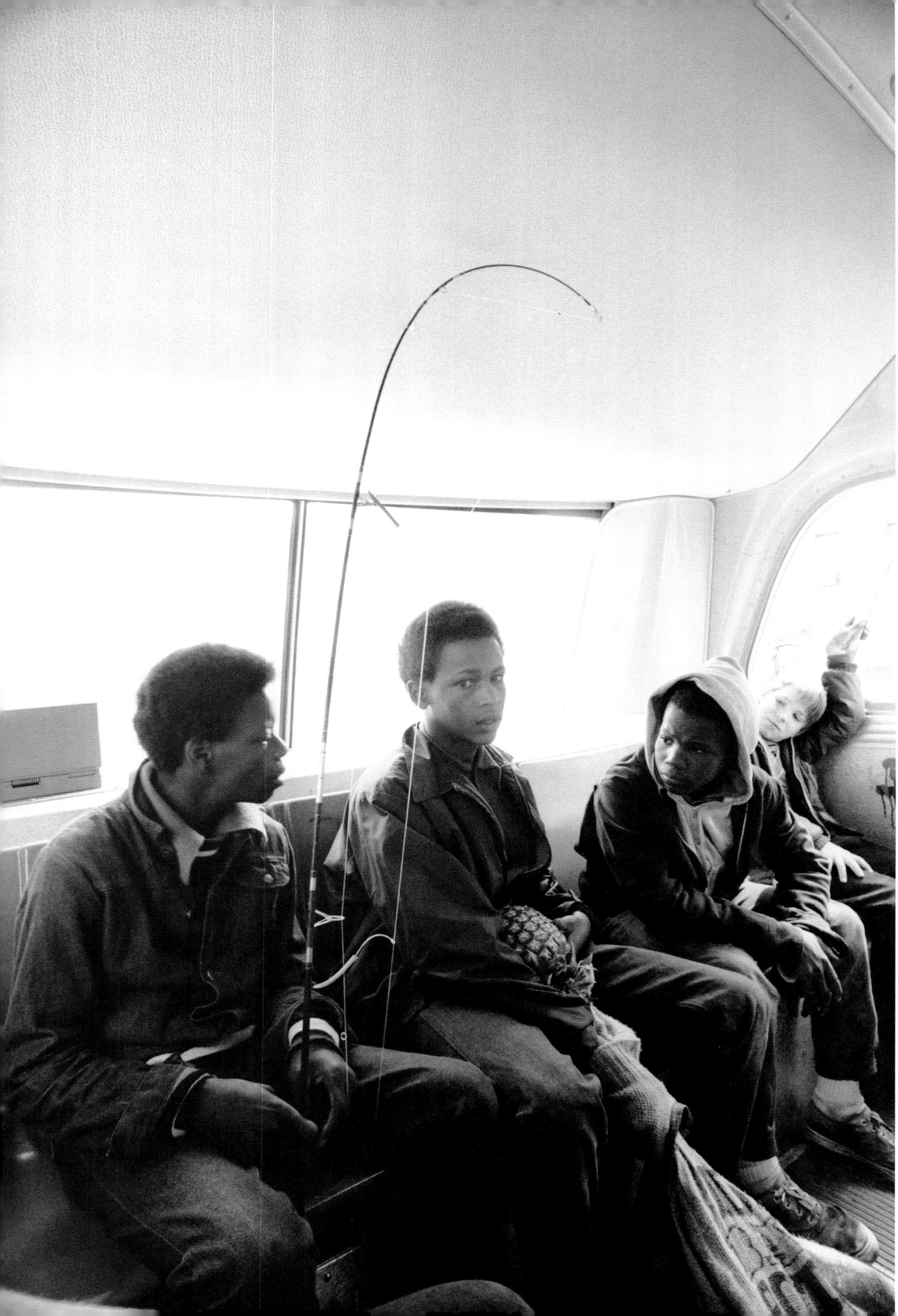

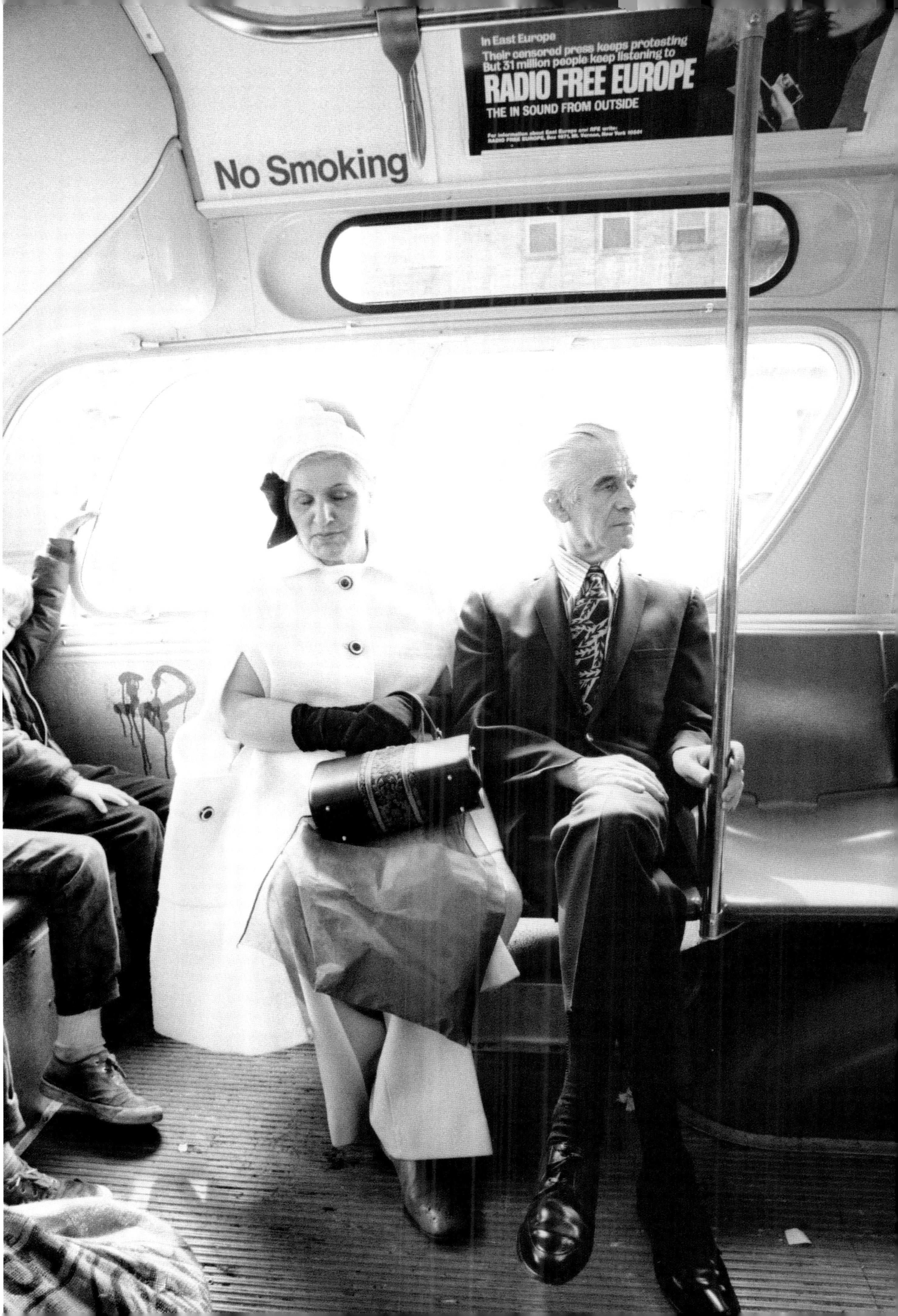
In East Europe
Their censored press keeps protesting
But 31 million people keep listening to
RADIO FREE EUROPE
THE IN SOUND FROM OUTSIDE
No Smoking

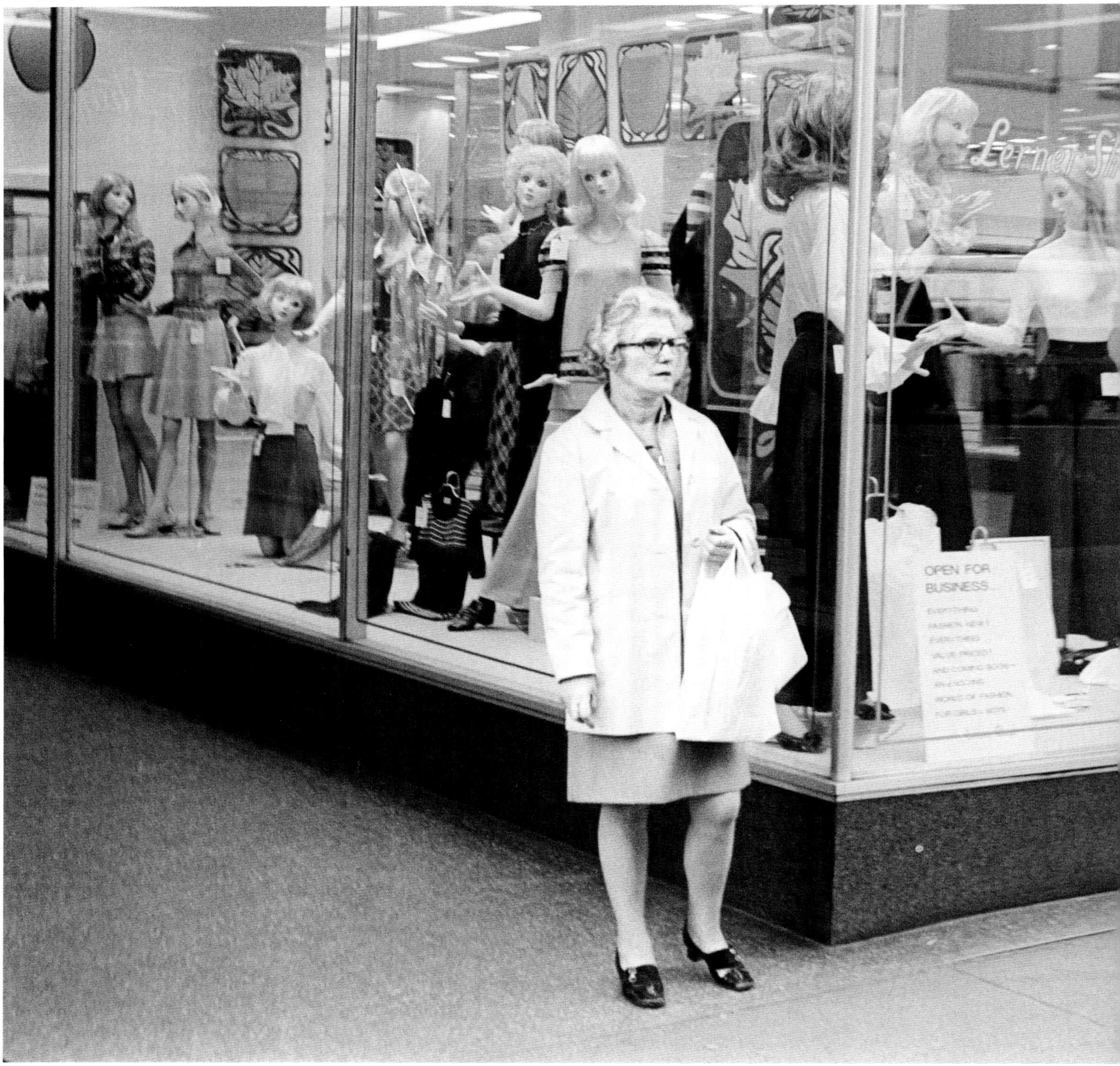

PREVIOUS PAGES:
On the bus, Ocean Avenue, Brooklyn. The kids were probably coming back from a fishing expedition at Brighton Beach, hence the poles and sacks.

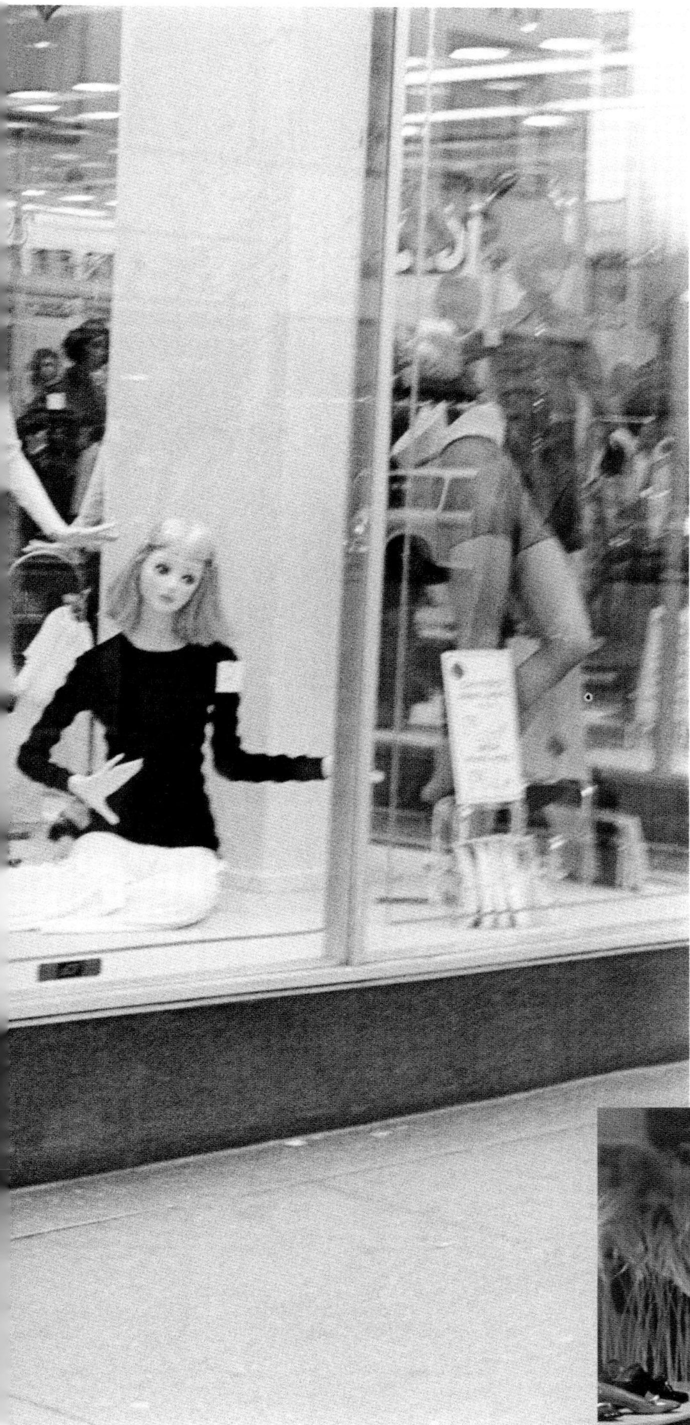

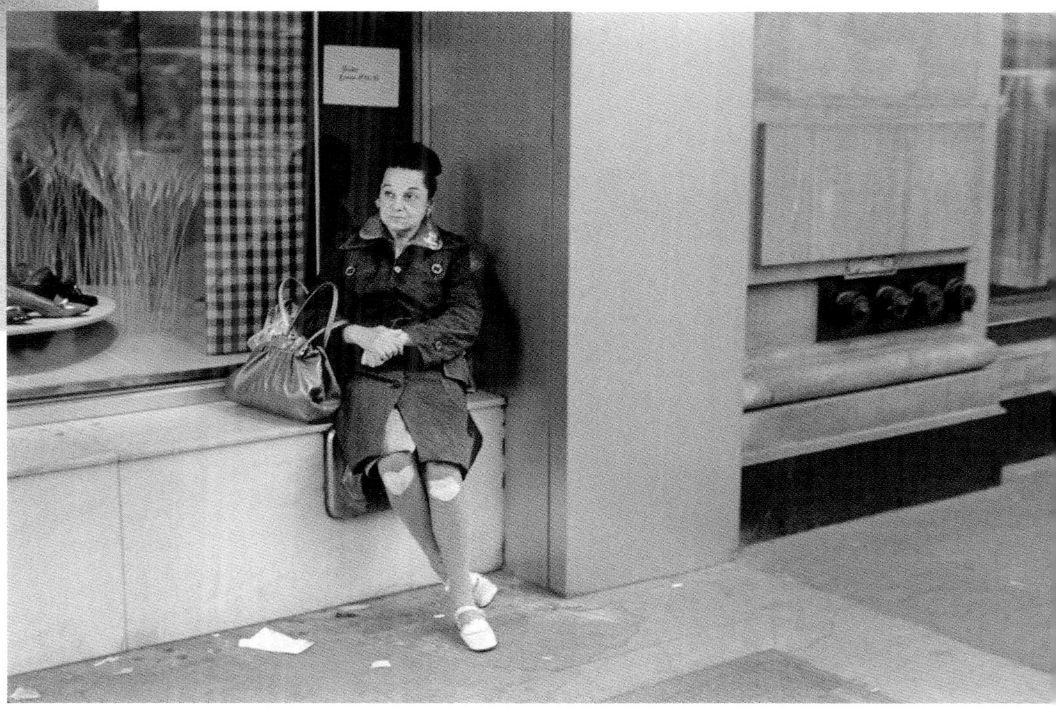

Shoppers.

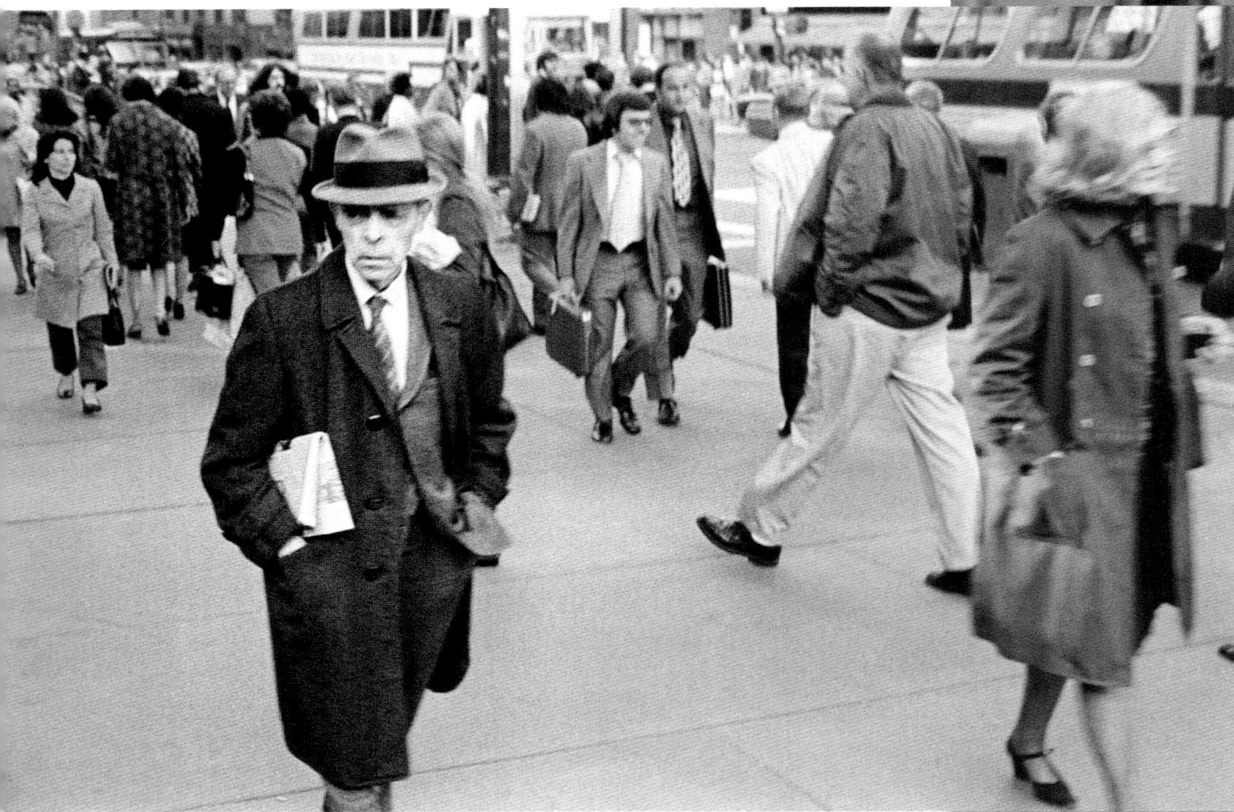

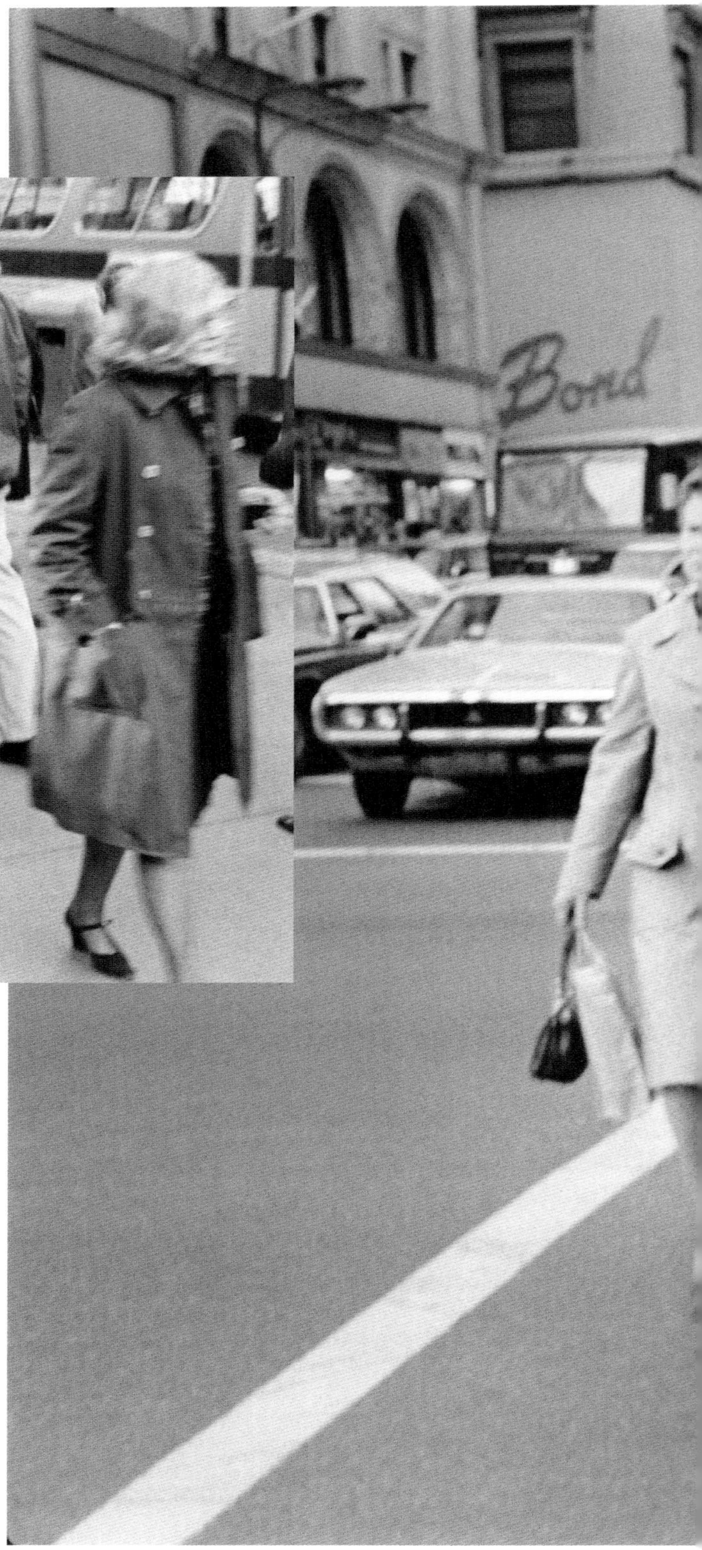

Midtown.

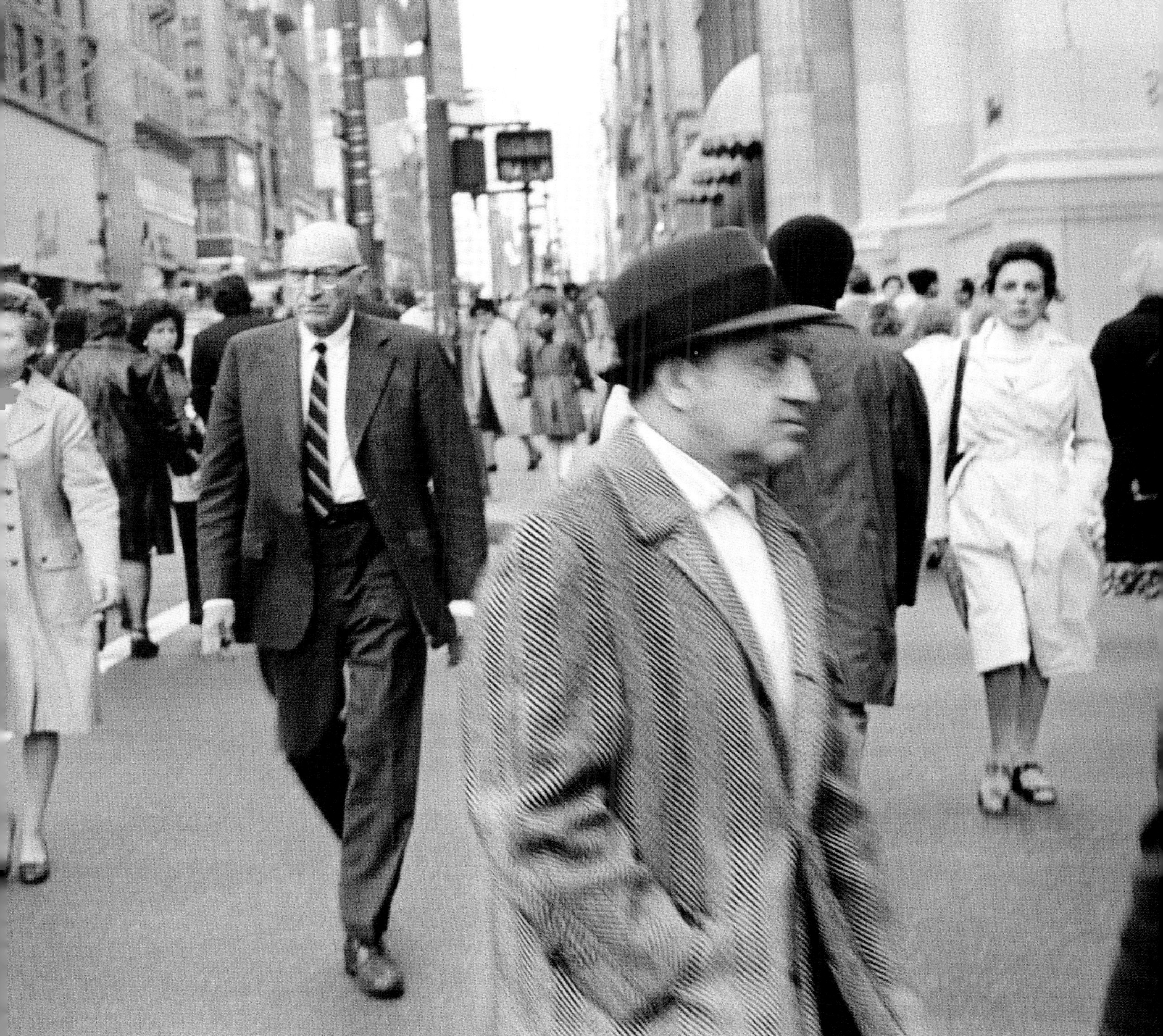

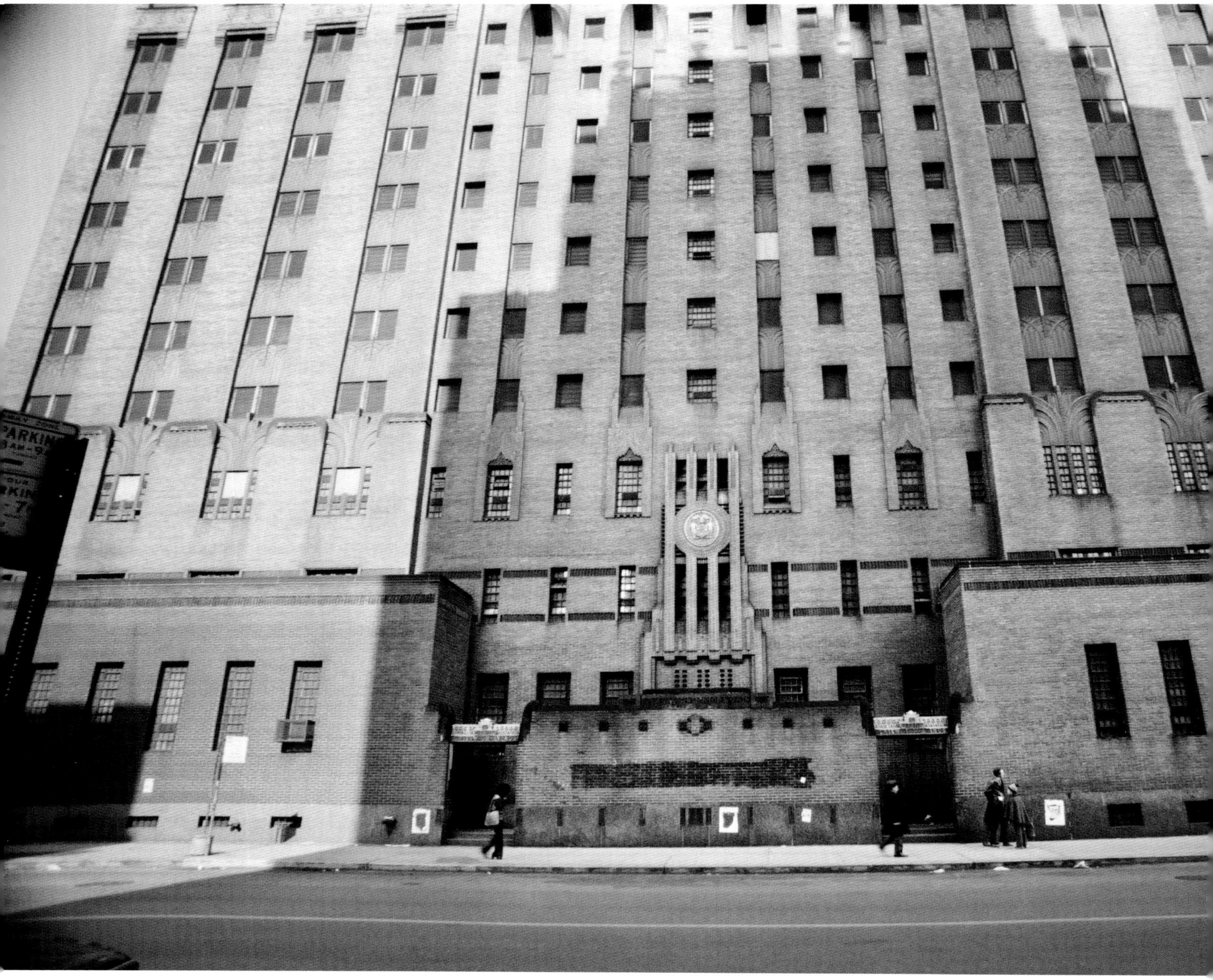

FOLLOWING PAGES:
A *Death in Venice* moment at Hudson River piers, all the way west. I've always heard that the debris that's just under the water levels at the side of the river embankment is a vast wall of broken glass, discarded pistols, and everything else one might imagine.

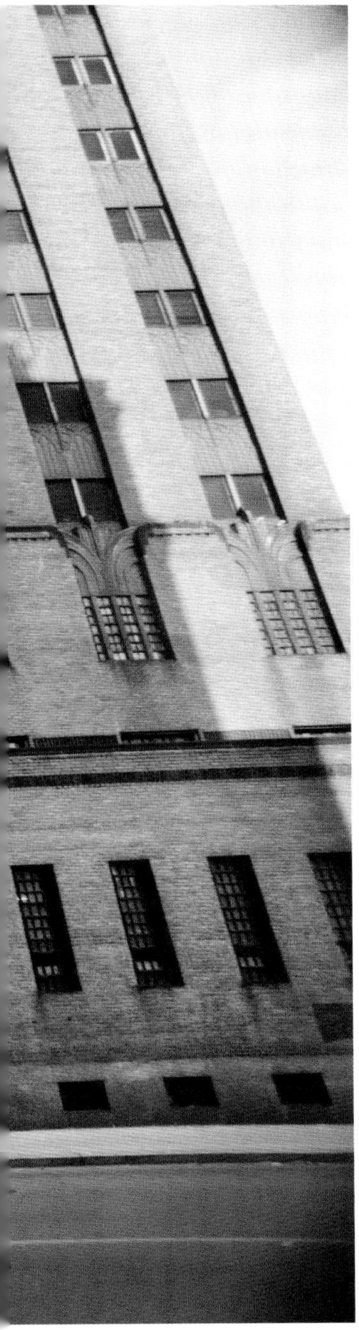

WOMEN'S HOUSE OF DETENTION

The Women's House of Detention was a women's prison in the middle of Greenwich Village at 10 Greenwich Ave. that existed from 1932 to 1974. It was a really grim and potent symbol of female oppression—an absurdly Orwellian-looking structure. Inmates included Angela Davis, Ethel Rosenberg, and activist Dorothy Day, who was considered for canonization by the Catholic Church. Day cofounded the *Catholic Worker* in 1933 and various acts of civil disobedience saw her jailed in the fifties.

Even by the mid-sixties, the area around the jail on Greenwich and Sixth Ave. was pretty hip and upscale, and the existence of the prison was ironic and awkward.

There was an odd scene that went on around the prison. Guys—boyfriends, husbands—would collect on the sidewalk below the windows and engage in shouted conversations with the inmates. I actually saw girls lower long strings so the guys could tie cigarettes to them and have them pulled up into the barred windows.

The House of D was finally demolished in 1973–74 under Mayor John Lindsay and replaced by a garden.

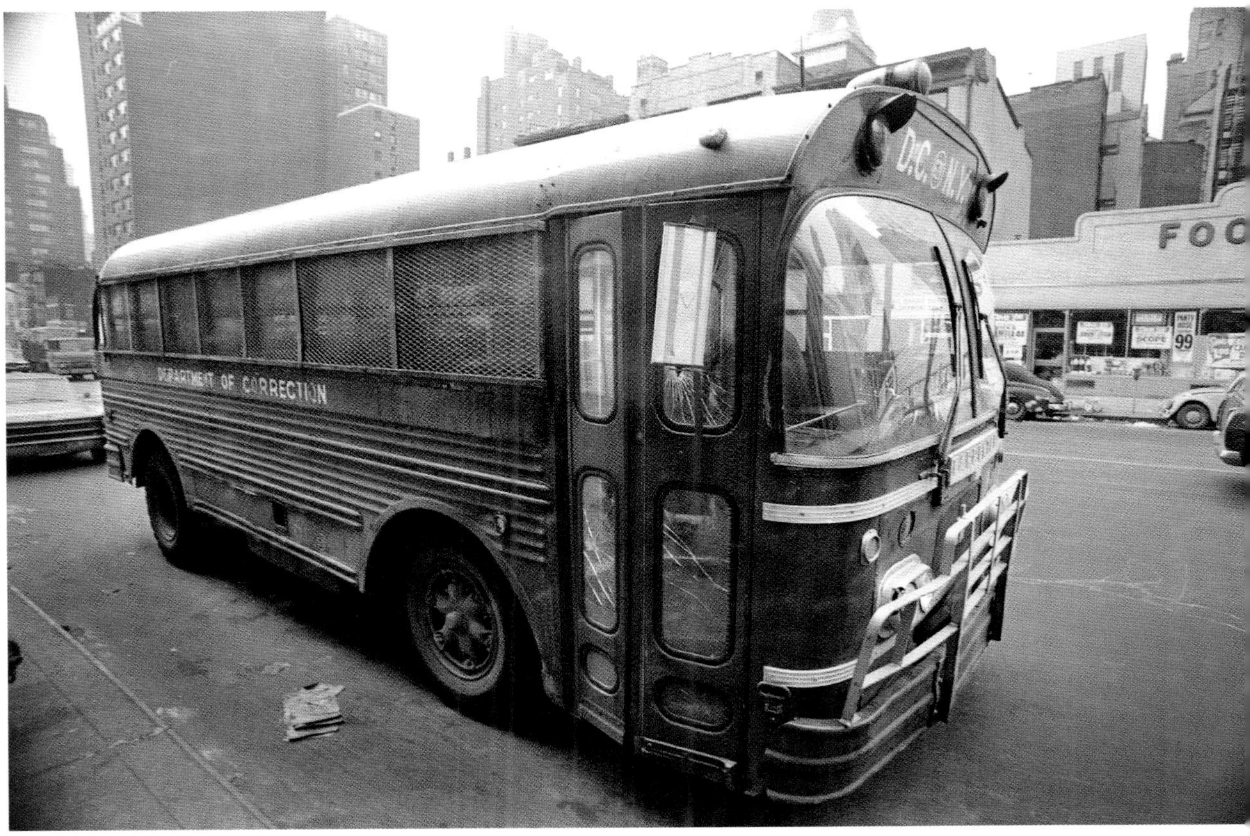

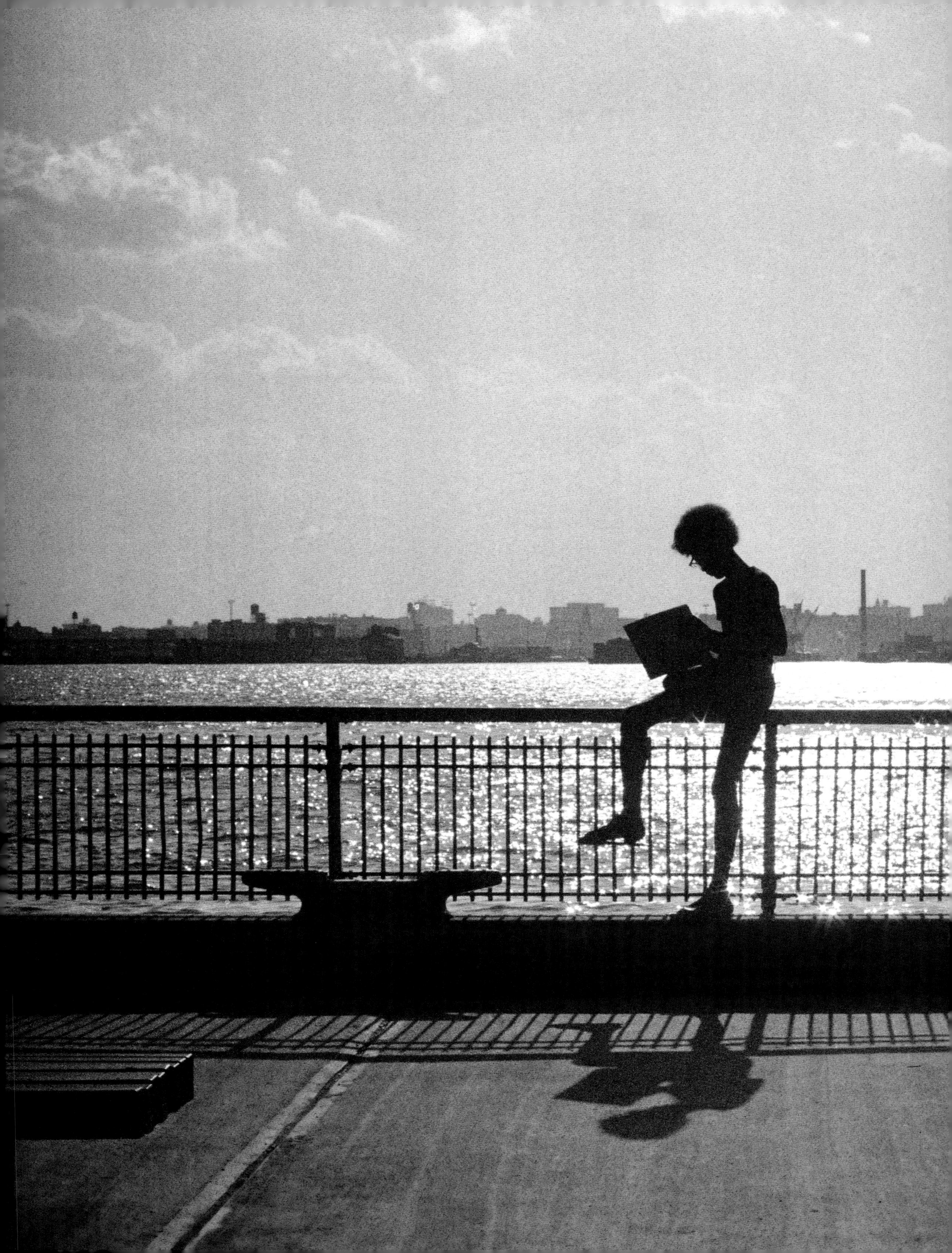

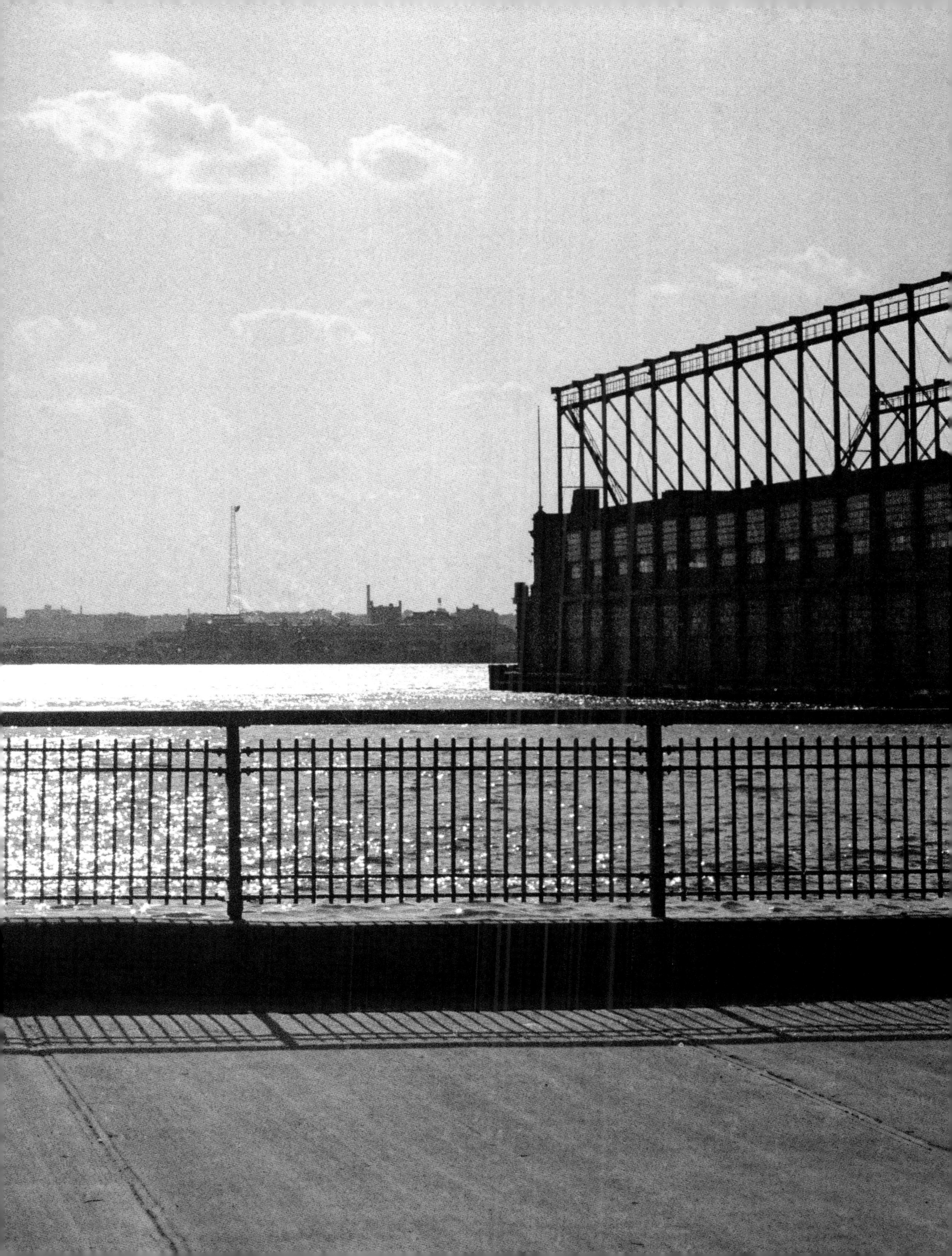

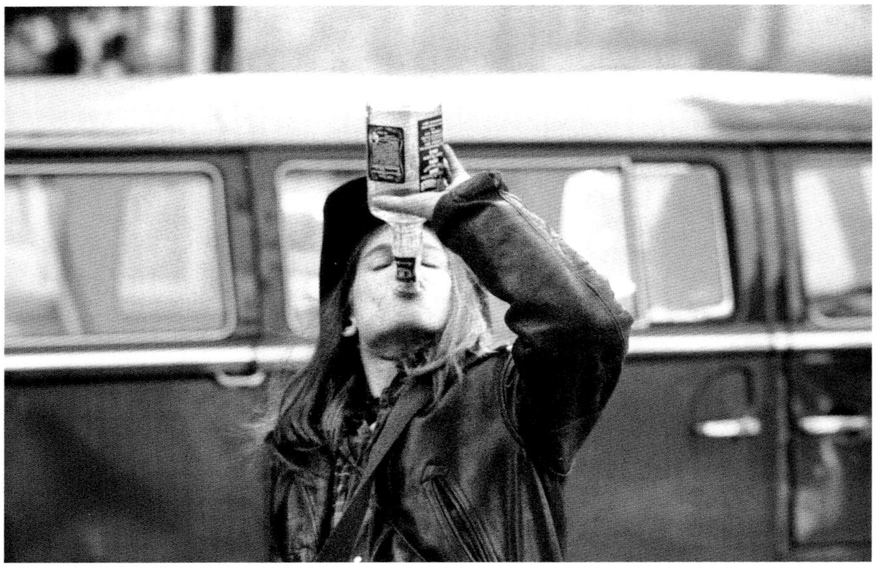

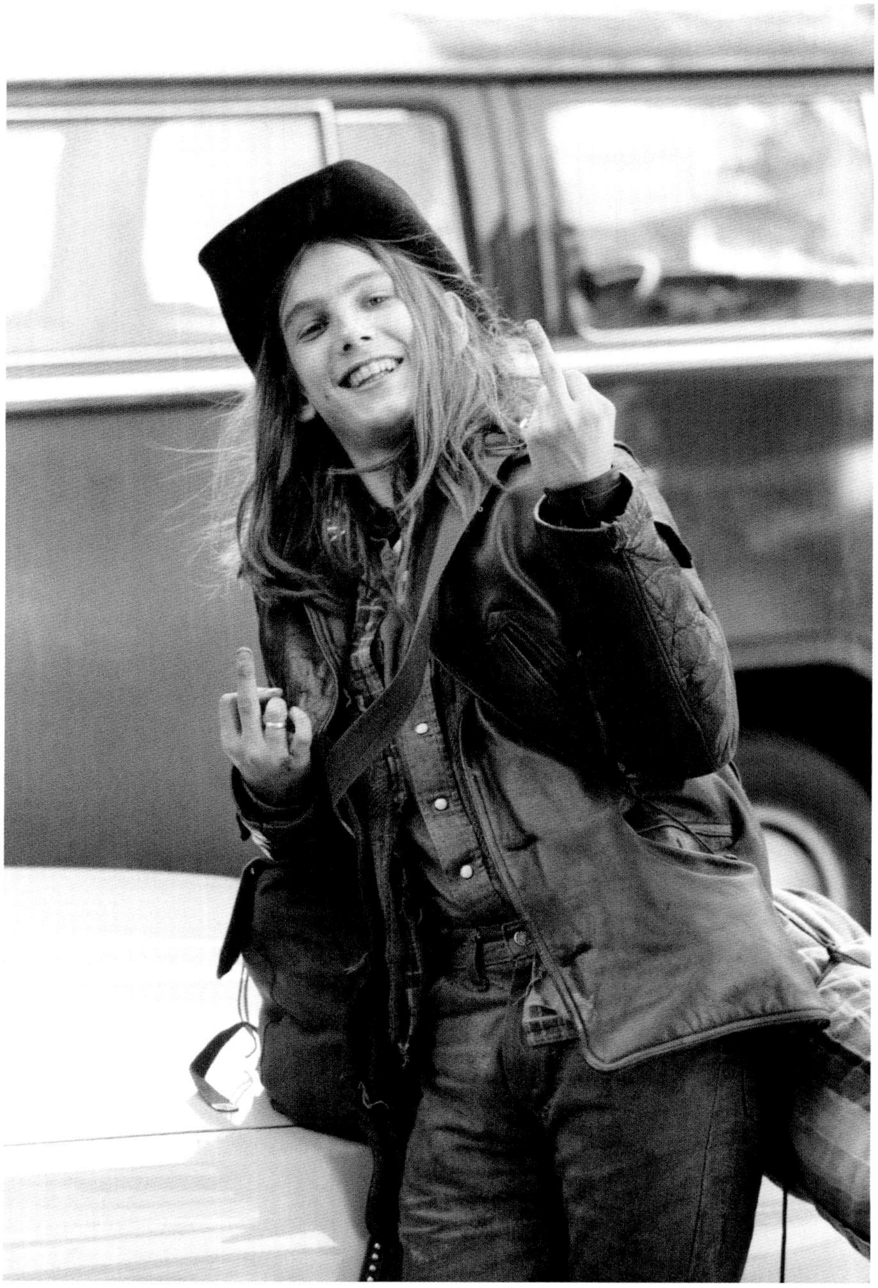

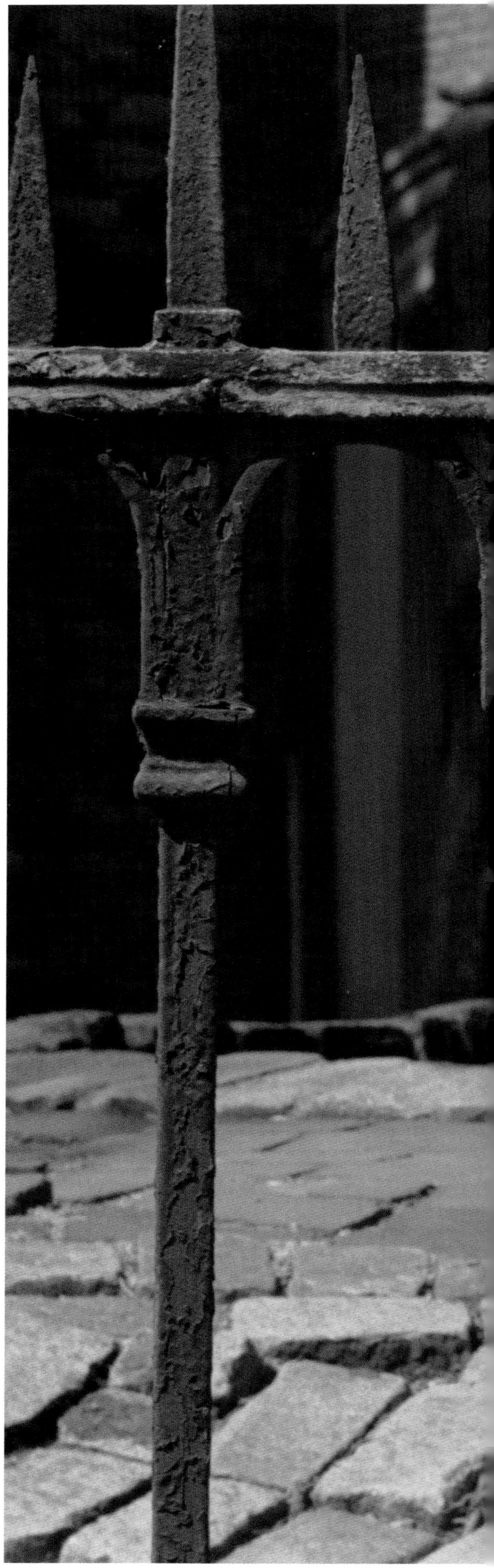

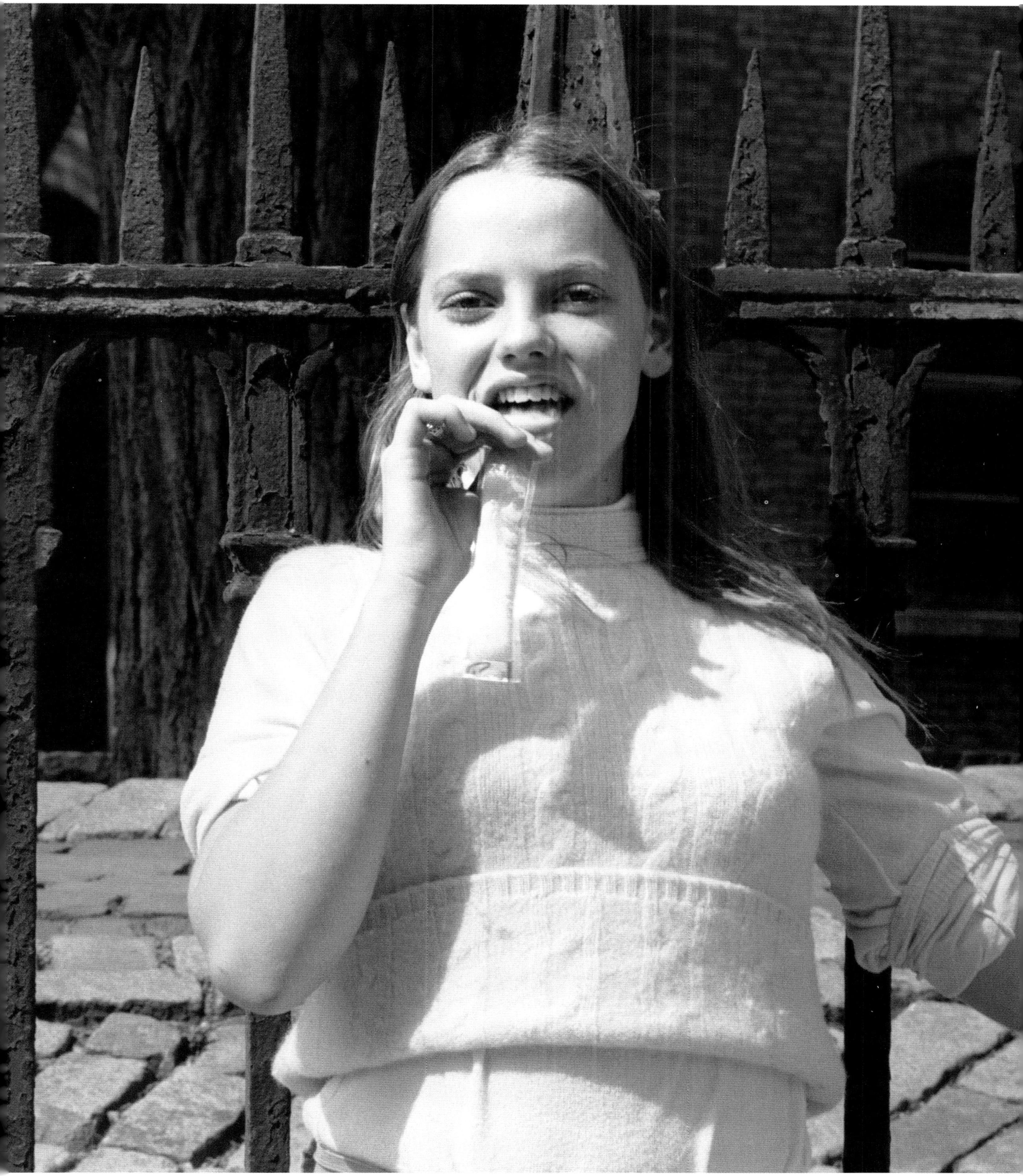

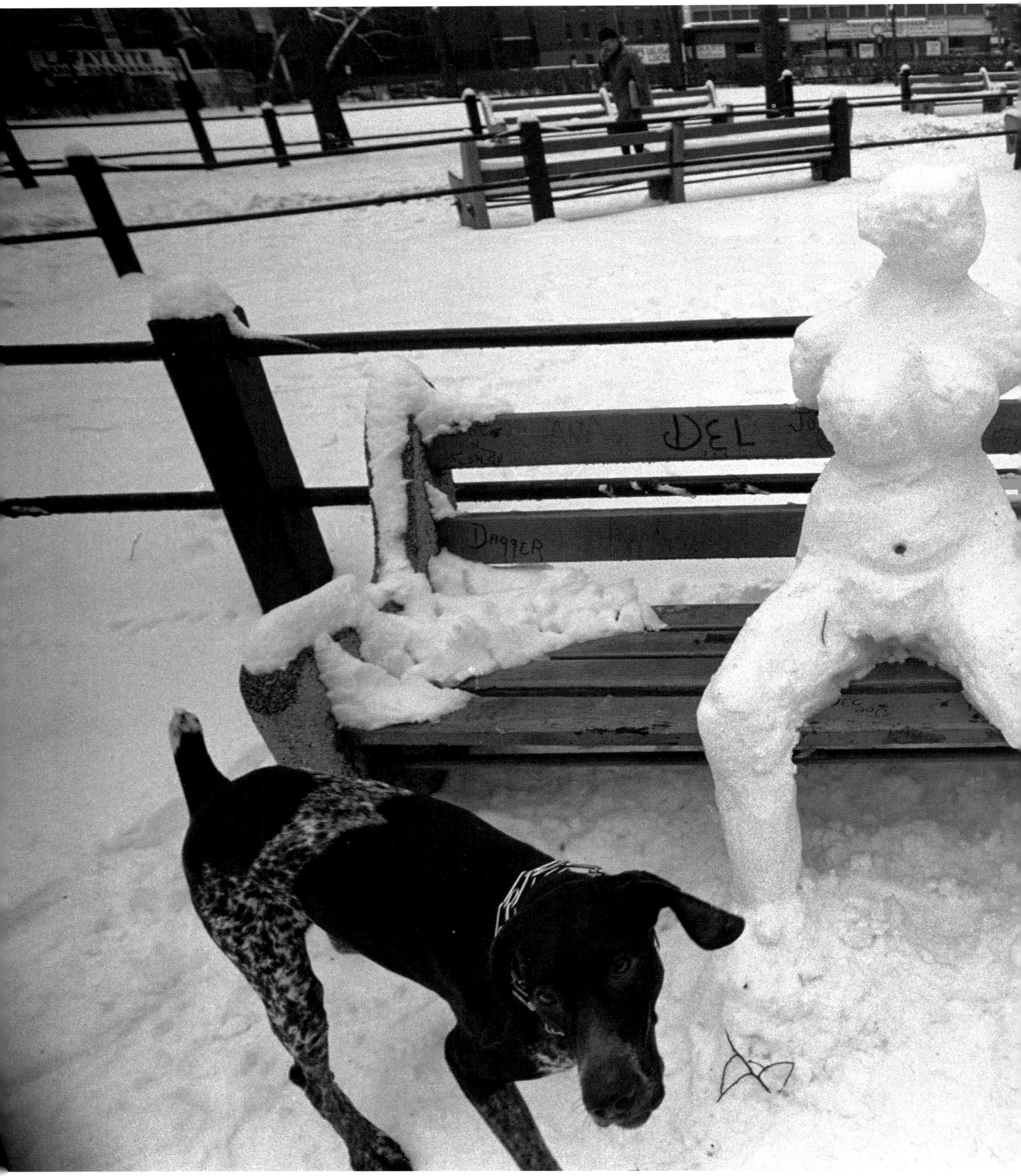
DEL
Dagger

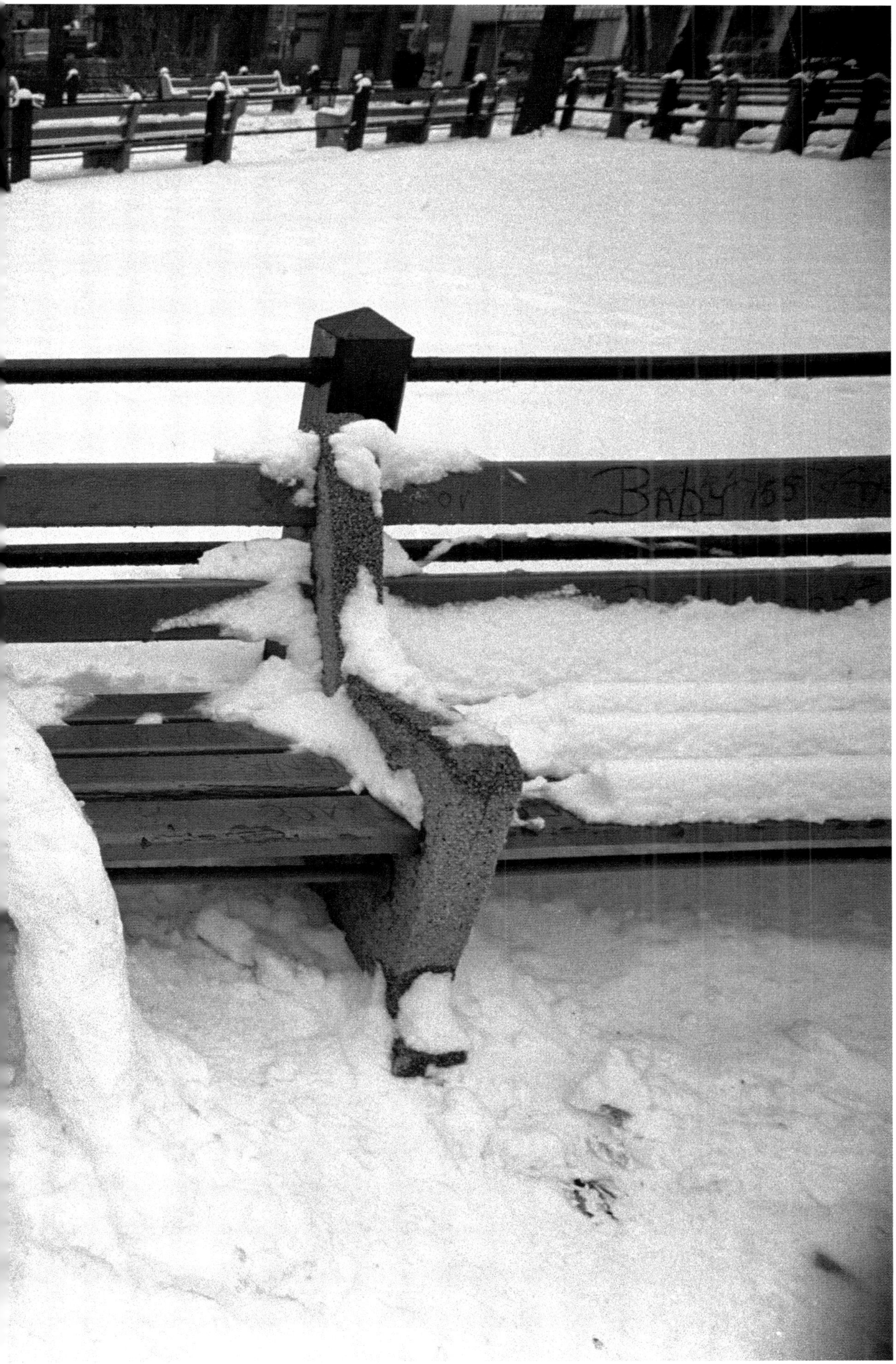

PREVIOUS PAGES:
Kids on the street along my route to and from the School of Visual Arts on East 23rd Street.

I was fascinated by a group of street kids that used to hang around the Lower East Side, known as the STP family. They all had a ragged brown dress motif and would have STP patches sewn onto their clothing everywhere. I'd frequently see them camped out with dogs and sleeping bags in front of Saint Mark's Bowery Church. This boy, though not an STP family member, has that look.

I recall seeing the first Gaping Banana Outfitters type clothing stores opening up, and being amazed that the clothes in the window were the sort of bland uniforms that up to that point were the province of thrift stores—the dress code no one really wanted to wear.

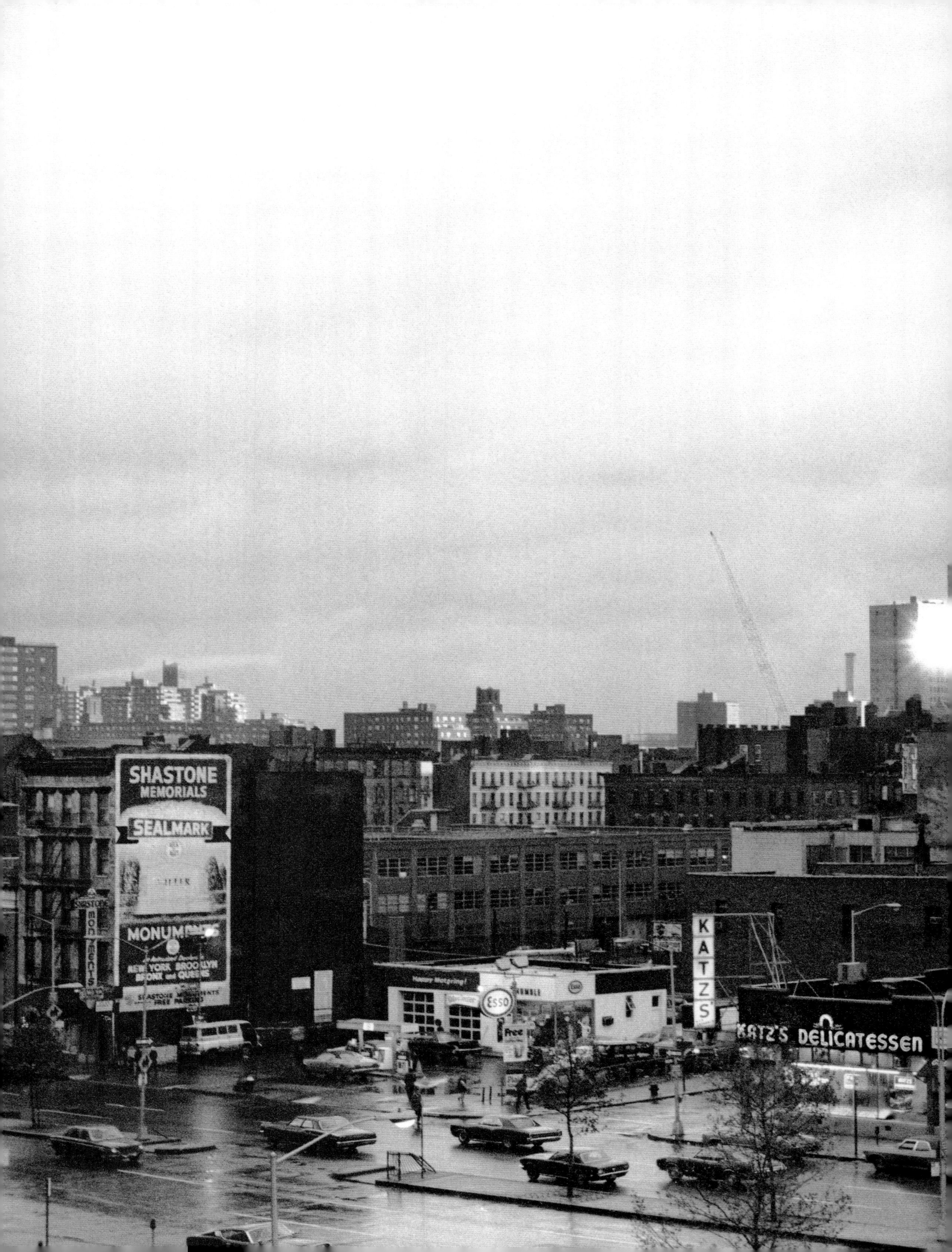
SHASTONE
MEMORIALS
SEALMARK
NEW YORK BROOKLYN
BRONX and QUEENS
ESSO
KATZ'S
KATZ'S DELICATESSEN

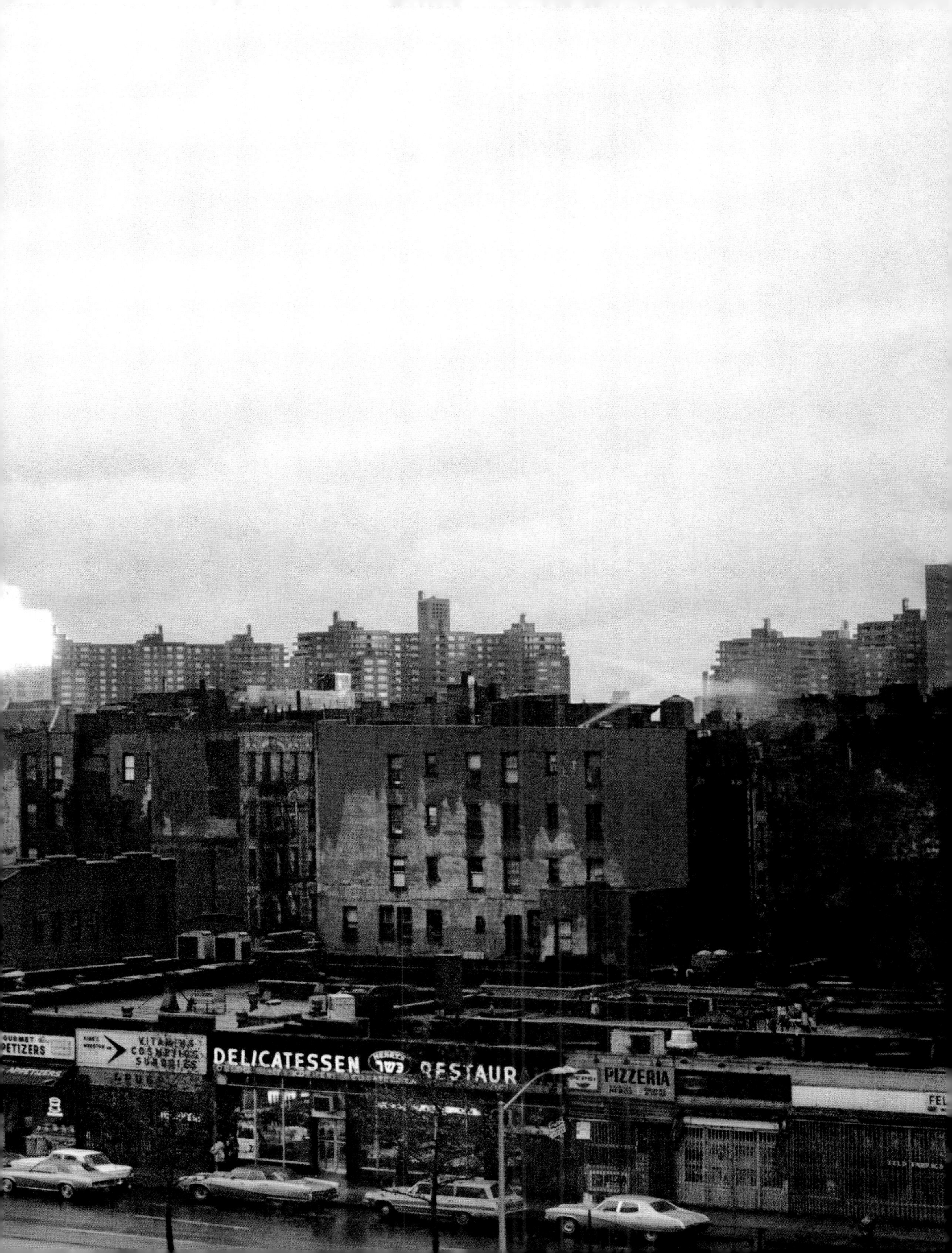
PETIZERS
DELICATESSEN
כשר
RESTAUR
PEPSI
PIZZERIA

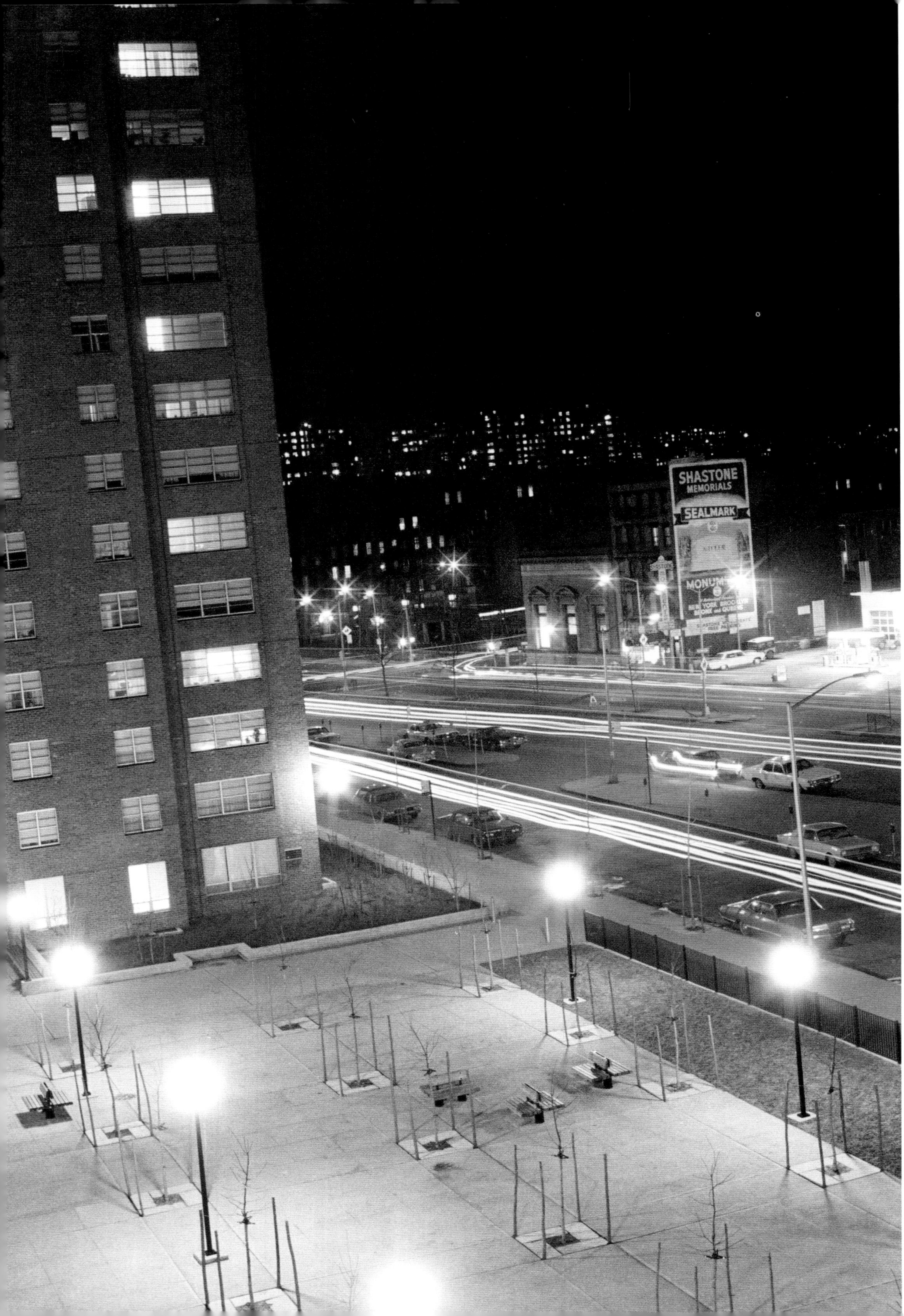
SHASTONE
MEMORIALS
SEALMARK

THE APARTMENT

In 1969 I was staying with my mother in Brooklyn. A girlfriend and I decided to look for an apartment together in Manhattan. She was British and Polish and she easily charmed the rental manager of this building at 18 First Avenue, right at First and First, a location that has some *Seinfeld* significance—I don't know, I never watched much of it.

The people in the building were almost exclusively working-class families, this being long before hipster invasion or gentrification.

The fifth-floor apartment had, up until our tenancy, been functioning as a sort of clubhouse for the manager dude and his buddies. I don't know exactly why he was willing to surrender this space just based on my girlfriend being cute, but that's what happened. There were many holes in the rear-facing wall where a dartboard had been.

We moved in. The building looked out on the side of an abandoned tenement that faced Houston Street. At night the abandoned building was used as a shooting gallery for addicts and street people who would come and go very casually. One night during the wee hours the old building caught fire and burned very extravagantly. It was only maybe twenty feet away from our building, and the apartment was brightly lit and hot. By morning the flames had been extinguished and the place was destroyed but still standing. About a month later a wrecking crew showed up and a great power shovel that reminded me a lot of Godzilla proceeded to demolish what was left of the old tenement. Shortly thereafter my girlfriend and I broke up and I was left with the apartment, which now had a great view of Houston Street.

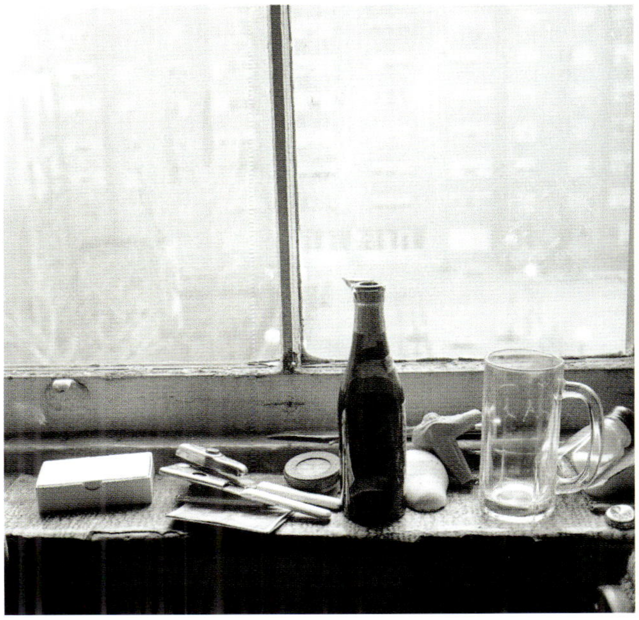

The rent was around ninety bucks when I moved in and went to almost one twenty by the time I finally left. The nice old lady next door, whom I rarely saw, paid forty dollars a month.

The people in the building initially thought I was normal. They soon figured out the grim truth. By 1972 I was hanging out in the rock scene at Max's and Mercer Arts Center, going to art school, and inviting a lot of freak types over on a regular basis.

I had made friends with Warhol 'superstar' Eric Emerson and his band, the Magic Tramps. Eric had been living with Warhol superstar Jane Forth, and when they broke up he came to live with me at the apartment. Any craziness that I had produced in the 18 First Avenue environment on my own was now greatly expanded by Eric's presence. Eric would come around to the rear of the building and yell up at the apartment windows, "THROW MY WORKS DOWN! THEY'RE IN THE DRAWER!" All the lights in the building would turn on and heads would emerge from windows. Eric entertained as many women as he could; girls came and went. I had other friends who would hang out just to see Eric's successes with the ladies.

It was a hot summer night, and Eric and I were alone in the place. It must have been two or three in the morning. I was in the front when I heard him yelling, "Come here! Look at this!" I ran to the rear window. The apartment overlooked Katz's Deli. As we watched, a street dude grabbed a trash can and after a couple of attempts managed to throw it through the giant plate-glass front window of Katz's. The dude then climbed through the hole the trash can had made. We just sat there watching for what seemed like a long time until the guy emerged, staggering under the weight of a cardboard box that he'd filled with salamis. He wobbled around the corner and walked downtown on Ludlow Street and at the *exact second* that he disappeared around the corner, a police car pulled up.

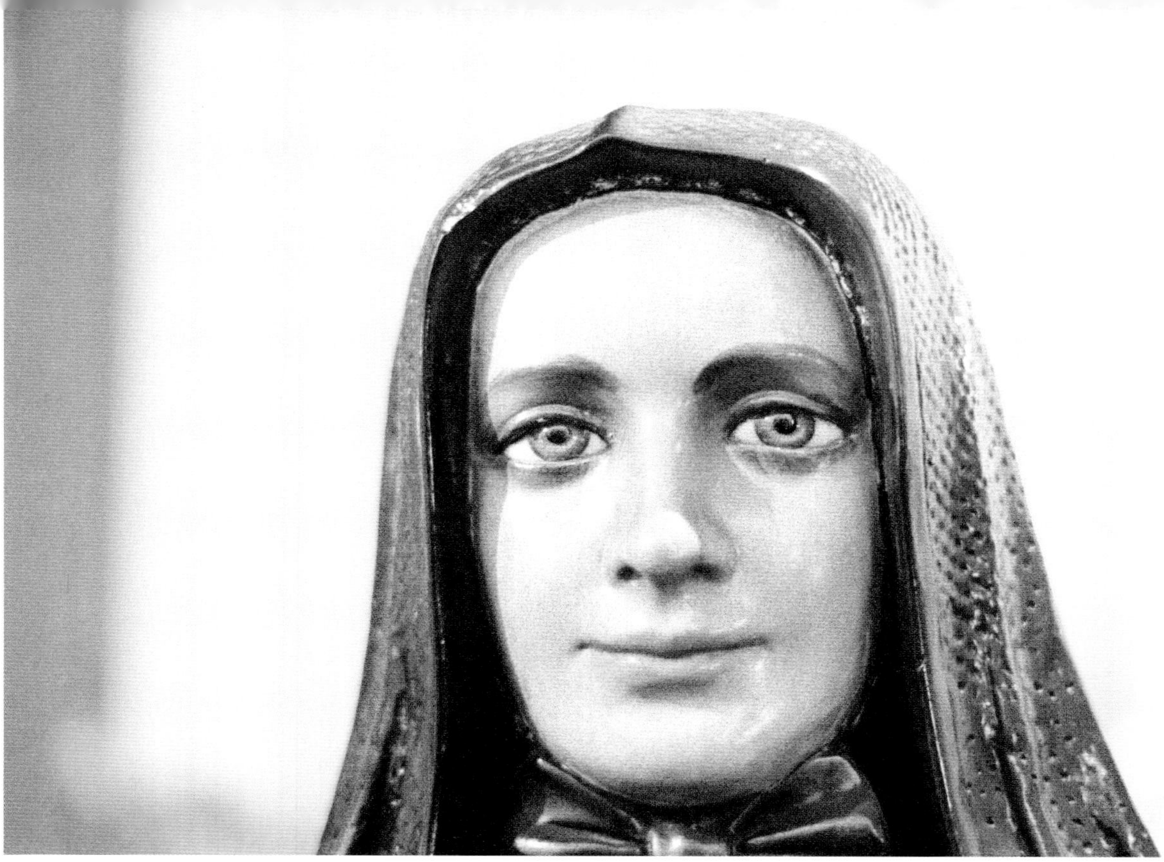

I still have a life-size Saint Mother Cabrini statue that I'd bought in a junk store on Second Avenue for ten bucks. It weighed a lot and I had to drag it back to the fifth floor apartment on a particularly hot day in the summer. When I got it the eyes were painted over, but on examination I saw that it had realistic glass eyes and I scraped the paint off them. I can't figure why someone would have painted them over except for creepiness factor. Later Dee Dee announced that he was afraid of it and stabbed some holes in it with a kitchen knife.

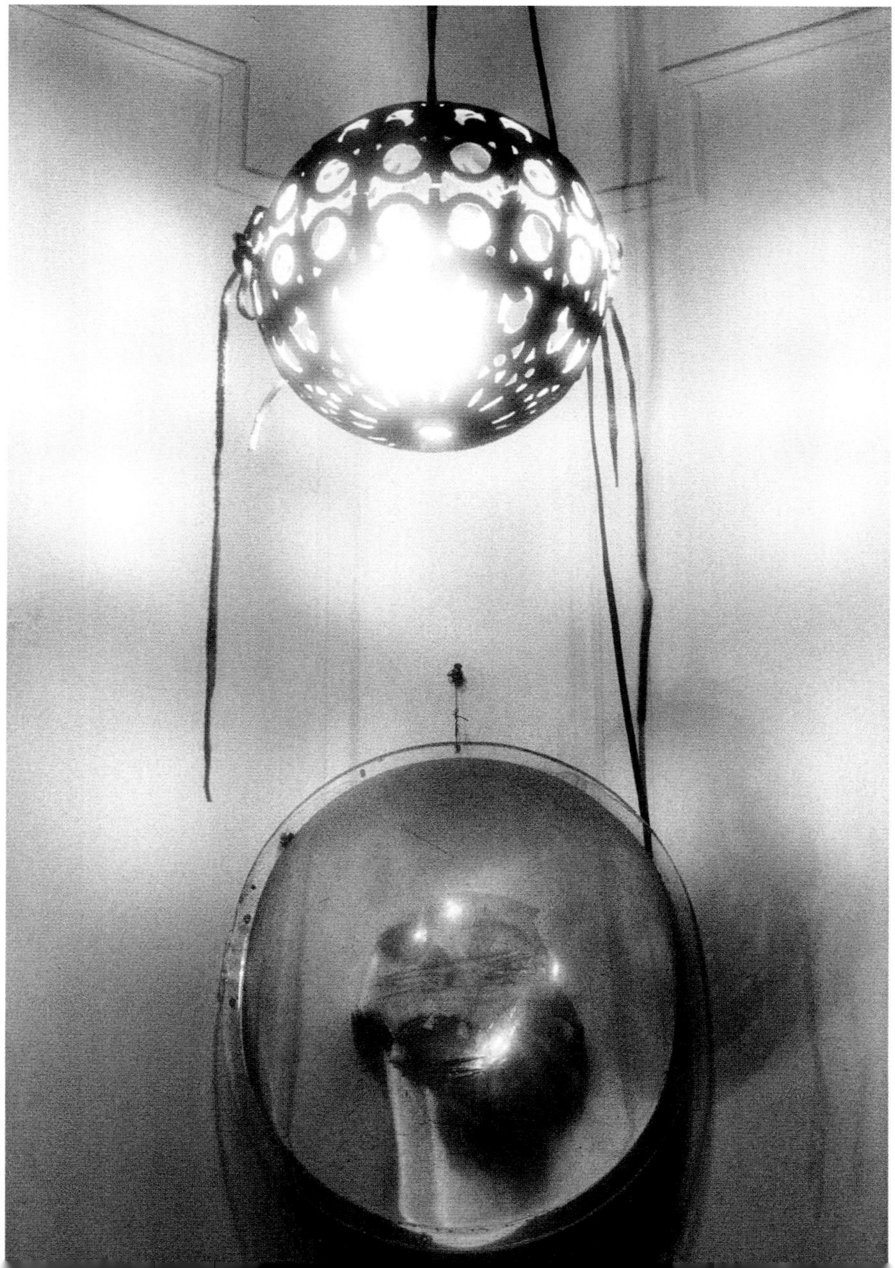

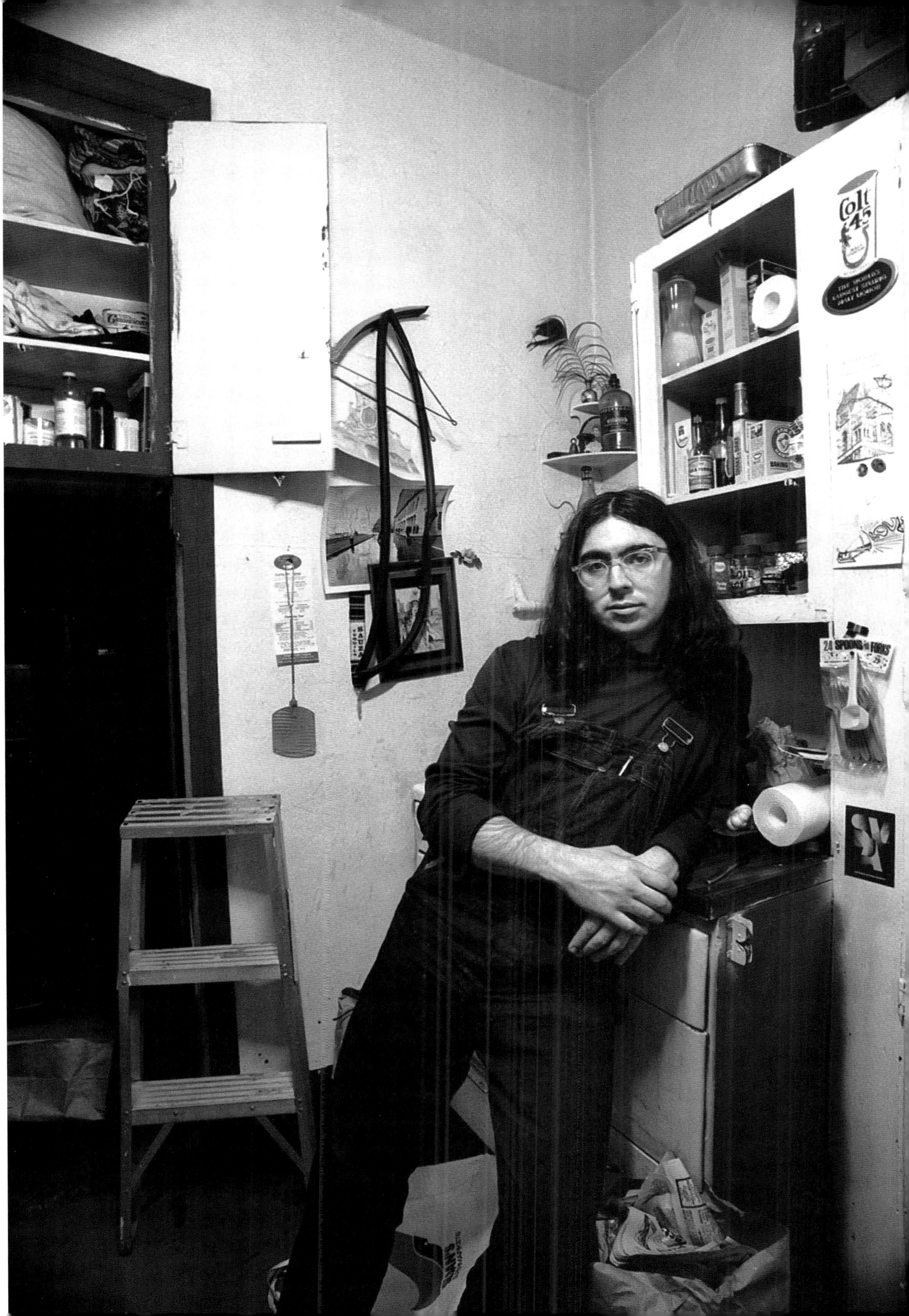
Colt 45

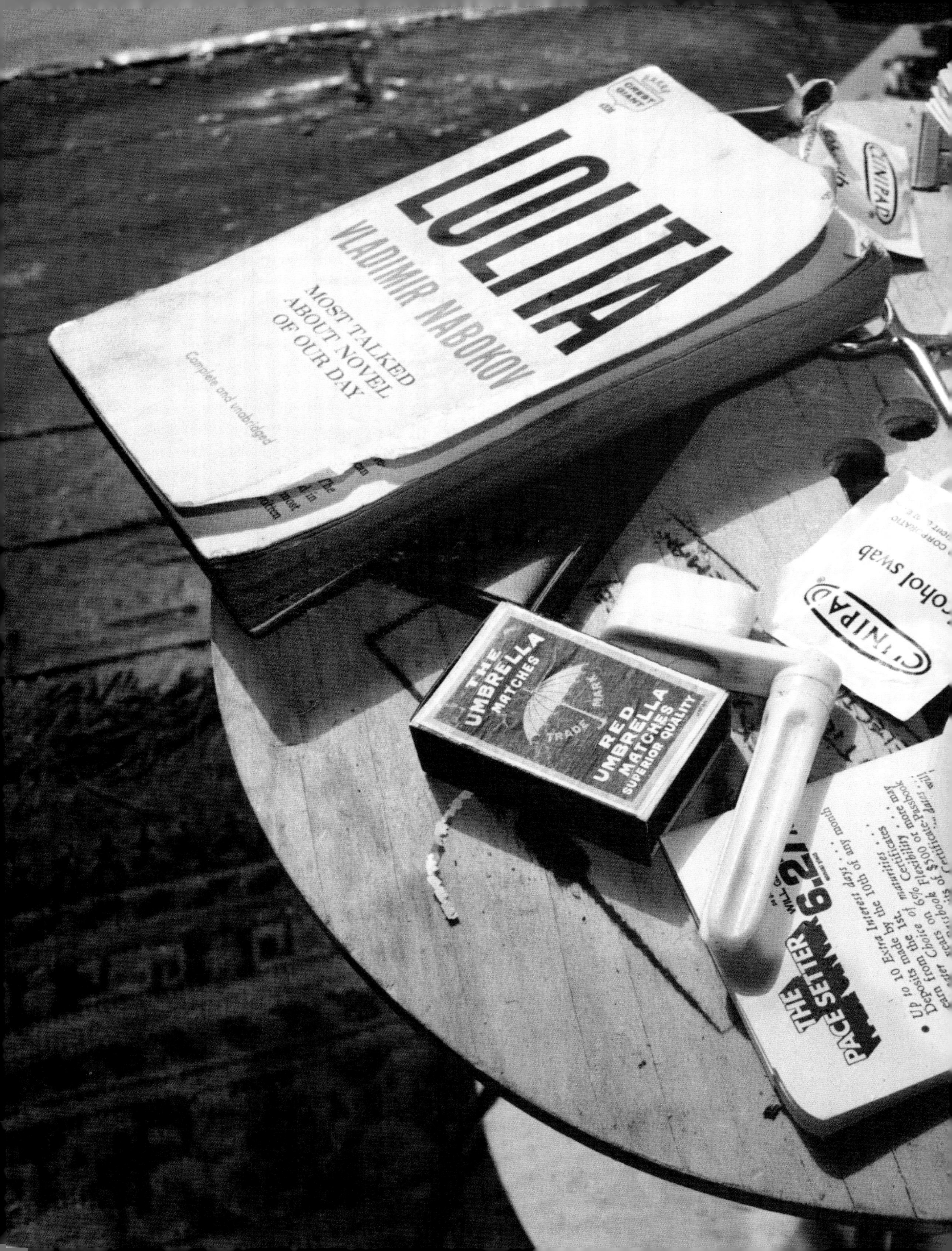
LOLITA
VLADIMIR NABOKOV
MOST TALKED ABOUT NOVEL OF OUR DAY
Complete and unabridged
THE UMBRELLA MATCHES
TRADE MARK
RED UMBRELLA MATCHES SUPERIOR QUALITY
CUNIPAD
THE PACE SETTER

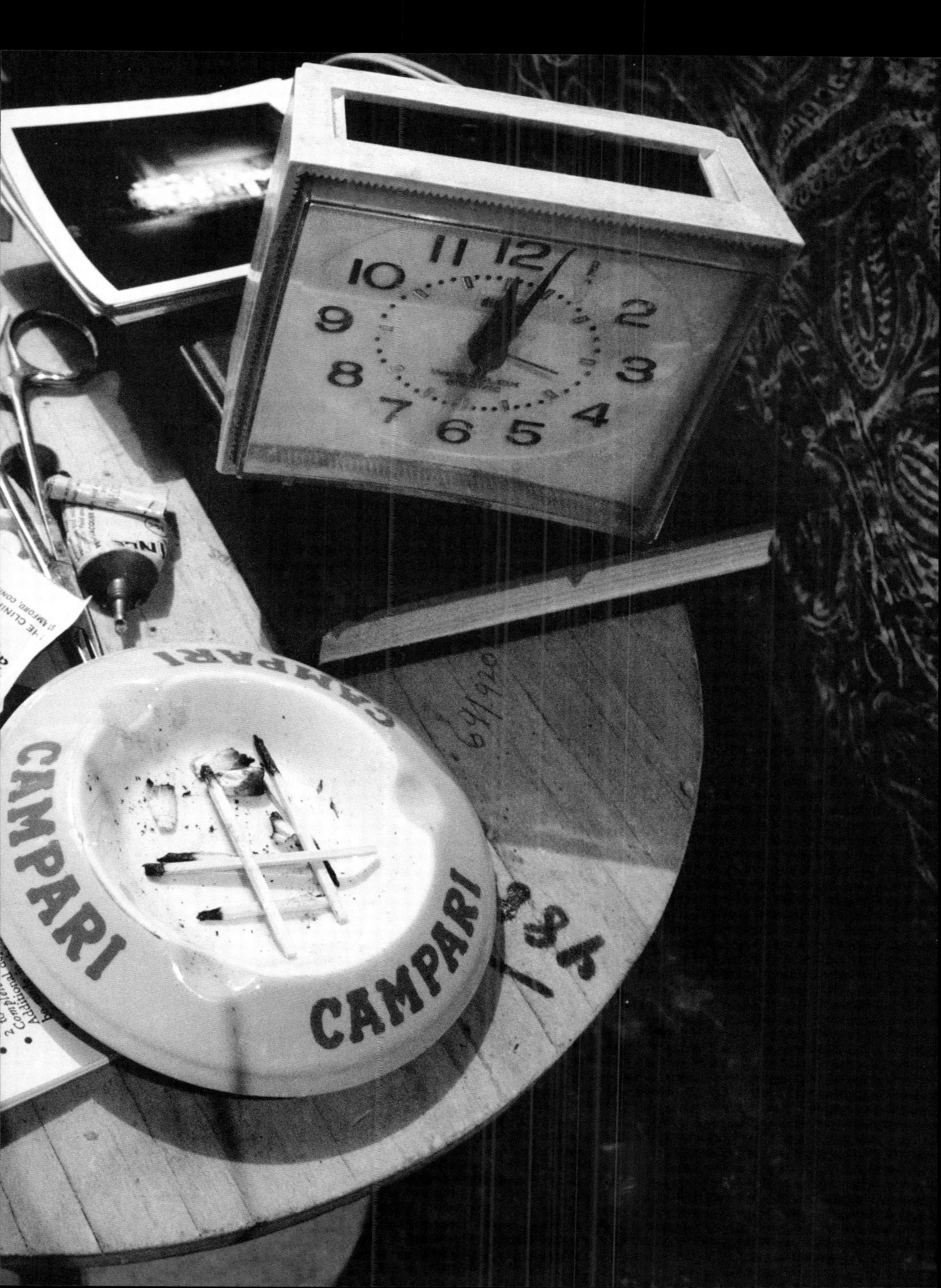
CAMPARI
CAMPARI
CAMPARI
CAMPARI

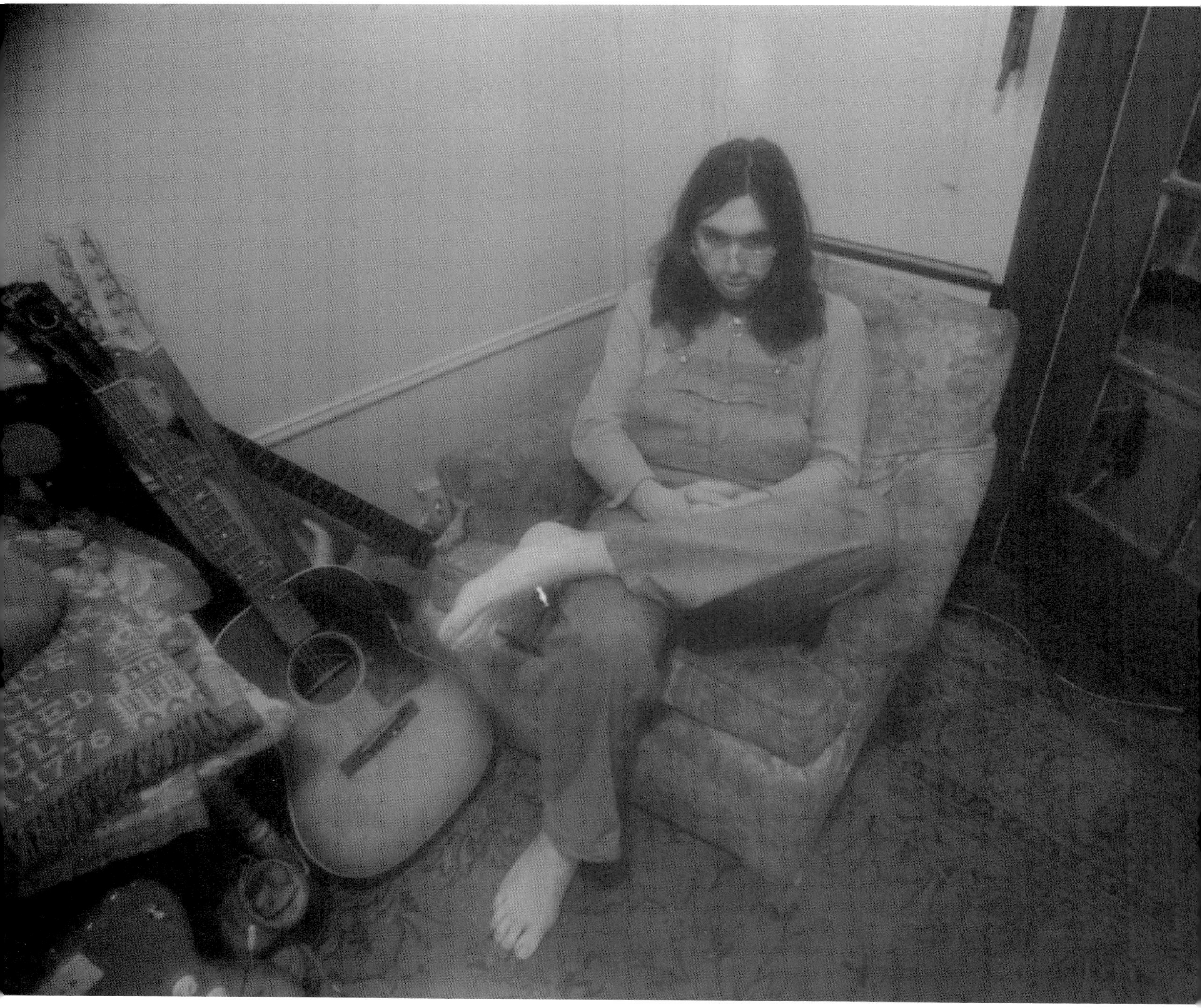

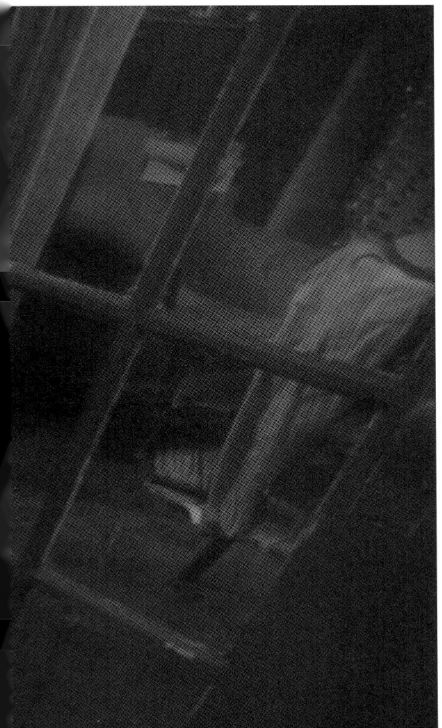

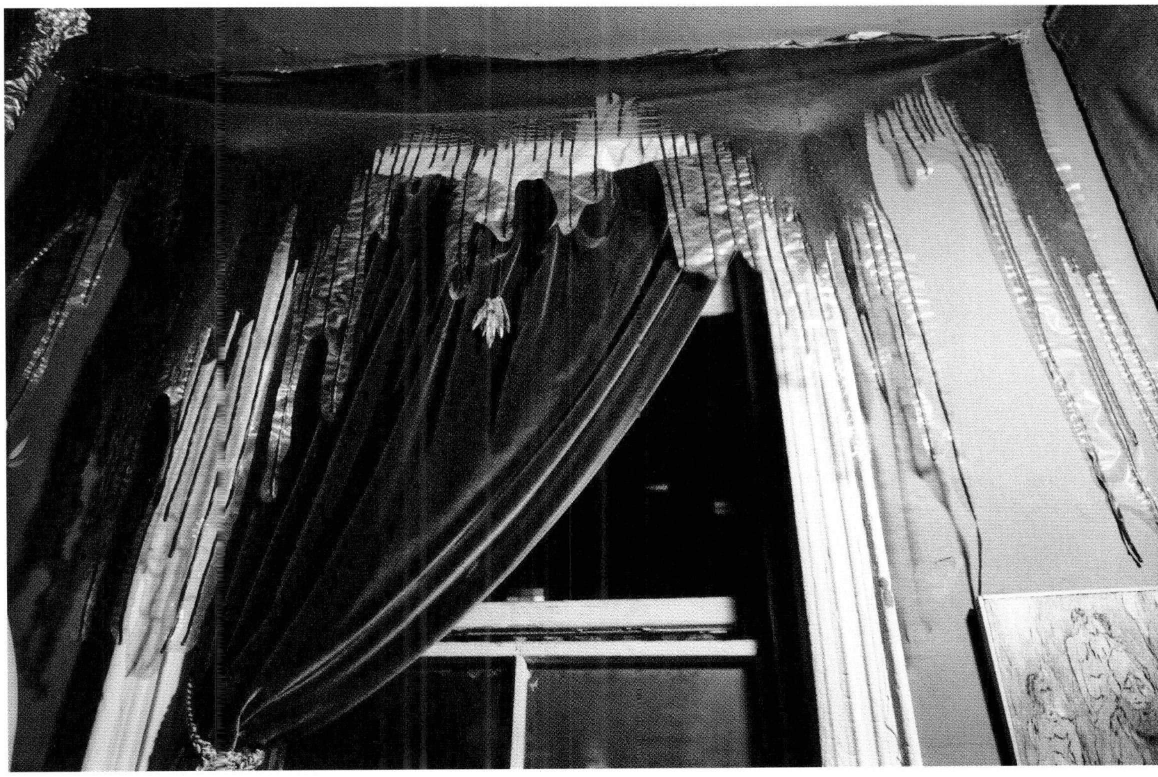

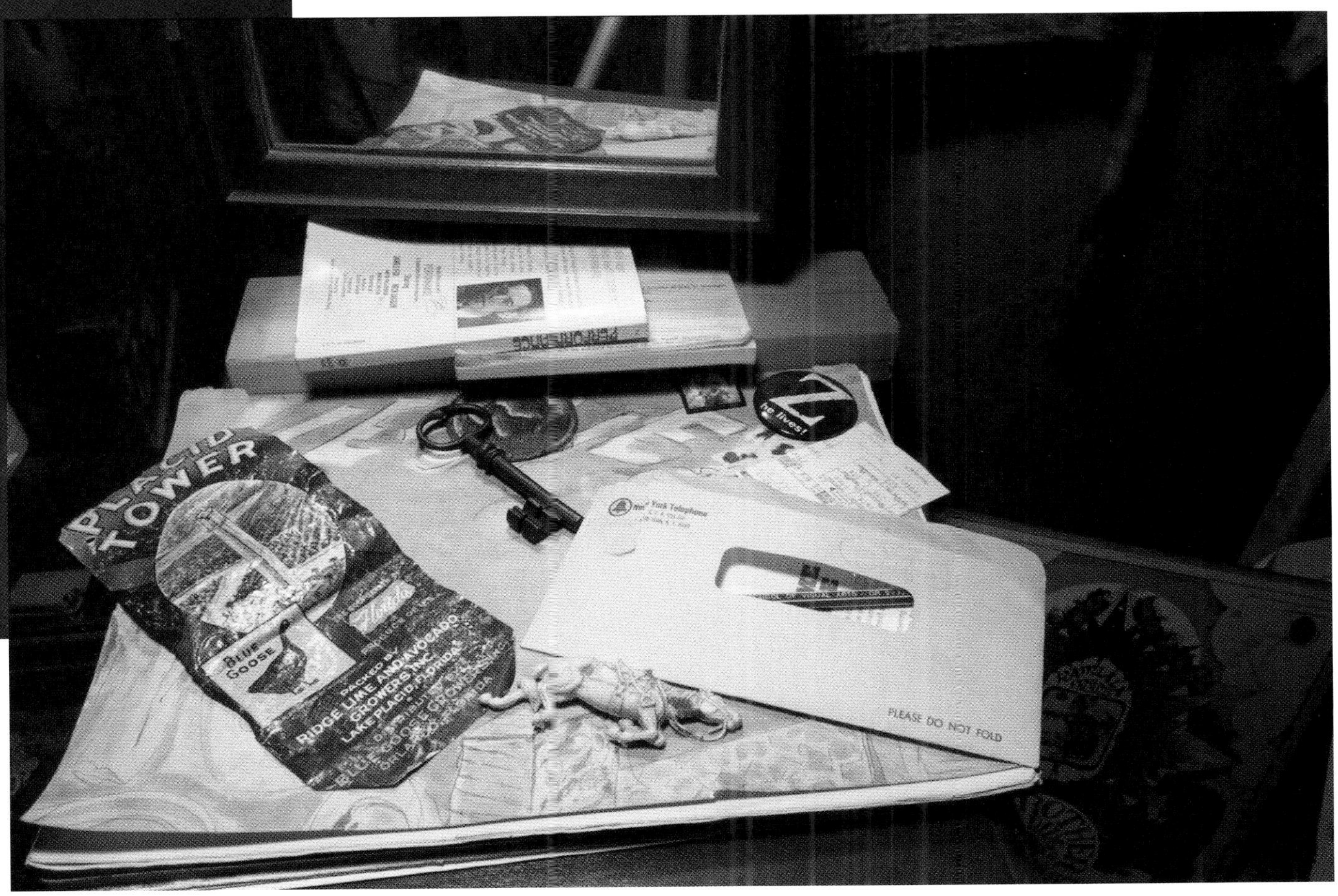
PLACID TOWER
BLUE GOOSE
PACKED BY
RIDGE LIME AND AVOCADO
GROWERS INC.
LAKE PLACID, FLORIDA
he lives!
PLEASE DO NOT FOLD

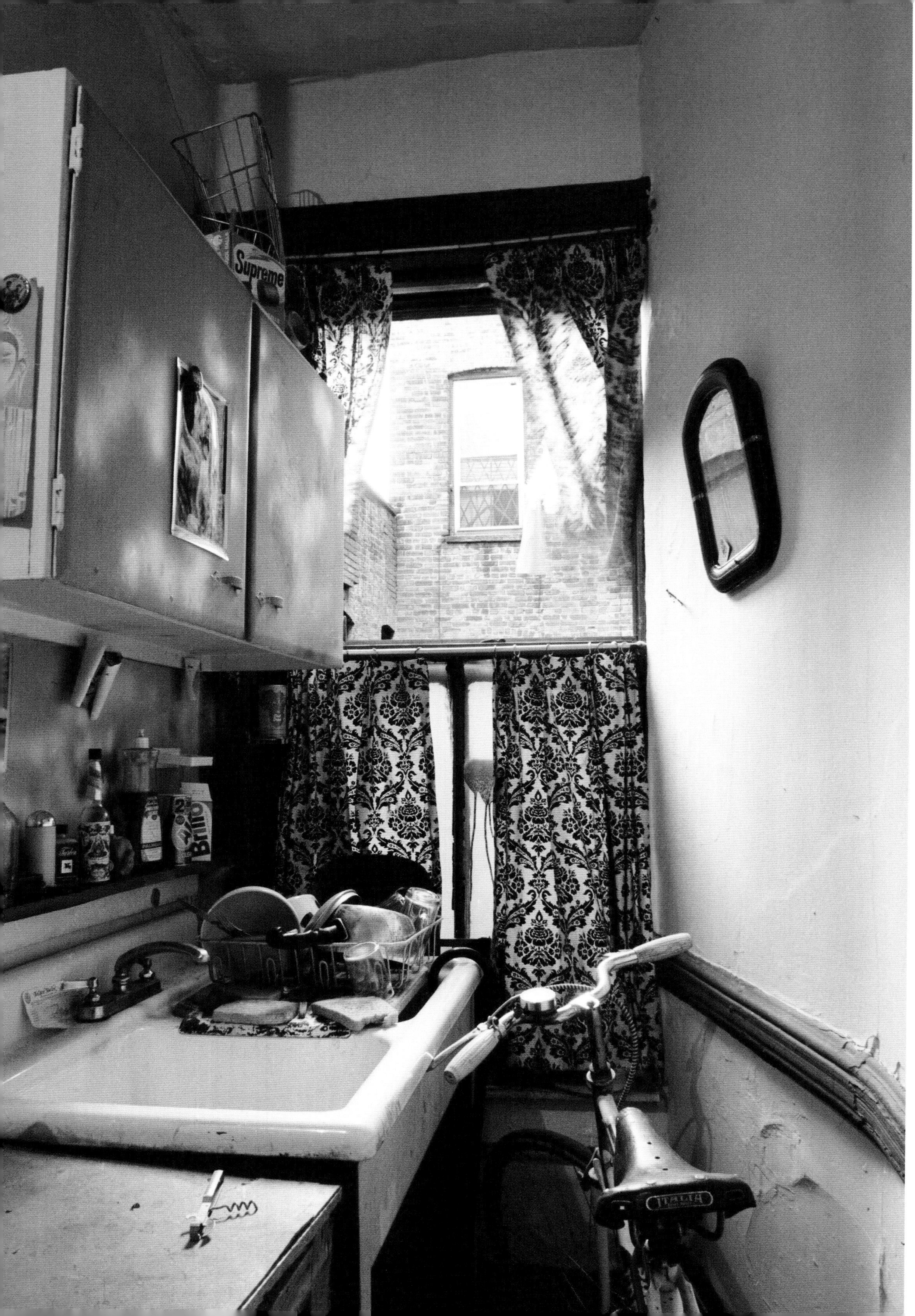
Supreme
Brillo
ITALIA

The cops got out waving flashlights into the hole in the window. If they'd just looked around the corner they would have caught the guy.

Eric and I were sitting around one day when we heard a rustling in a pile of old copies of the *Village Voice*. We investigated and it was a friendly gerbil that had mysteriously appeared—we assumed having escaped from another apartment. He ran around the apartment for a few months until he finally drowned in the toilet. I still feel bad about it forty-five years later.

Eric eventually moved on to live with Edgar Winter's ex Barbara, I met Debbie and started staying with her on the West Side, and Tommy Ramone took over the apartment. Tommy stayed there together with bandmate Dee Dee, but it was mostly Tommy.

I remember the last time I was in the apartment, getting ready to leave. There was a big pile of debris on the living room floor, all abandoned stuff. I did find Dee Dee's draft card that I still have somewhere.

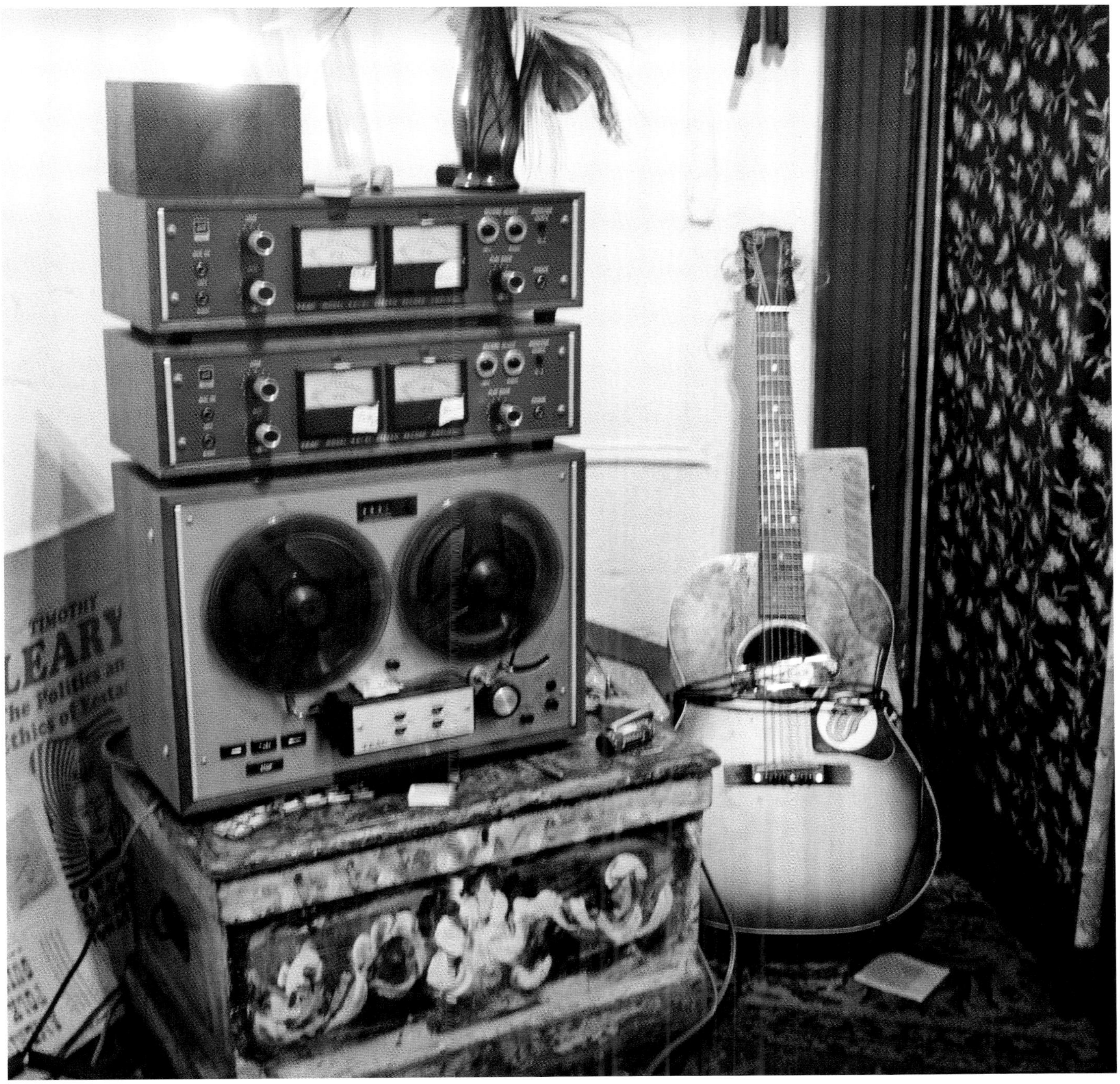

Me shooting antique video on a rooftop in Hell's Kitchen, 1972. This was a very early cable TV show that my friend Joey Freeman and I made with some of our downtown cronies. Fayette Hauser, Gorilla Rose, Screaming Orchid, and Tomata DuPlenty were the stars. Carol Thompson, a friend of Vali Myers, at the same moment on the roof. I can't remember exactly what went on in these tapes; we shot around five episodes, all of which were lost in a fire at this same location.

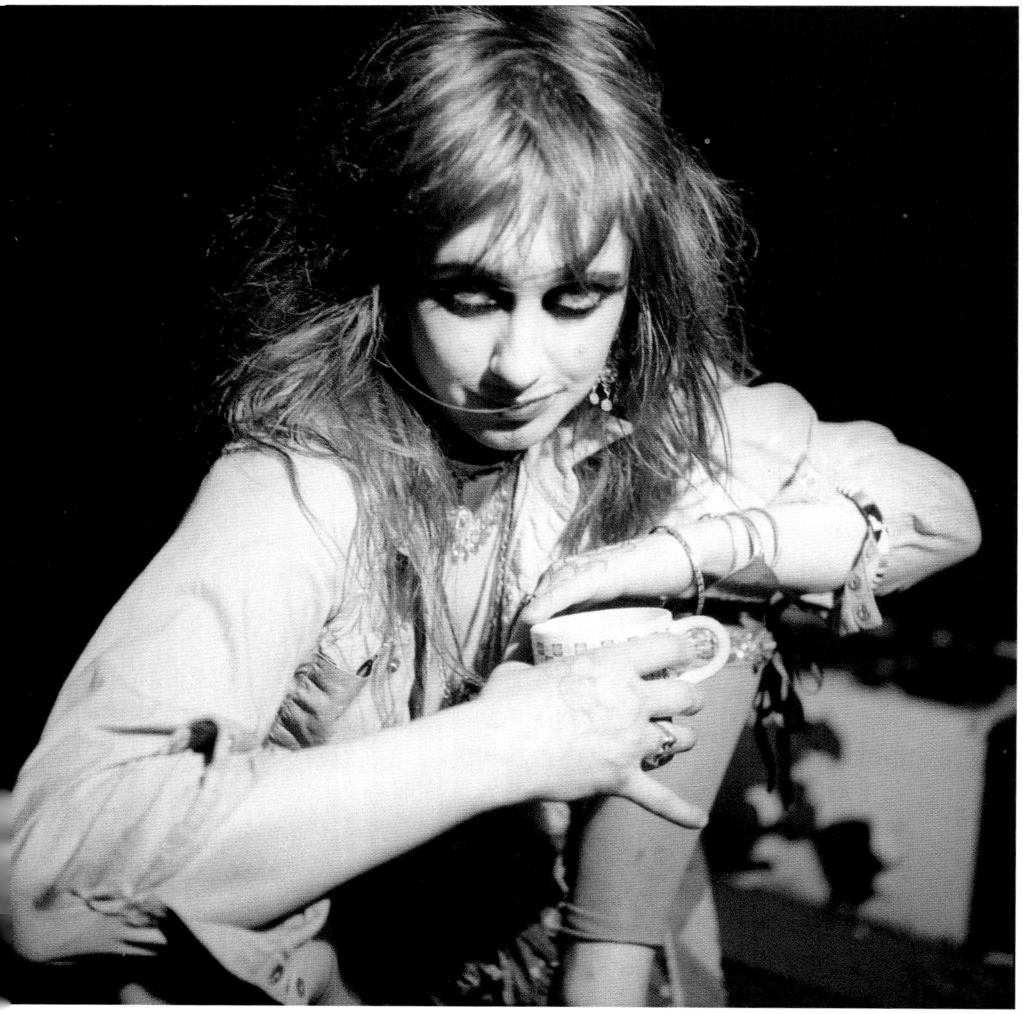

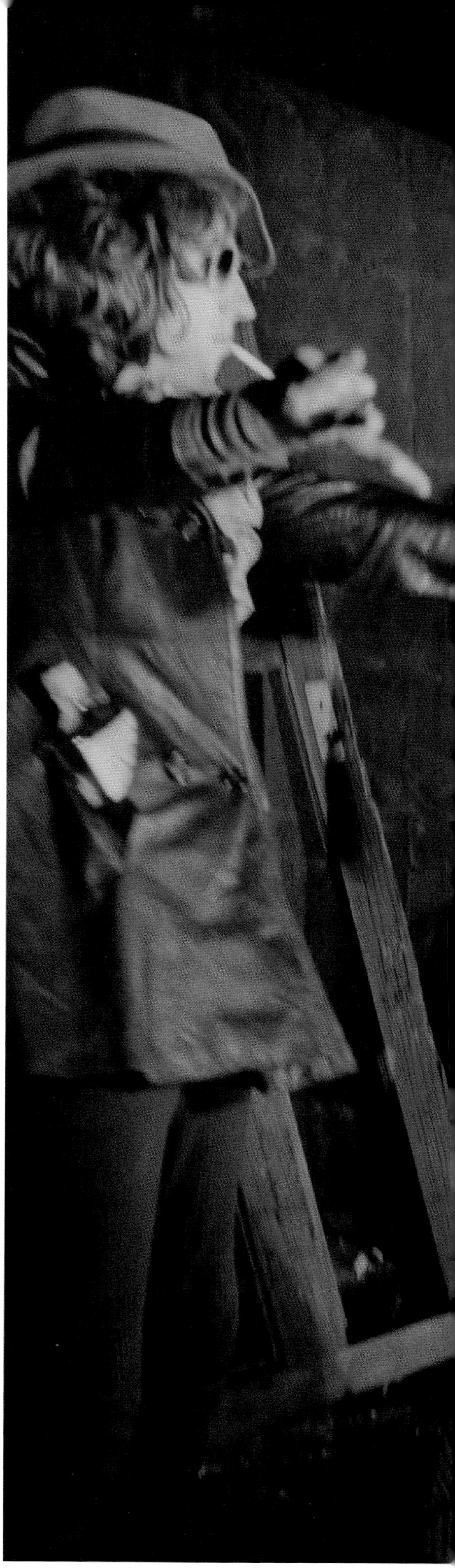

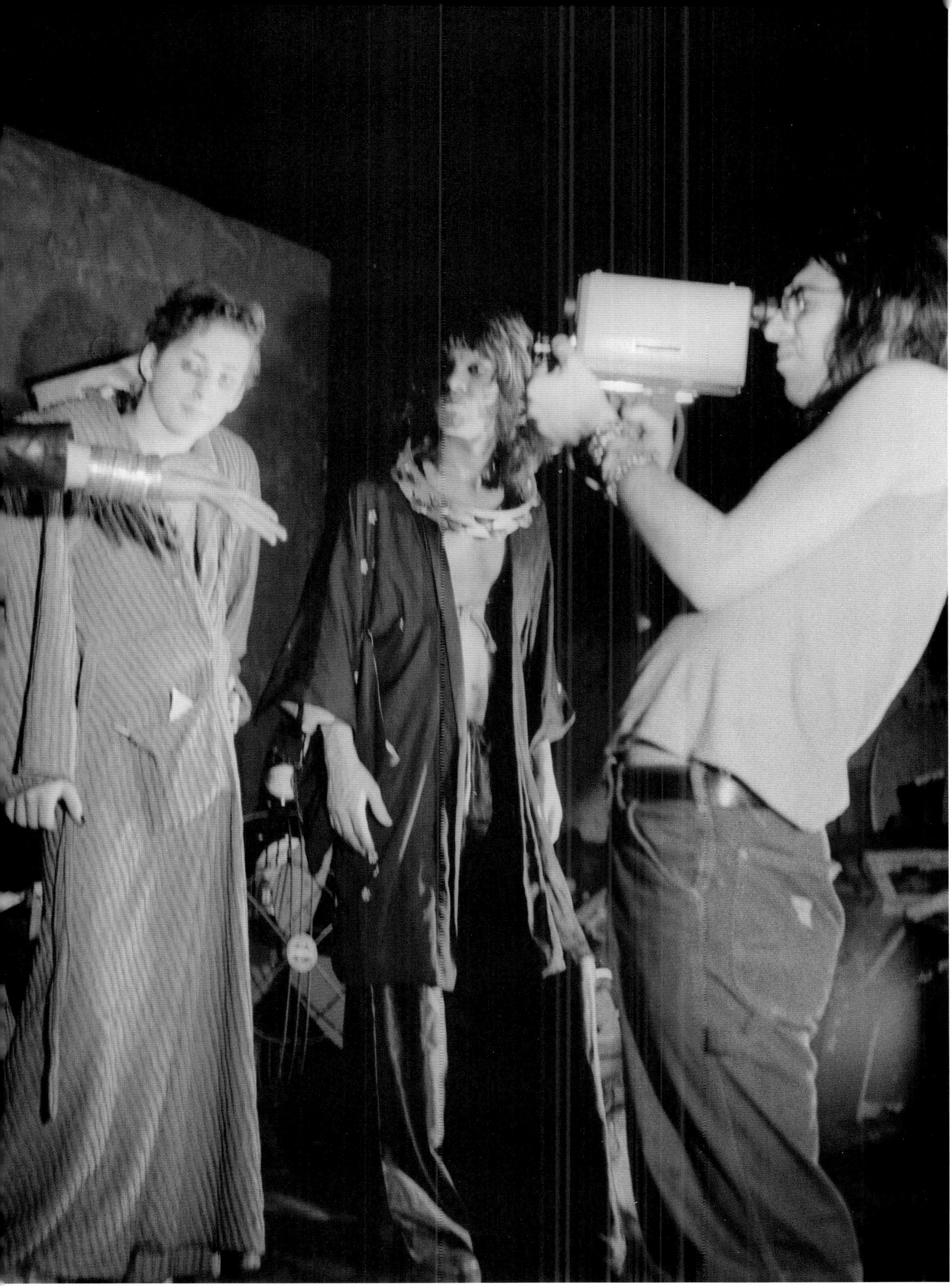

ERIC EMERSON, 1974

Eric bought a tattoo machine and worked on himself and whoever else was willing to let him have a go. He spent a week or so tattooing before he got bored. The impressionist dagger was his tattoo work, but the word *stilletoes* was just written on with a marker. Eric liked this picture. He gave me one of the silver bracelets that he's wearing here. I wore it for the longest time after he died. When we were doing our big New Year's Eve show in Bangkok in 1977–78, I was talking to a little kid before our soundcheck. I shook hands with him, and before I even noticed he'd

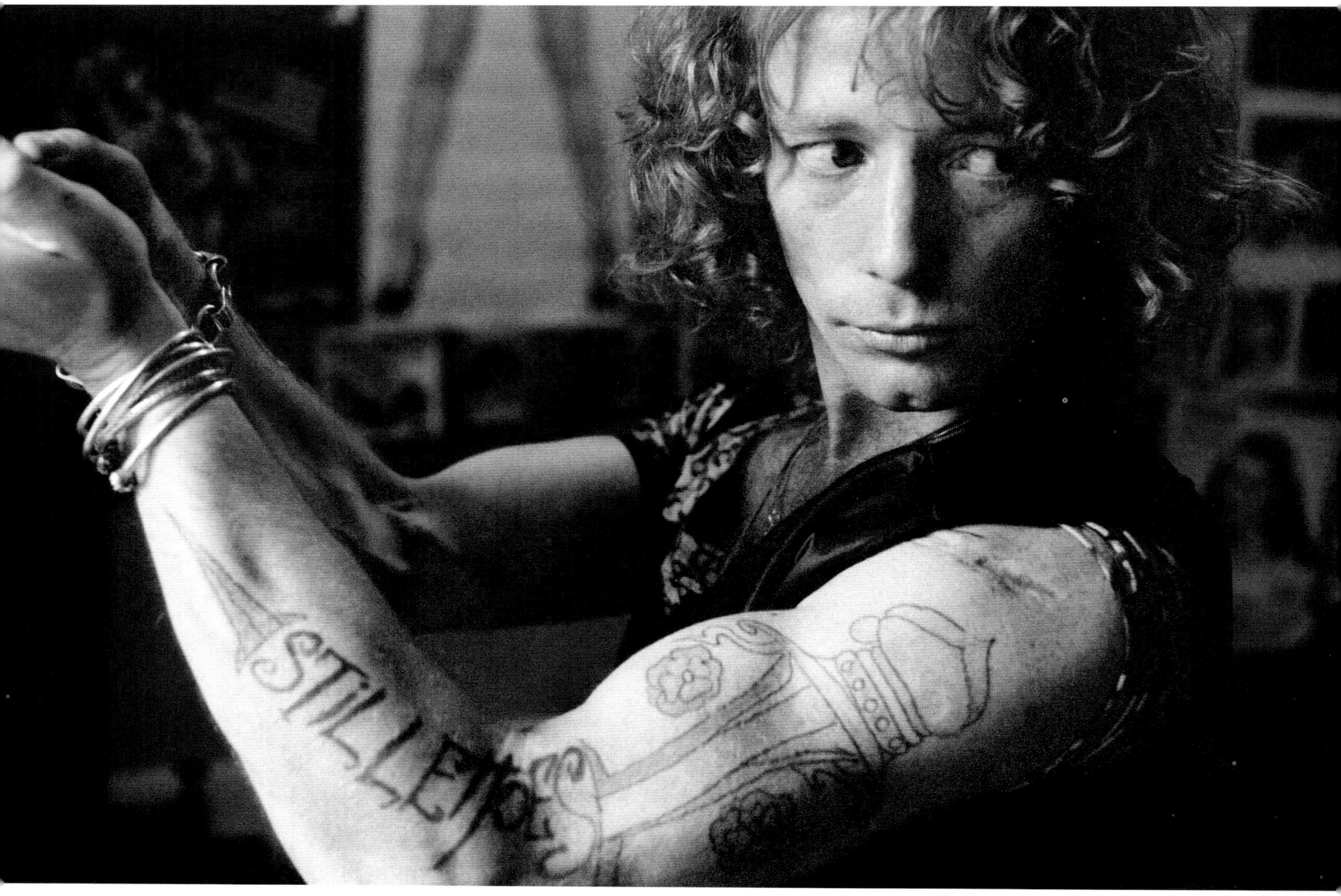

slipped off the bracelet. He was a pro. I wound up giving him a harmonica to get the bracelet back.

On Halloween in 1973, the Dolls, who did frequent Halloween shows, played at the ballroom in the Waldorf Astoria. Eric, though not listed on the bill, was an opening act. By this time the Magic Tramps and Eric had split, even though Eric still worked with various Tramps members. For the Halloween gig, Eric was on doing his solo act. He was tripping heavily and dressed in his usual gold glitter outfit but wearing a fantastic set of huge and very realistic white feather angel wings that someone had made for him. His act involved songs that often used stream of consciousness–based lyrics accompanied by his gold glitter covered, nylon string guitar. This night he just kept going, and wouldn't respond to people offstage indicating that he should wrap it up. Finally, one of the promoters—I've always heard it was the Limbo King, Mike Quashie, who had associations with everyone from Jimmy Page and Cosby to Hendrix—came onstage and attempted to remove Eric. Eric kept singing and ultimately, really distracted and annoyed, hit Mike over the head with his guitar and stormed off. The audience was about fifteen hundred and cheered wildly. Eric was seriously pissed. He grabbed the girl he was with, who happened to be the owner of a blue Ford Mustang. They left the Waldorf and Eric jumped into the car and sped off downtown. He got to

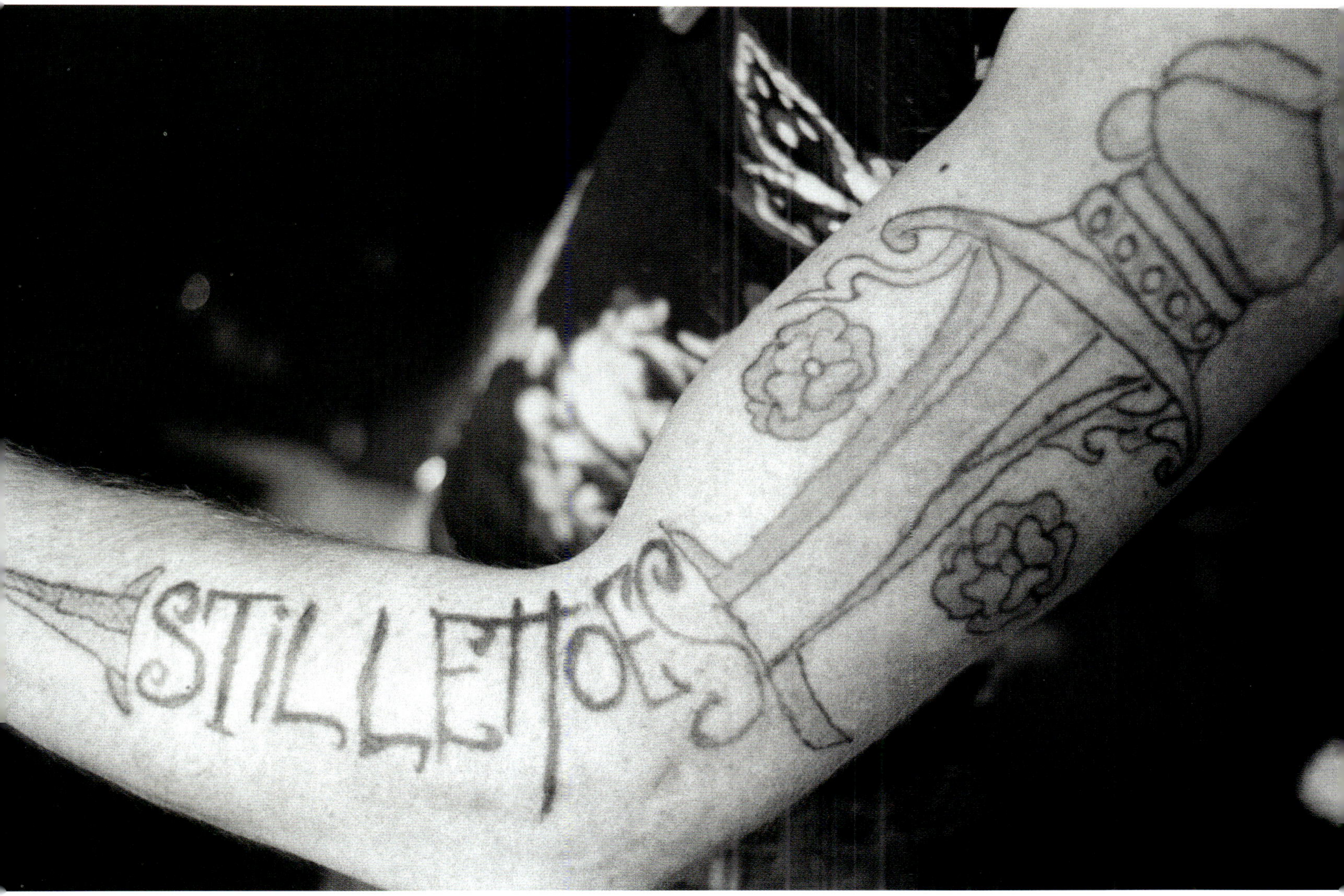

the Holland Tunnel and blew into it, driving like a maniac. He was actually bumping off the walls of the tunnel as they went, and I picture the sparks flying.

The cops were waiting on the Jersey side, all lined up with guns drawn. The Mustang screeched to a halt, and out comes this gold angel with gigantic wings. Eric wound up in jail in New Jersey.

A few months earlier, he had met Barbara Winter, the ex of Edgar Winter. Eric called her and she bailed him out.

I've always skirted the issue of Eric's death to try and save feelings, but I'm fairly certain that he overdosed. Debbie and I were among the last people to see him alive. It was really the end of an era on many levels.

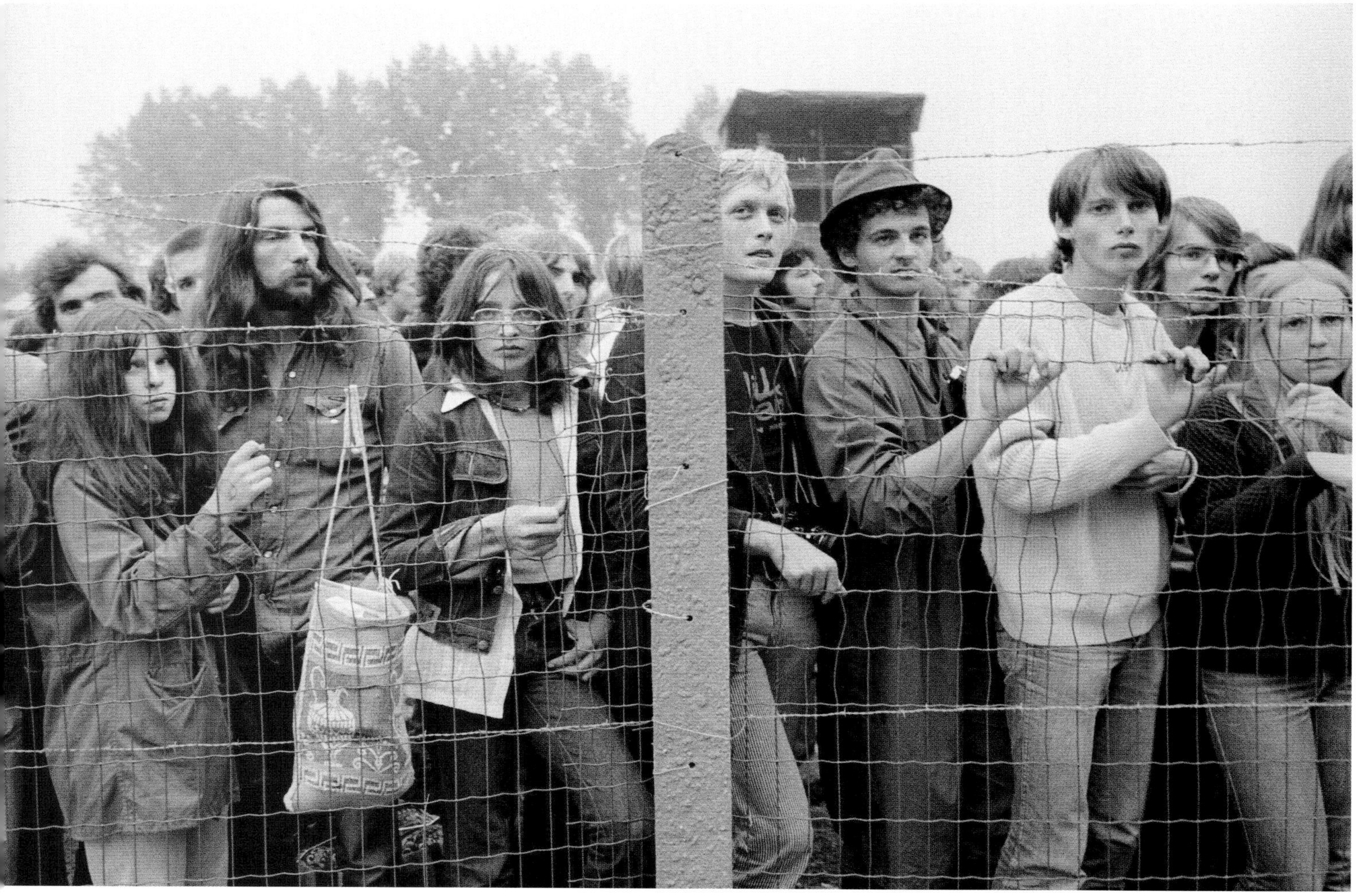

Cages.

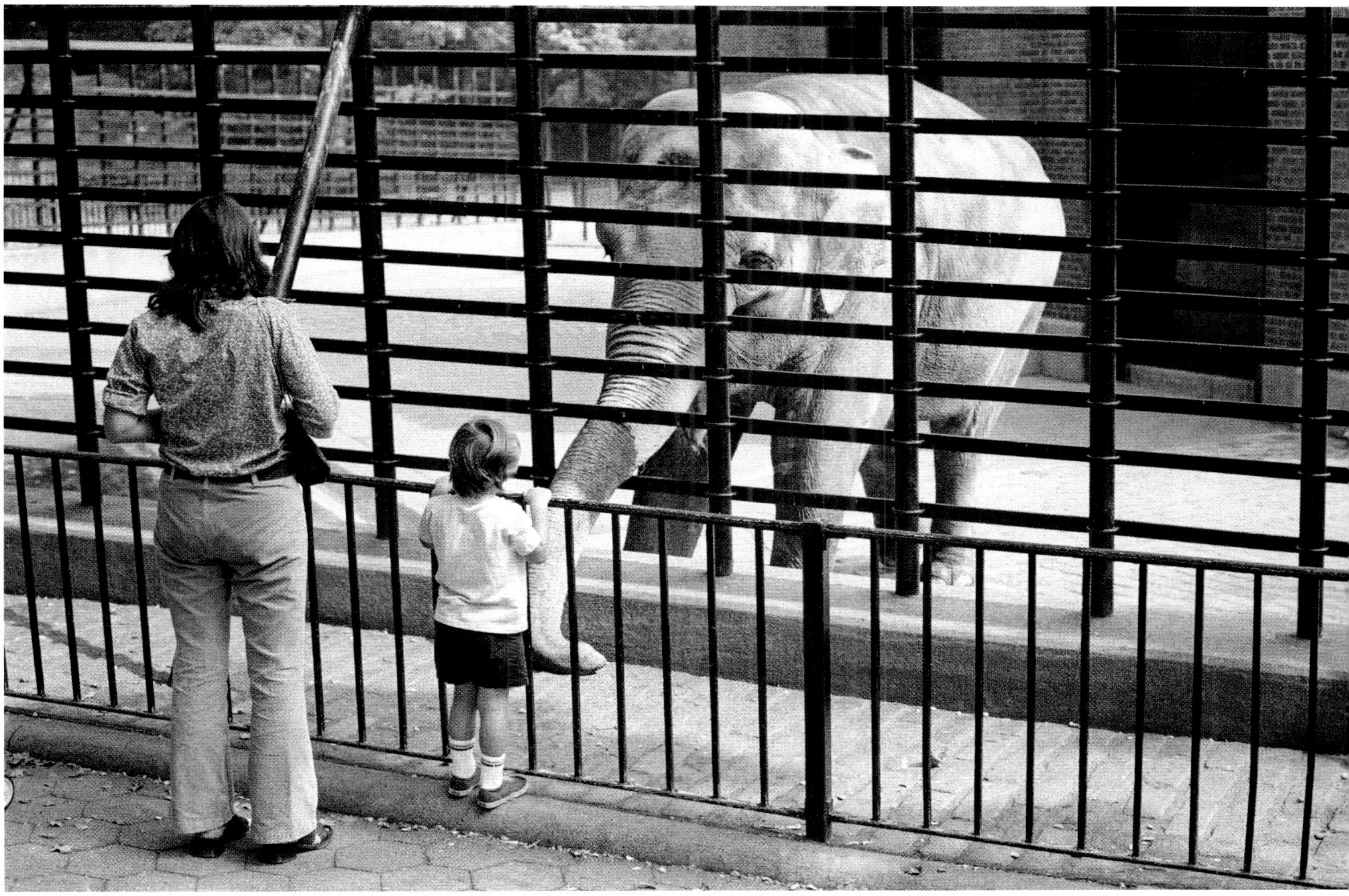

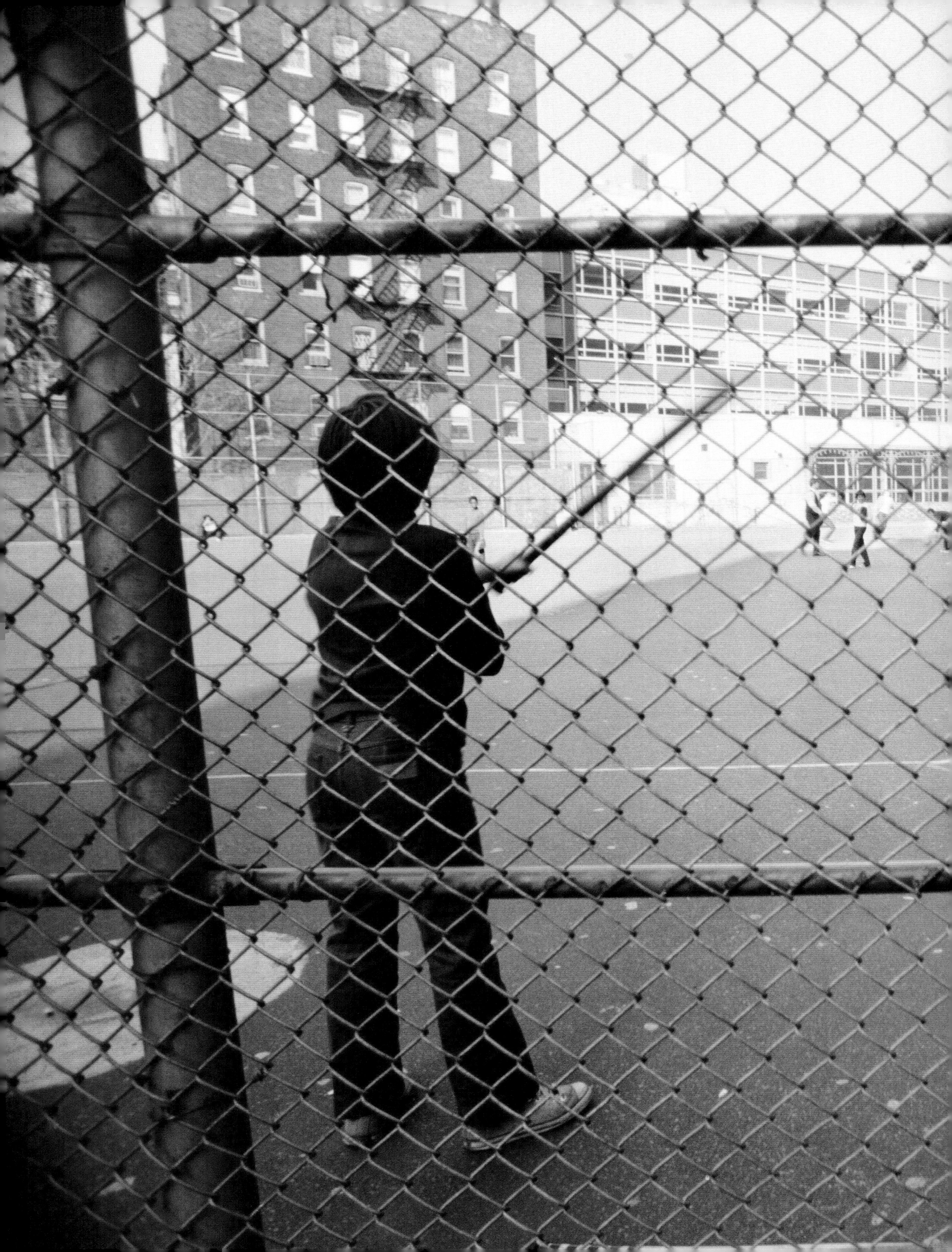

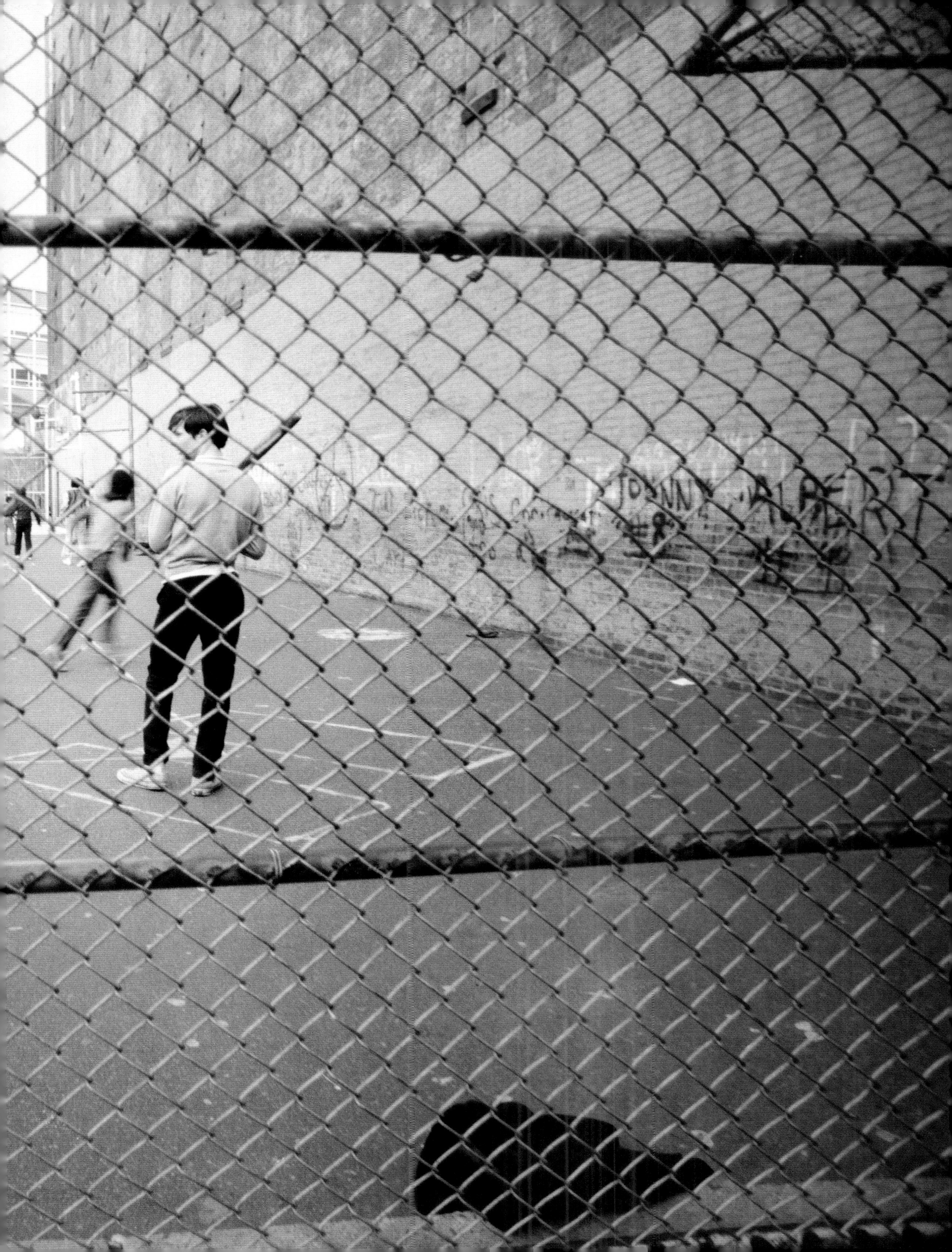
JOHNNY
ALBERT

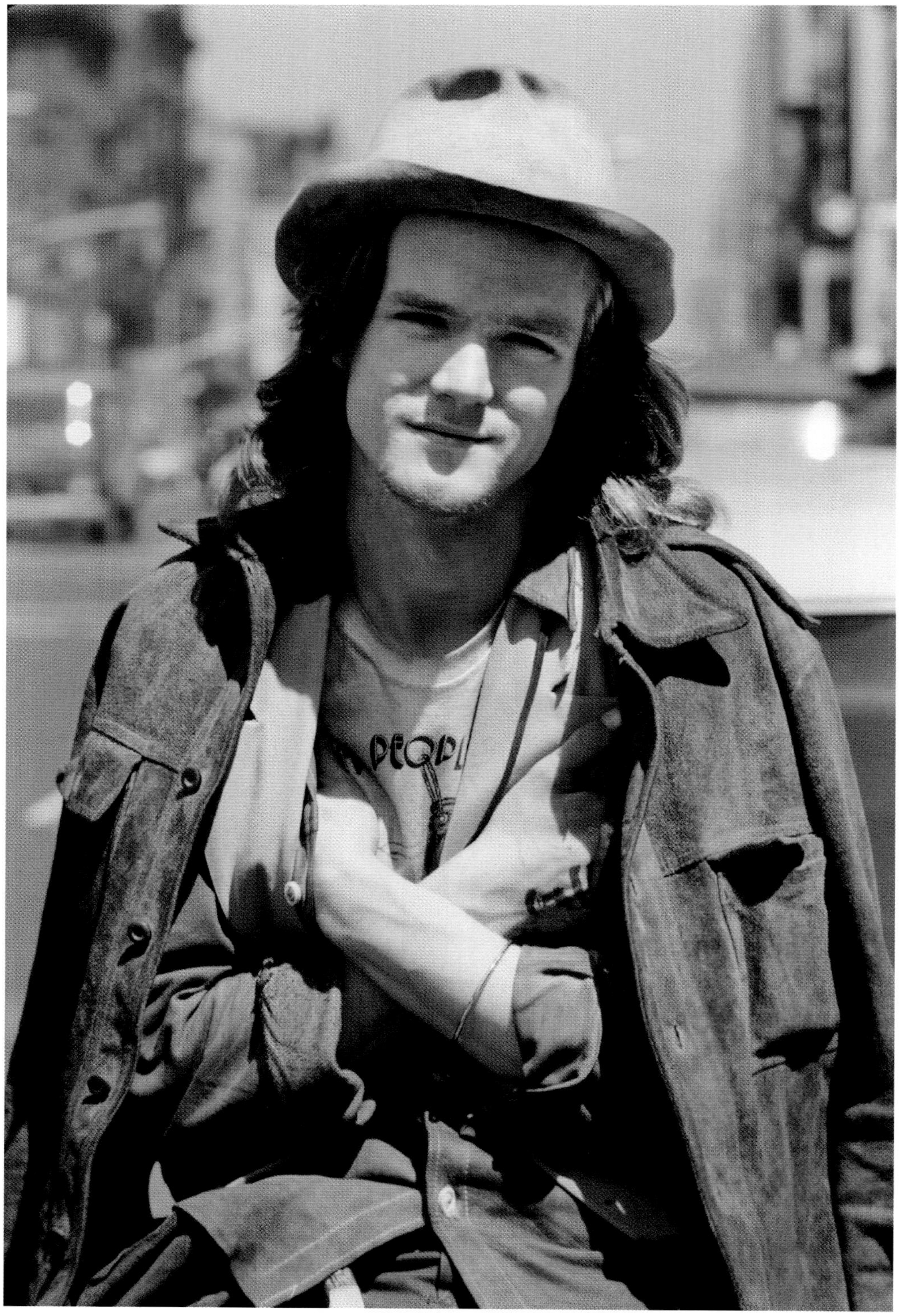

TREASURE HUNT

One day I left my apartment and saw a kid I knew from the streets hanging around in my neighborhood. He told me he'd found a "treasure" way over on Avenue C and that I would "appreciate" it. I left my camera home before heading east. The kid was carrying a medieval-style battle axe that was one of those objects designed as a decorative wall hanger. He was dressed in a sort of take on biker style that one would see at the time. We trekked east, and it turned out that the treasure was a demolished first floor apartment with the windows wide open. We climbed in and dug around the debris but I don't remember coming across anything of note. I did wish that I'd brought my camera though.

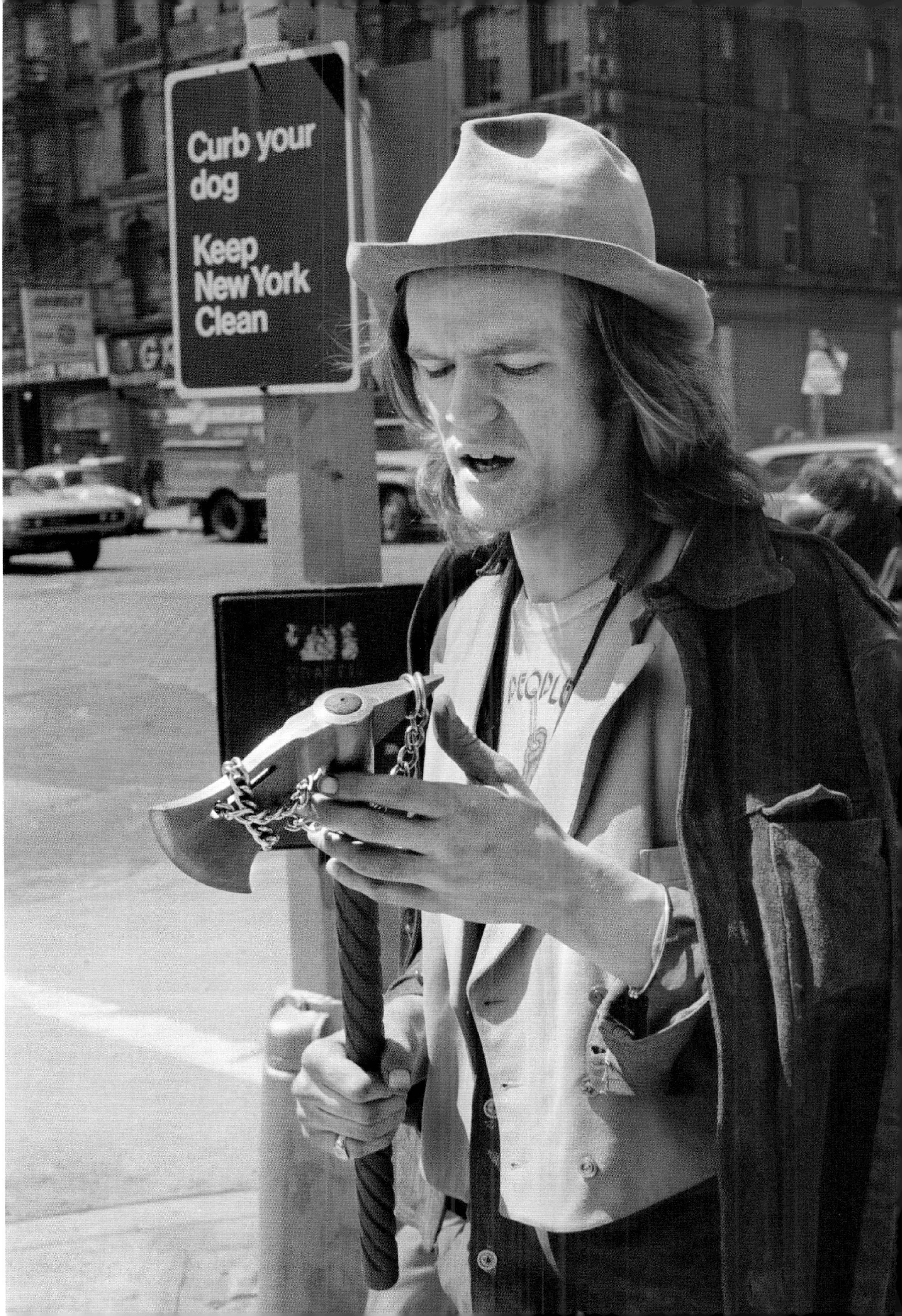
Curb your dog
Keep New York Clean

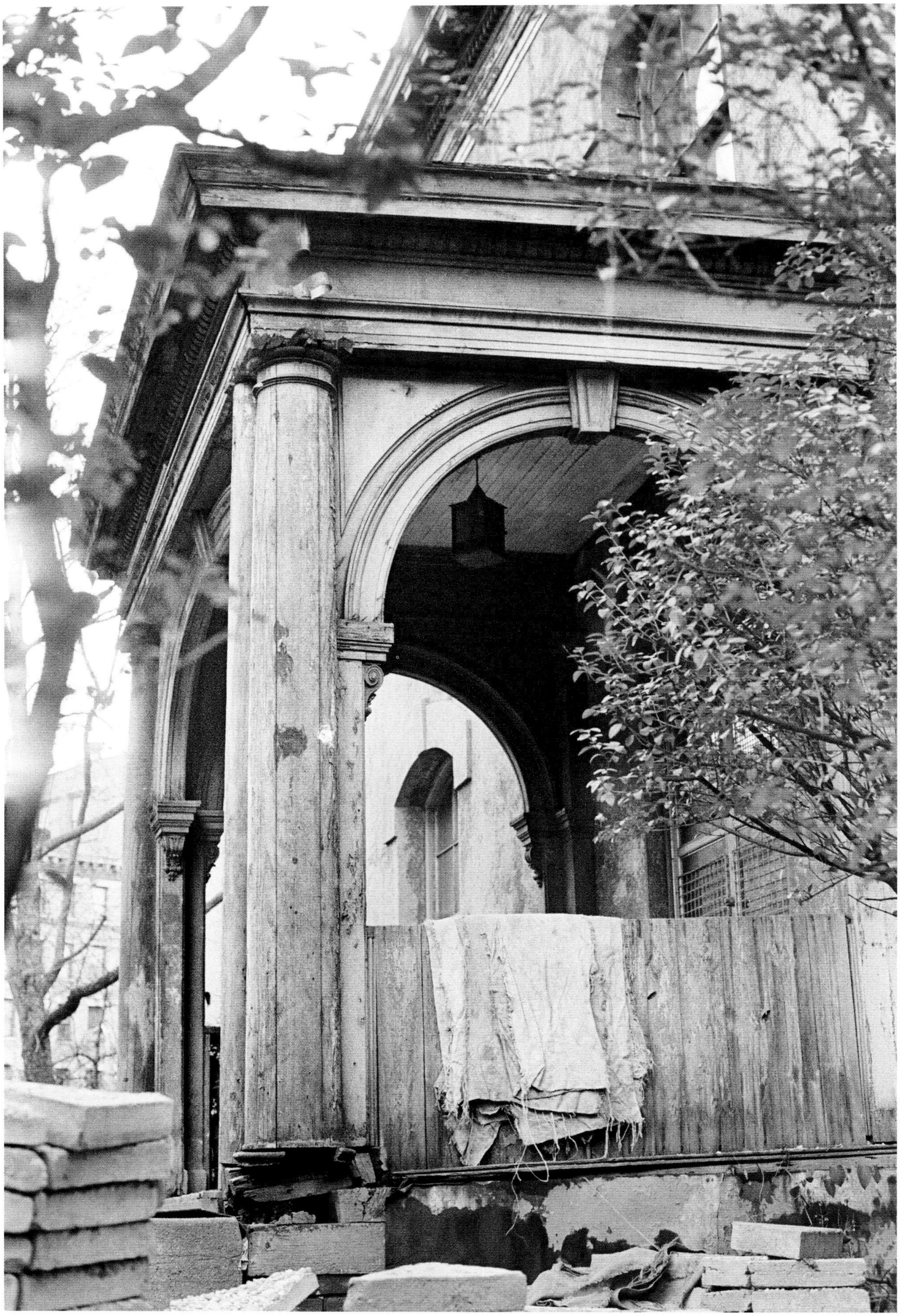

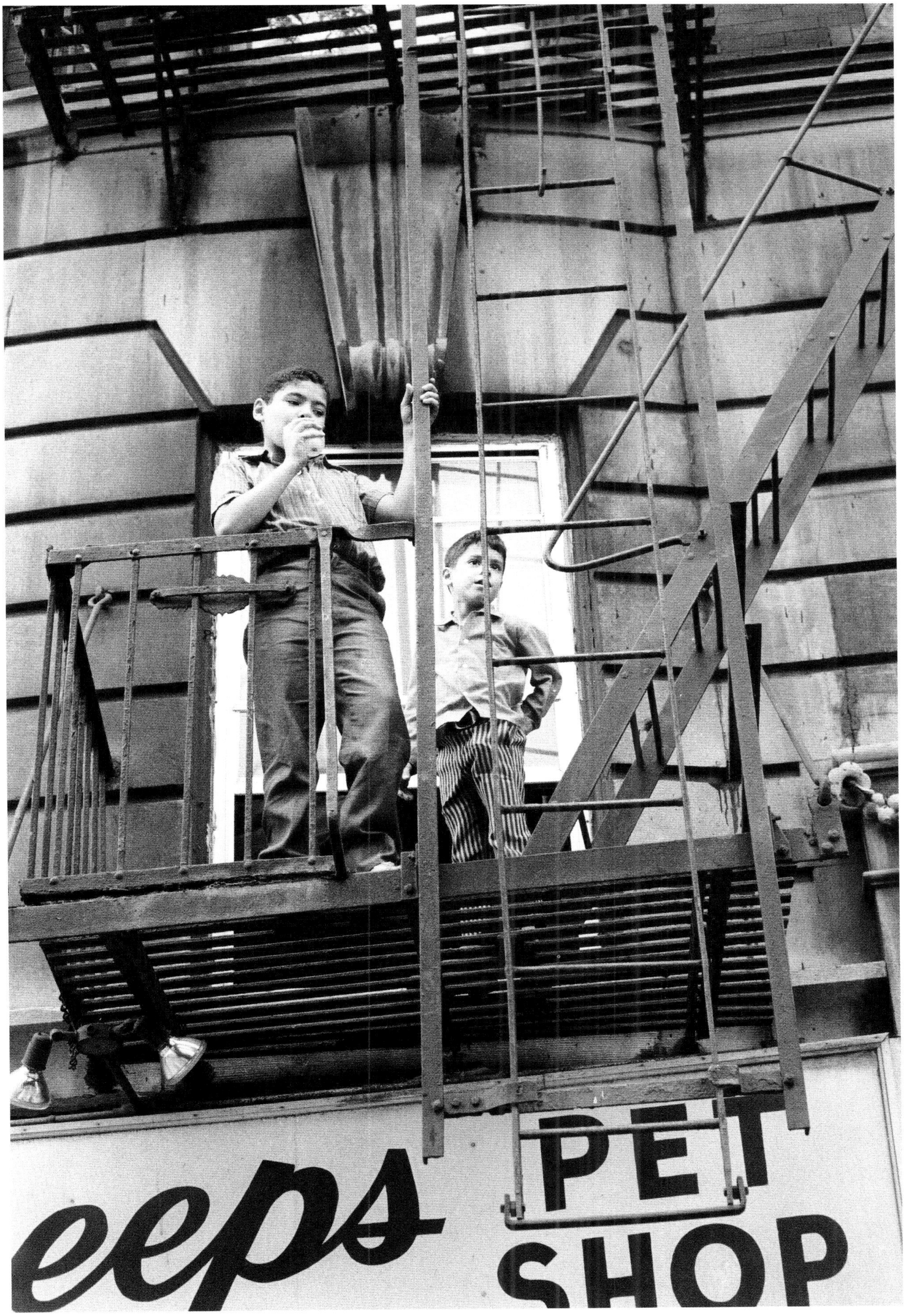
eeps
PET
SHOP

PREVIOUS PAGES: View of Saint Marks Church in the Bowery.

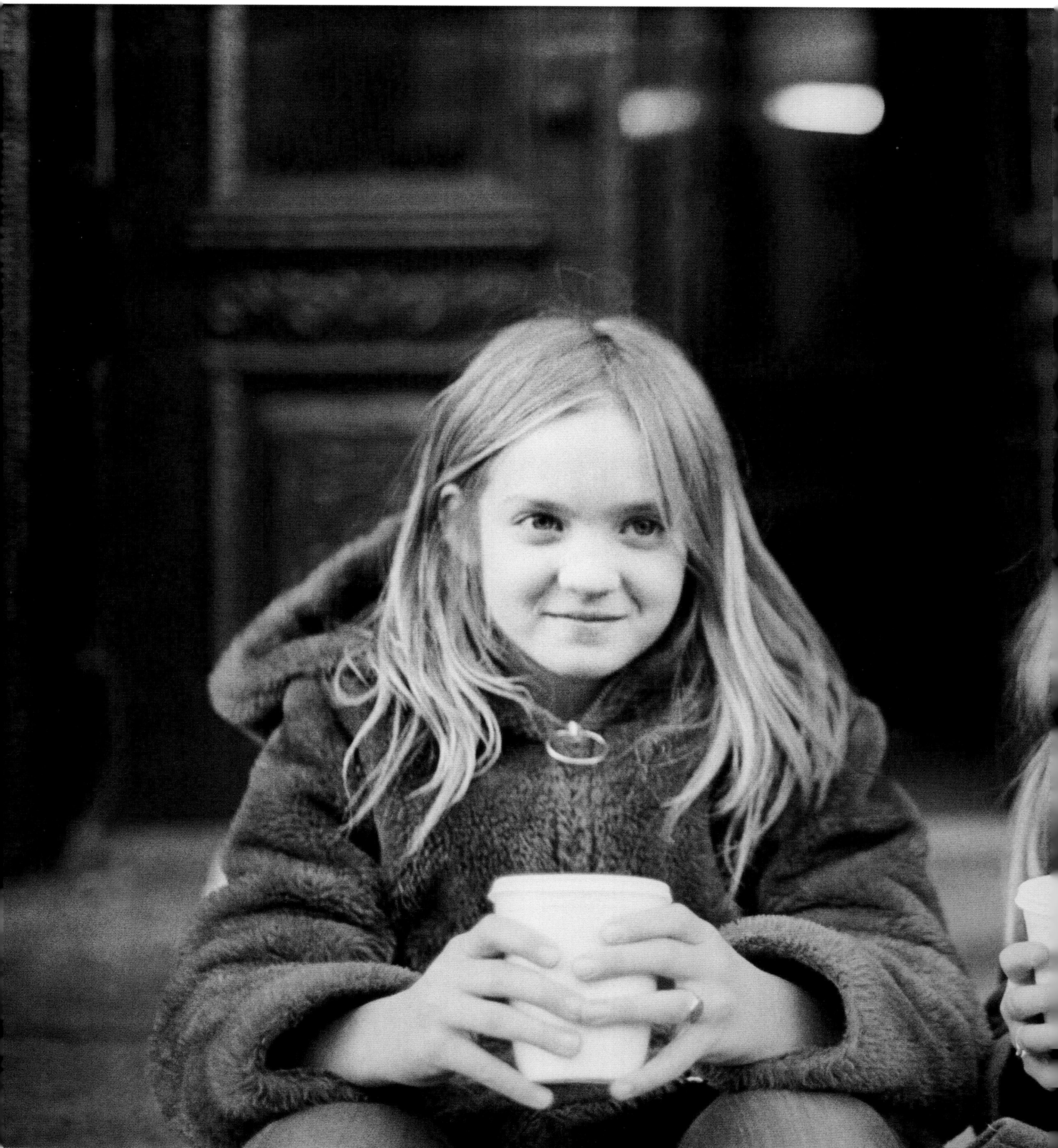

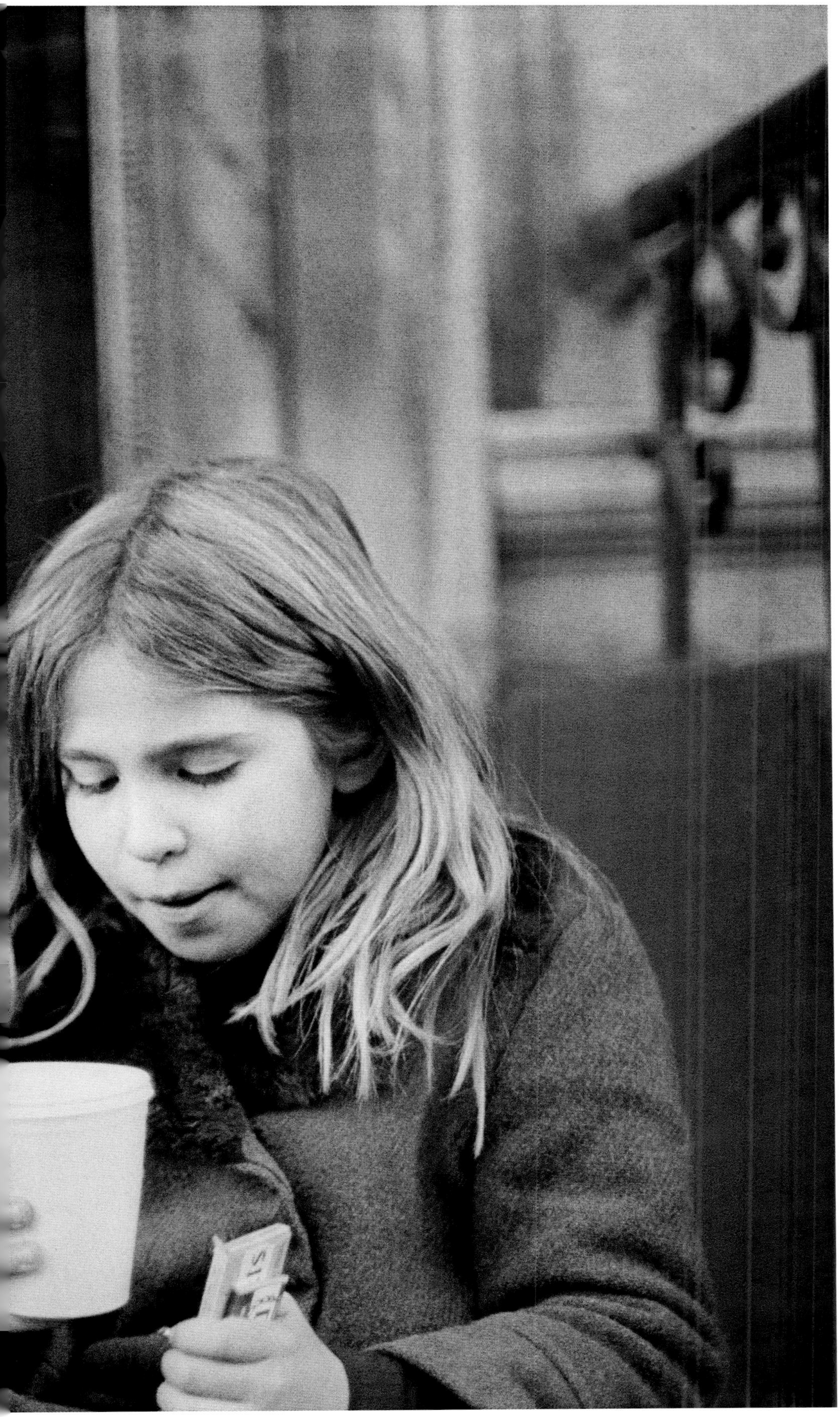

KIDS ON A STOOP, 1971–72

I really don't like Facebook. Mostly I hate the way it looks. It looks like a utility bill, customs form, or some horribly boring clothes catalog. Maybe they'll figure it out in my lifetime. I also get confused by the trend of people telling their very personal problems to what are pretty much complete strangers.

But some great stuff does come from the connectivity. (There's also a Facebook group I really like called Manhattan Before 1990. I've spent hours looking at the pictures people post on it, and had several shot locations identified by group members.) So I link my Instagram feed to Facebook, and pictures wind up on Facebook too. Within a few hours of posting this picture I had responses from both these girls, now adults. It really was exciting, as I've been looking at them anonymously, this image, for years.

Left is Marisa Perhaes Gorman, who went on to serve for almost twenty years in the NYPD, rising to the rank of sergeant during the height of the drug epidemics of the eighties and nineties. She wrote a book about her time as a patrol cop and her struggles in a male-dominated field, called *When I Was Blue*. Karen Trachtenberg, right, is a working actor.

The stoop they're on is on Second Avenue between 18th and 19th Streets. It was on the route I would take back and forth to the School of Visual Arts.

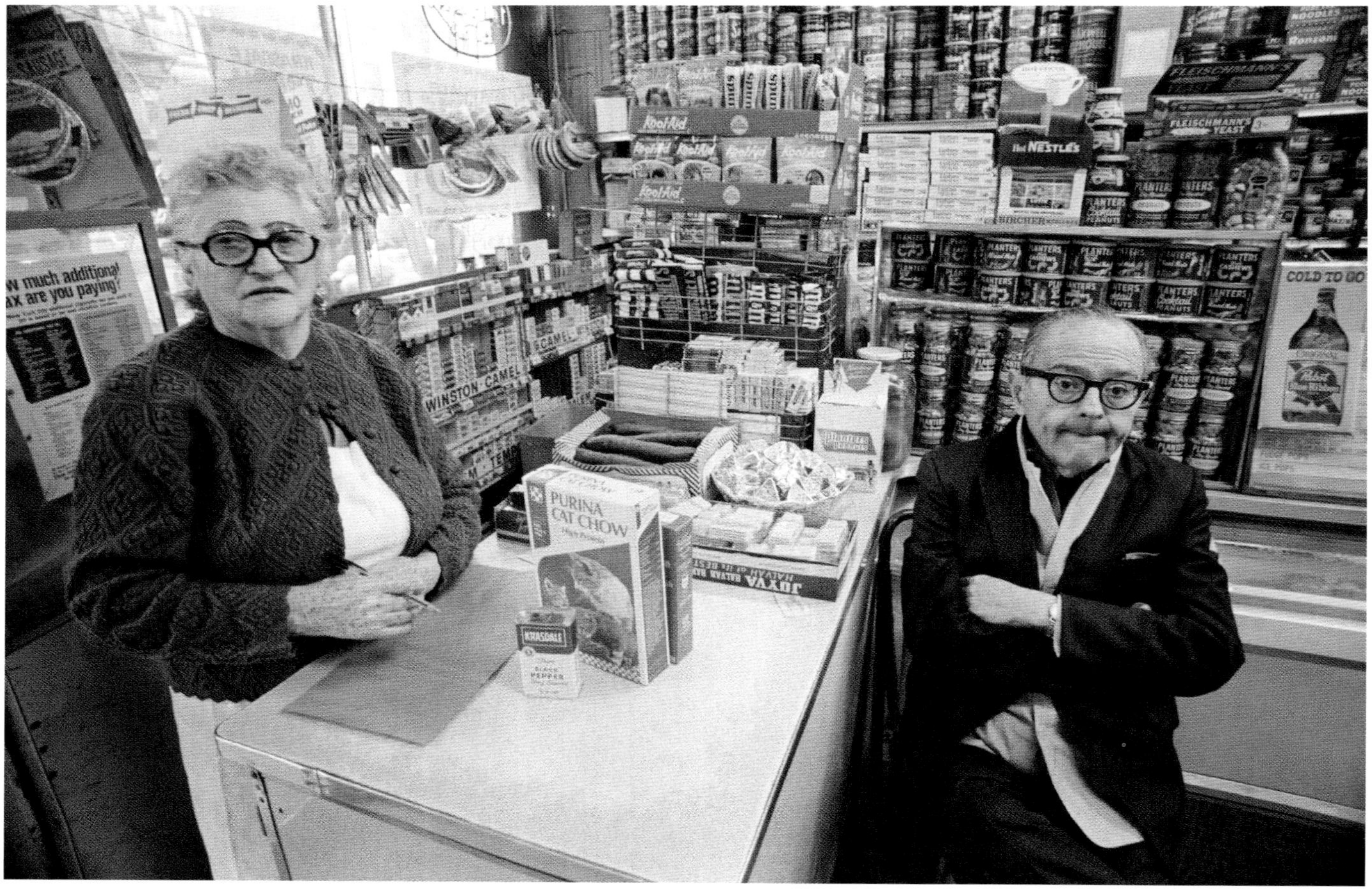
PURINA
CAT CHOW
WINSTON
CAMEL
KoolAid
NESTLE'S
FLEISCHMANN'S
PLANTERS
COLD TO GO

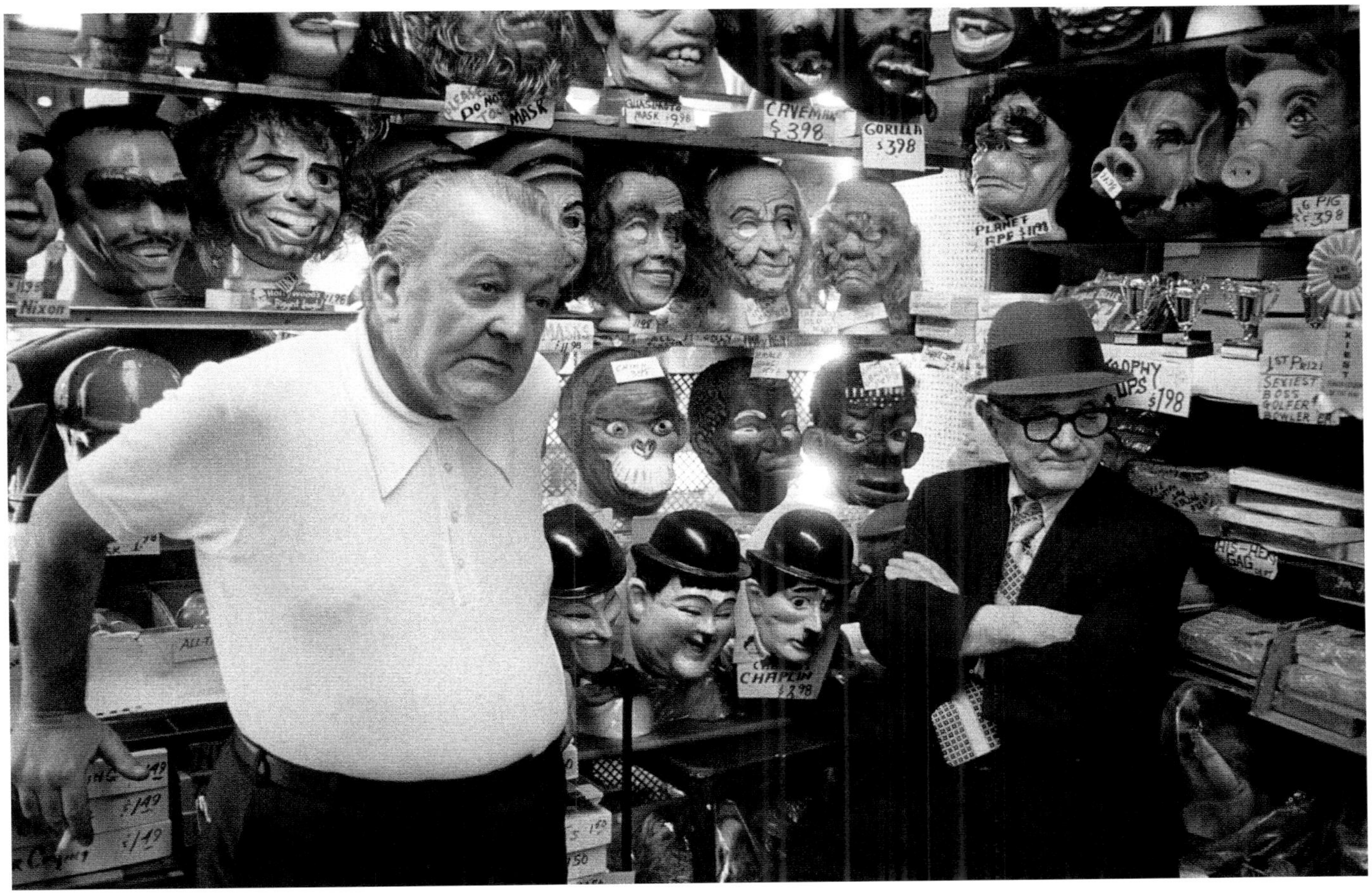
MASK
CAVEMAN $398
GORILLA $398
Nixon
CHAPLIN $398
$198
SEXIEST BOSS GOLFER BOWLER

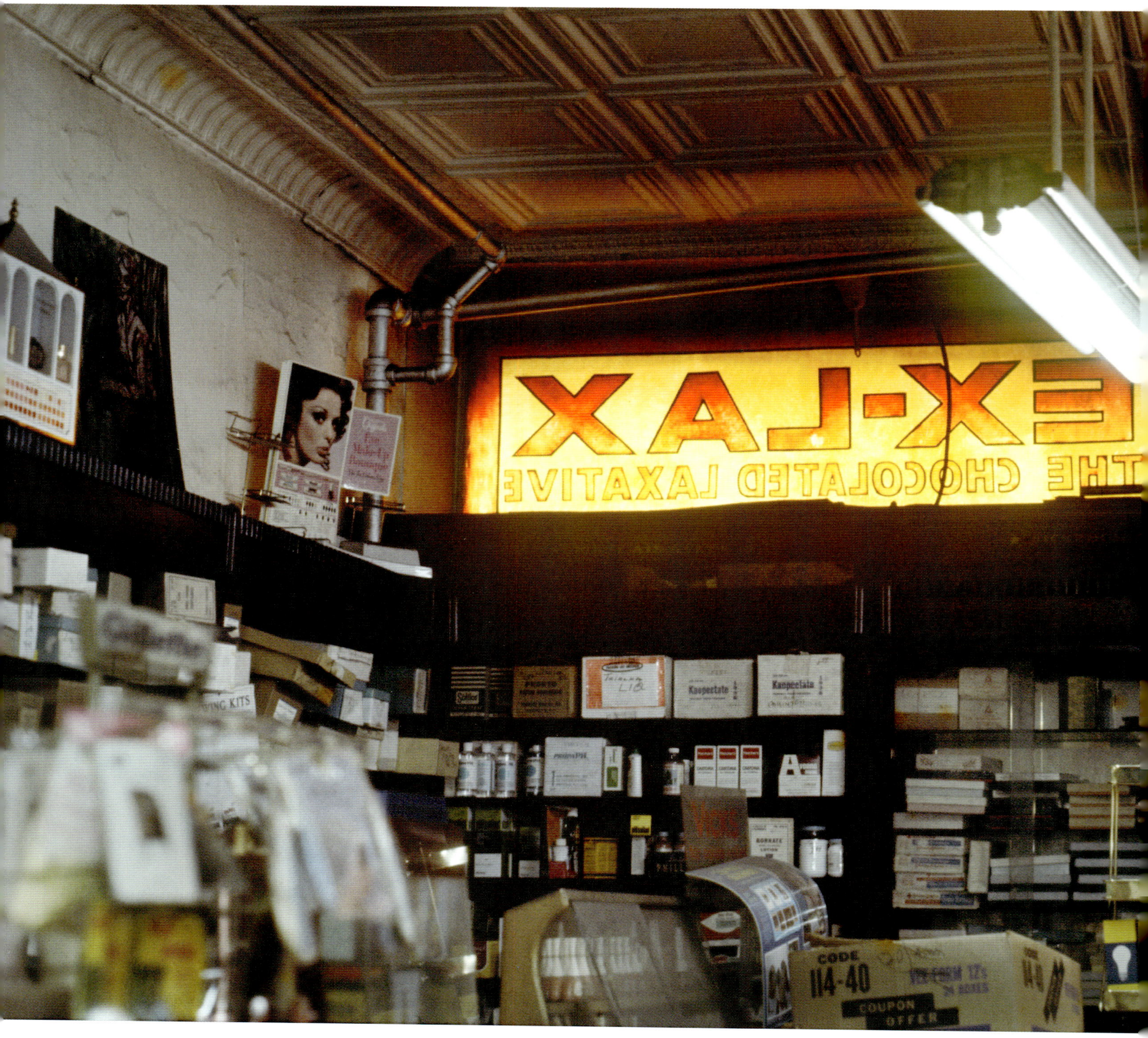
EX-LAX
THE CHOCOLATED LAXATIVE
Kaopectate
CODE
114-40
COUPON
OFFER

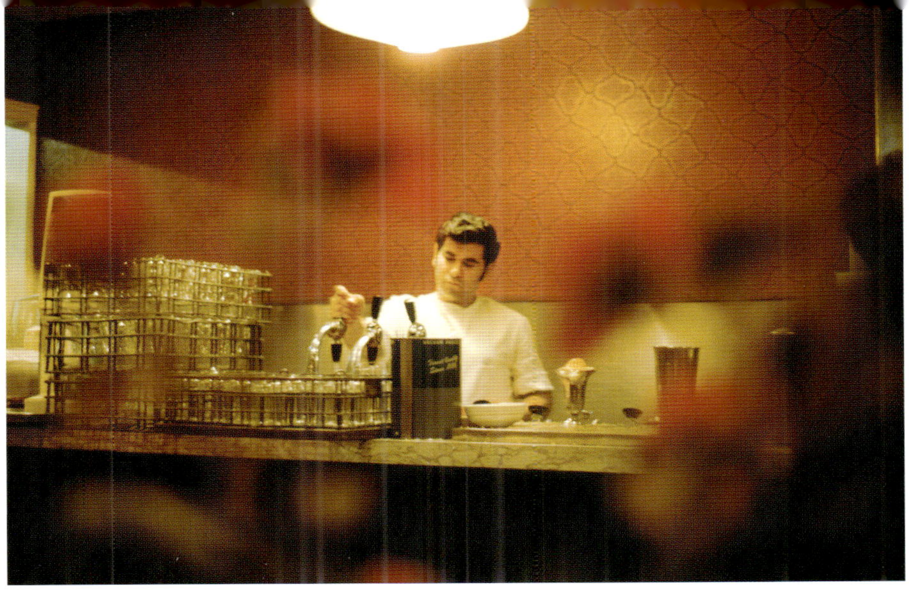

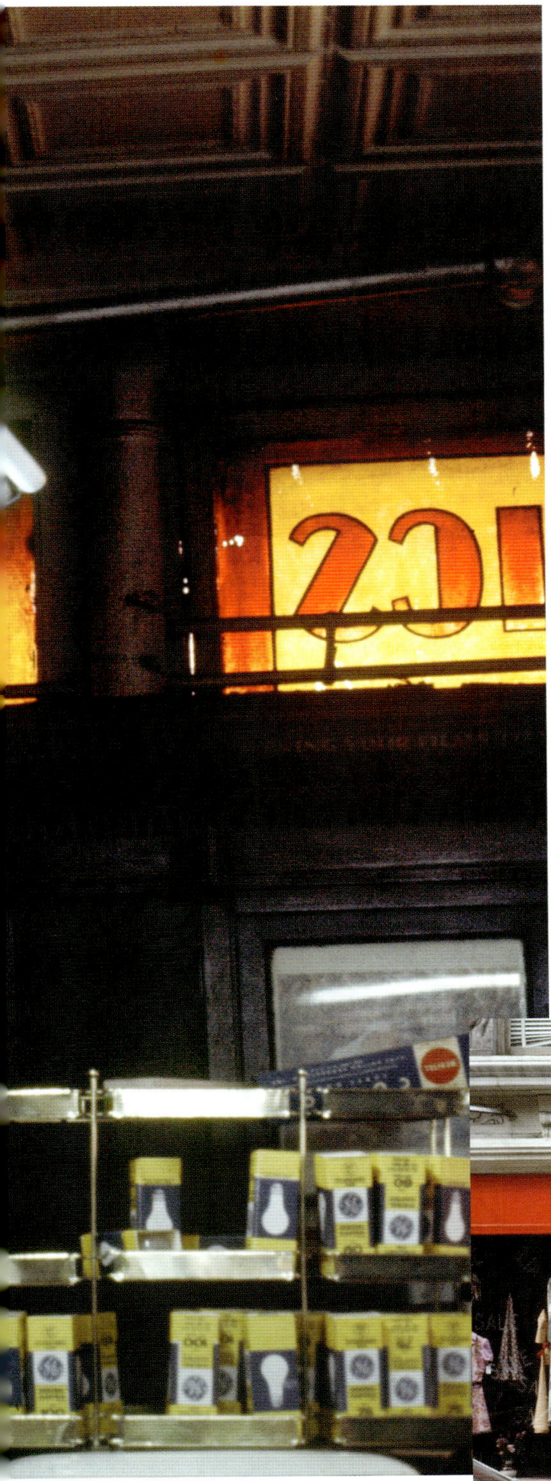

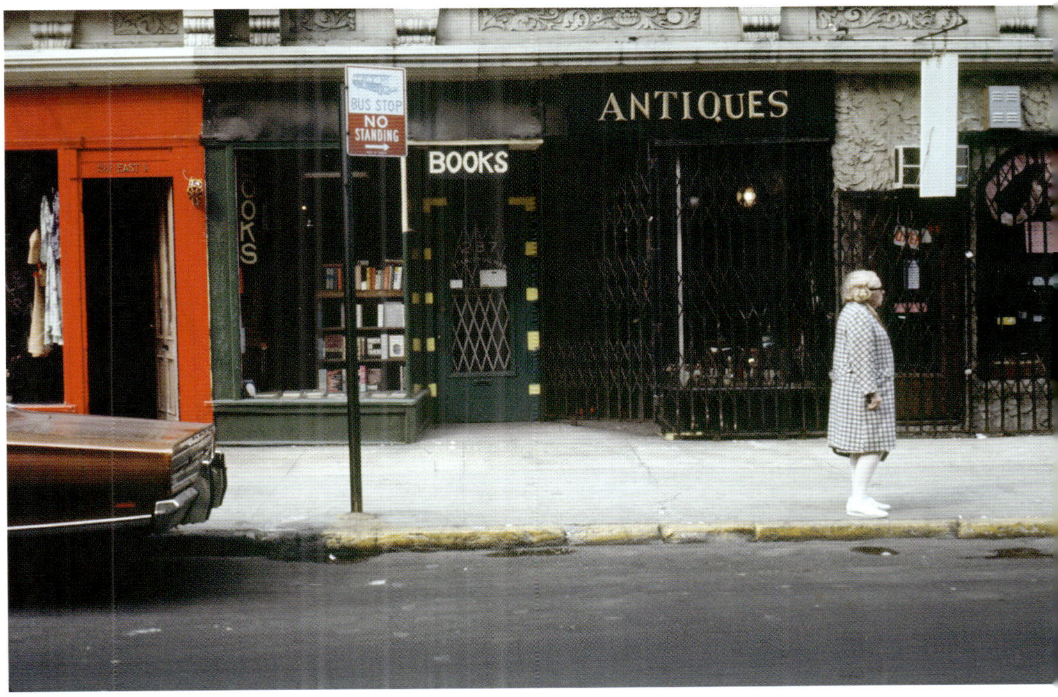
BUS STOP
NO STANDING
BOOKS
ANTIQUES

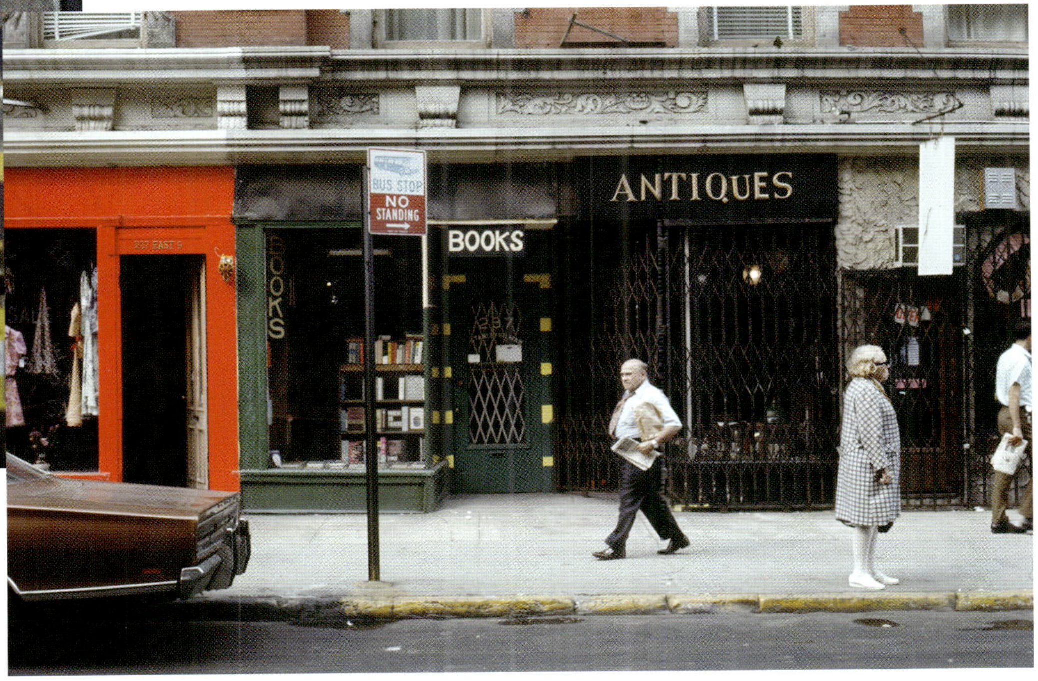
BUS STOP
NO STANDING
BOOKS
ANTIQUES

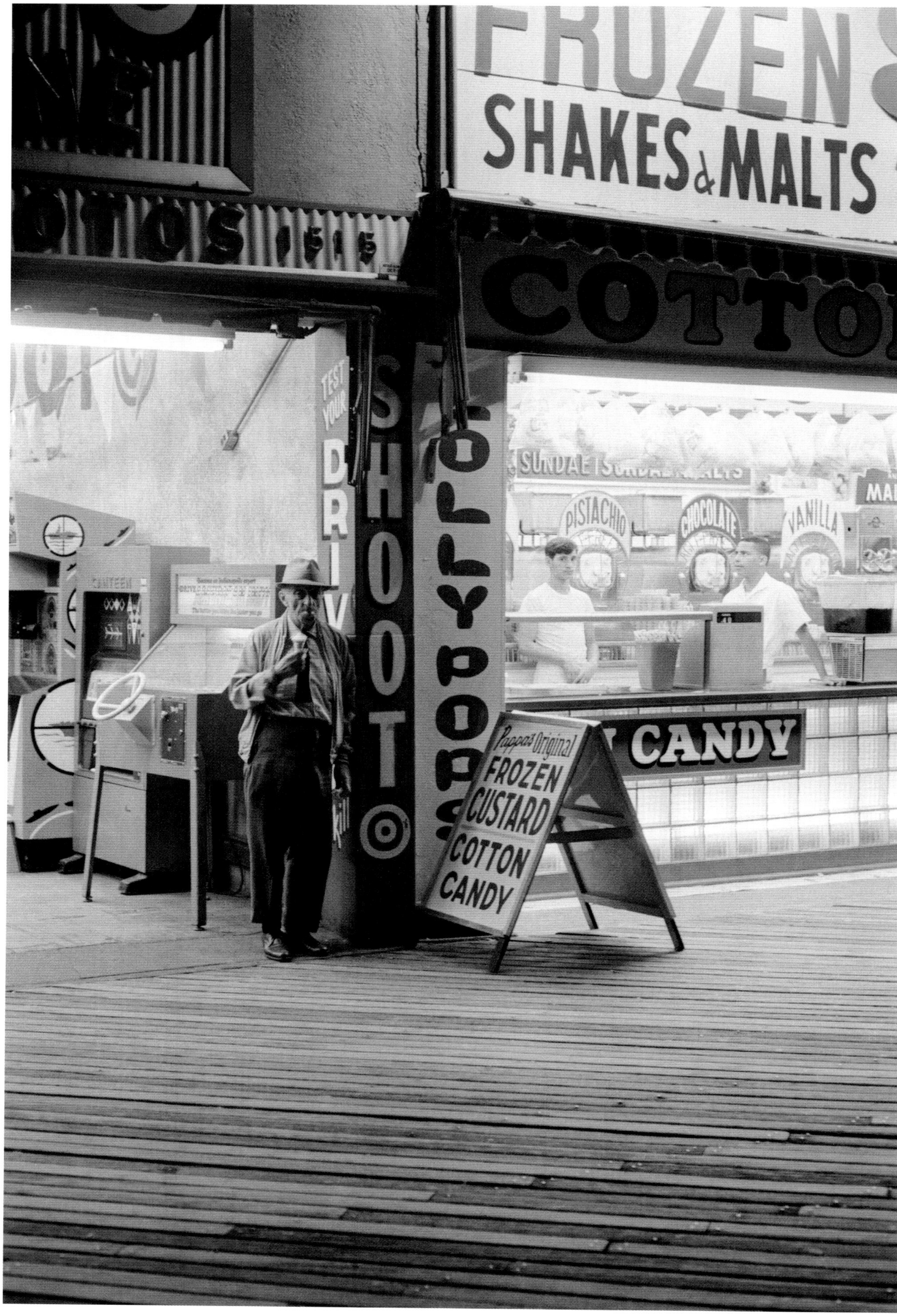
FROZEN
SHAKES & MALTS
COTTO
SHOOT
LOLLYPOPS
TEST YOUR DRIV
SUNDAE SUNDAE MALTS
PISTACHIO
CHOCOLATE
VANILLA
MALT
CANDY
Pappas Original
FROZEN
CUSTARD
COTTON
CANDY

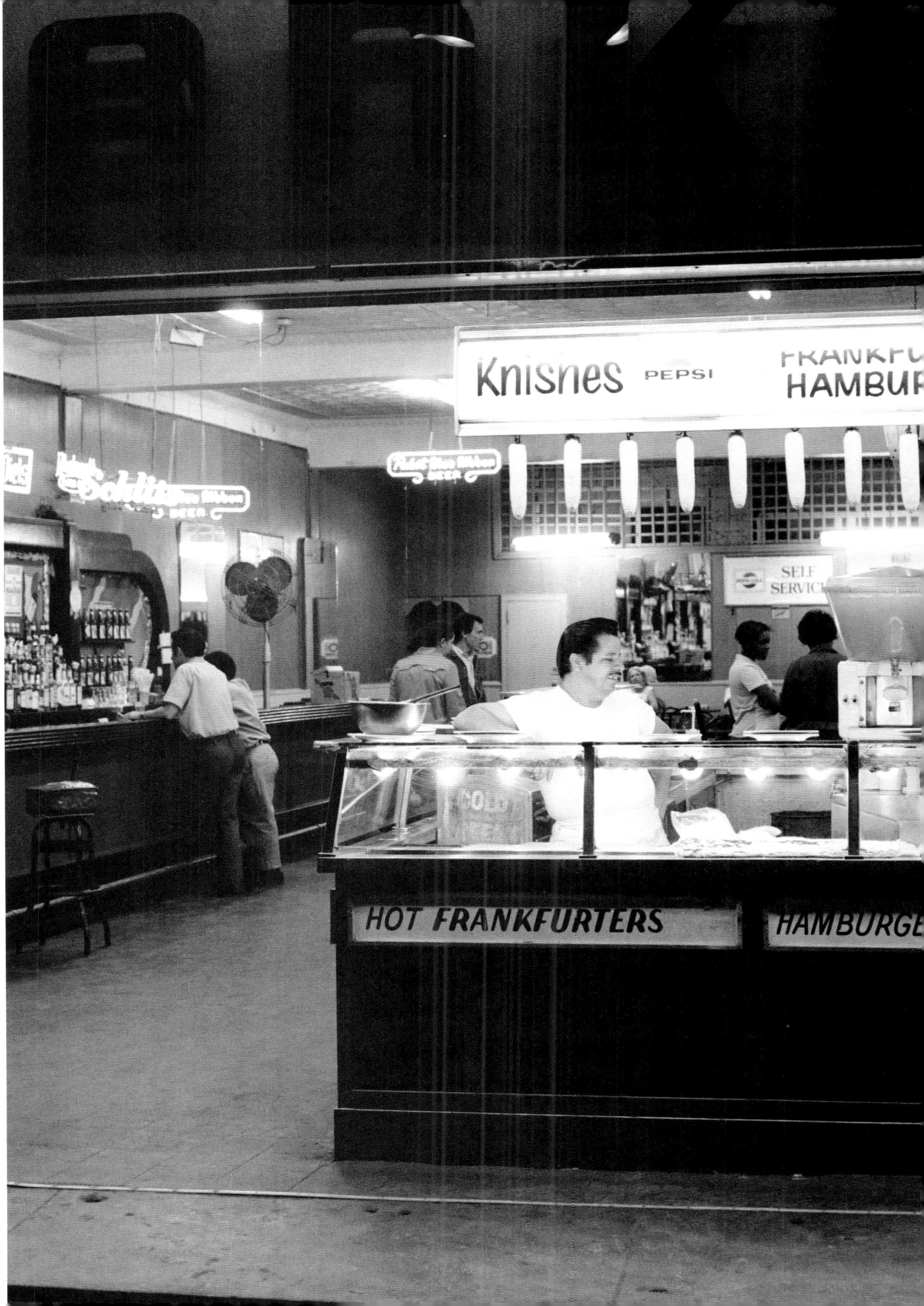
Knishes
PEPSI
HOT FRANKFURTERS

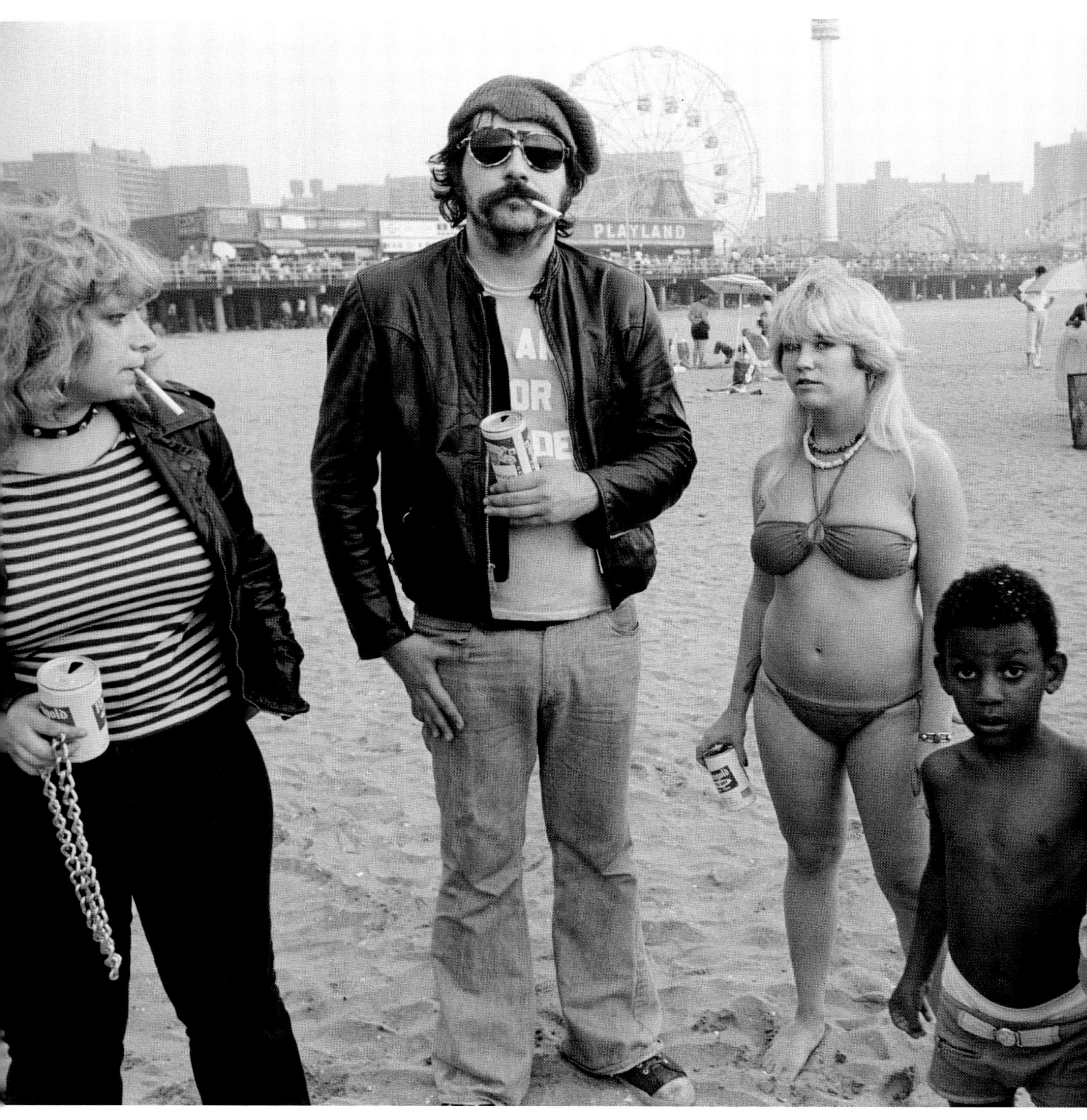
PLAYLAND

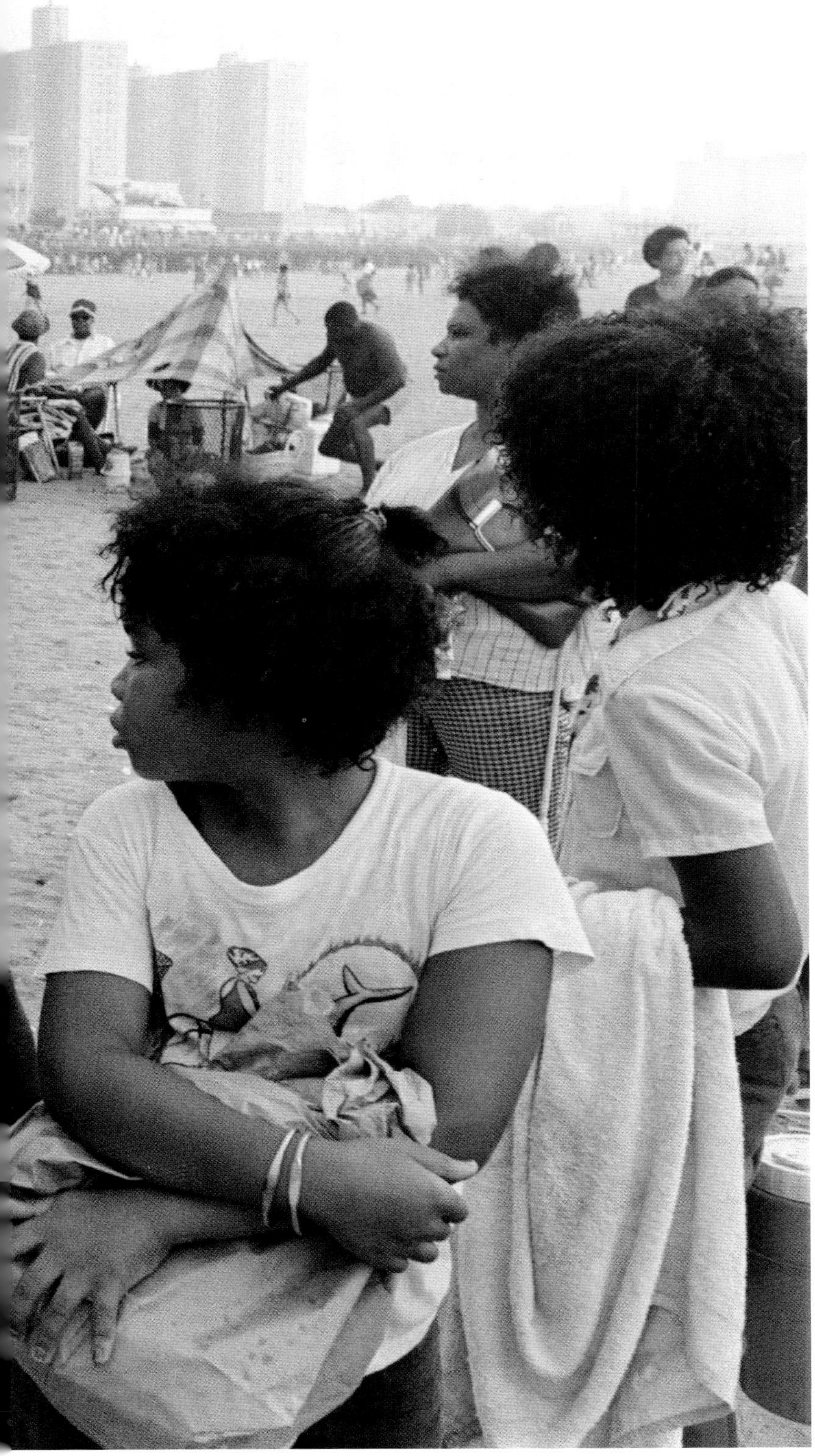

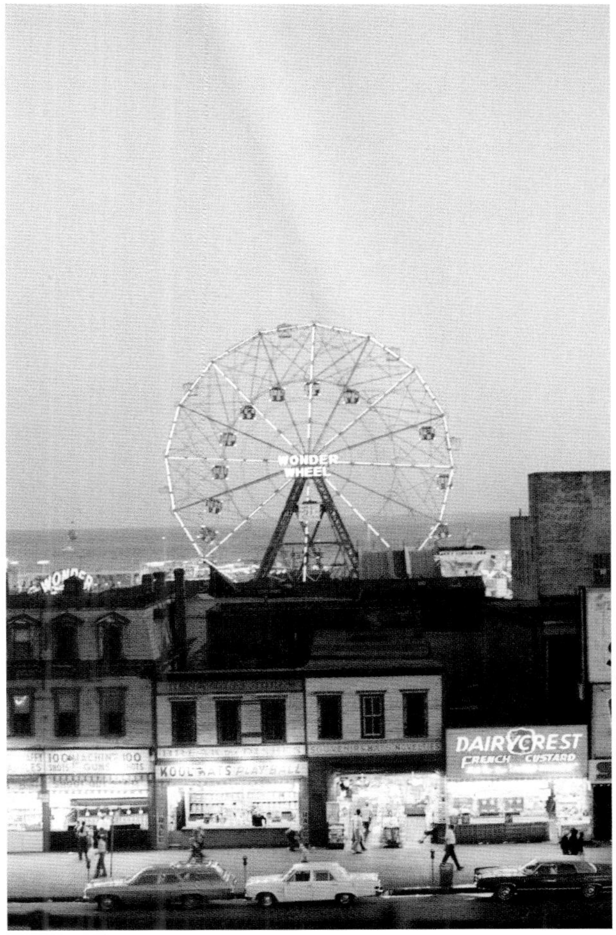

Punk magazine outtake, 1976. Lester Bangs on the beach at Coney Island. The girl in the striped shirt is Jessie Blue of the Slander Band; the girl in the bikini has only been identified as Frankie the Shark Woman.

CONEY ISLAND

My parents and I would frequently go to Coney Island in the late fifties. It's still very evocative; the Coney Island of the Mind is with us all. It still has a vibe, and recently Debbie and I were king and queen of the Mermaid Parade. So all these years later, full cycle, even more connection.

I must have been around ten when my parents and I were waiting on line for food at Nathan's one hot summer day. We finally got to the counter, and the server guy at the potato station was chanting "FRENCH FRIES AND SALT!" like it was a gospel song. He looked me in the eye as he handed the fries to me and said, "You're never gonna forget this." I never forgot it.

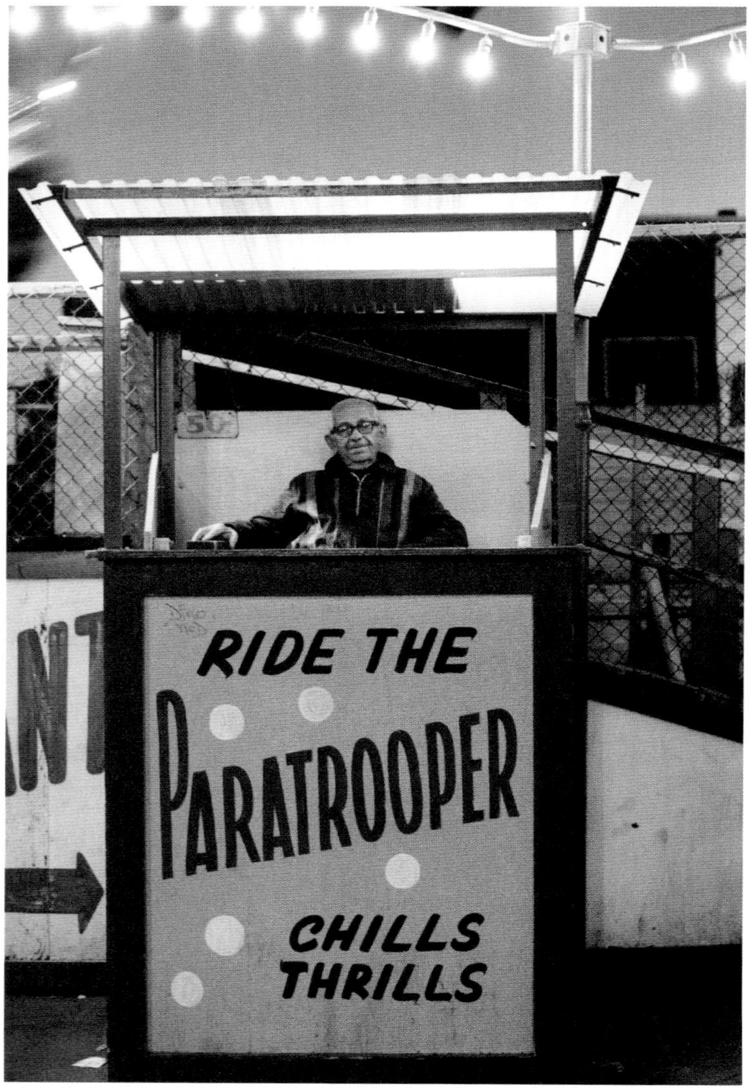

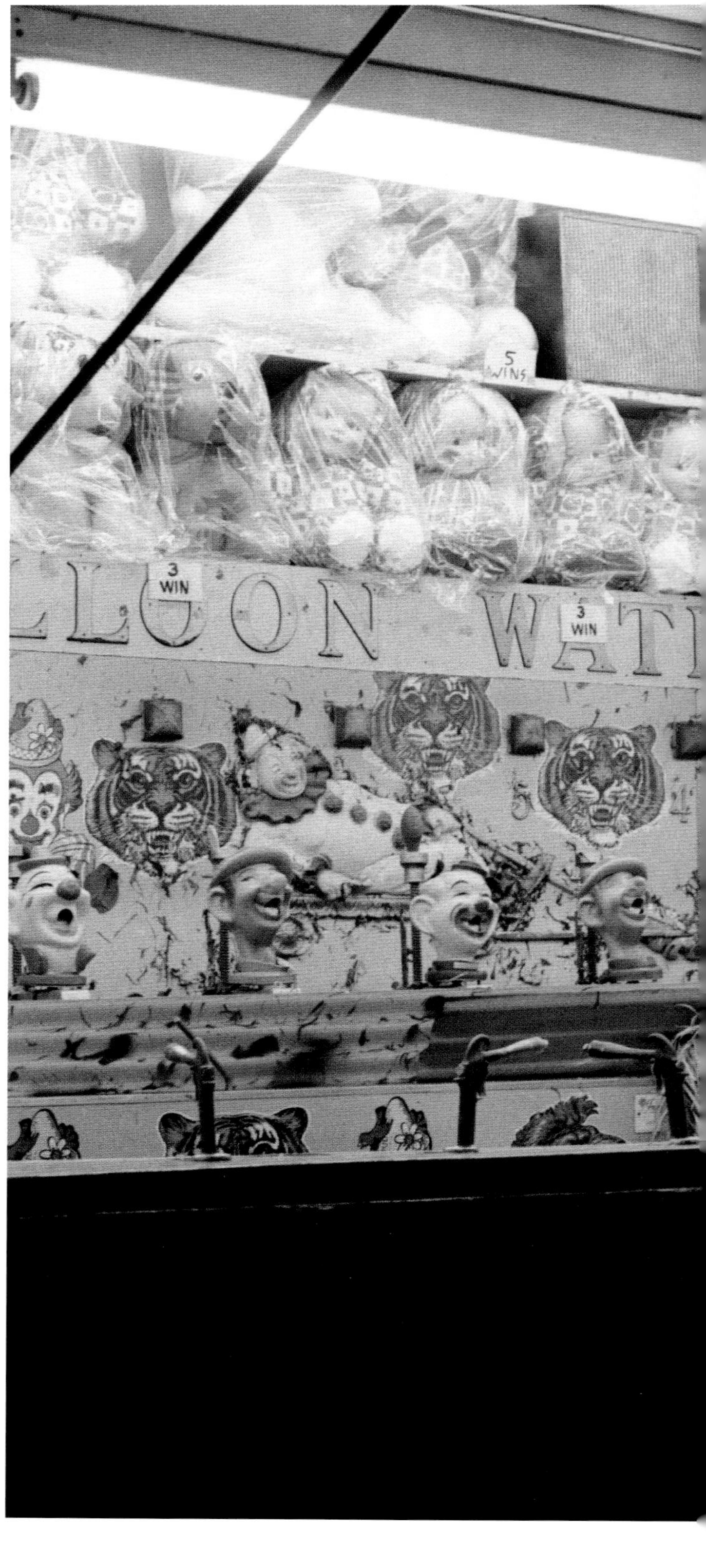

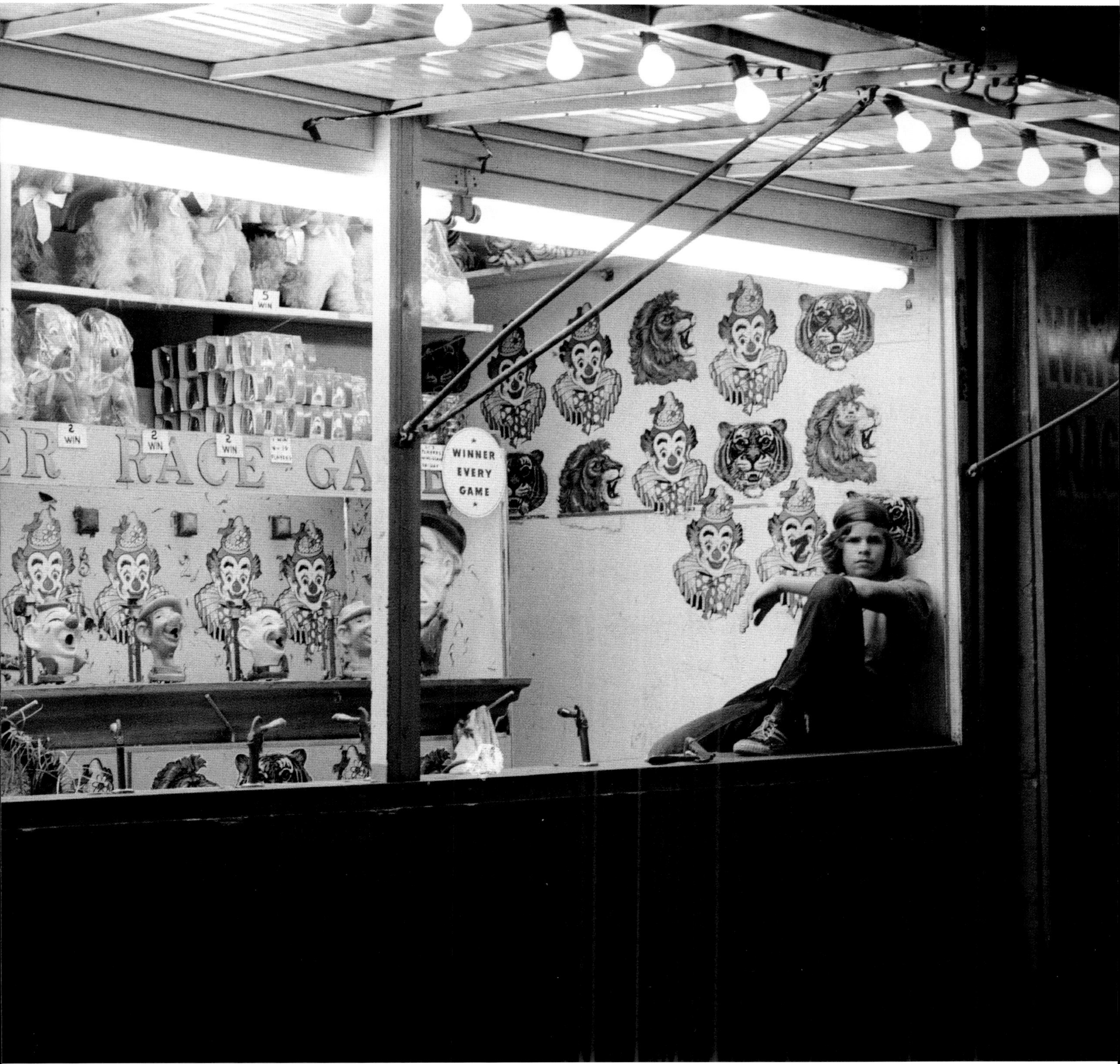
5 WIN
2 WIN
2 WIN
2 WIN
WINNER EVERY GAME

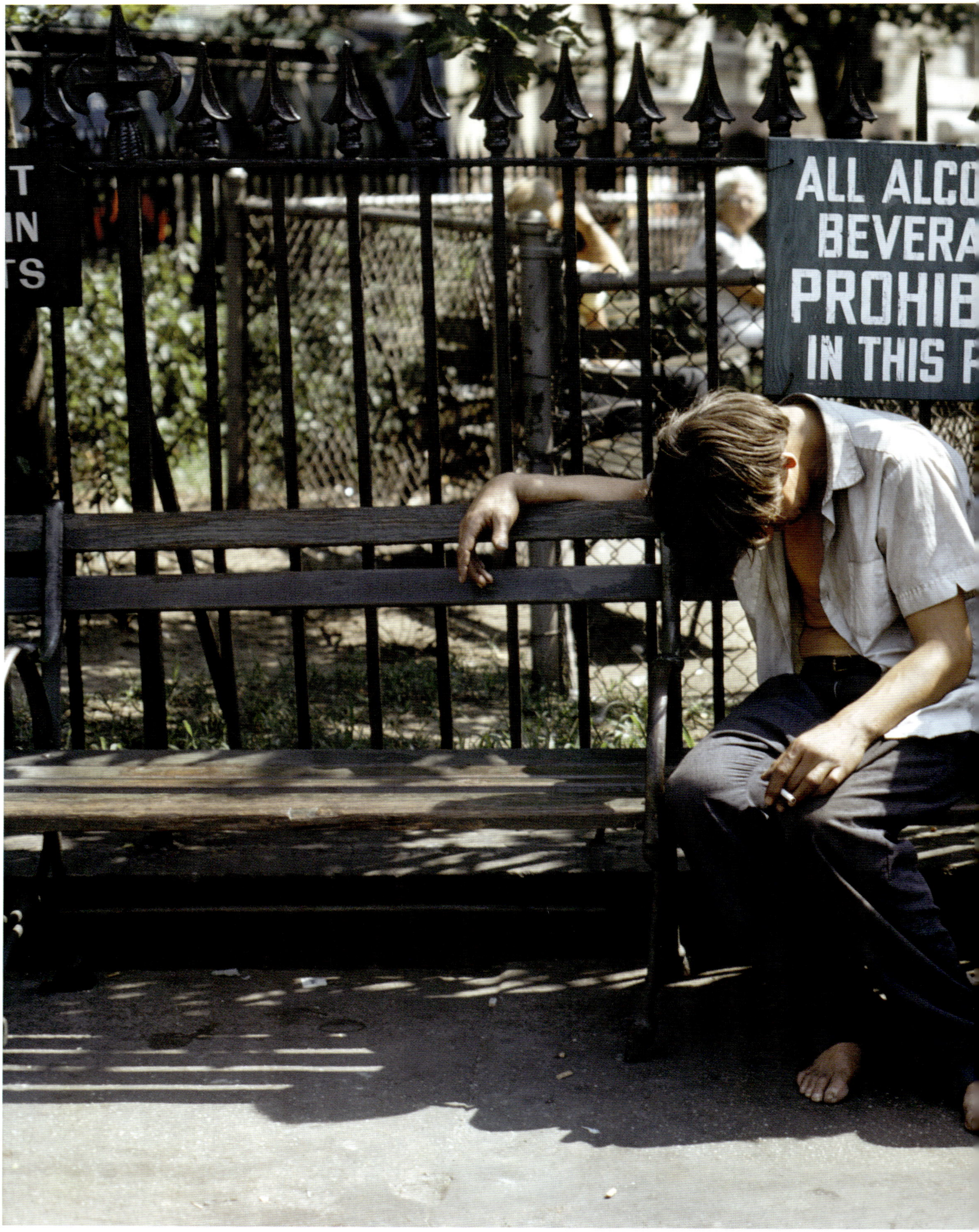
ALL ALCO
BEVERA
PROHIB
IN THIS

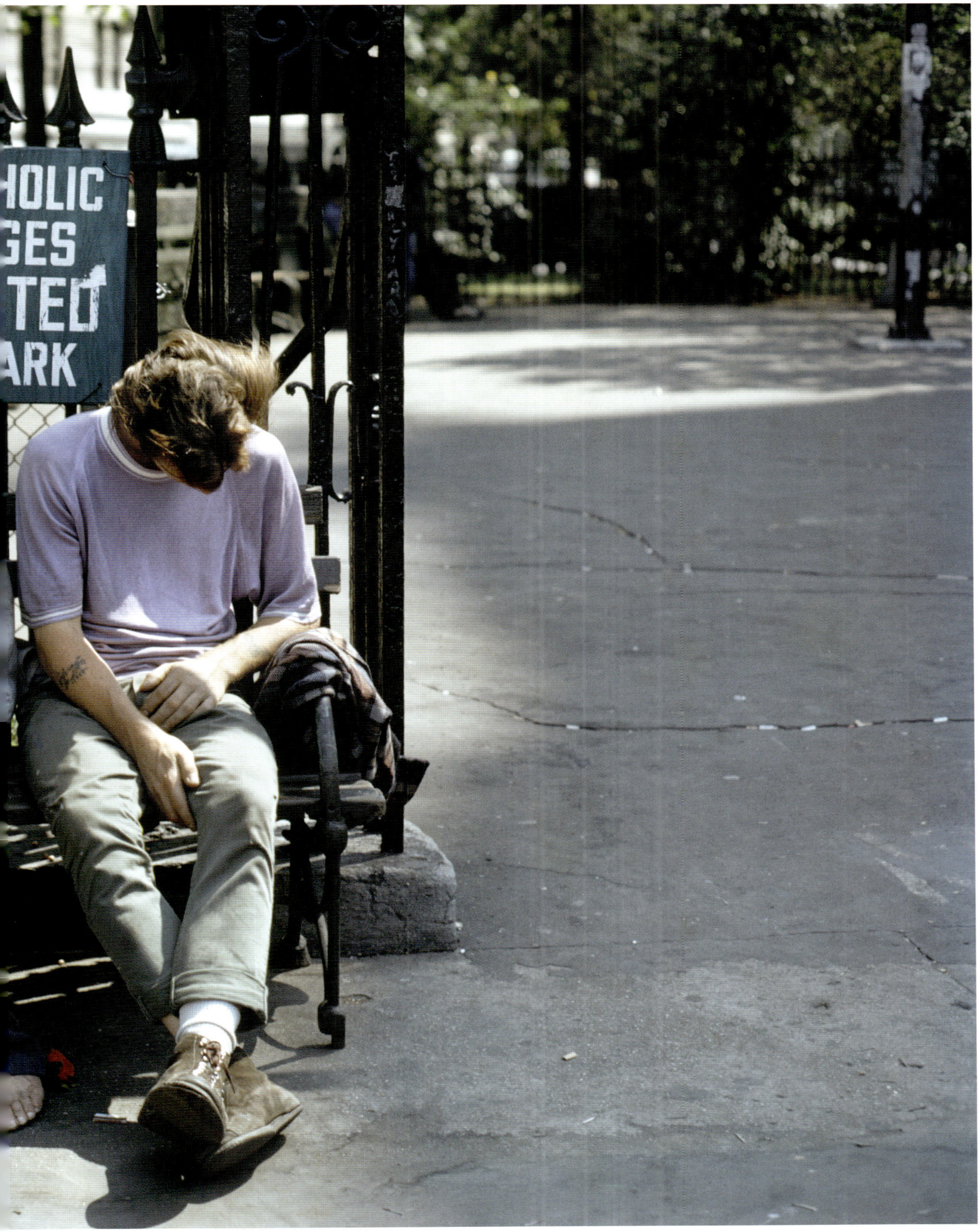
HOLIC
GES
TED
ARK

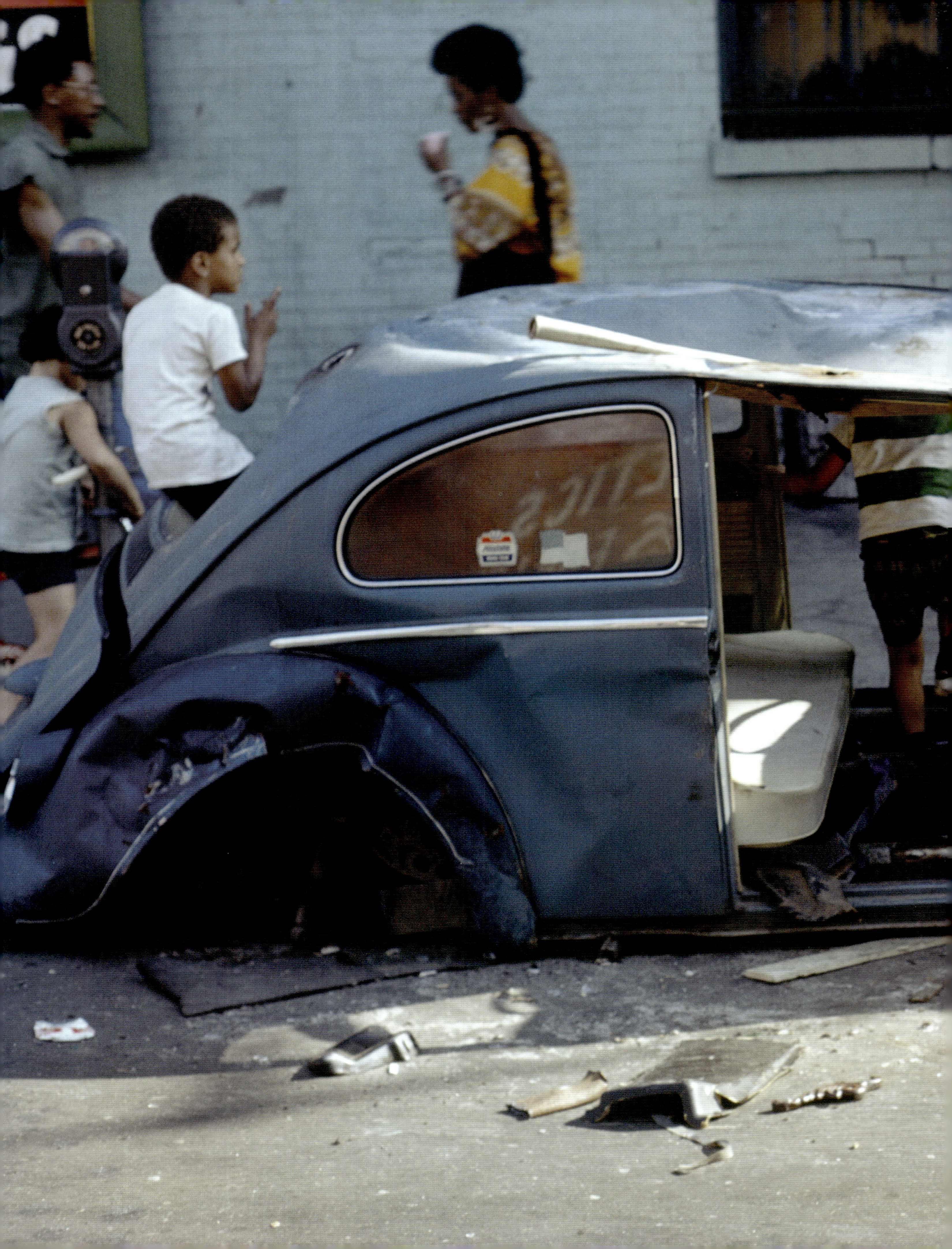

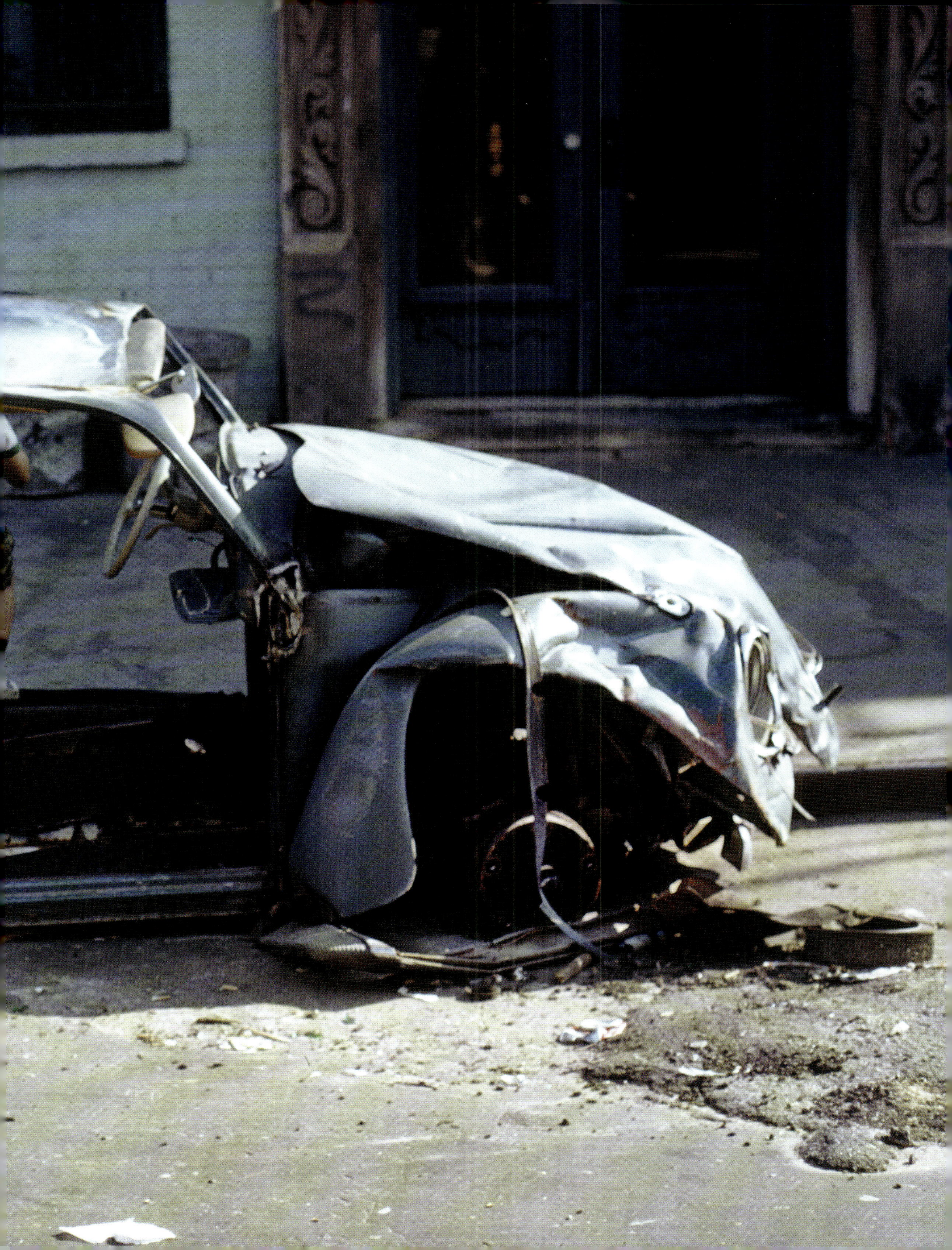

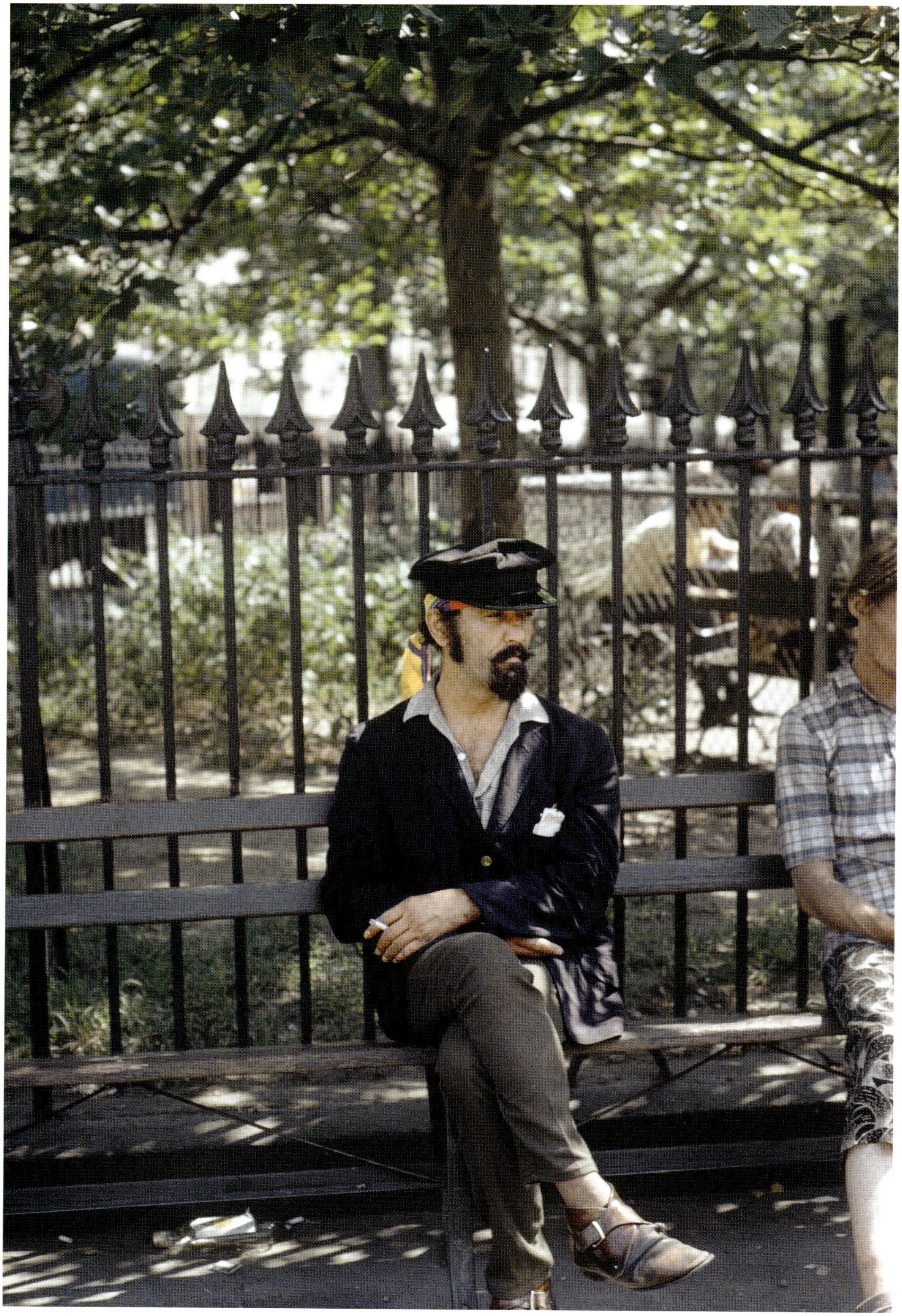

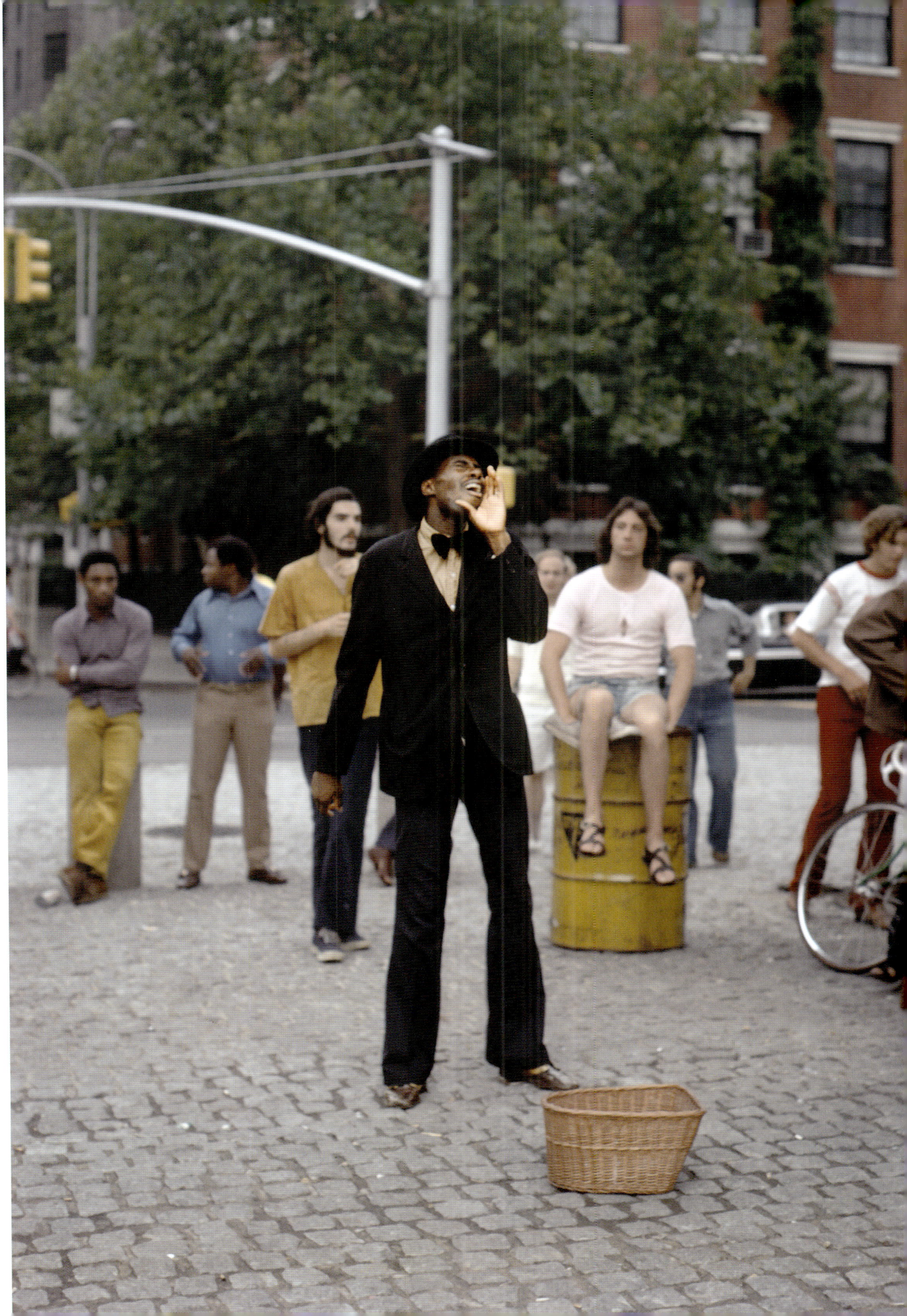

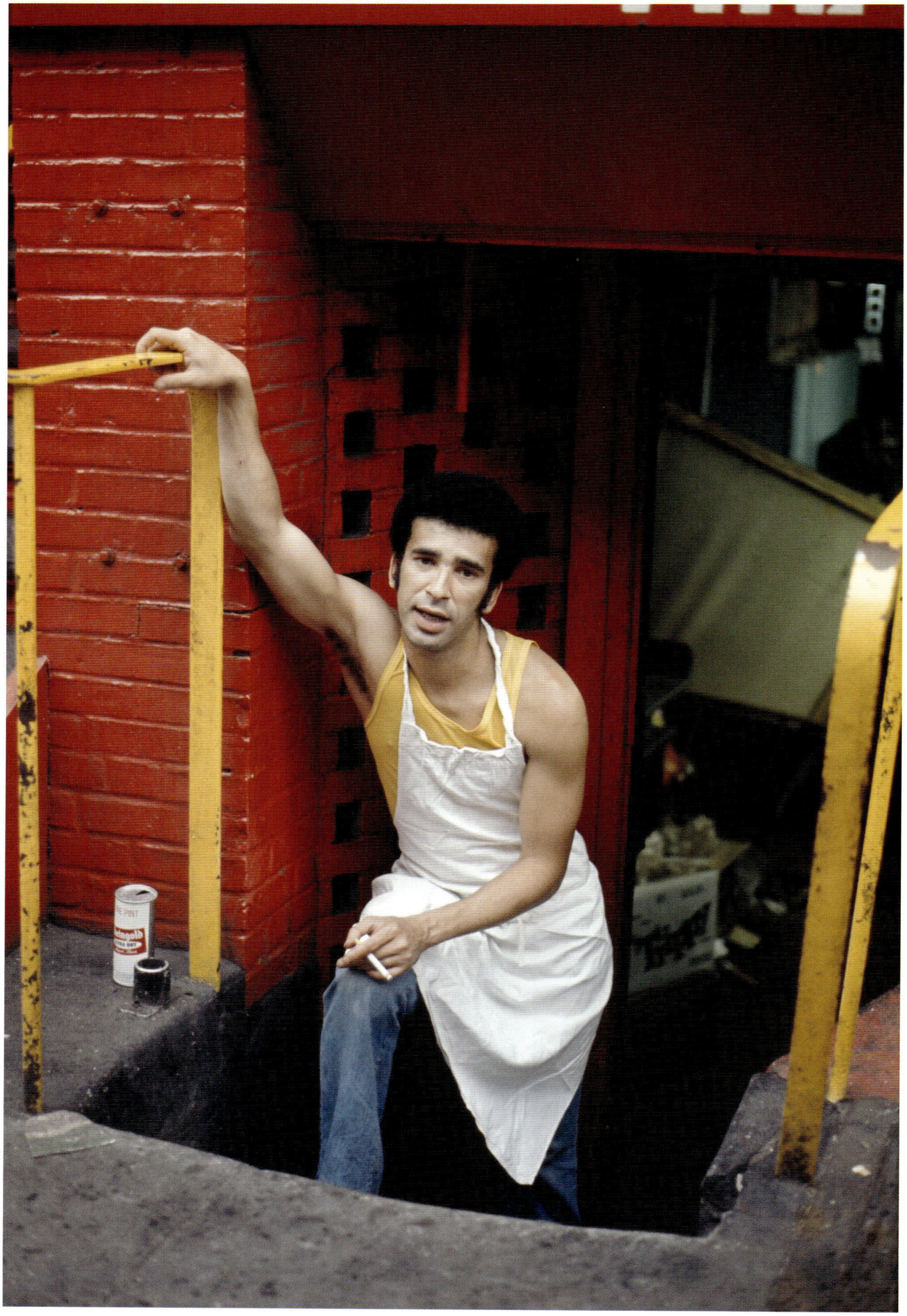

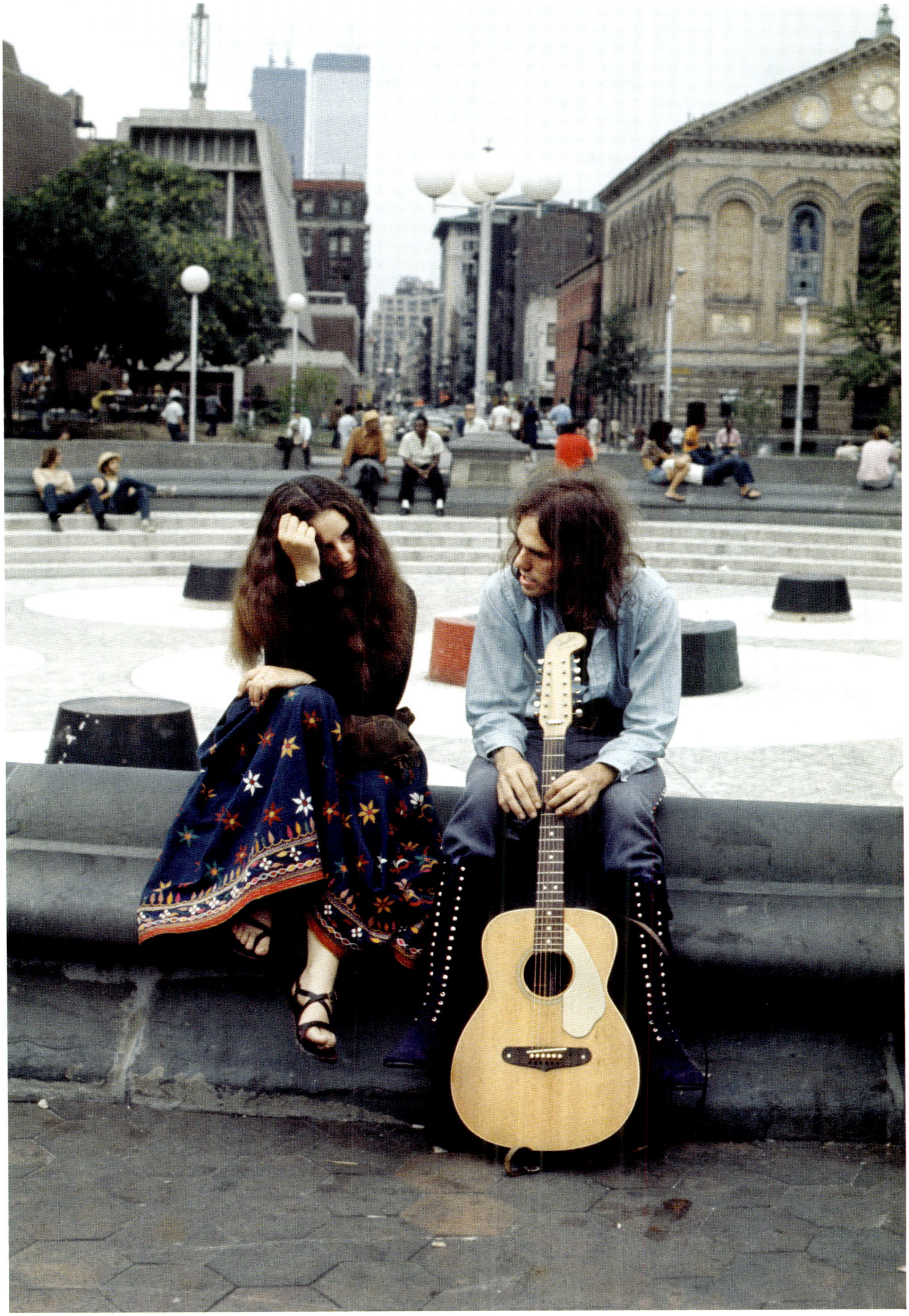

CAR FIRE, LOWER EAST SIDE

I can only guess the events here. I must have been wandering around after dark taking pictures. This would have been odd, since getting mugged was standard and I was cautious about the camera. Earlier my friend and I got held up by a couple of guys with knives in my hallway. After grabbing my friend's watch and the same camera I took this photo with, they demanded we pull our pants down. We looked at each other: if they're gonna stab us in the balls, we'll have to fight them. But it was a mugger's technique to keep the victims from chasing them as they made their getaway. We pulled up our pants and ran after them along Houston Street. We somehow came in contact with a cop who joined us in the pursuit. He caught up to the guy with the camera on Ludlow Street just past Katz's Deli. The cop grabbed the guy's shoulder and the guy instantly slipped out of his jacket. The cop was left standing there holding the camera and the jacket. I was very grateful, and the cop was amused. My friend Bob lost his watch, though. The camera did in fact get stolen for good, a year or so later, when I must have left the apartment door open and some random passerby reached in and took it. I never figured out what happened to it.

A car fire wasn't that big of a deal. Stuff was always burning and falling apart. I obviously waited for the fire department guys to show up and douse the flames while standing around and talking; another day on the job.

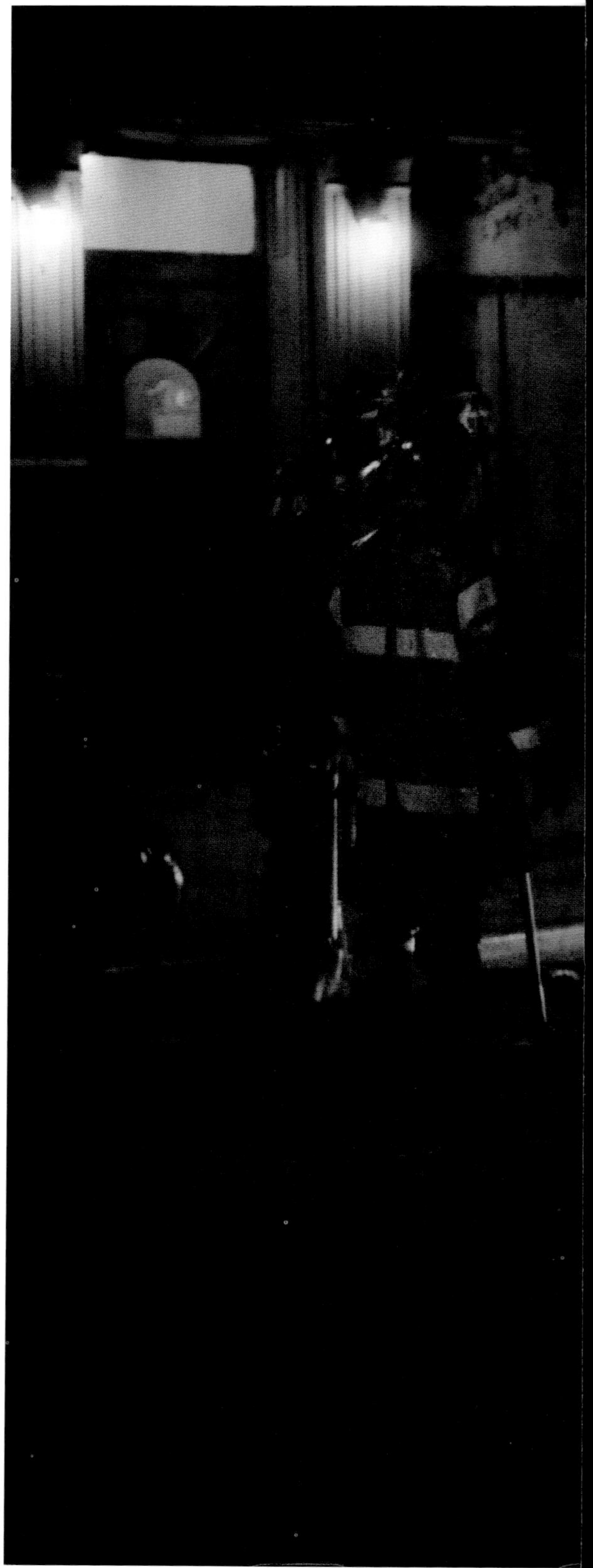

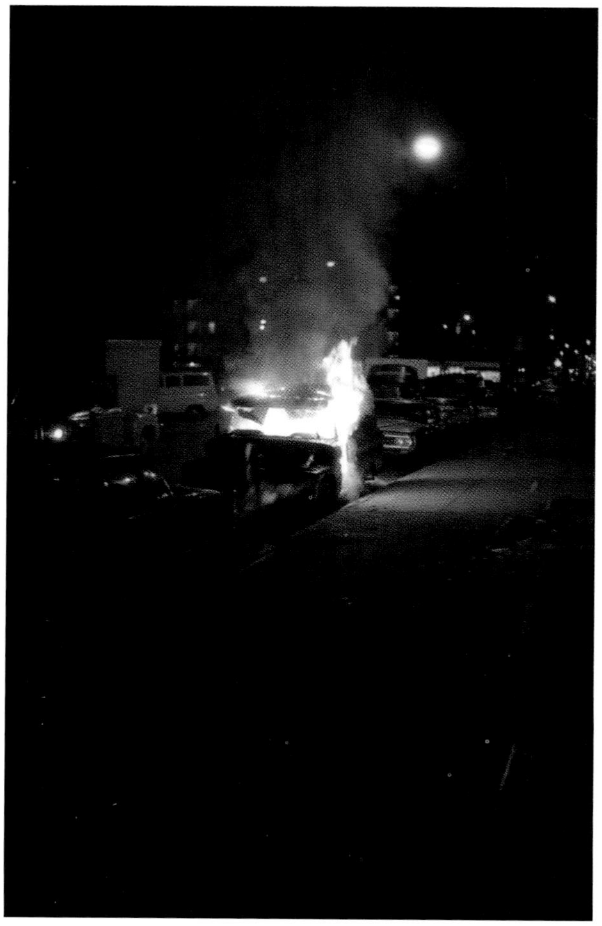

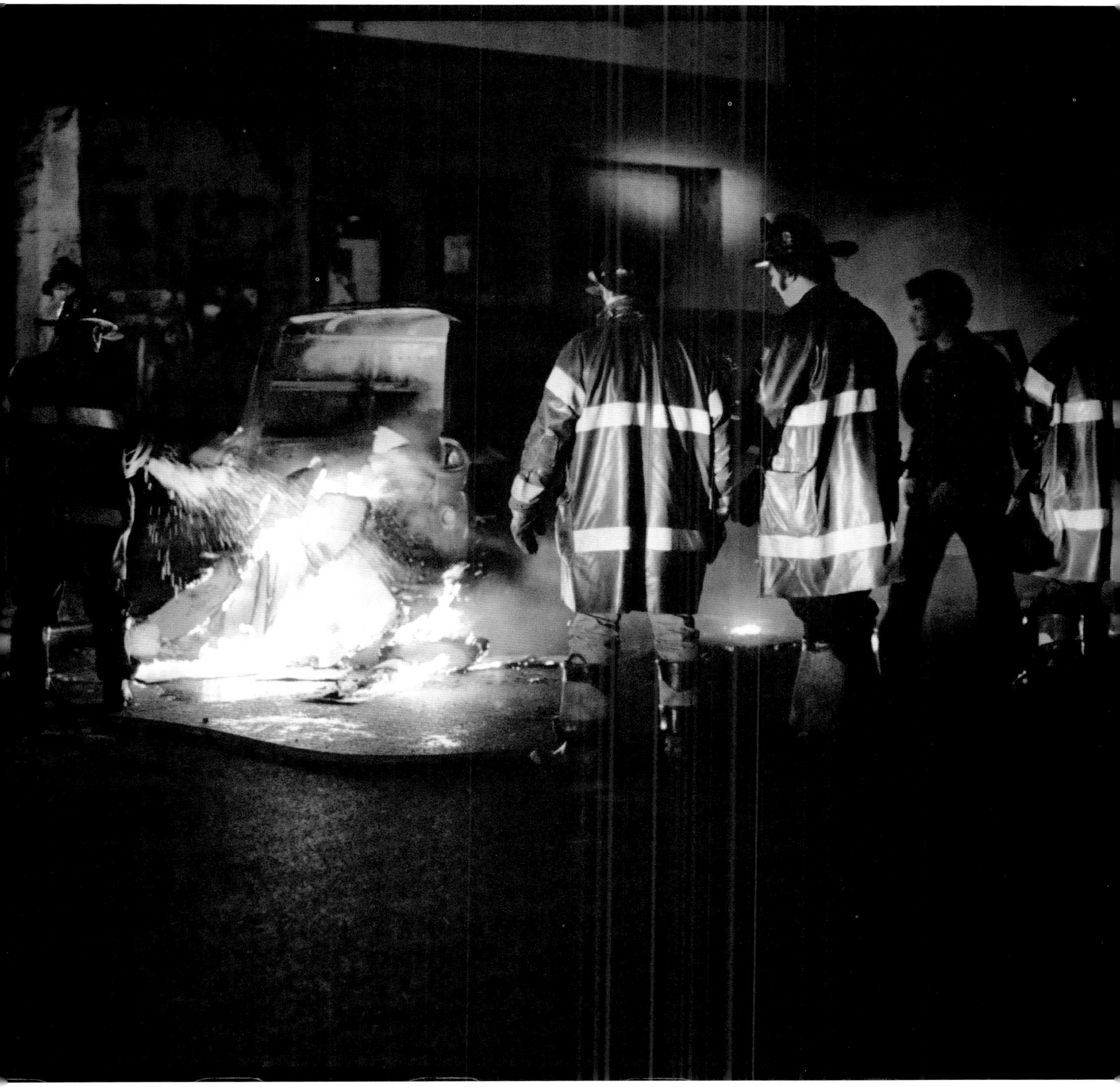

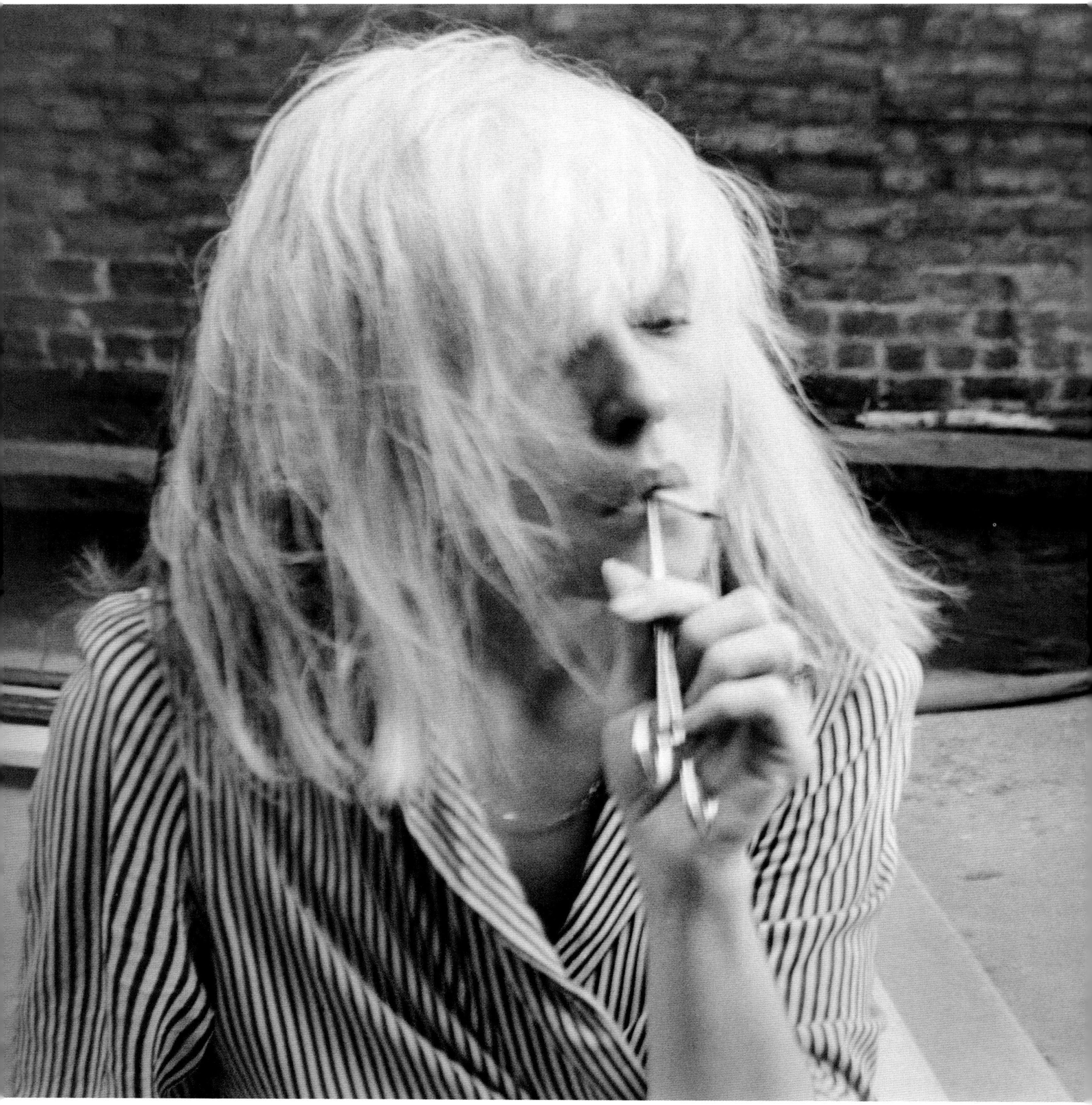

Debbie on the roof of our place on 17th Street. This is above the kitchen where we took the well-known burned dress / flaming frying pan shots. This is also where we first heard a Blondie song on the radio.

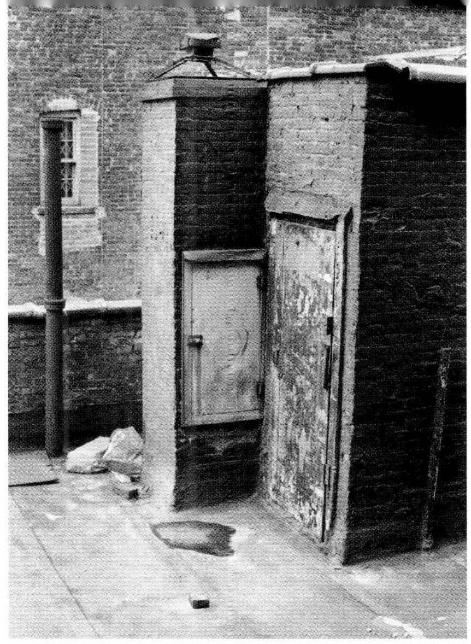

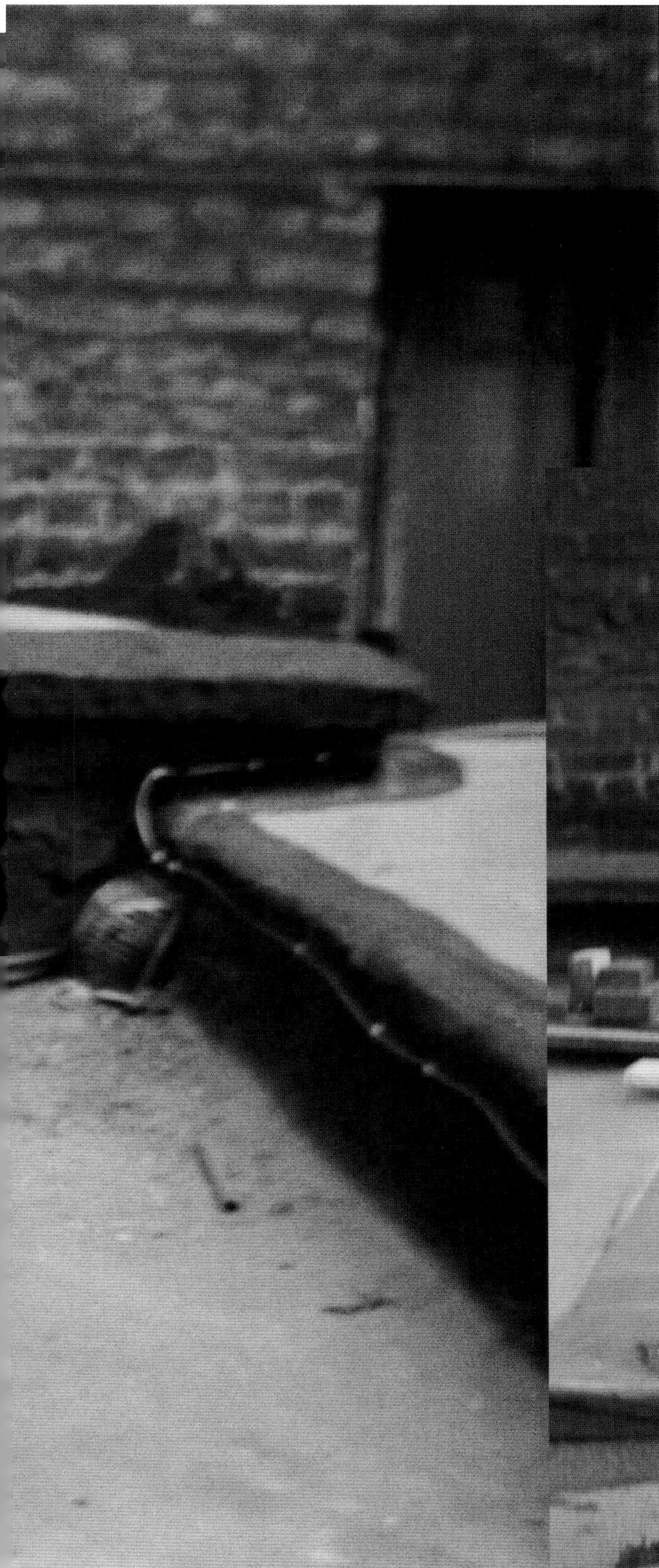

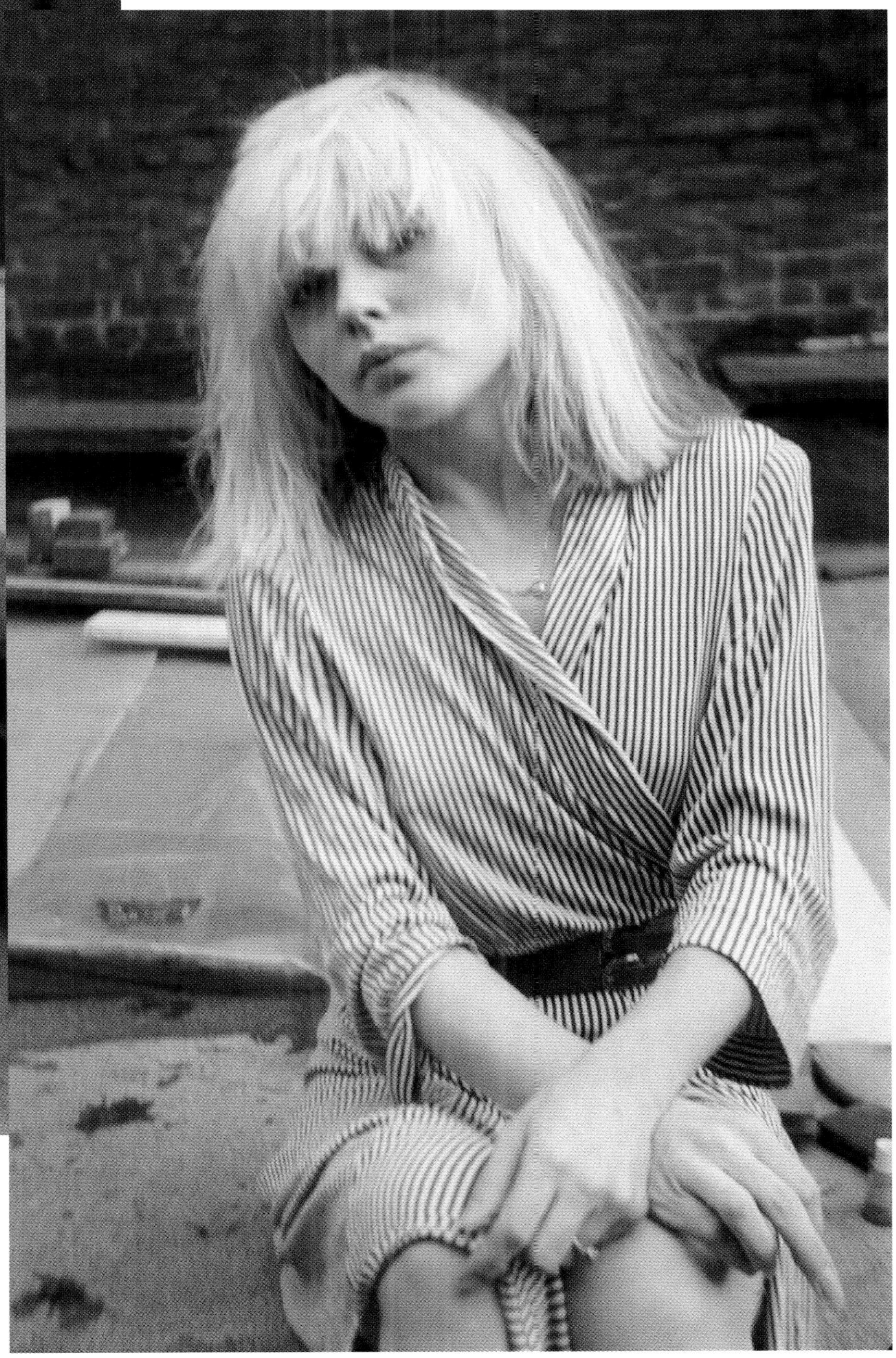

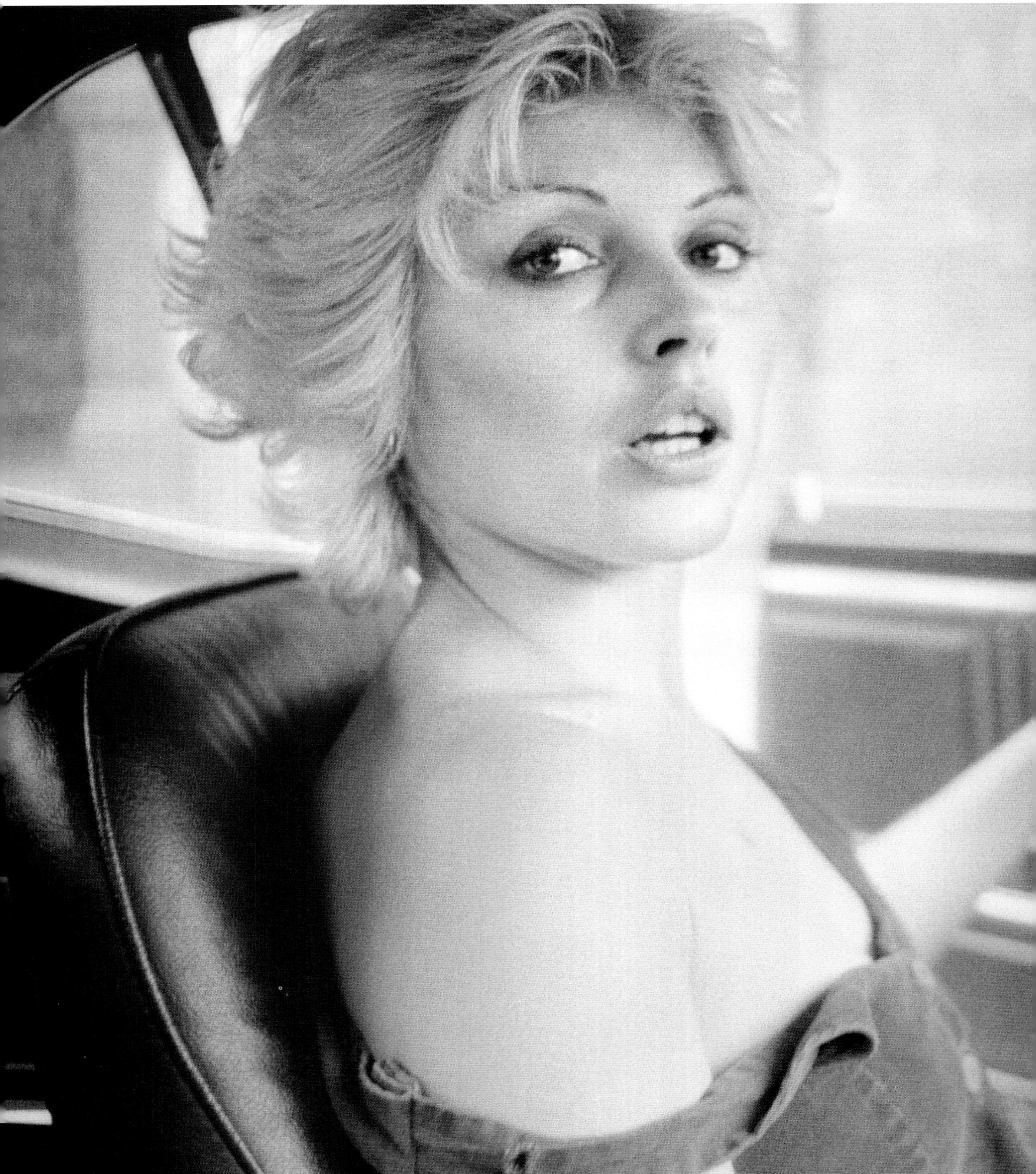

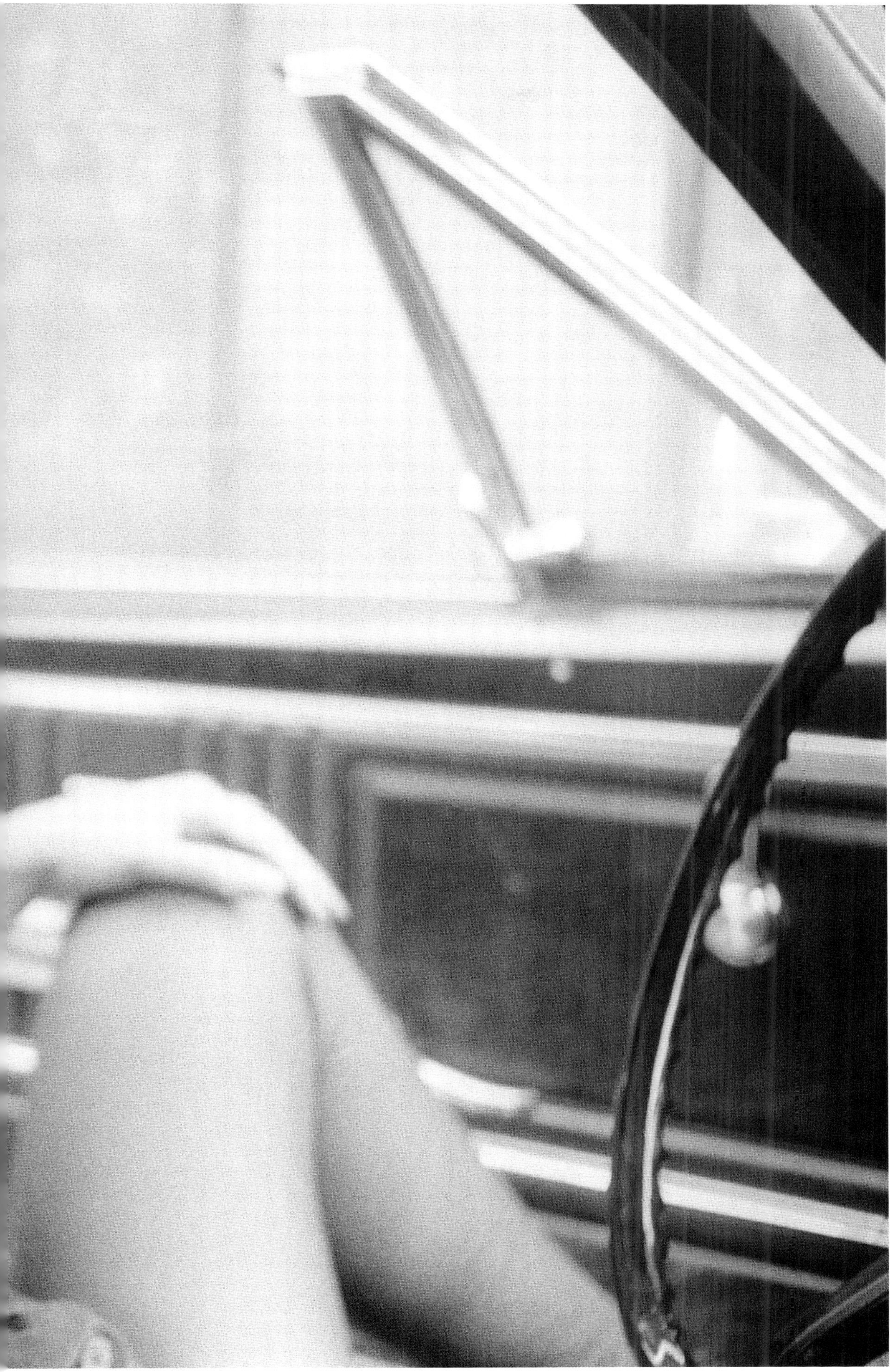

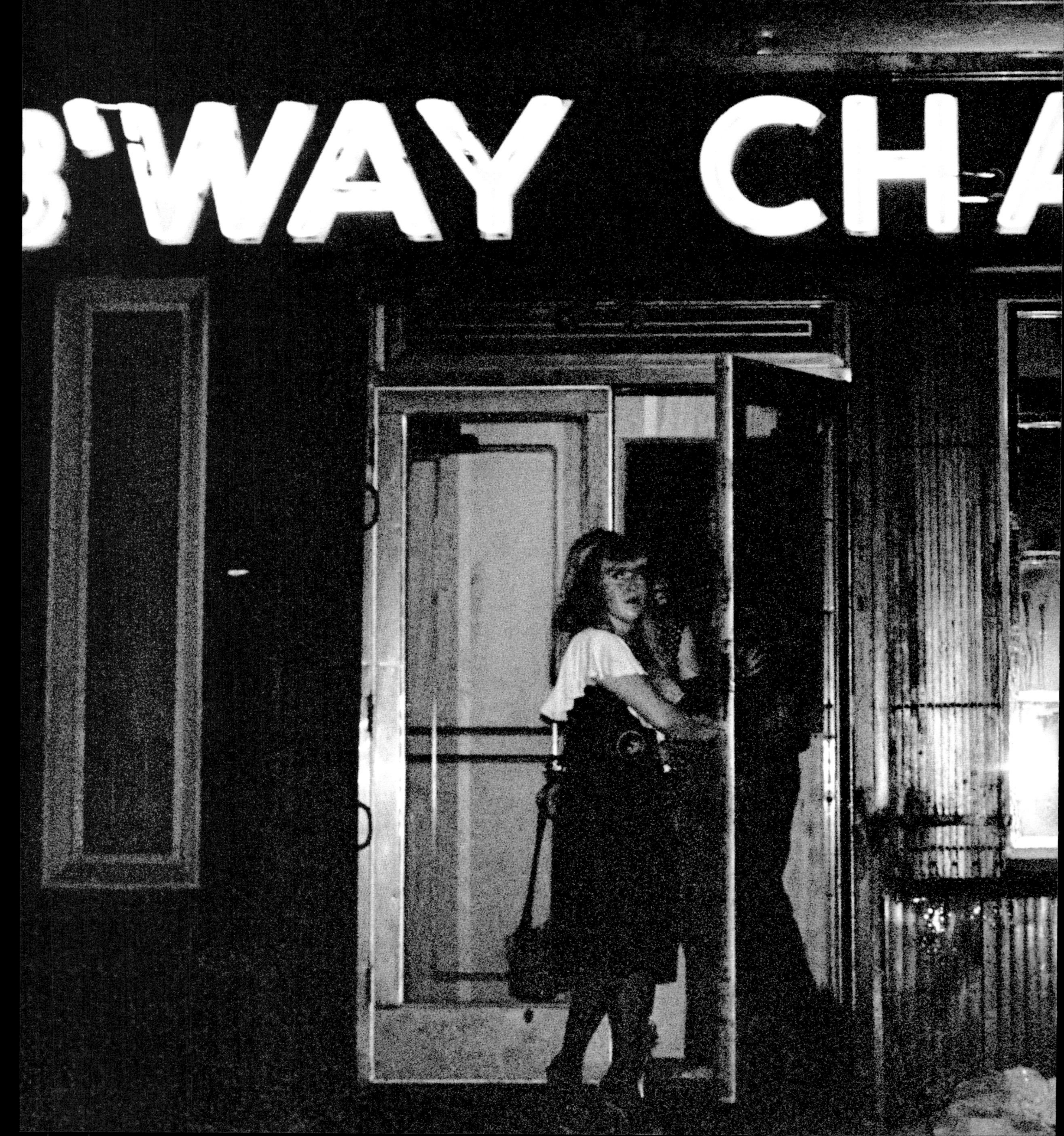
B'WAY CHA

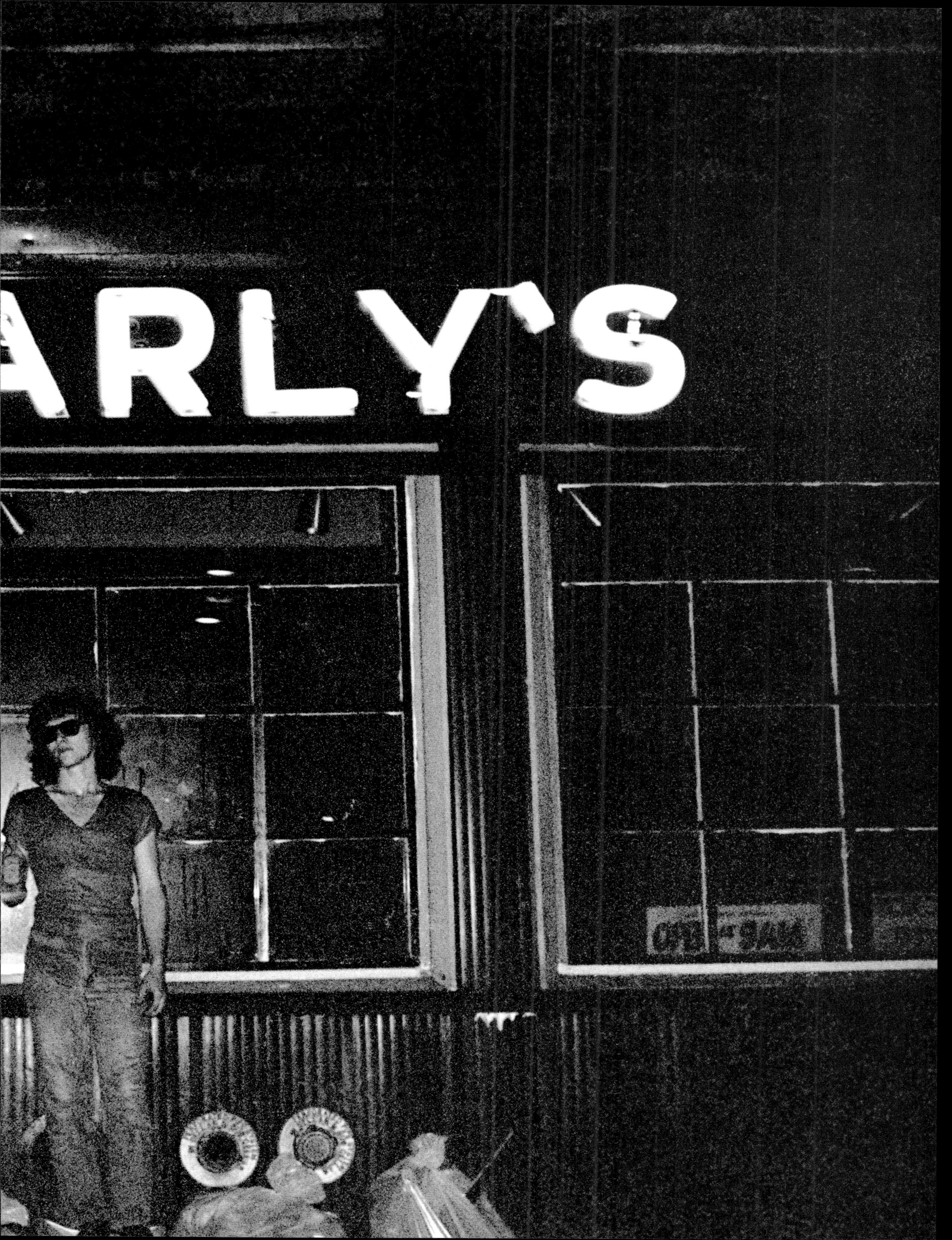
ARLY'S

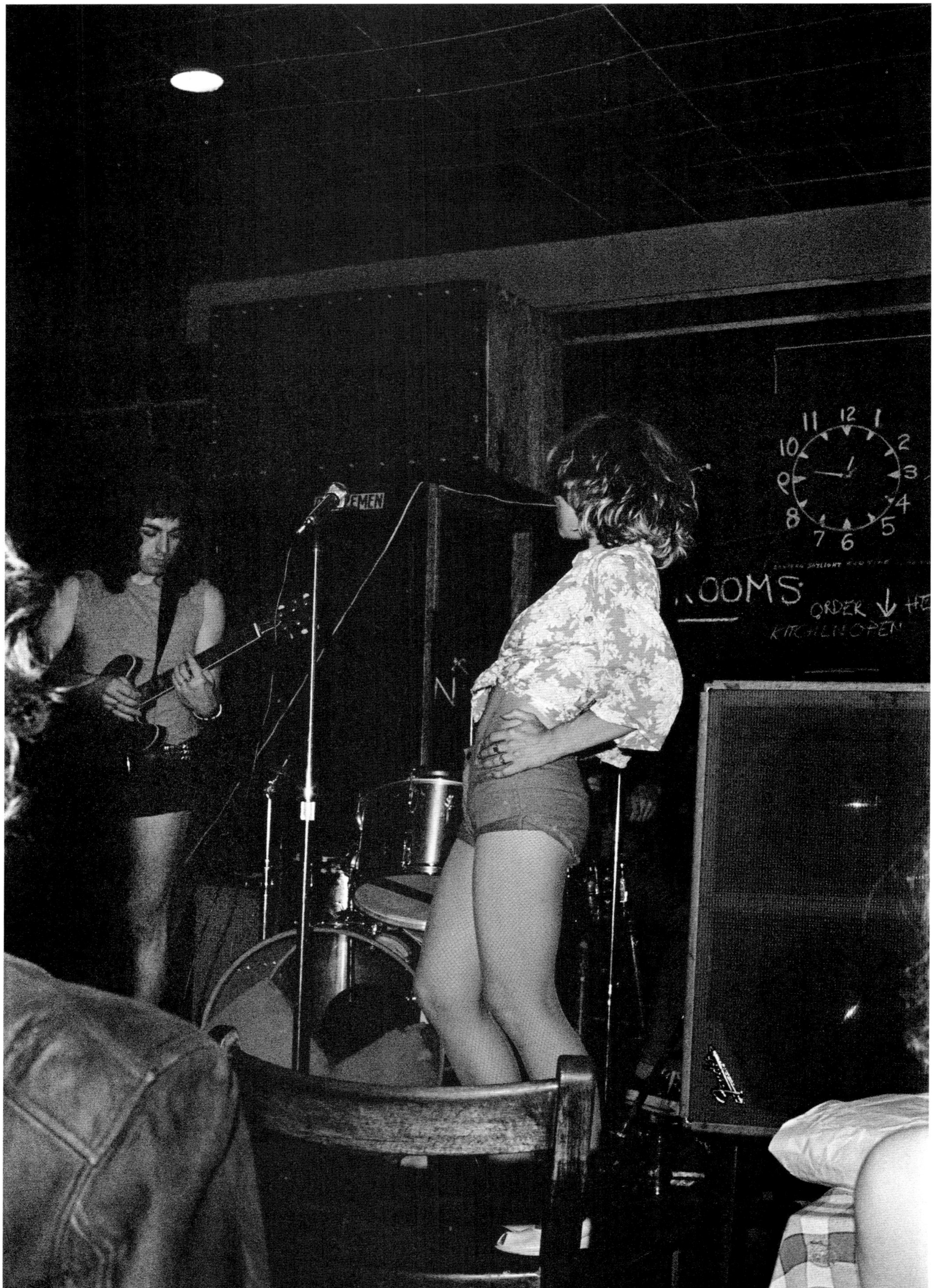
ROOMS
ORDER

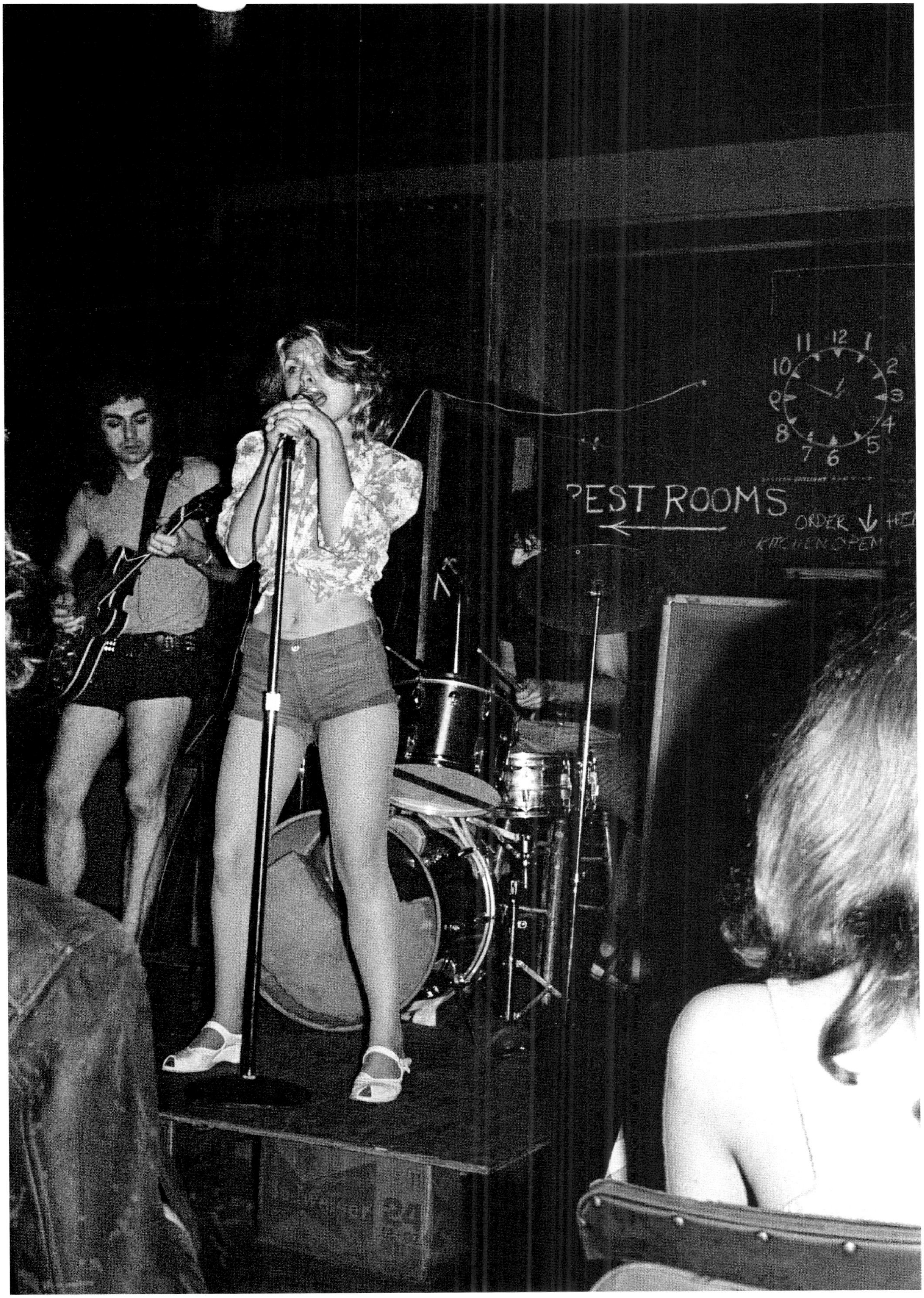
ORDER

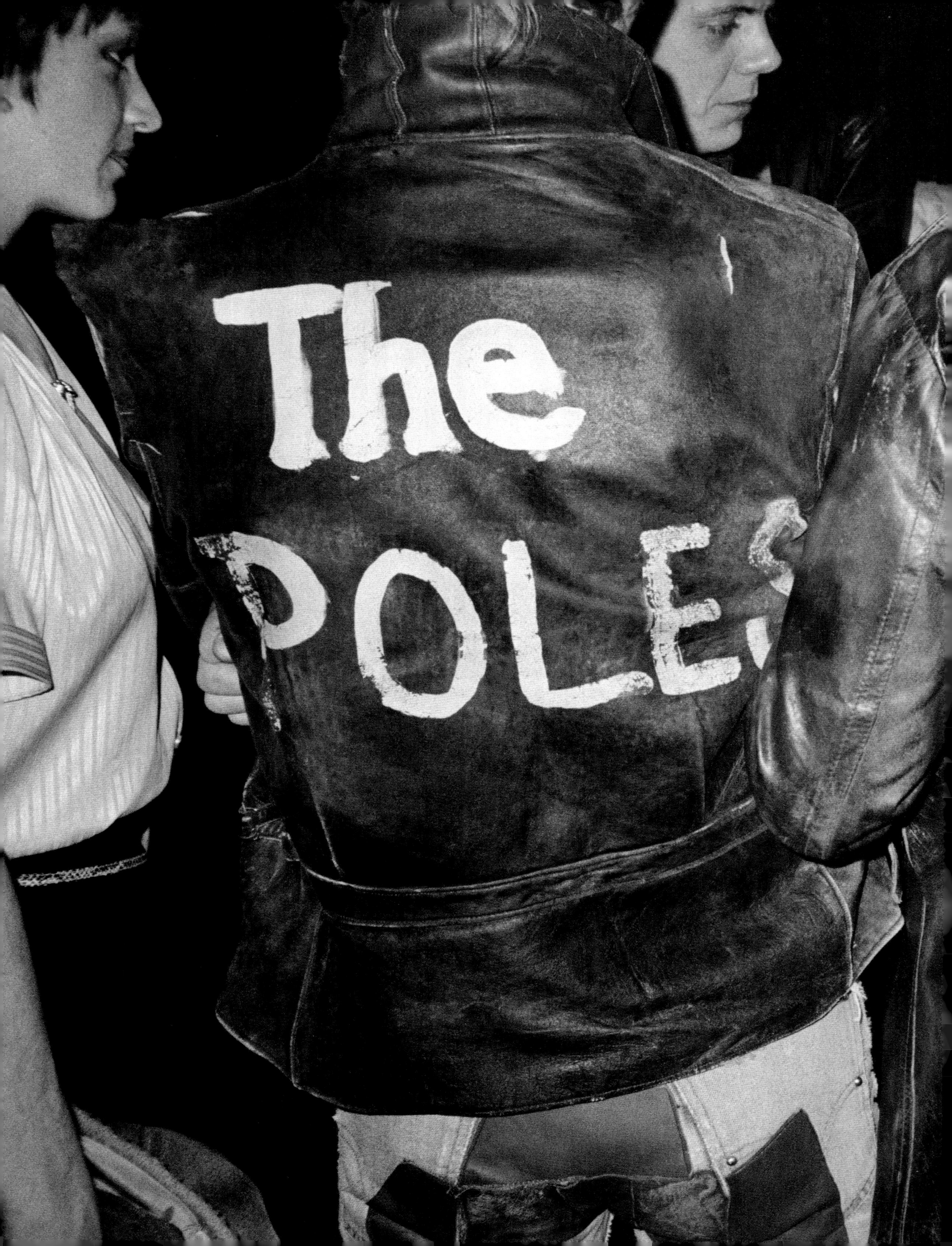
The
POLES

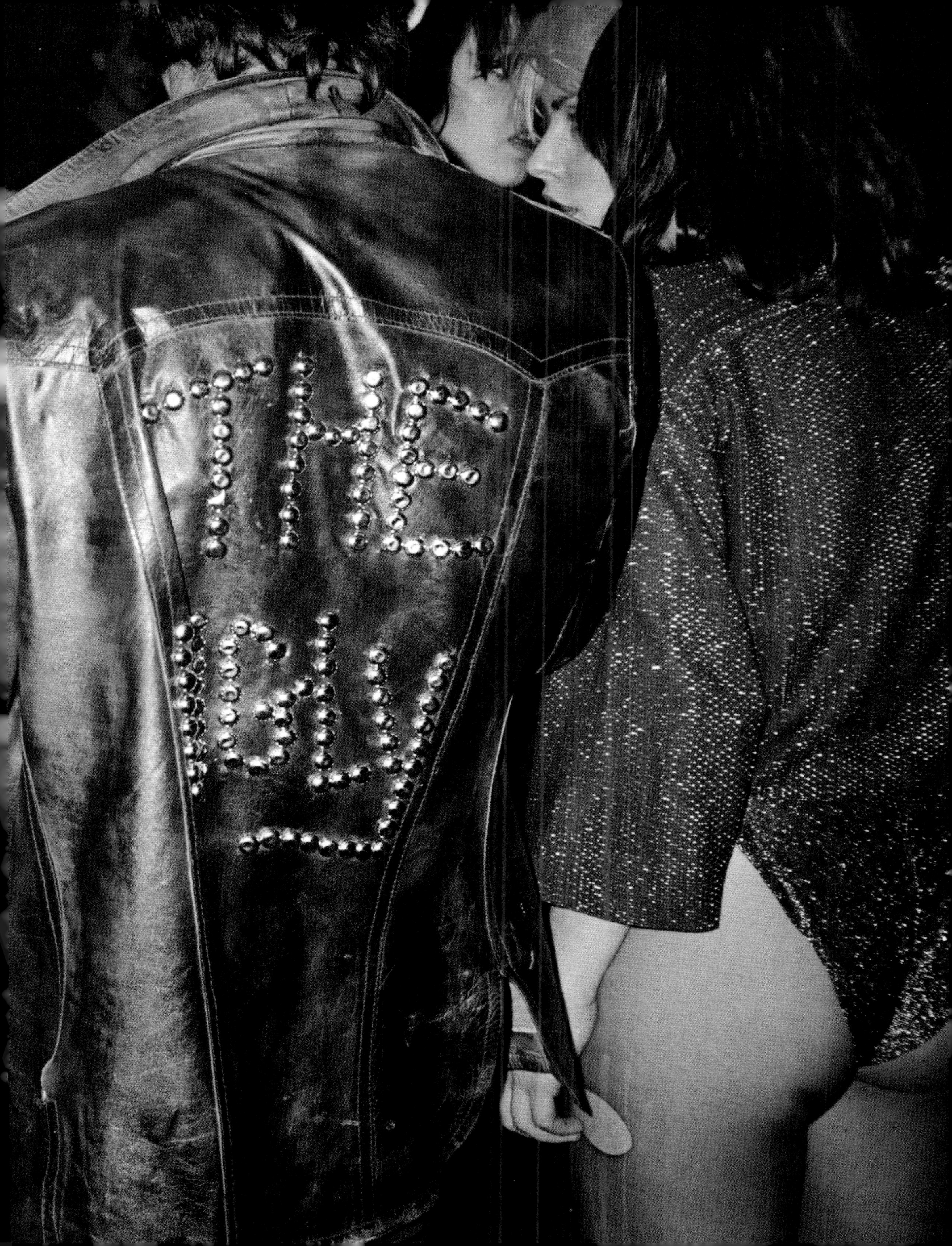
THE

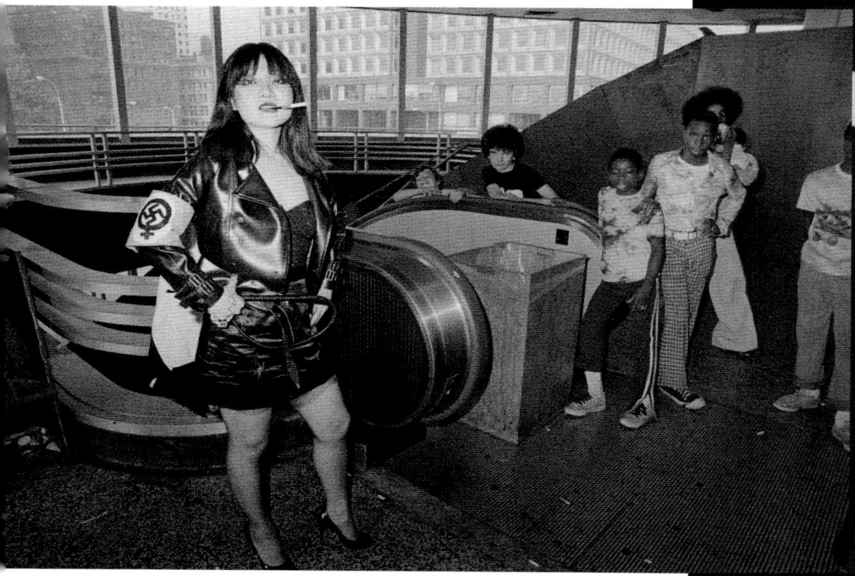

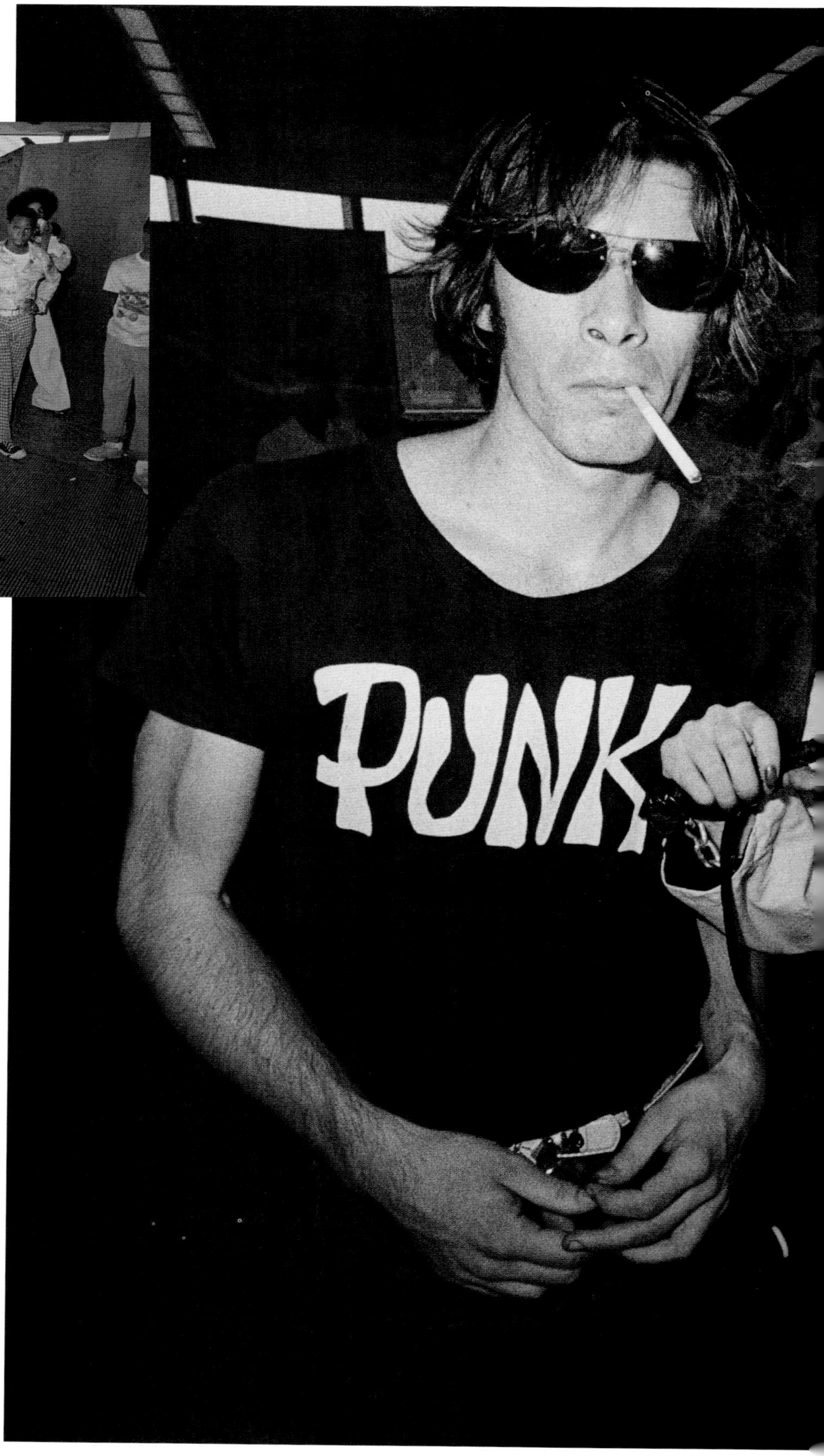

Legs McNeil, Anya Philips, and Debbie on the Staten Island ferry (and Anya alone at the terminal). More *Punk* magazine outtakes, 1976.

PAGES 96–99:
Broadway Charly's I'm pretty sure was on Third Avenue, around 12th Street. I would give the camera to people and ask them to shoot us, so I have these images from the first Blondie show that had Gary and Clem in the band, from the summer of 1975.

PREVIOUS PAGES:
Debbie with fans of the Poles and the Ugly.

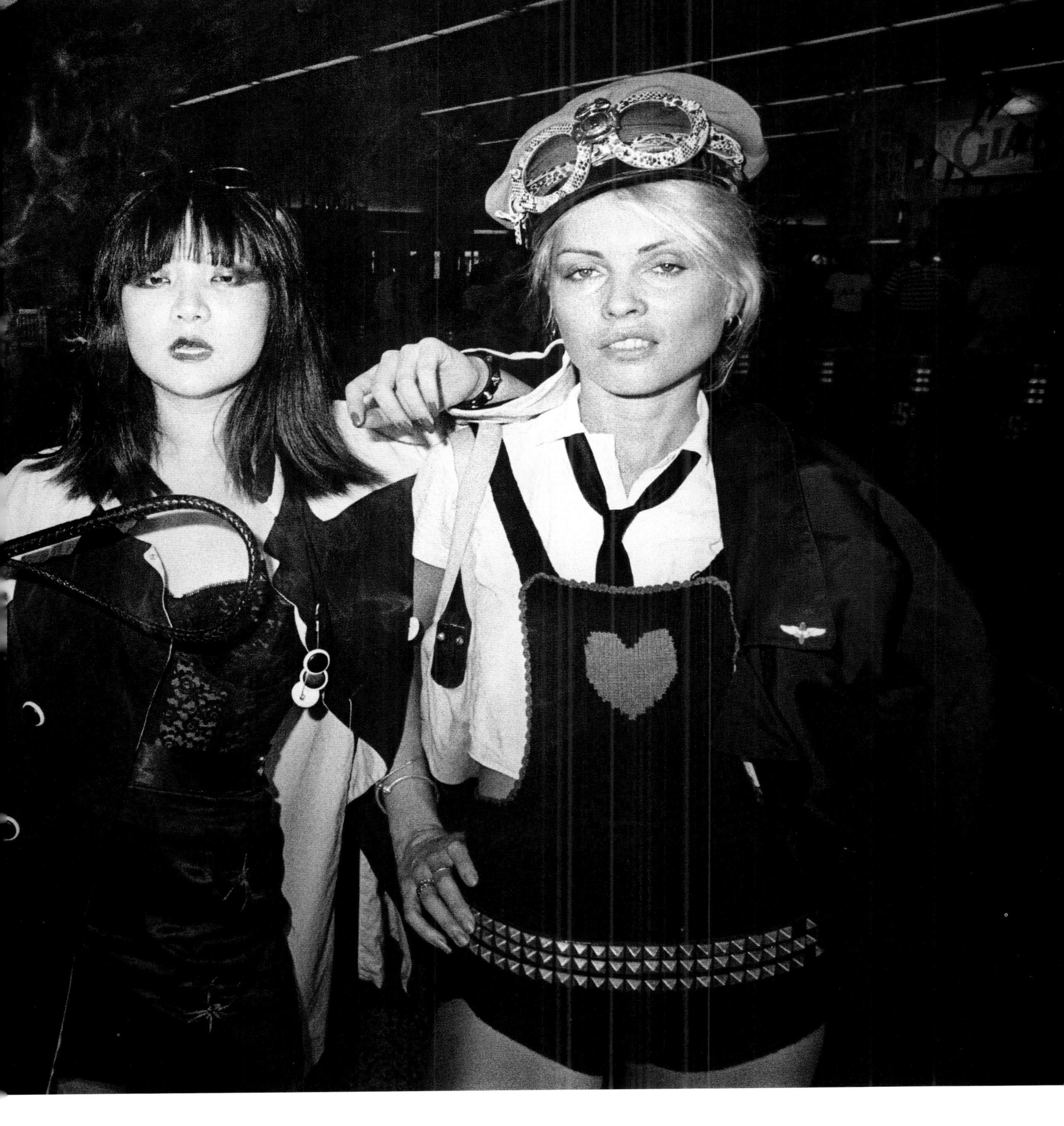

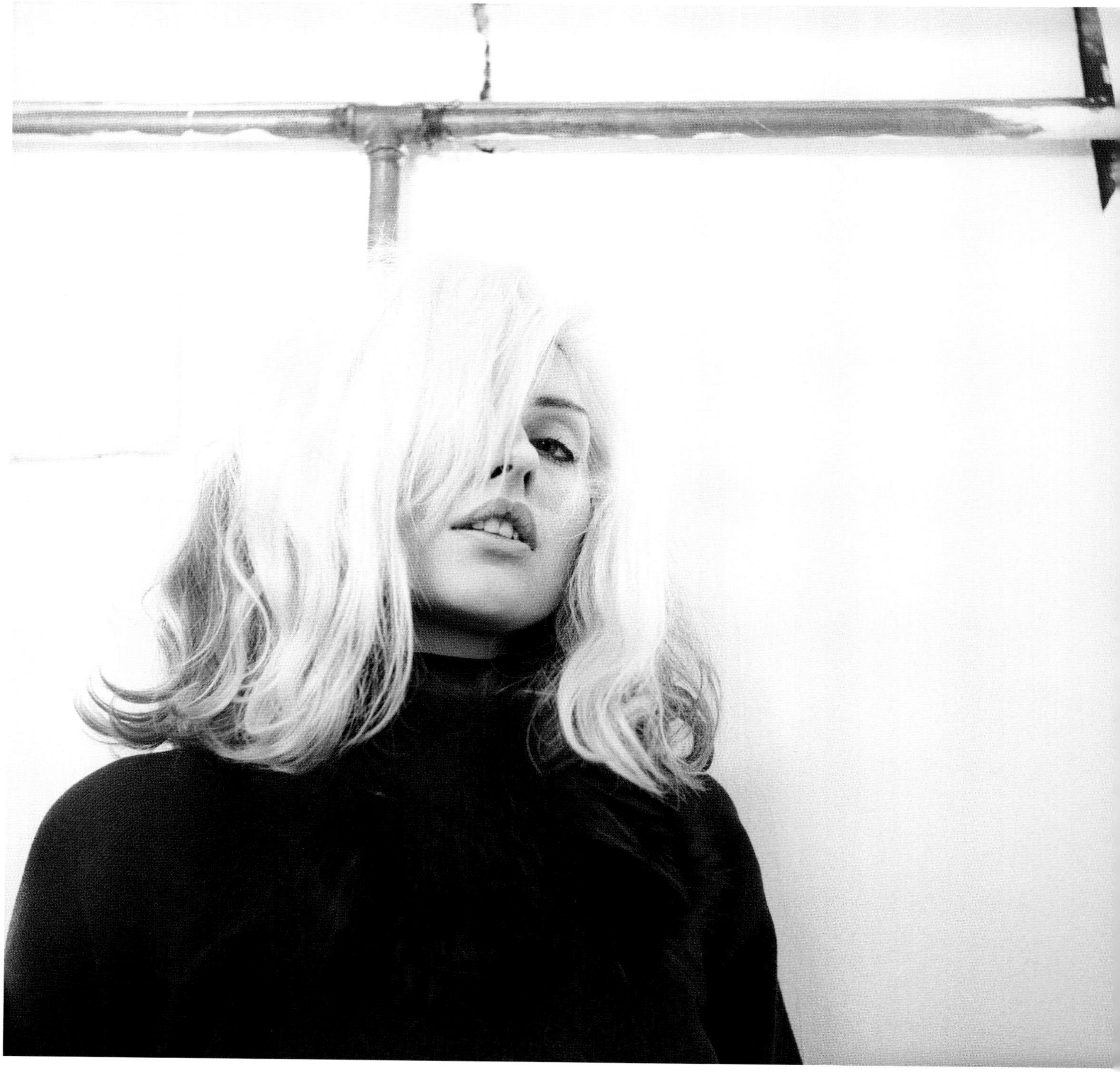

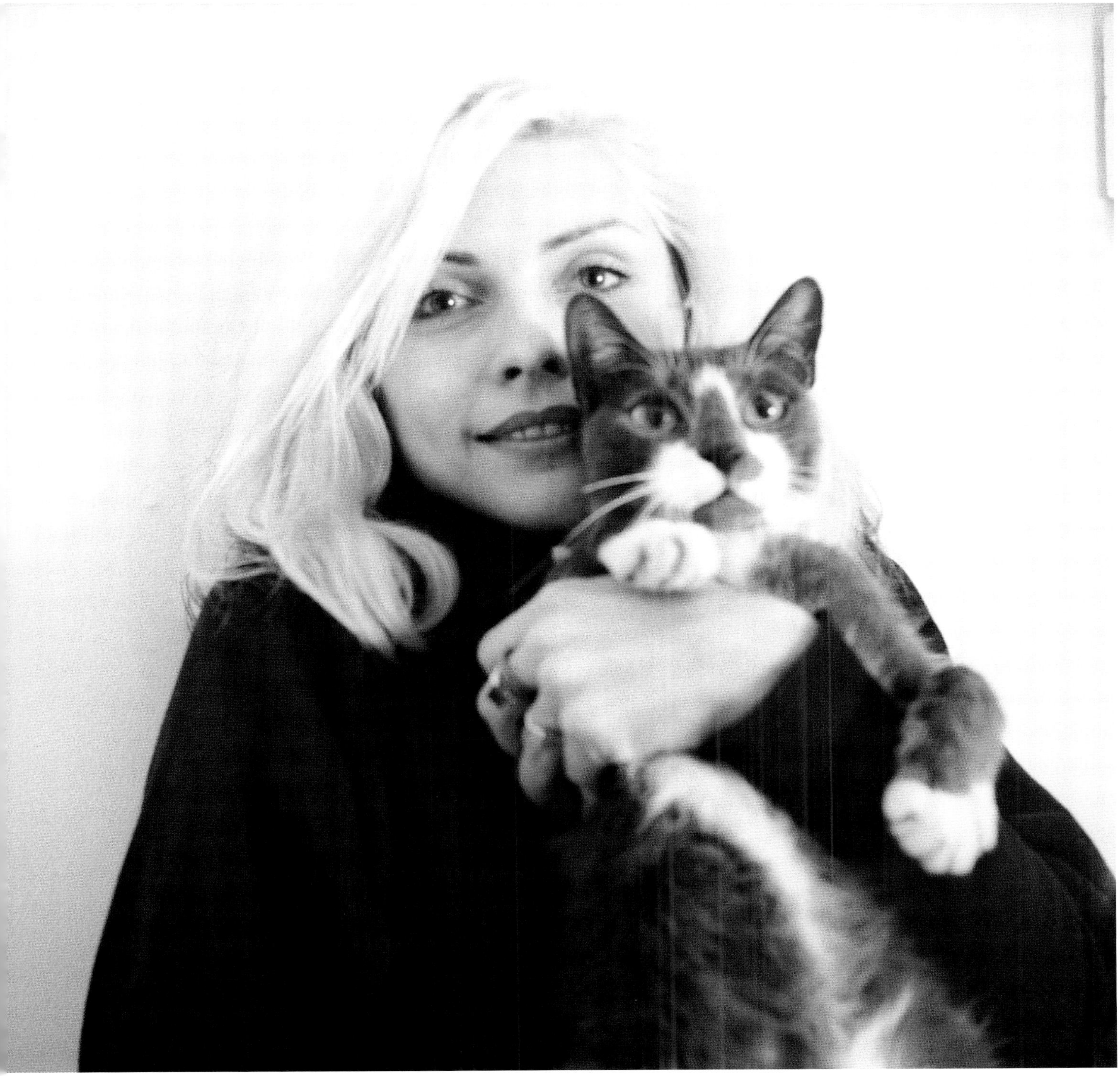

Debbie on the Bowery with Daniel, who was the leader of her squad of three cats. The other two were Sunday Man and Grey Girl. Sunday Man is the one that 'Sunday Girl' is somewhat about.

FOLLOWING PAGES:
Merch at a concert.

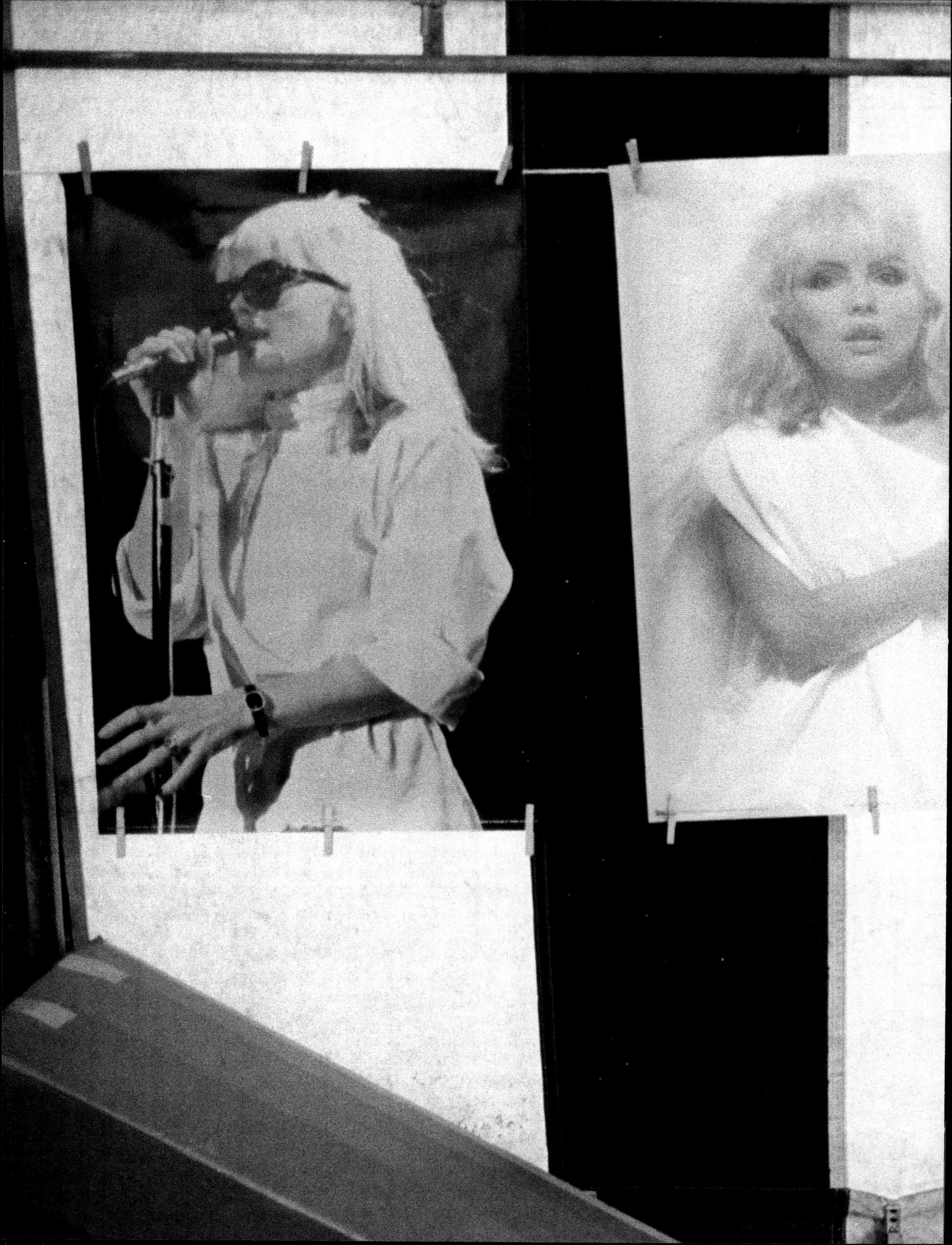

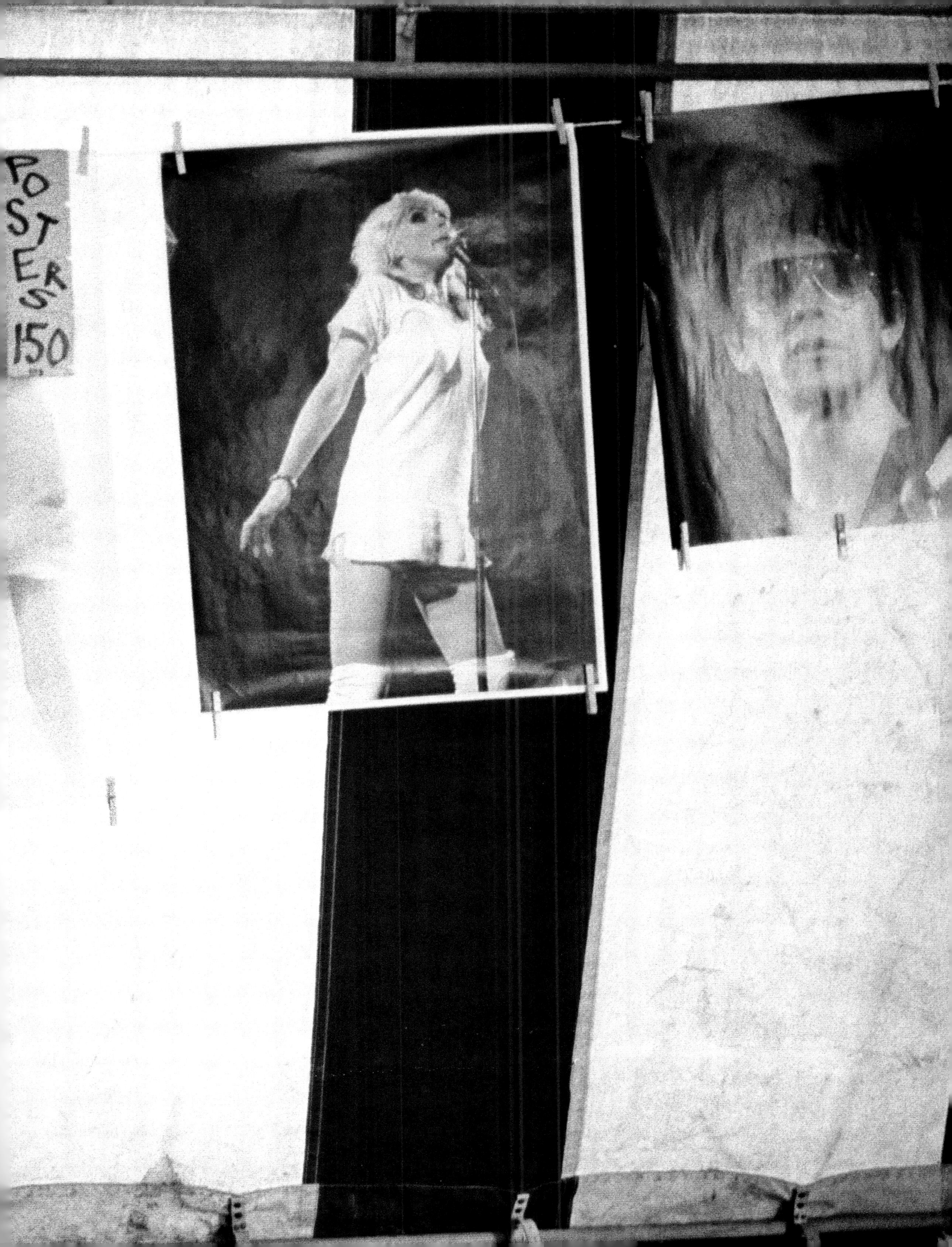
POSTERS
150

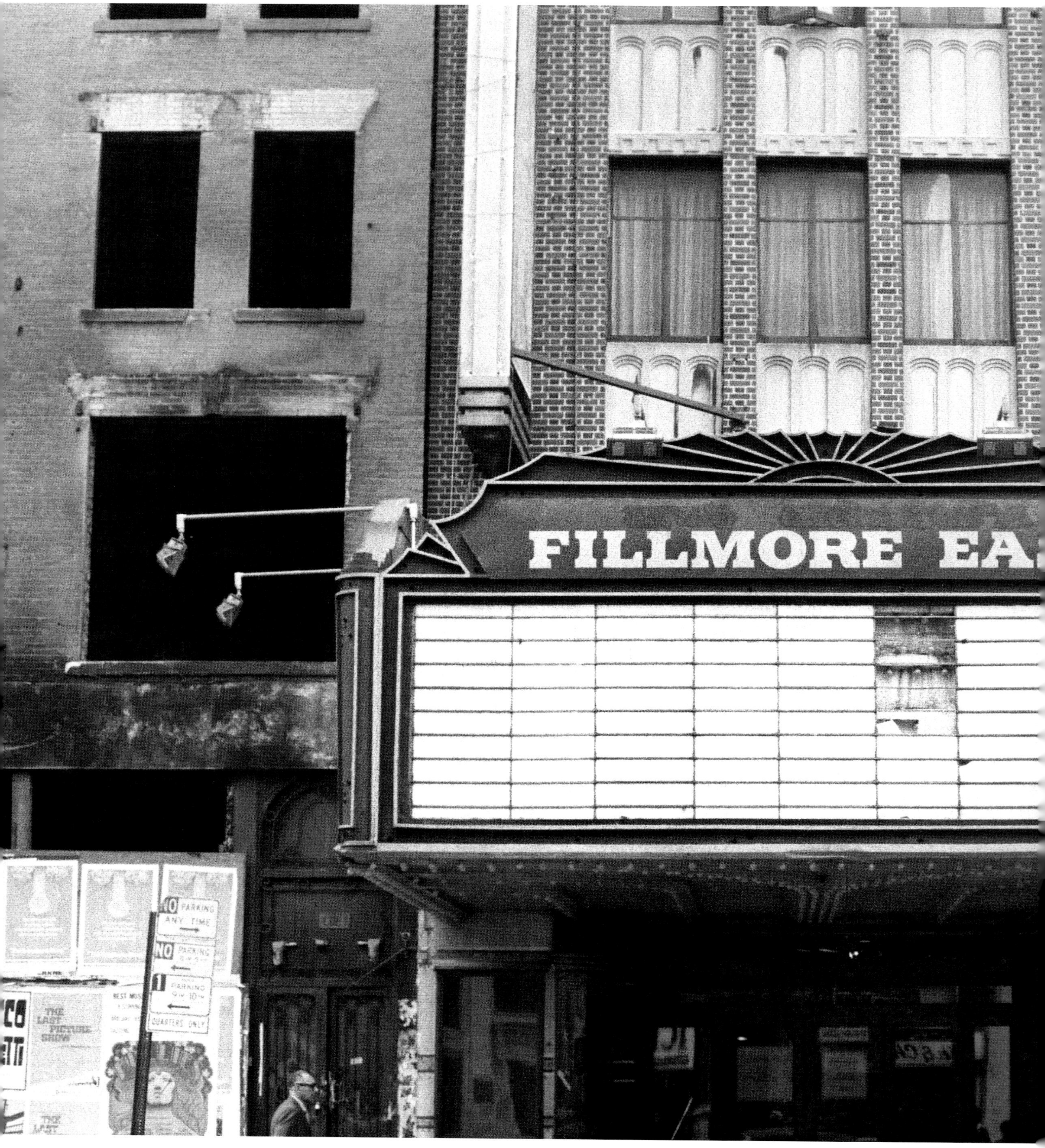
FILLMORE EA
NO PARKING ANY TIME
NO PARKING
QUARTERS ONLY
THE LAST PICTURE SHOW

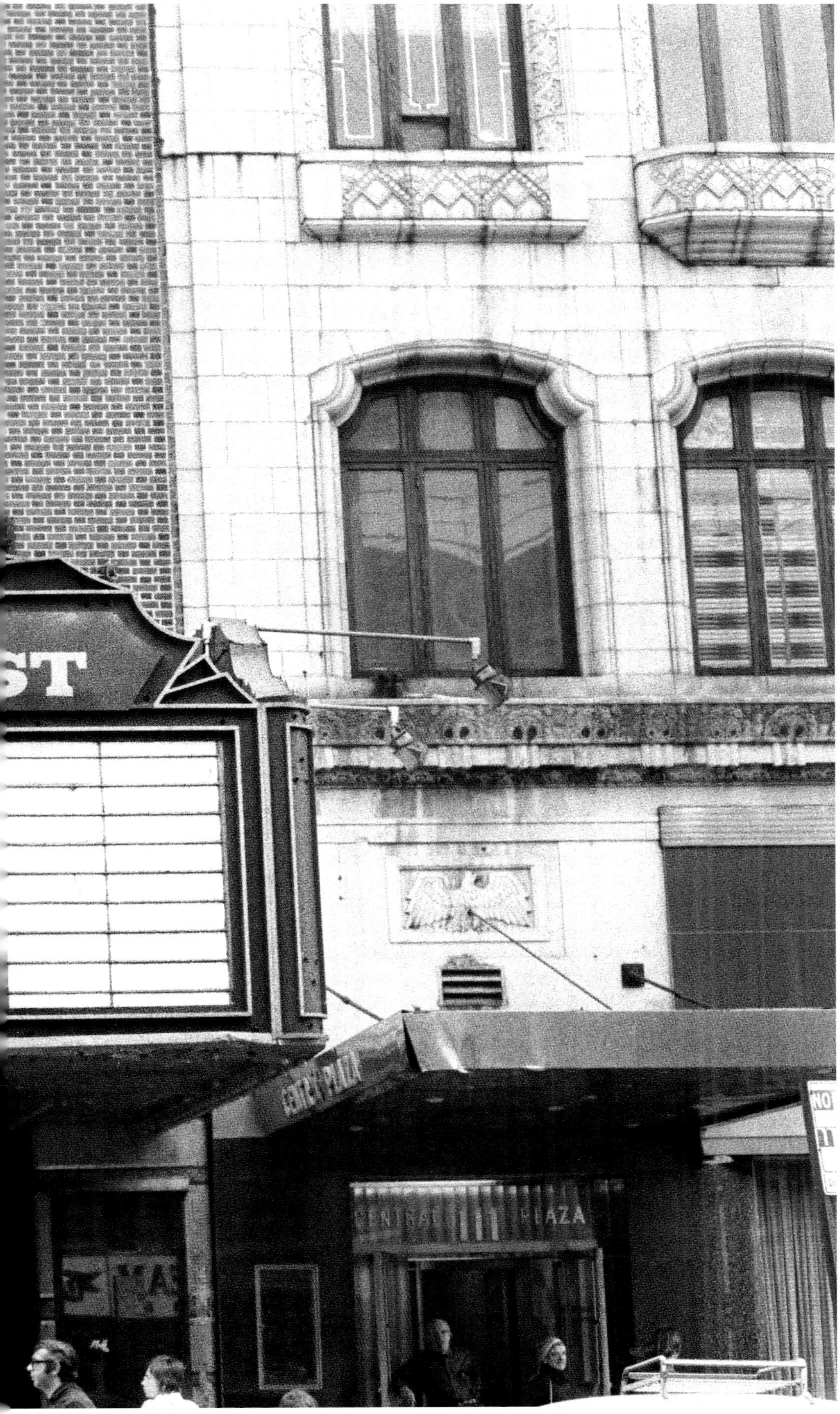

THE FILLMORE EAST, 1971–1972

I saw a lot of amazing stuff at the Fillmore East when I was younger. I was at Janis Joplin's first public show in New York City there (she'd played one show prior for the Hells Angels). It must have been 1969, which was the craziest year for me. I was wandering around the city tripping heavily and found myself by the Fillmore. I looked like a freak with very long hair and wearing a long black cape. I just walked into the Fillmore unchallenged and headed toward the stage. Frank Zappa was onstage with the Mothers of Invention. He was routining band members in a very weird and discordant horn part, mostly noise—I remember wondering if any of these guys were actually horn players. The stage was packed with odd equipment, little bicycle bells and chimes all miked and wired up. I climbed up onto the stage and started looking around. A huge roadie came out of nowhere and escorted me off. I climbed back up and was again led off by this guy, who was sort of Andre the Giant-sized. By this time Zappa noticed me and, holding his hand by his side so the roadie wouldn't see, made a beckoning gesture at me. I jumped back up onto the stage. By this time the giant roadie was showing signs of impatience and shoved me off the stage. Zappa was watching all of this unfold and gestured at me again. I climbed up again and was again shoved off. Was this some sort of inside band joke, to 'drive the roadie crazy?' I never found out. The last time I was escorted off the stage, the big guy just pointed at the exit and I left.

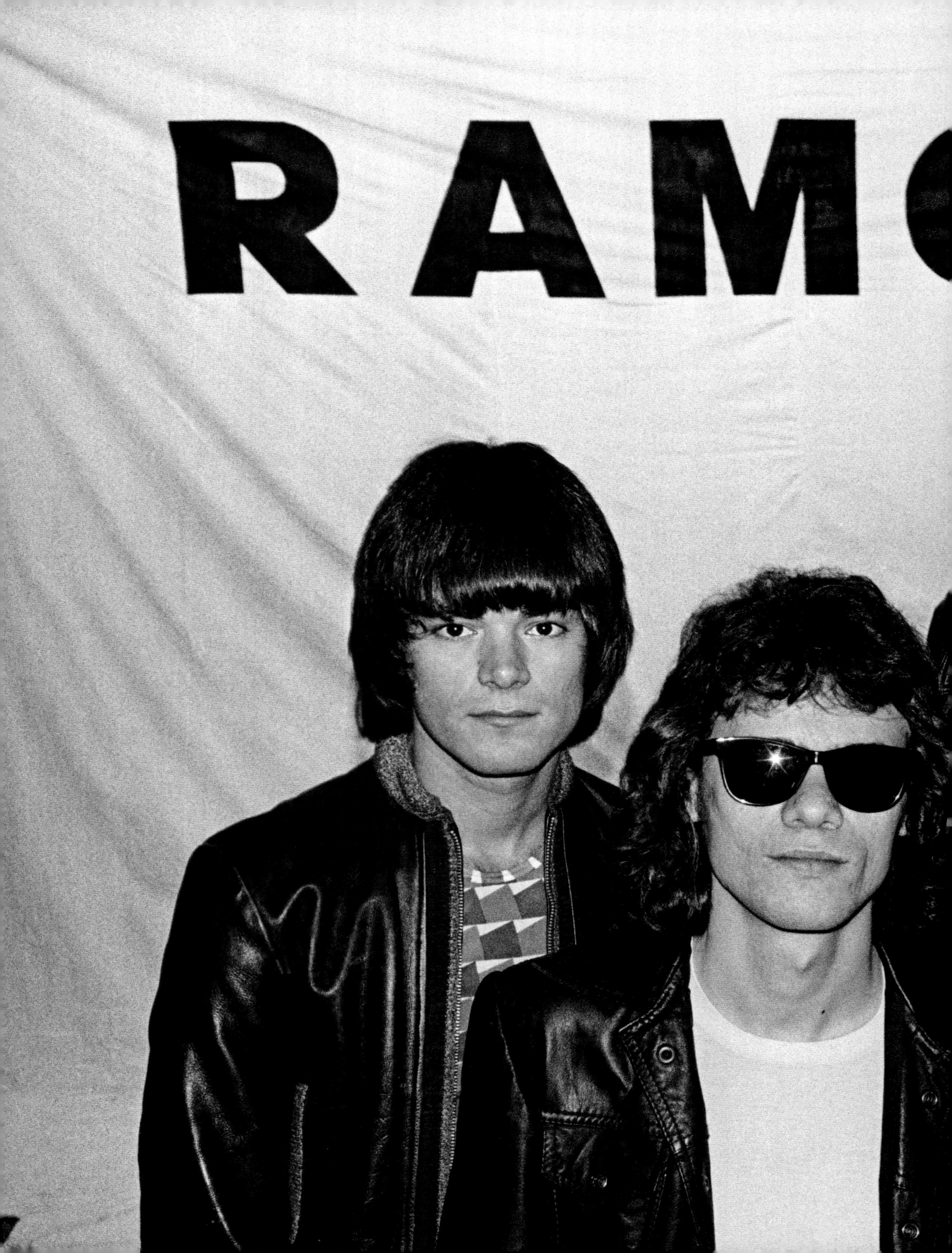
RAM

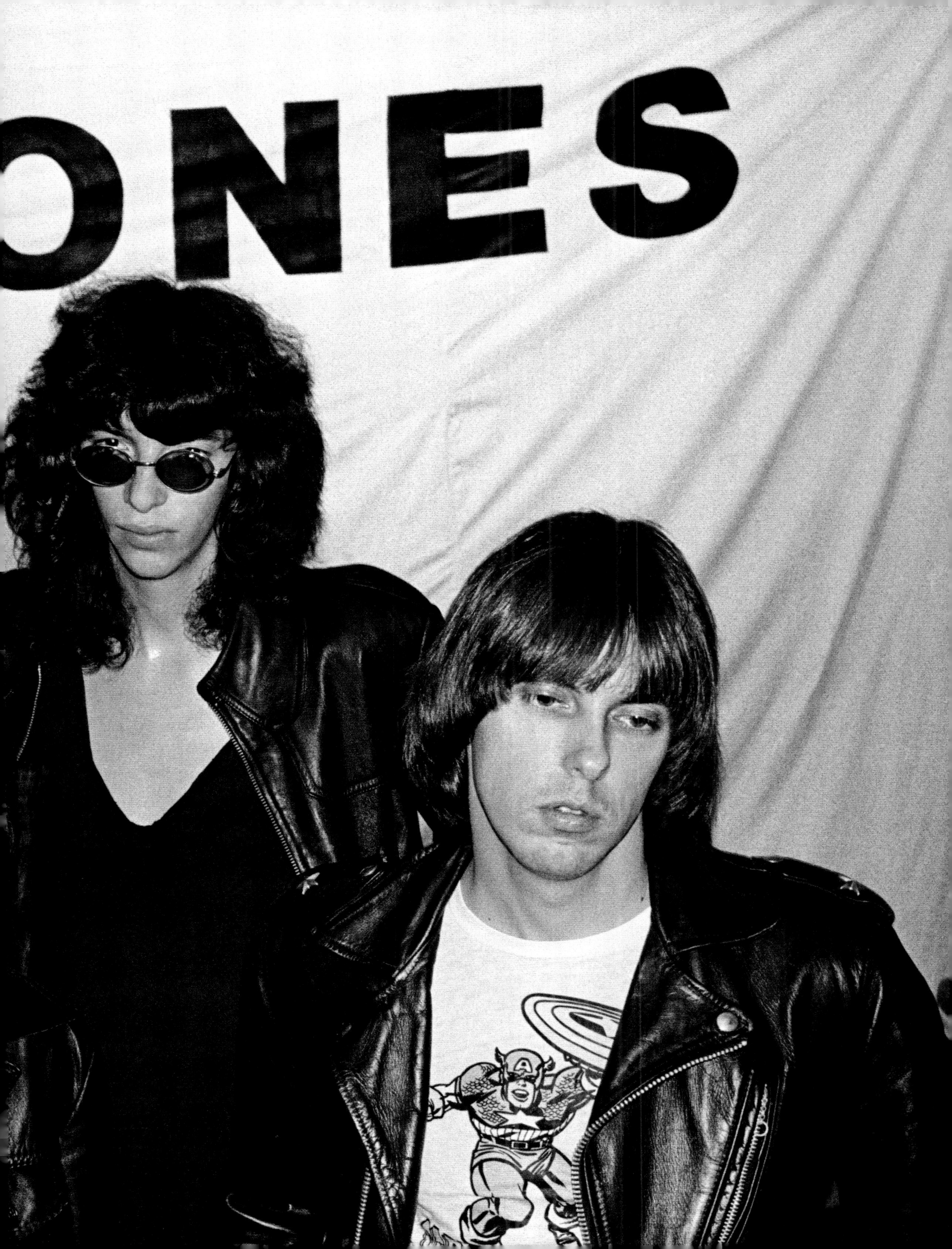
ONES

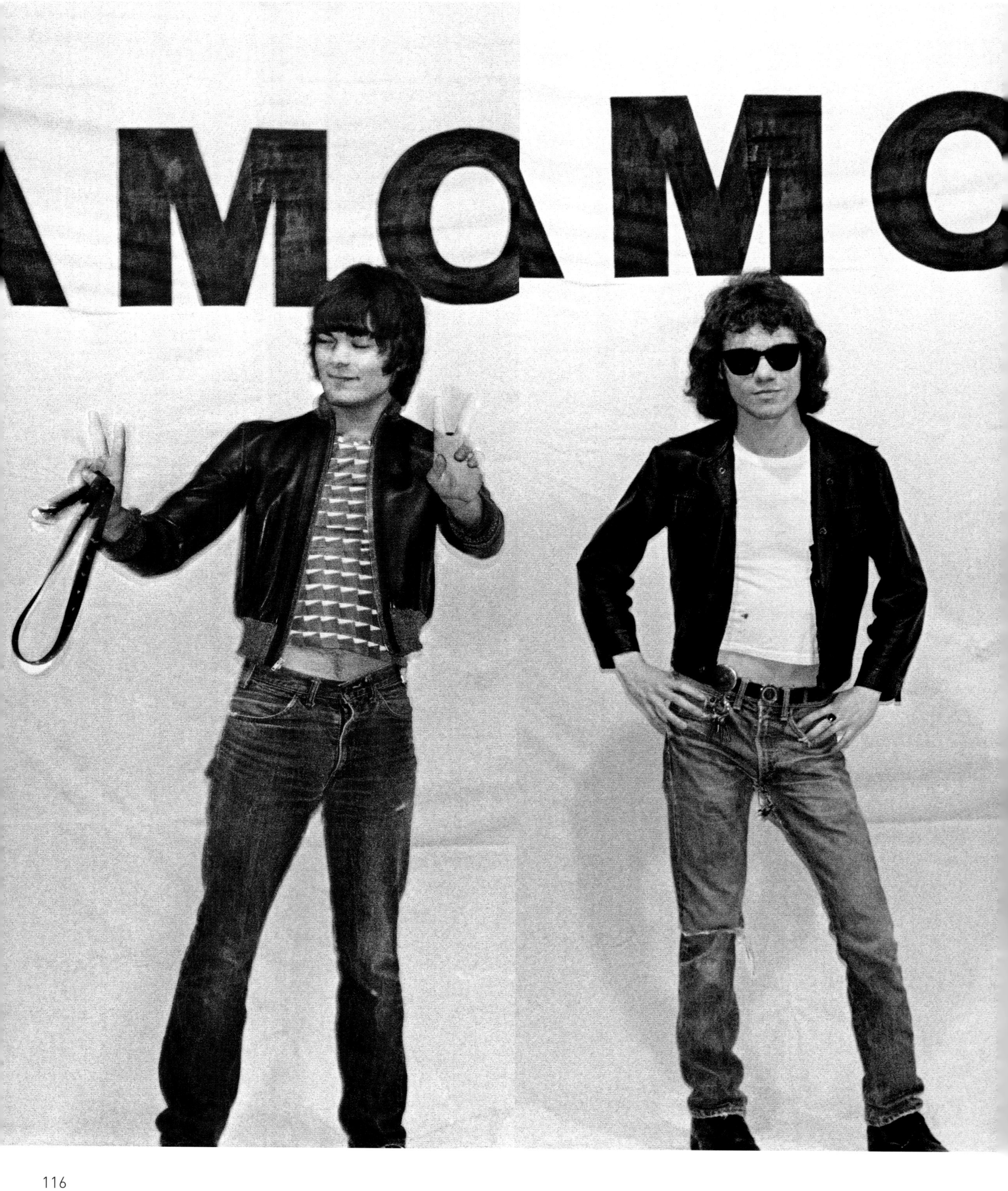

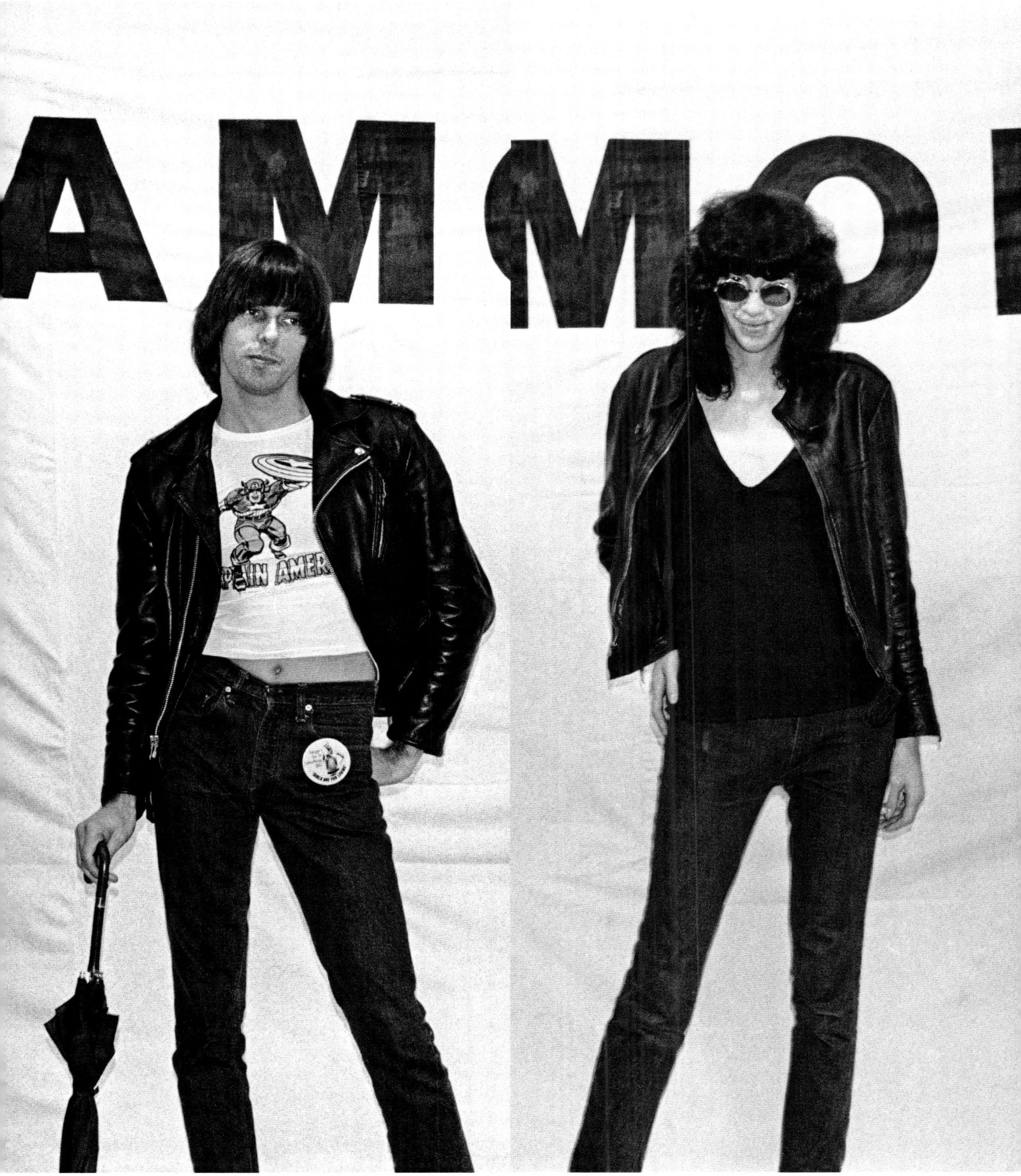
AMMO
IN AMER

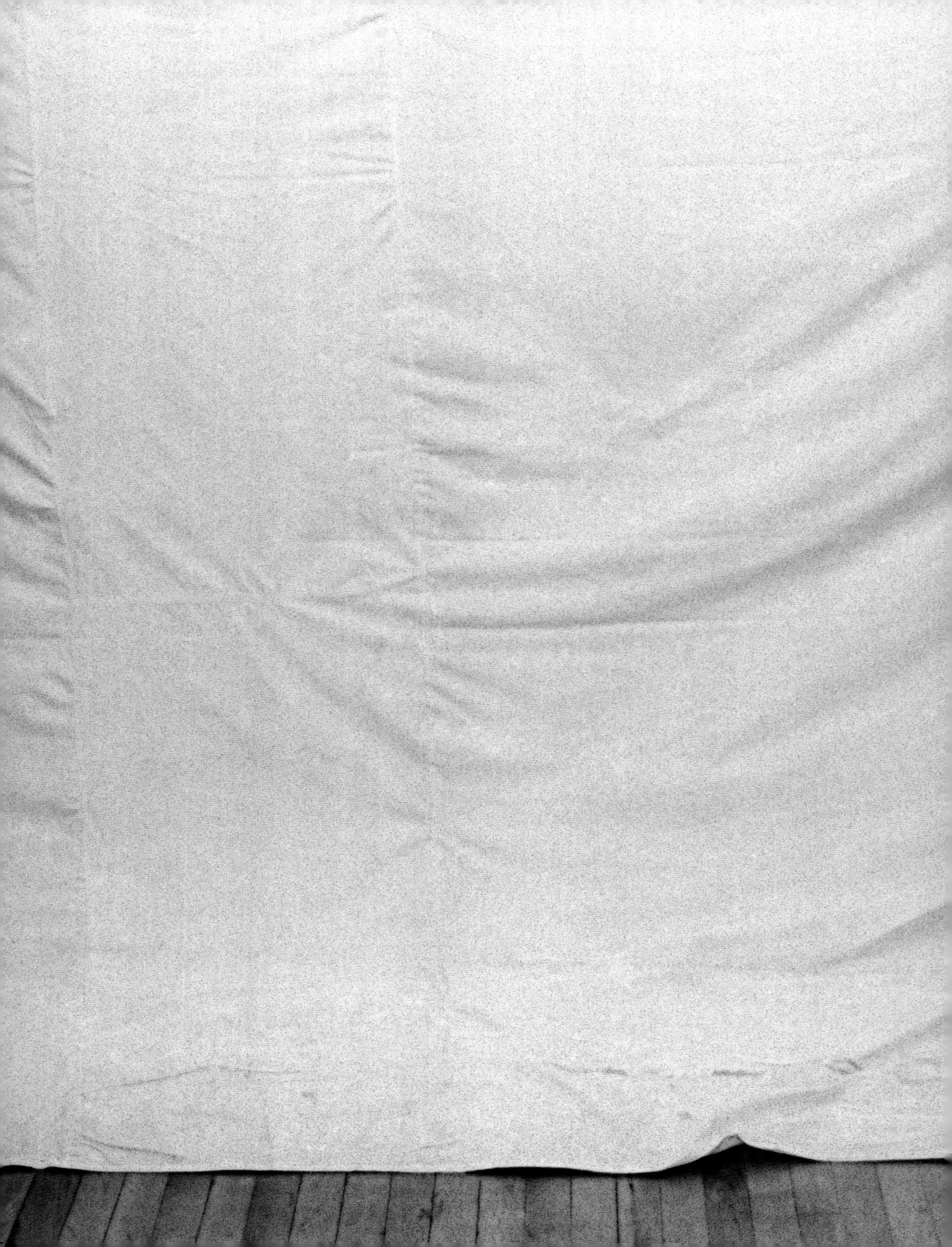

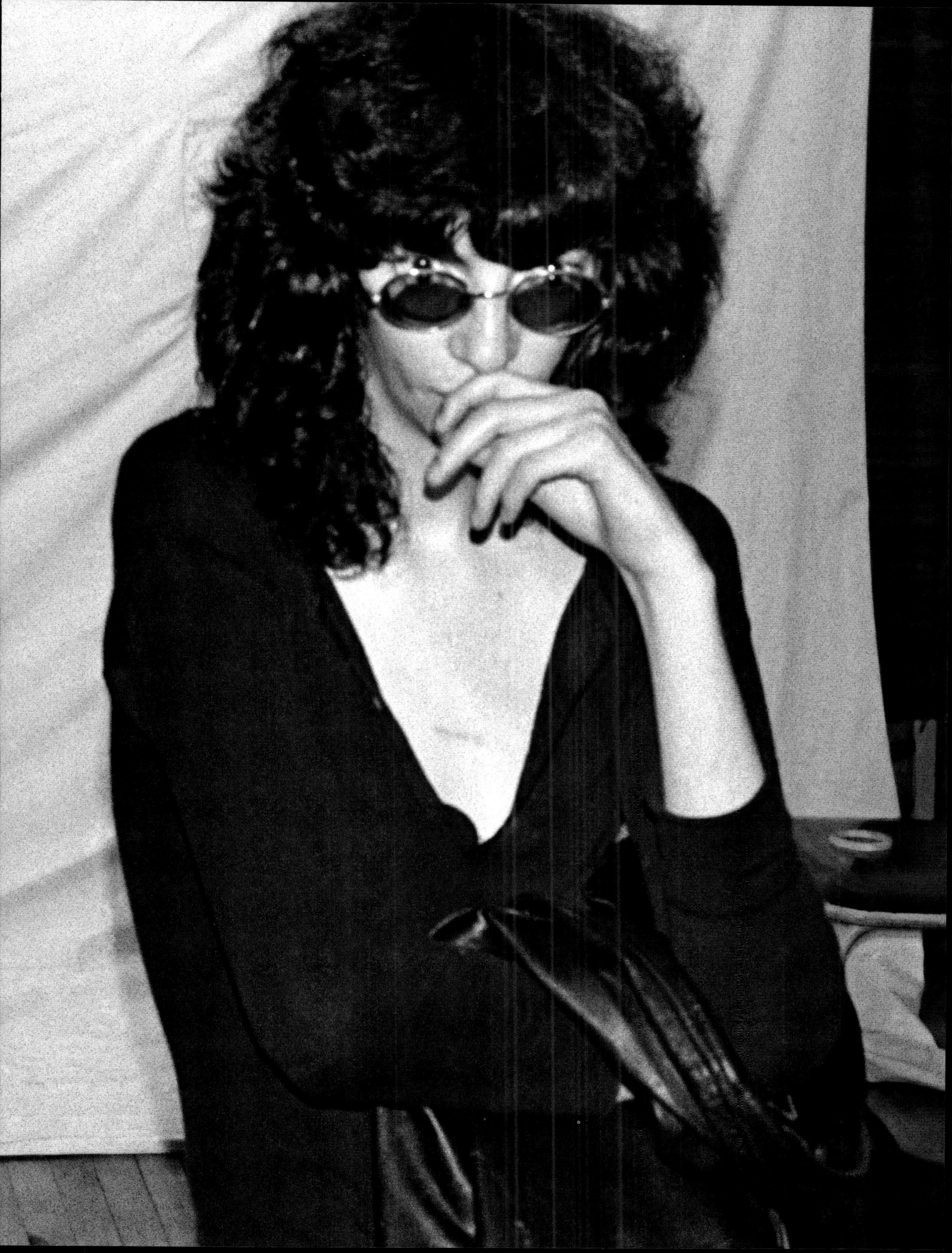

The Ramones at Arturo Vega's loft and in front of CBGB. I really vividly recall those summer nights spent on the street in front of the club. Here Johnny is putting his Mike Mathews Freedom Amp in the trunk of a car, no roadies.

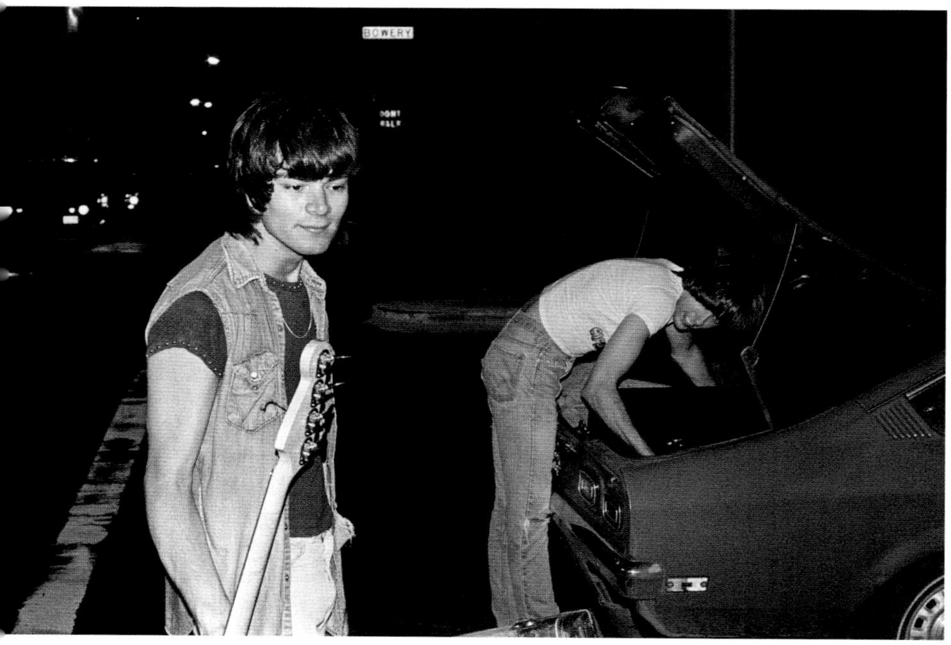

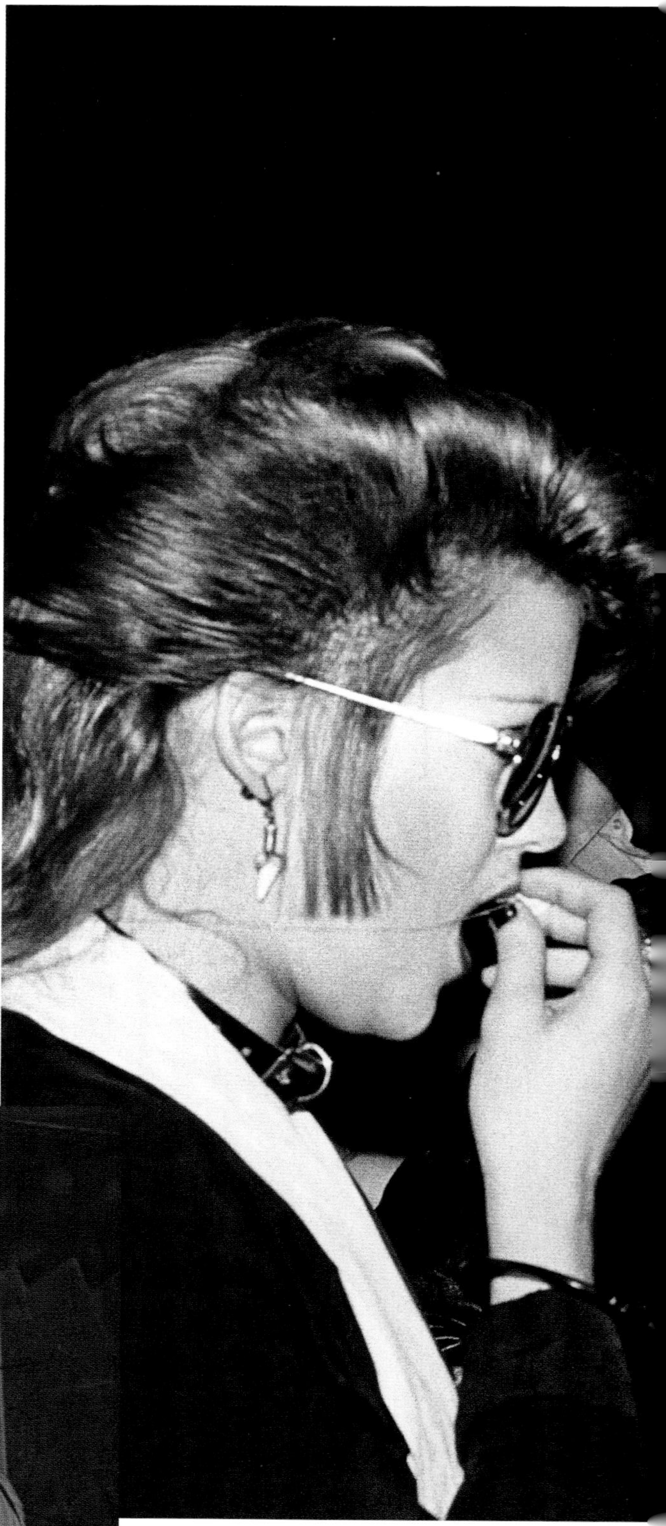

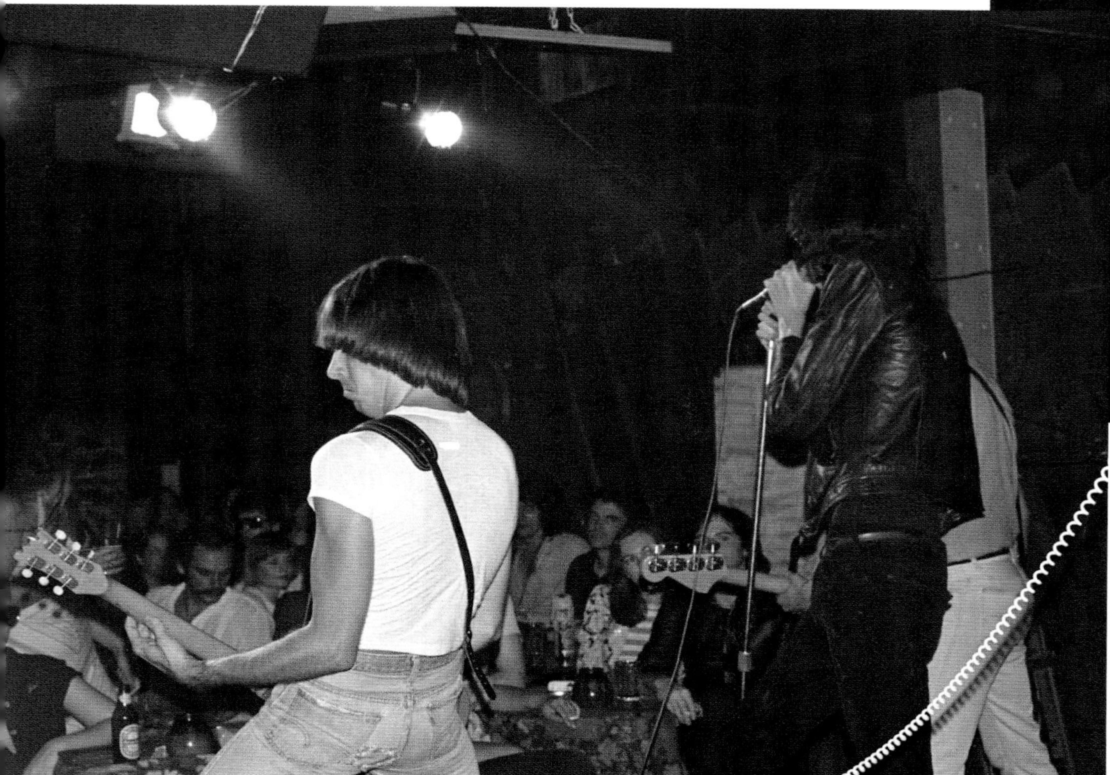

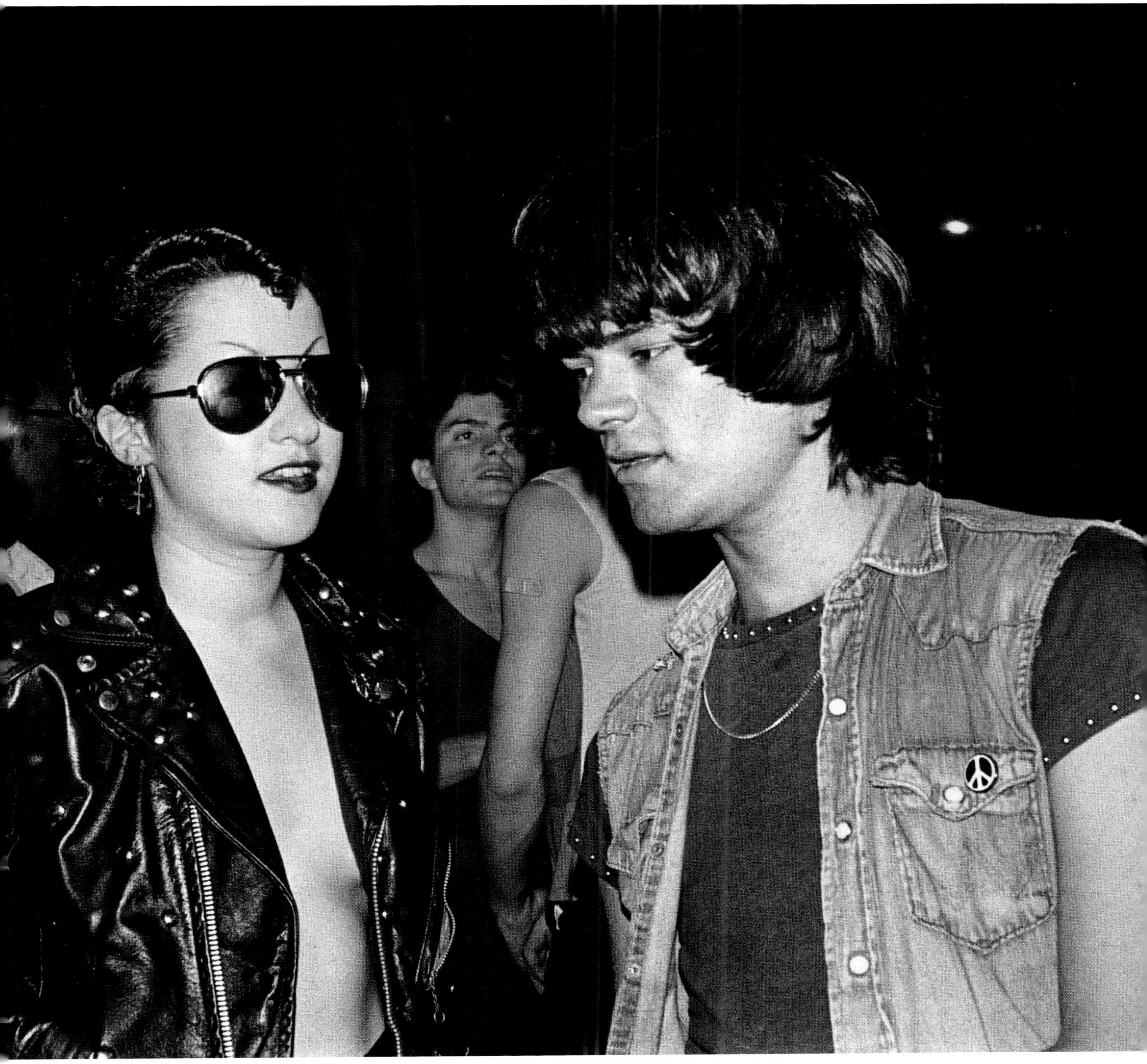

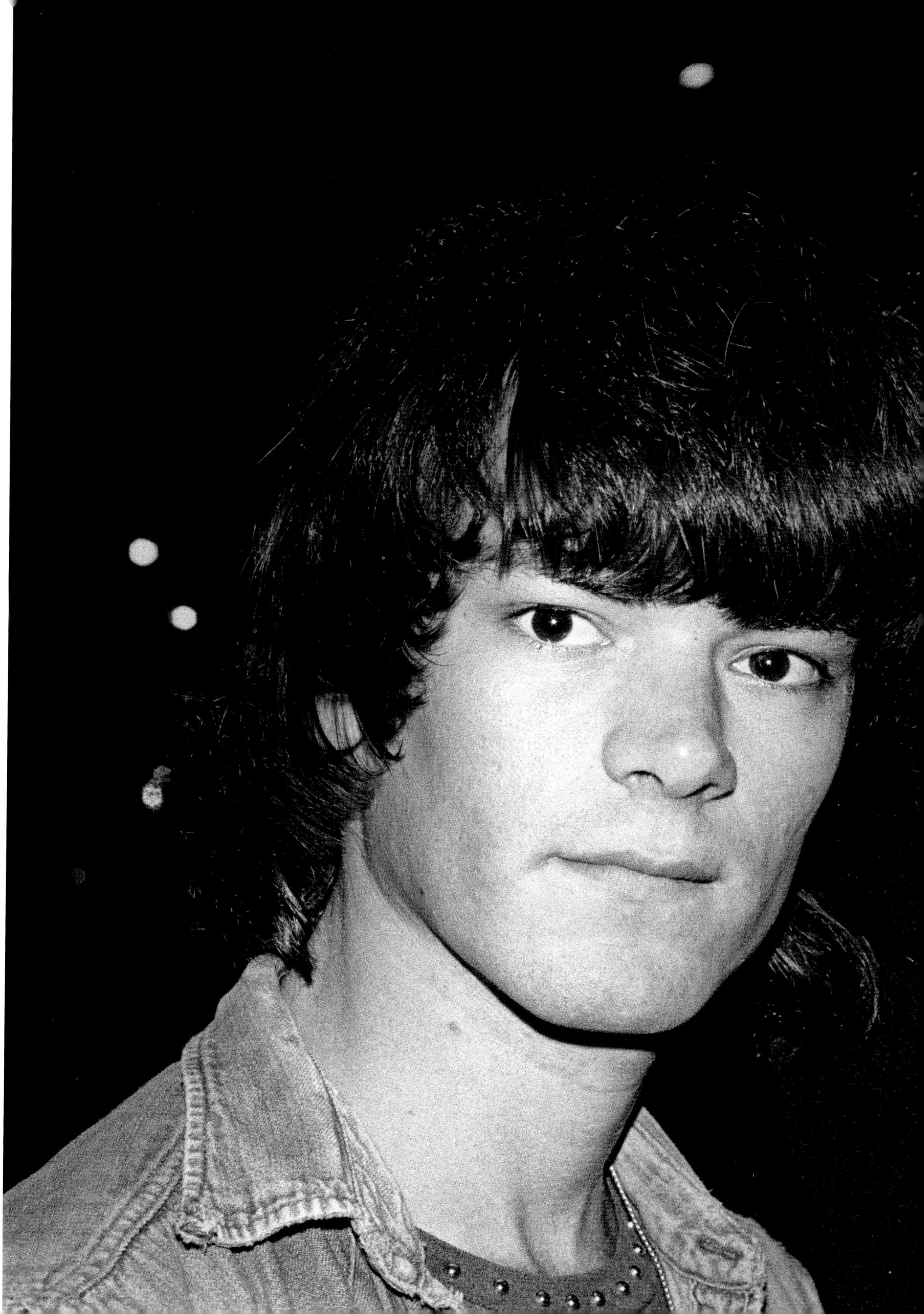

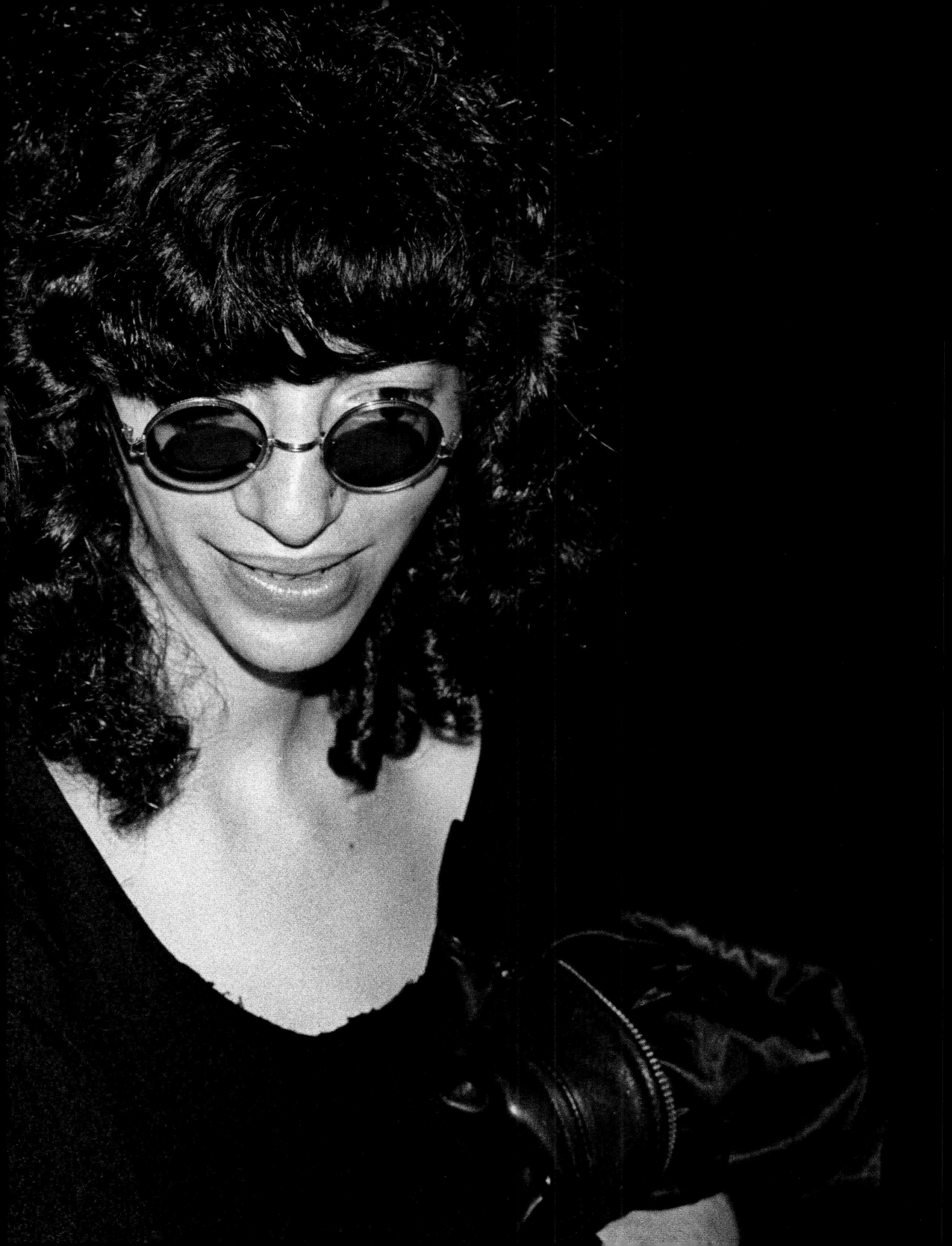

GASOLIO

WILLIAM BURROUGHS

In 1986, after the long, annoying illness I had, and having been in Manhattan for around three years without leaving, I went to spend a couple of weeks with Bill Burroughs at his house in Lawrence, Kansas. The local Lawrence punk club, the Outhouse, was very fringe. It was located on the edge of a really big cornfield. Kids at the club told me that when the police would show up at the club the patrons would run into the cornfield.

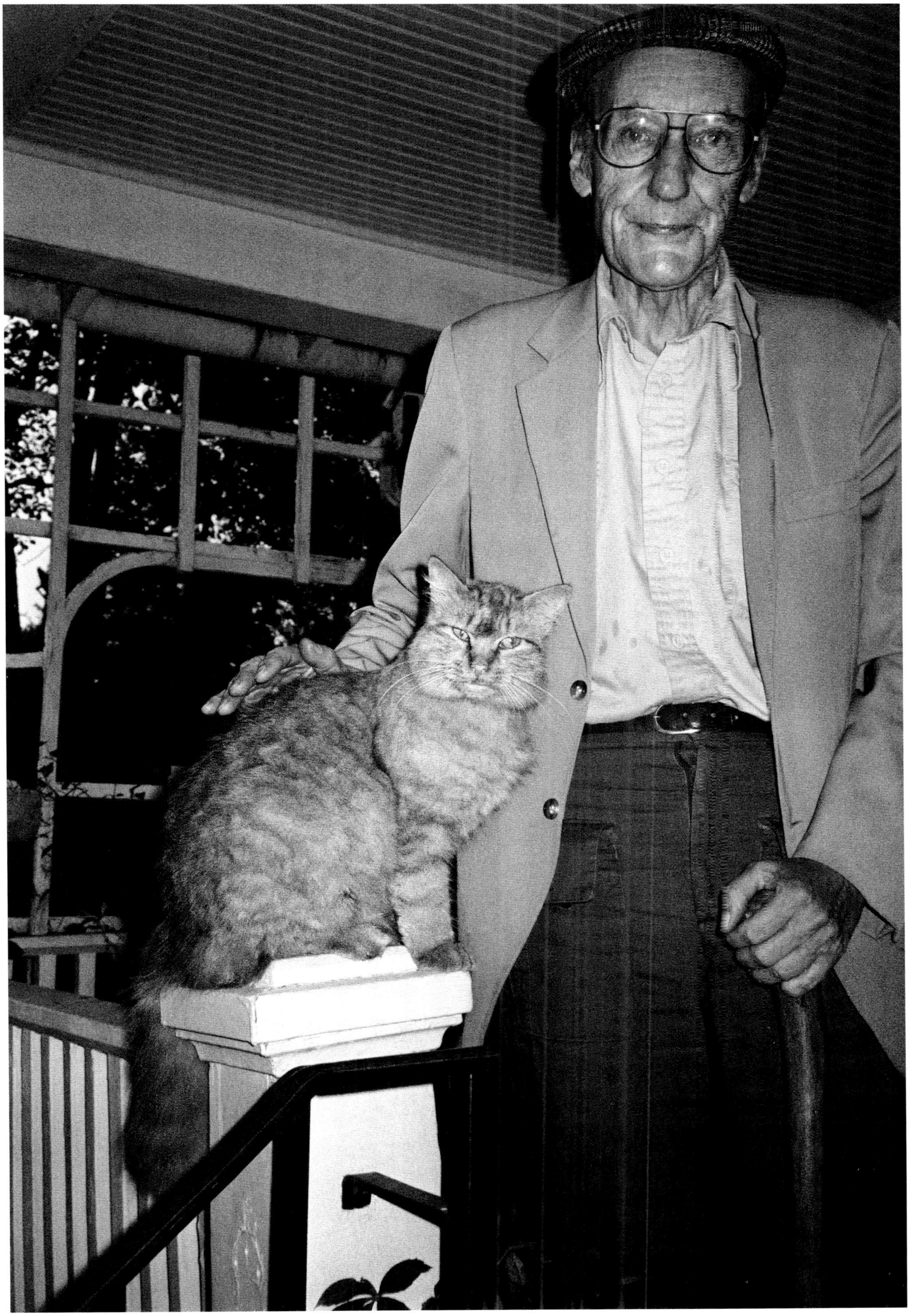

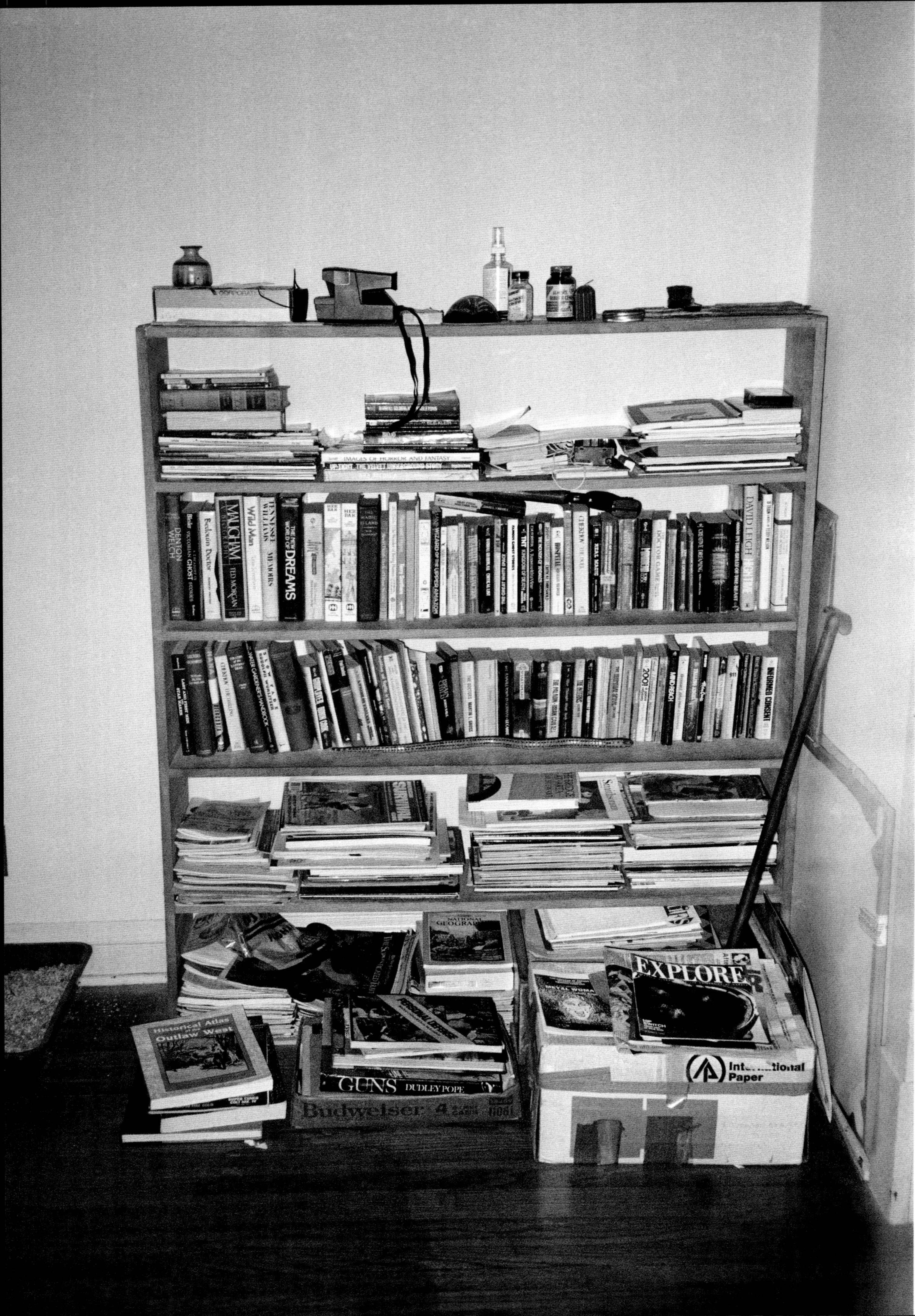
IMAGES OF HORROR AND FANTASY
UP-TIGHT THE VELVET UNDERGROUND STORY
DENTON WELCH
VICTORIAN GHOST STORIES
MAUGHAM
TED MORGAN
Wild Man
TENNESSEE WILLIAMS
MEMOIRS
THE NEW WORLD OF DREAMS
WIZARD OF THE UPPER AMAZON
DAVID LEIGH
INFORMED CONSENT
Historical Atlas of the Outlaw West
PERSONAL DEFENSE
GUNS
DUDLEY POPE
Budweiser
EXPLORE
International Paper

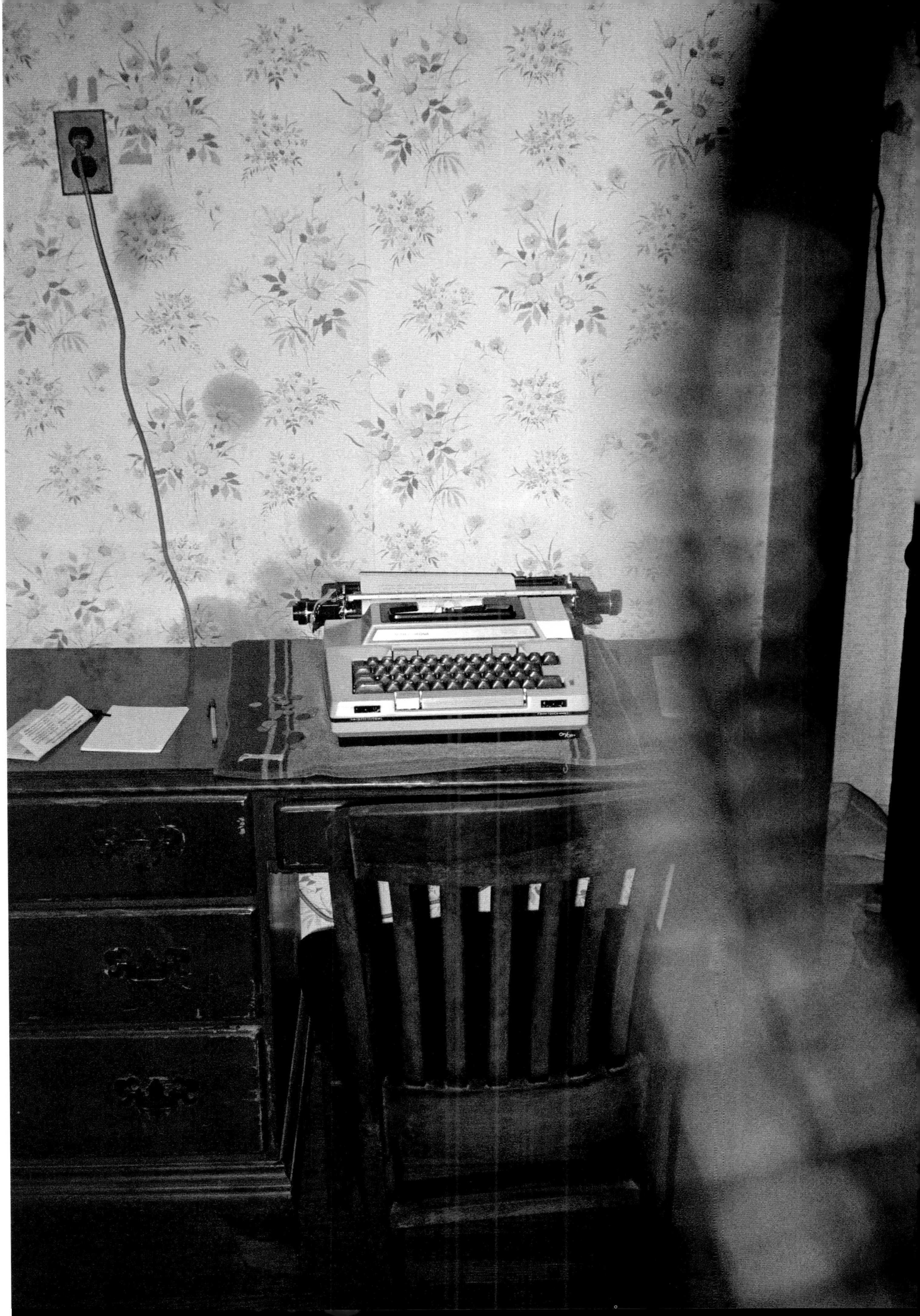

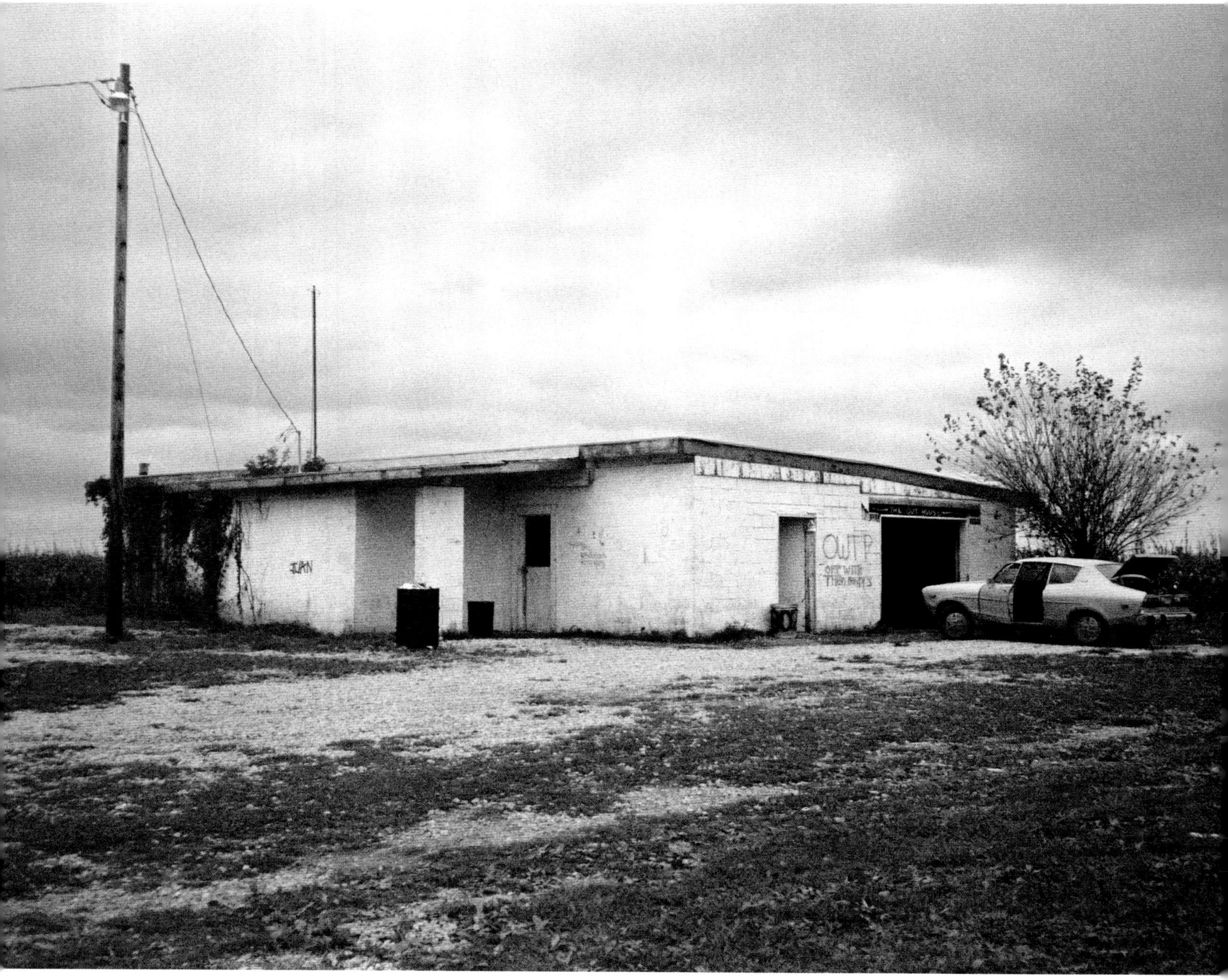
OWTP

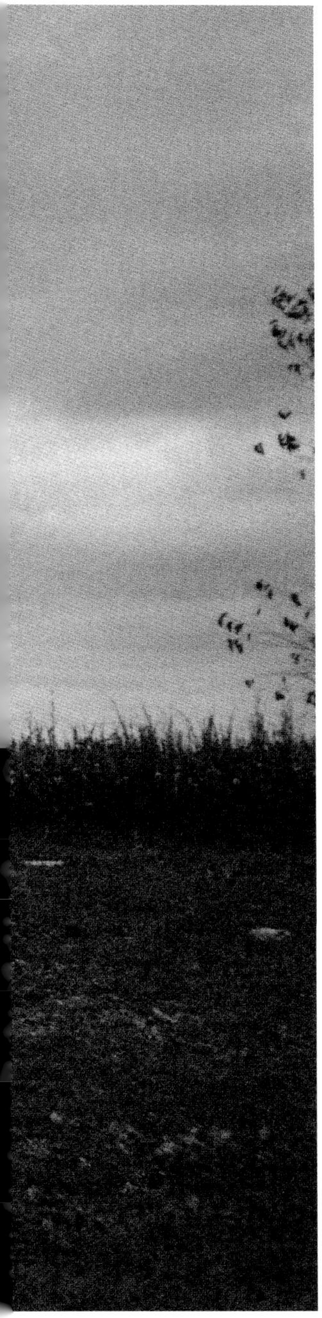

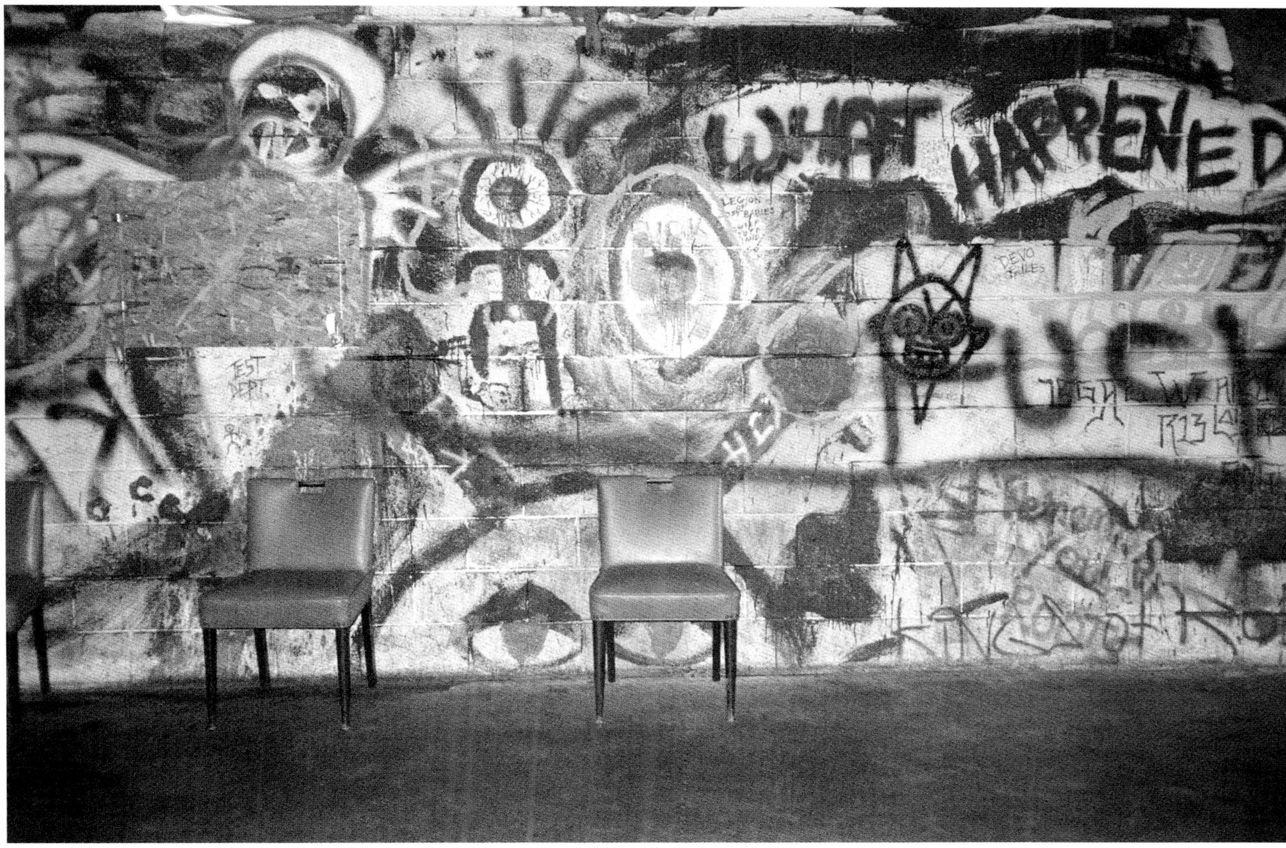

The Outhouse.

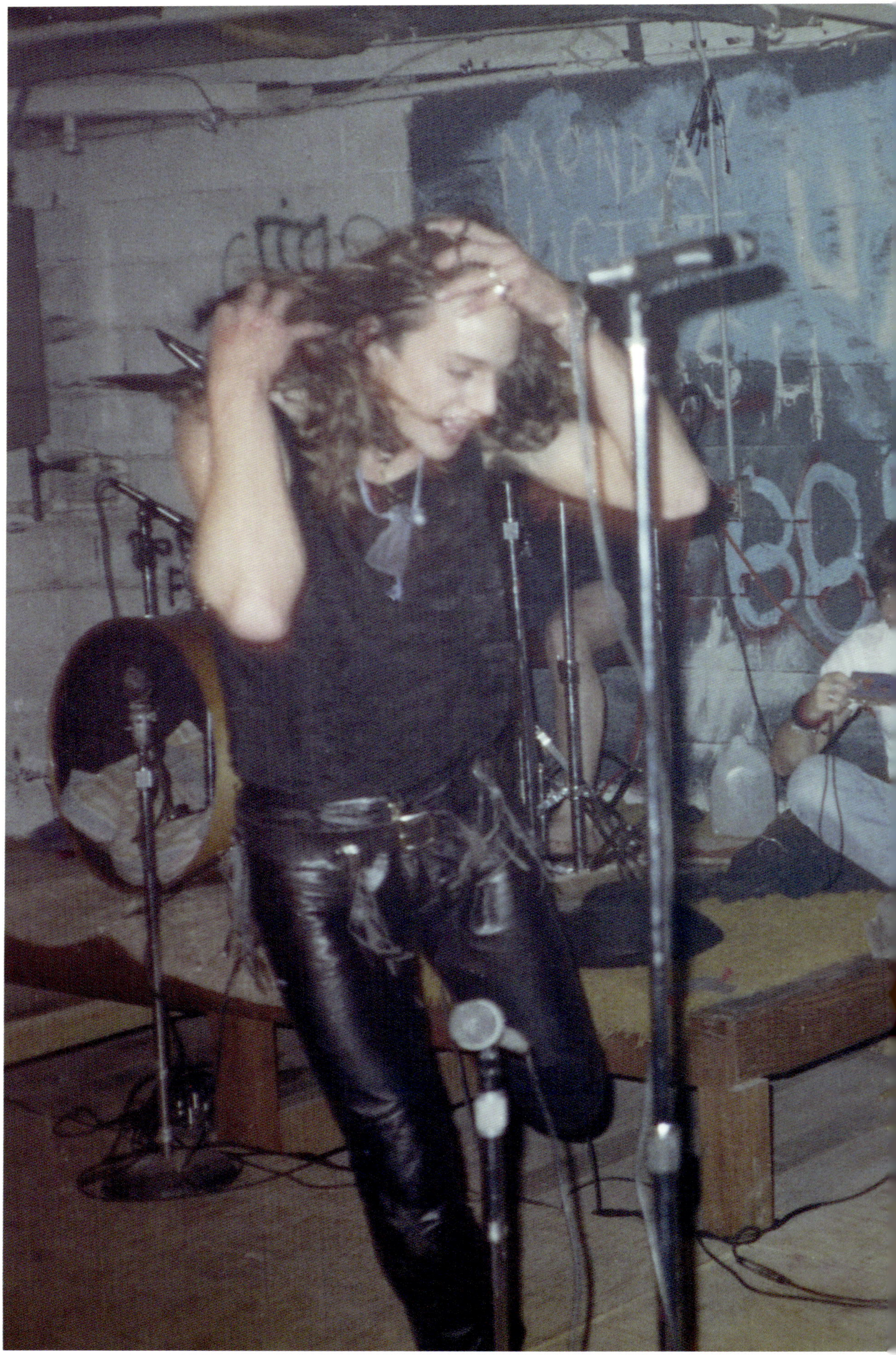

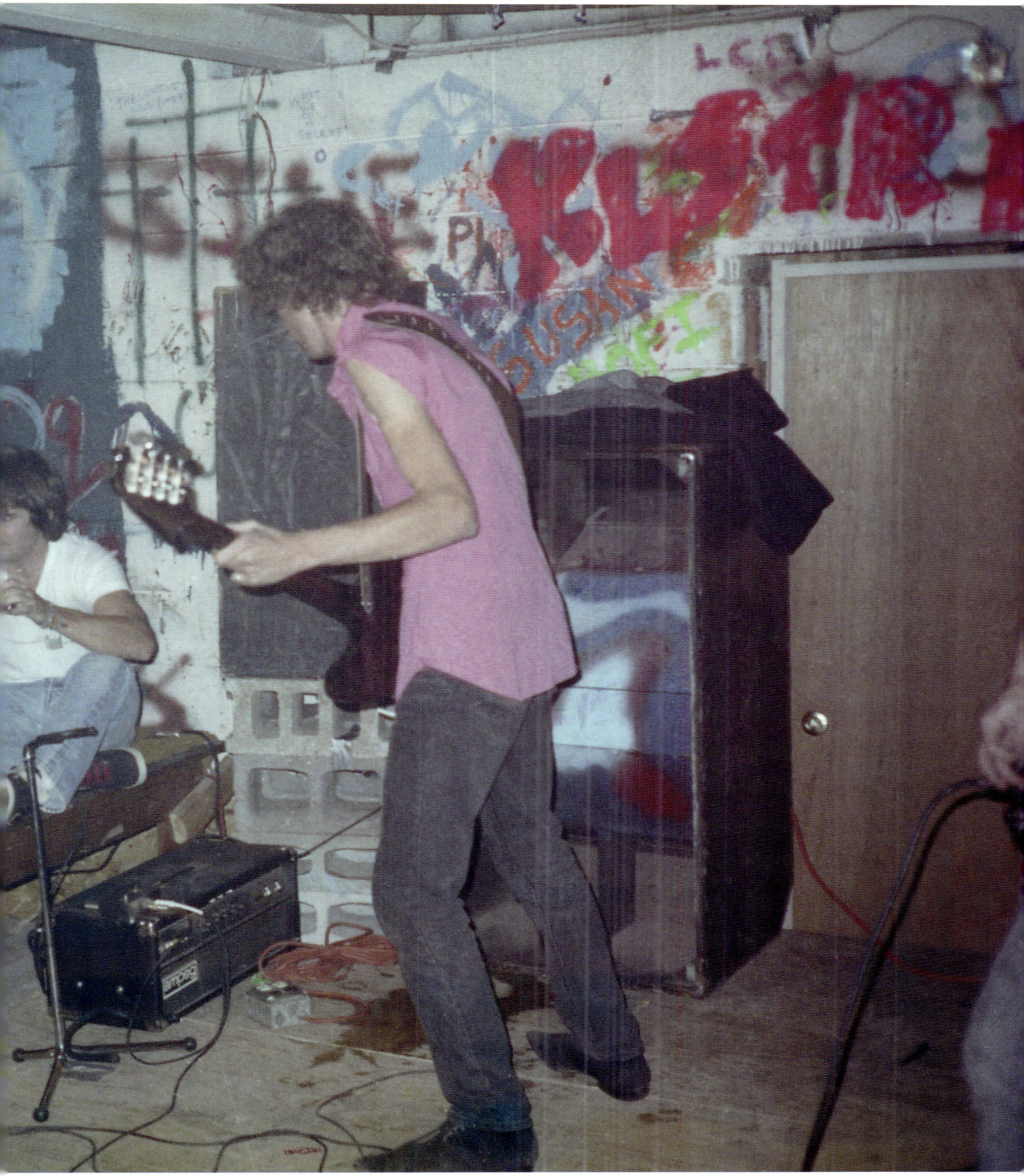

the spot
your golden ring
sticking me.
GRATEFUL
SONIC

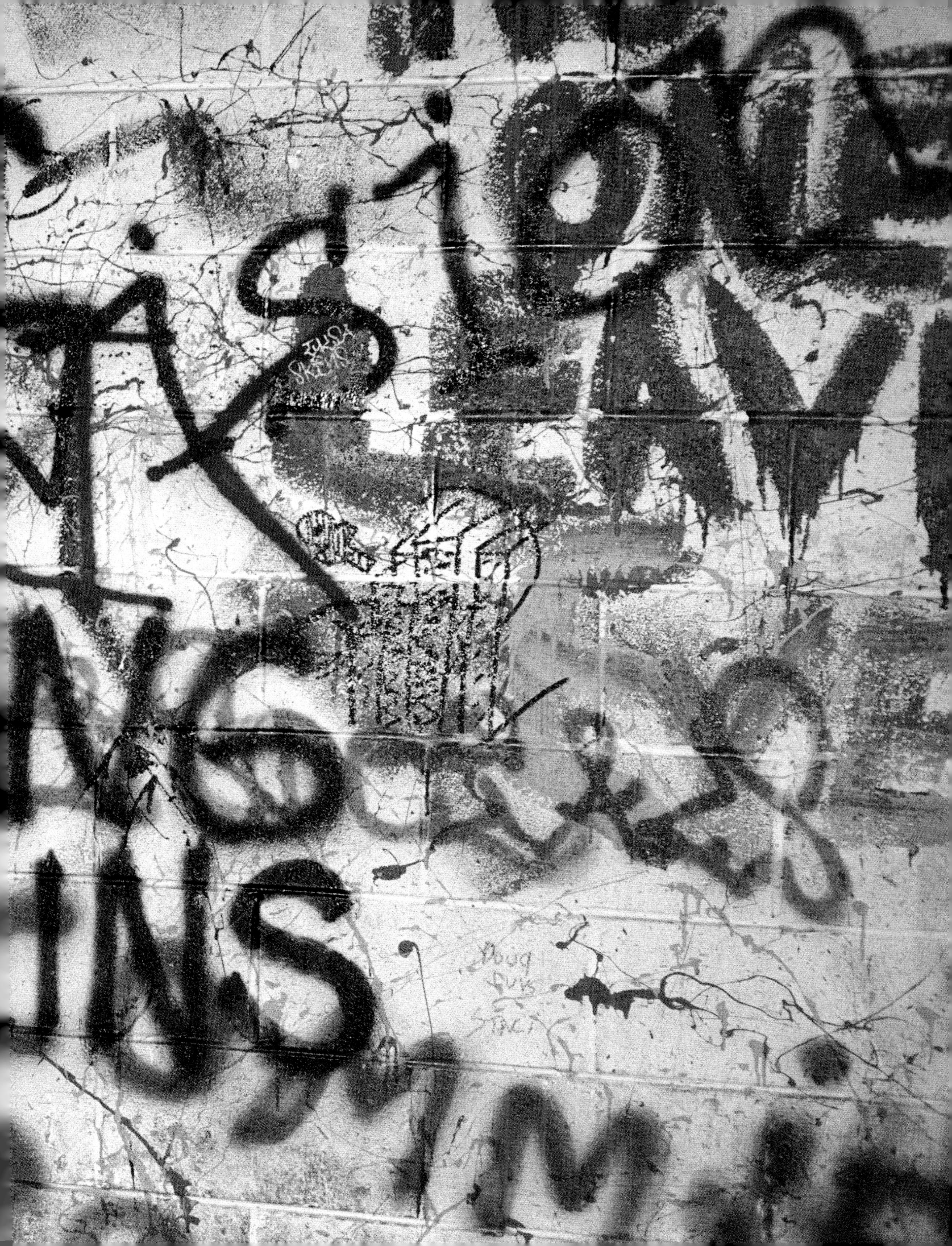

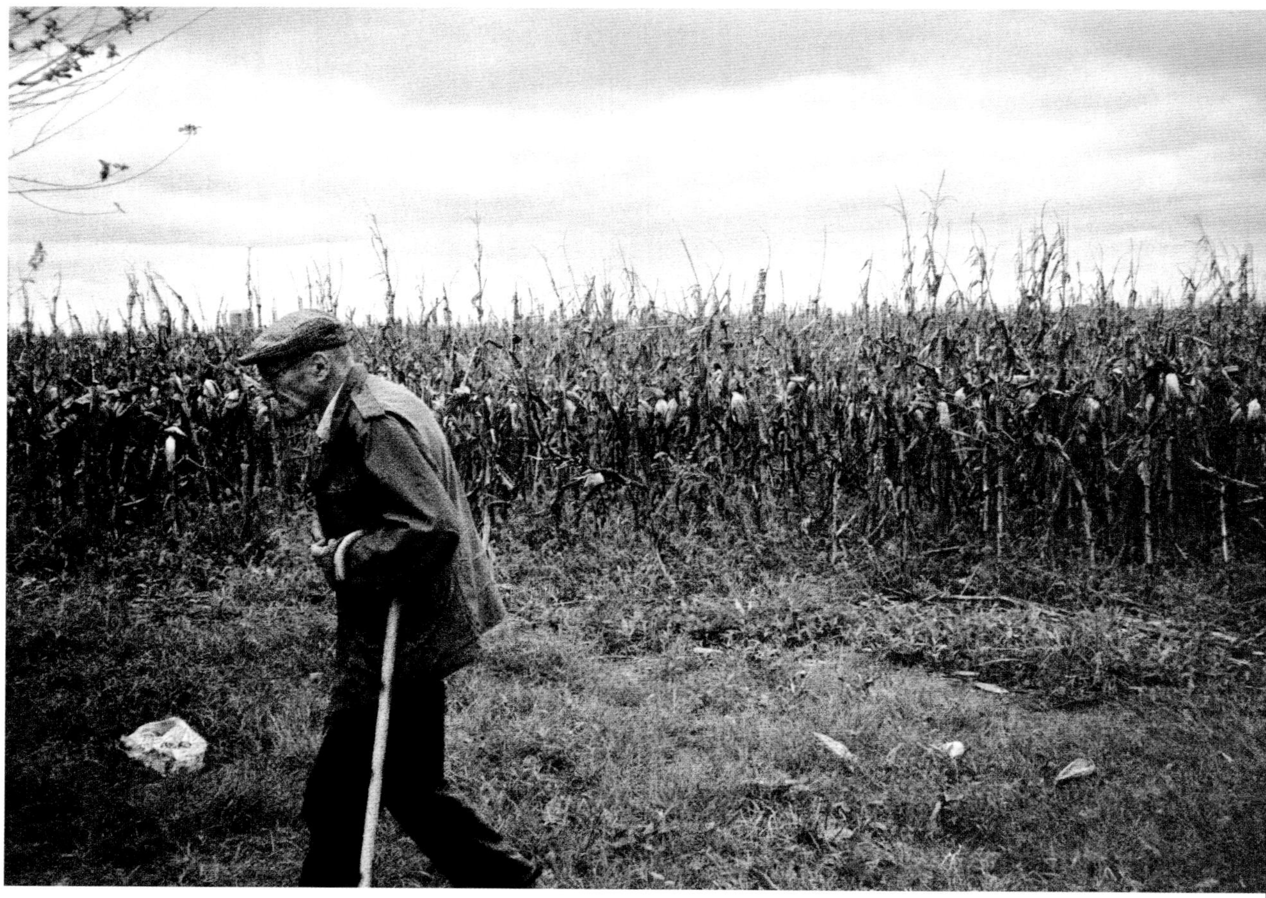

Bill walking and shooting in the cornfield outside the Outhouse.

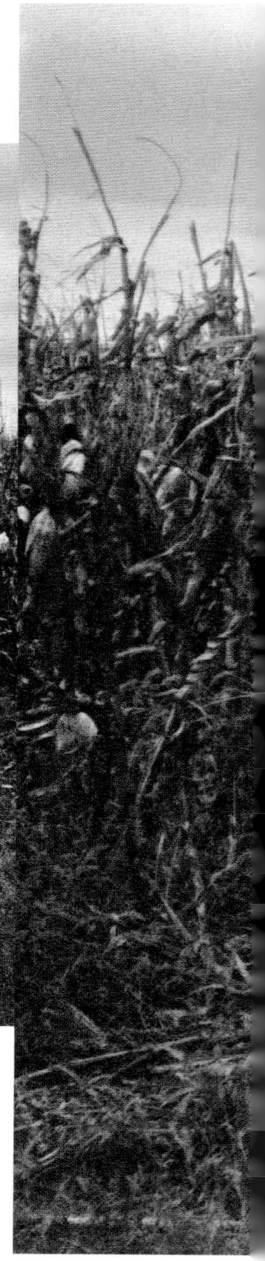

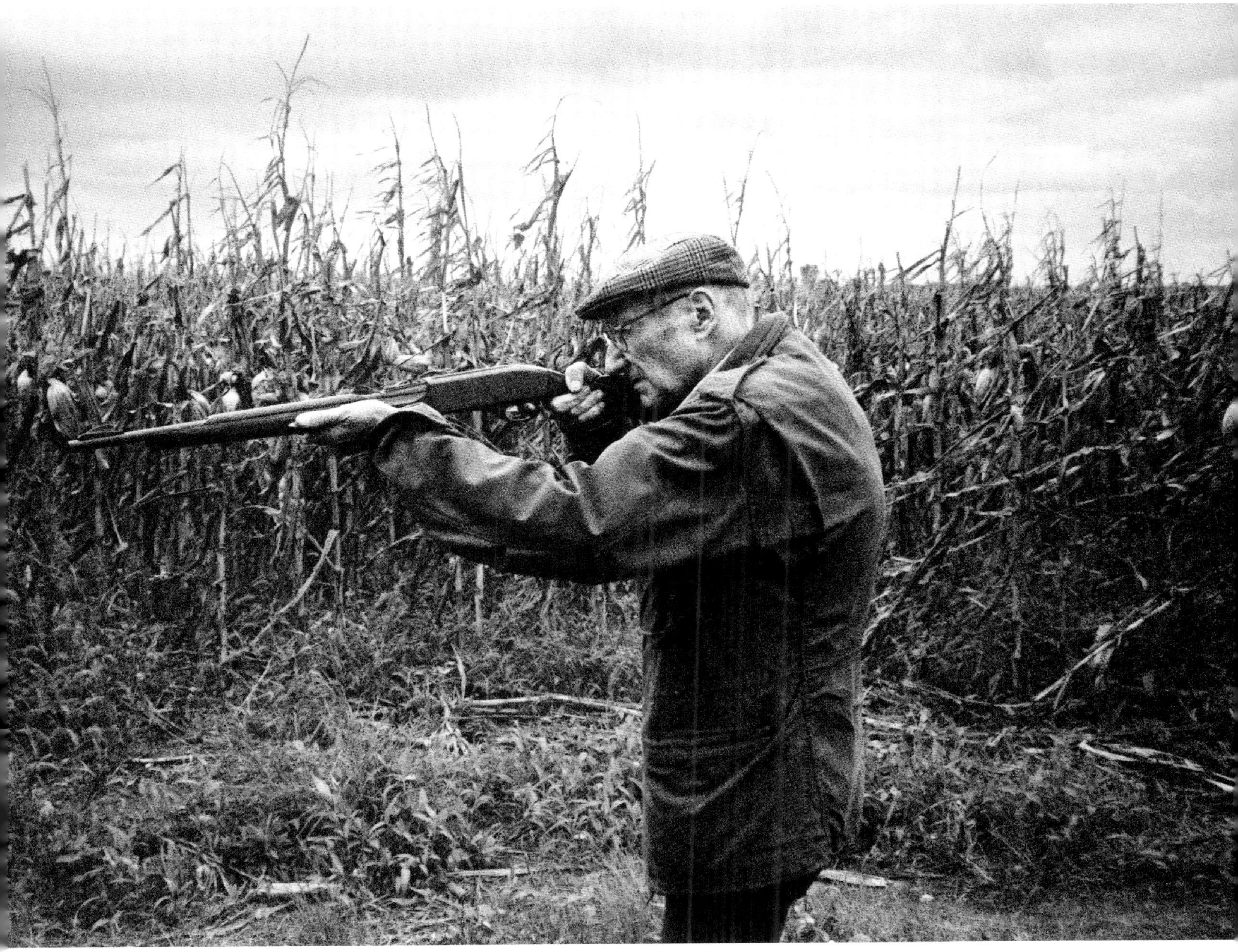

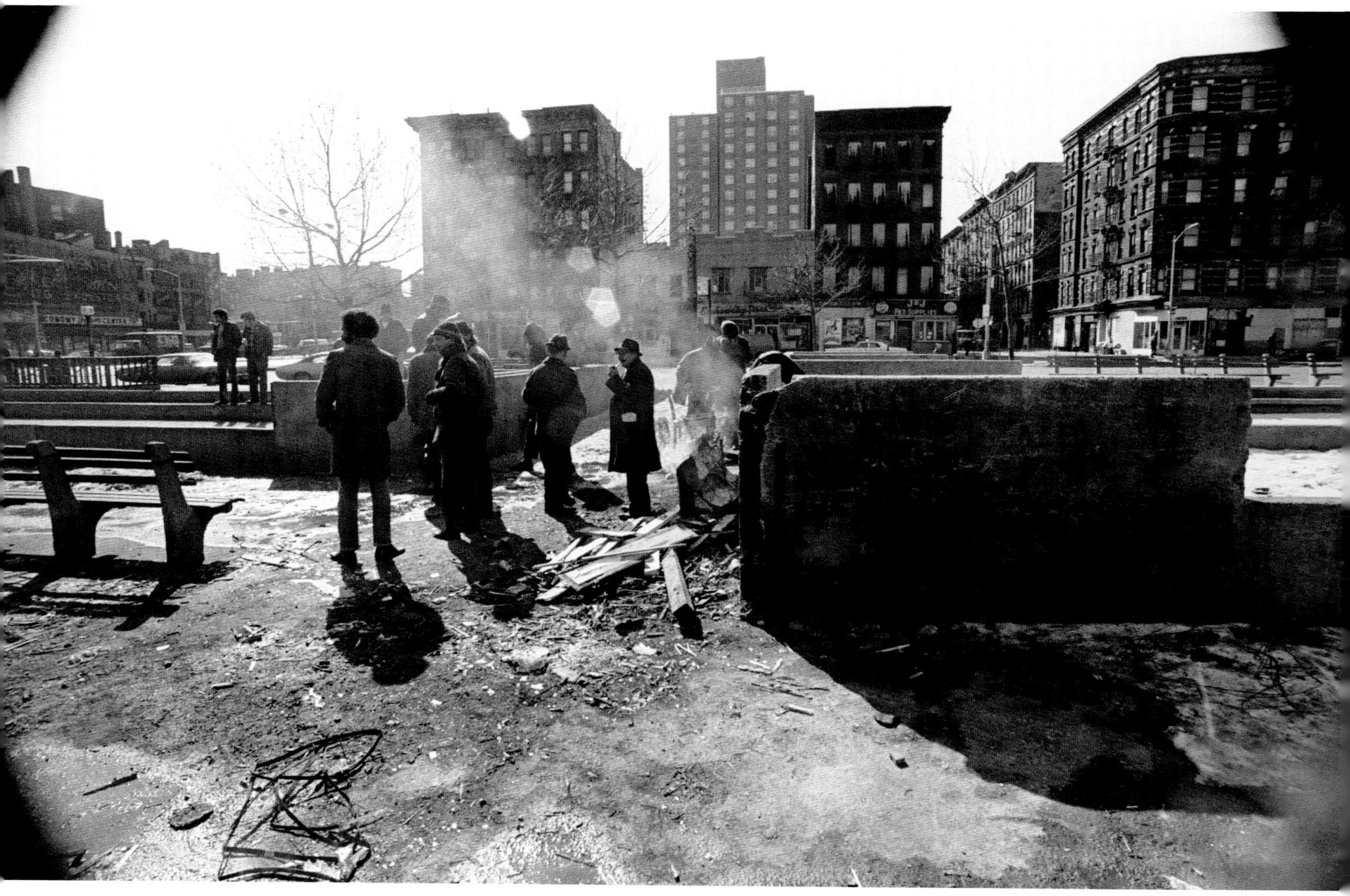

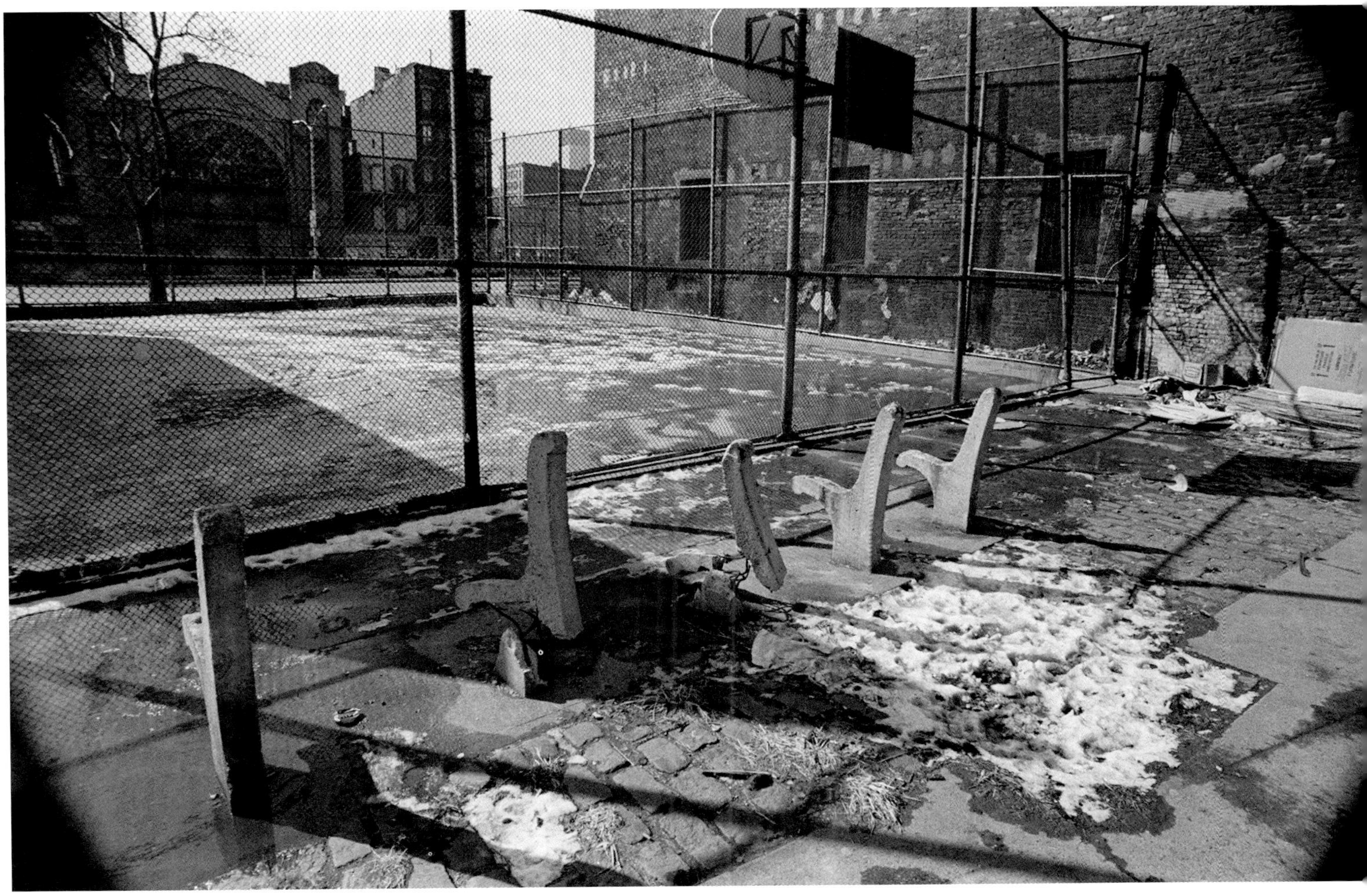

THE FENCE

Before I moved in with Debbie, I would make a daily trip along Houston Street over to her place on Thompson Street. I don't know what made me notice, but one day I saw a note in a chain-link fence I always passed on the uptown side of Second Avenue. I looked at it and it seemed to be 'written' by someone who was semi-literate and also slightly crazy. I kept the note and the next day found another. I passed the fence every day, and every day there'd be another note. The notes were sometimes written on the foil from a cigarette pack, on the white paper side, and sometimes written on pages pulled from a little pocket-sized spiral notebook. They were dated! A theme ran through them: the presumed author, one Andrew Creechy, and his niece Vernice Creechy were being denied social security monies that the government owed them. The writing would be partly readable, but would sometimes trail off into illegibility. The notes would always have a series of seemingly random numbers on them that I took to characterize social security numbers. I wound up with a really large collection of these notes. Sometimes there would be two or more in the fence, and I must have had a hundred or so. One day I thought I saw an old guy putting a note in the fence—was this Andrew? I couldn't be sure. I began to think that somehow, by my interaction in taking the notes, old Andrew was maintaining his audience and communication as it were. I was breaking the prime directive. If I'd left them there to pile up, maybe he'd have stopped posting them. I still have one that I pasted into a notebook someplace. When everyone finally left the First Avenue apartment, I think the majority of the notes wound up in the abandoned debris pile.

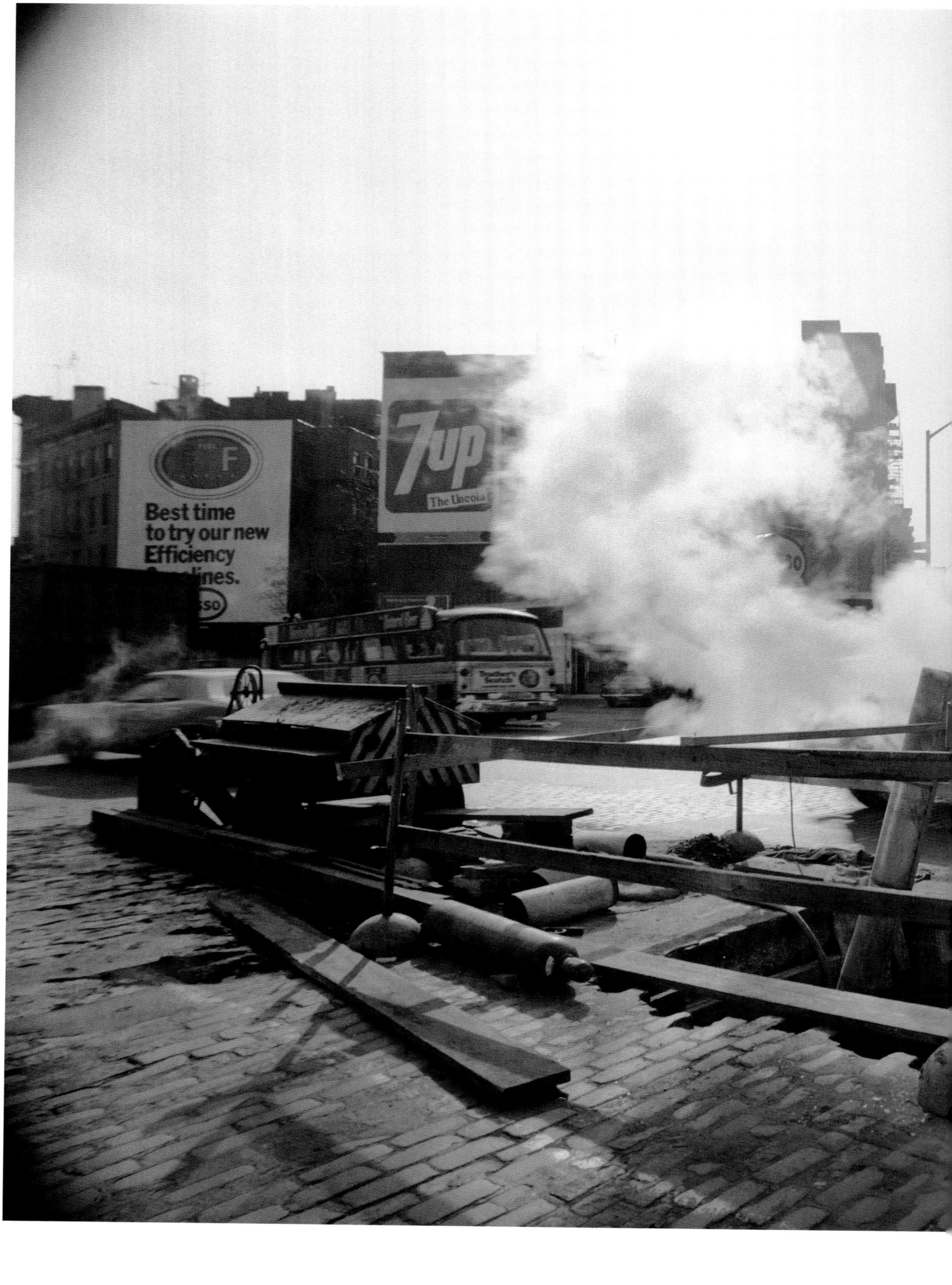
Best time
to try our new
Efficiency
7up

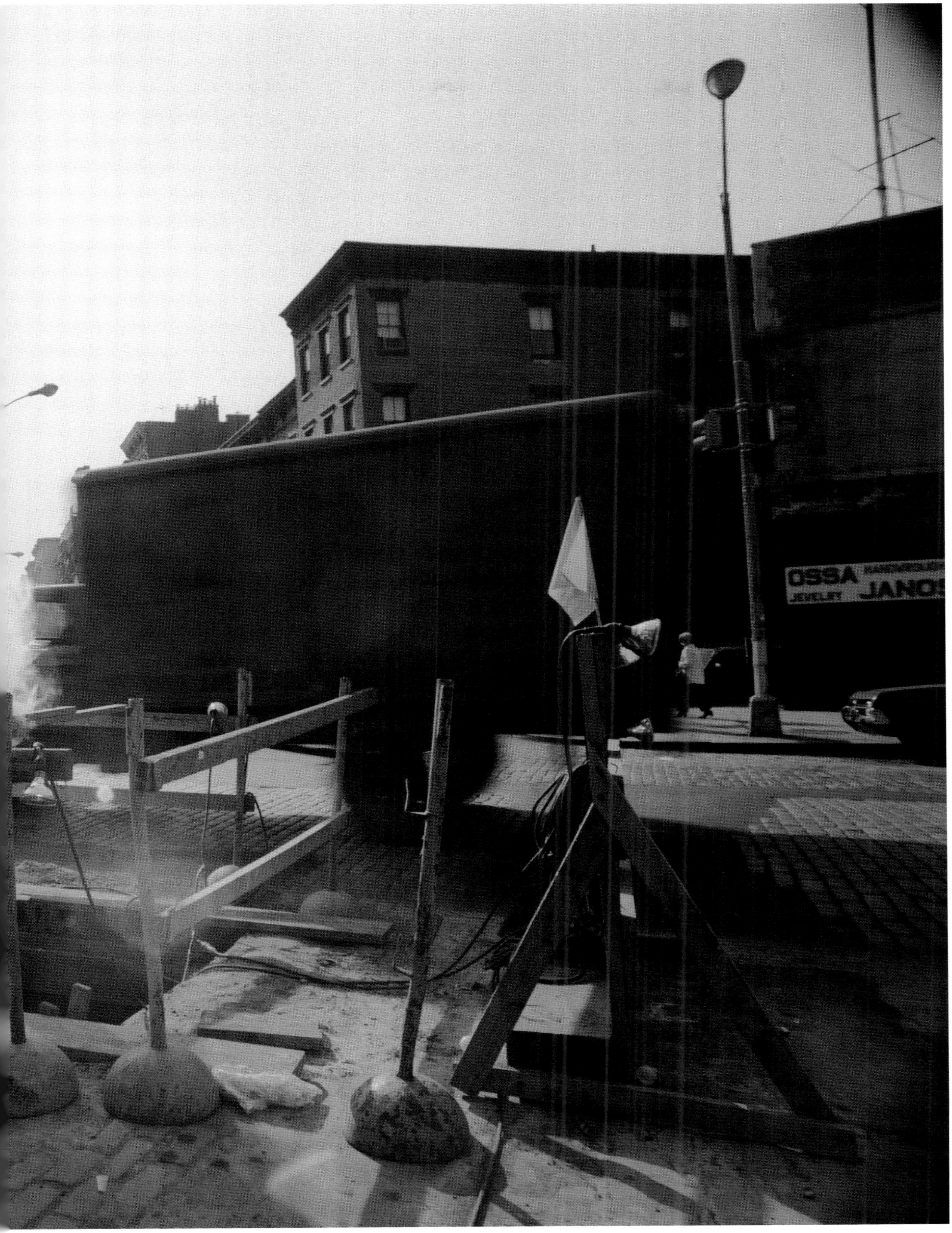
OSSA
JEWELRY
JANOS

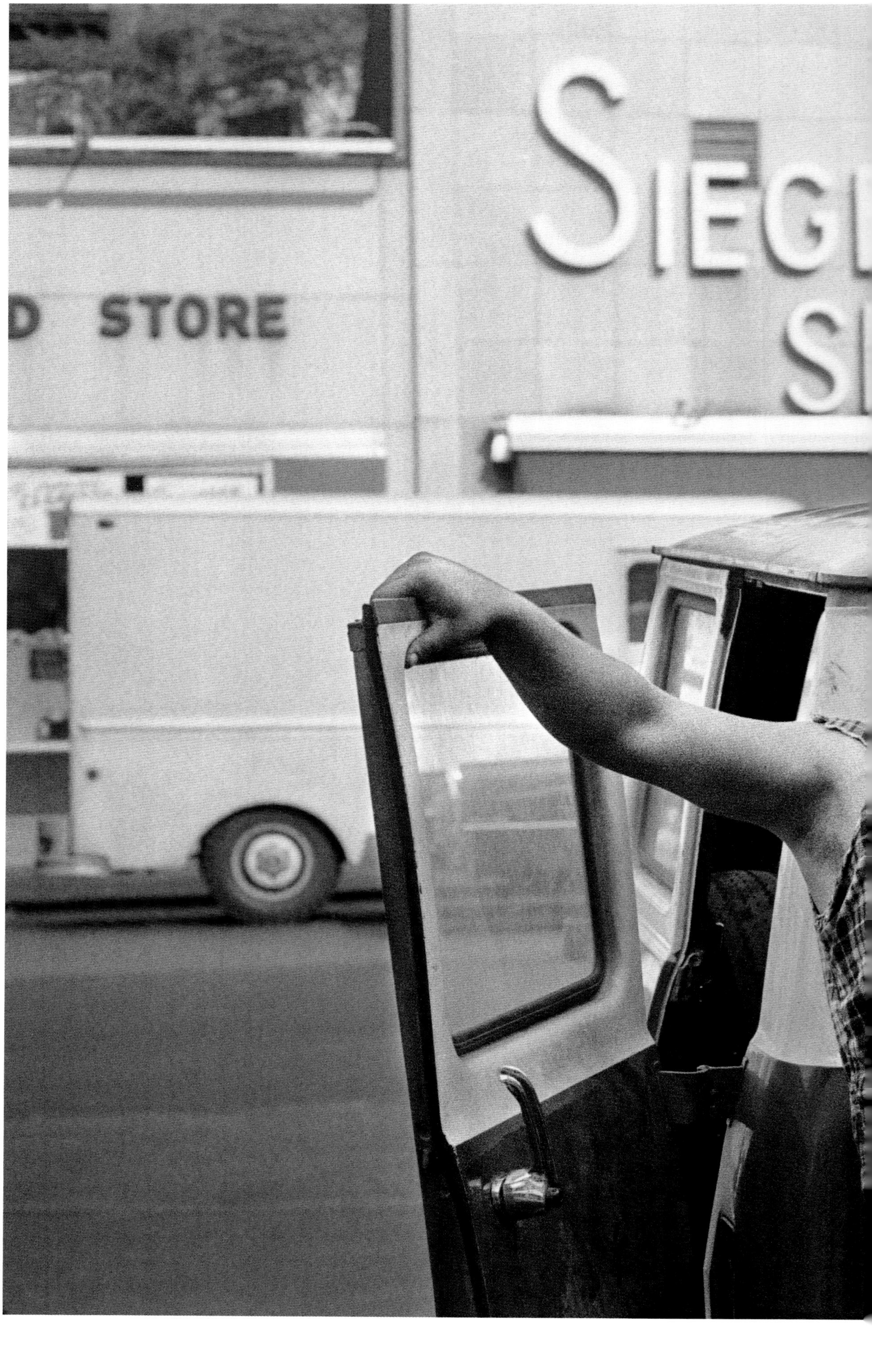
SIEG
D STORE

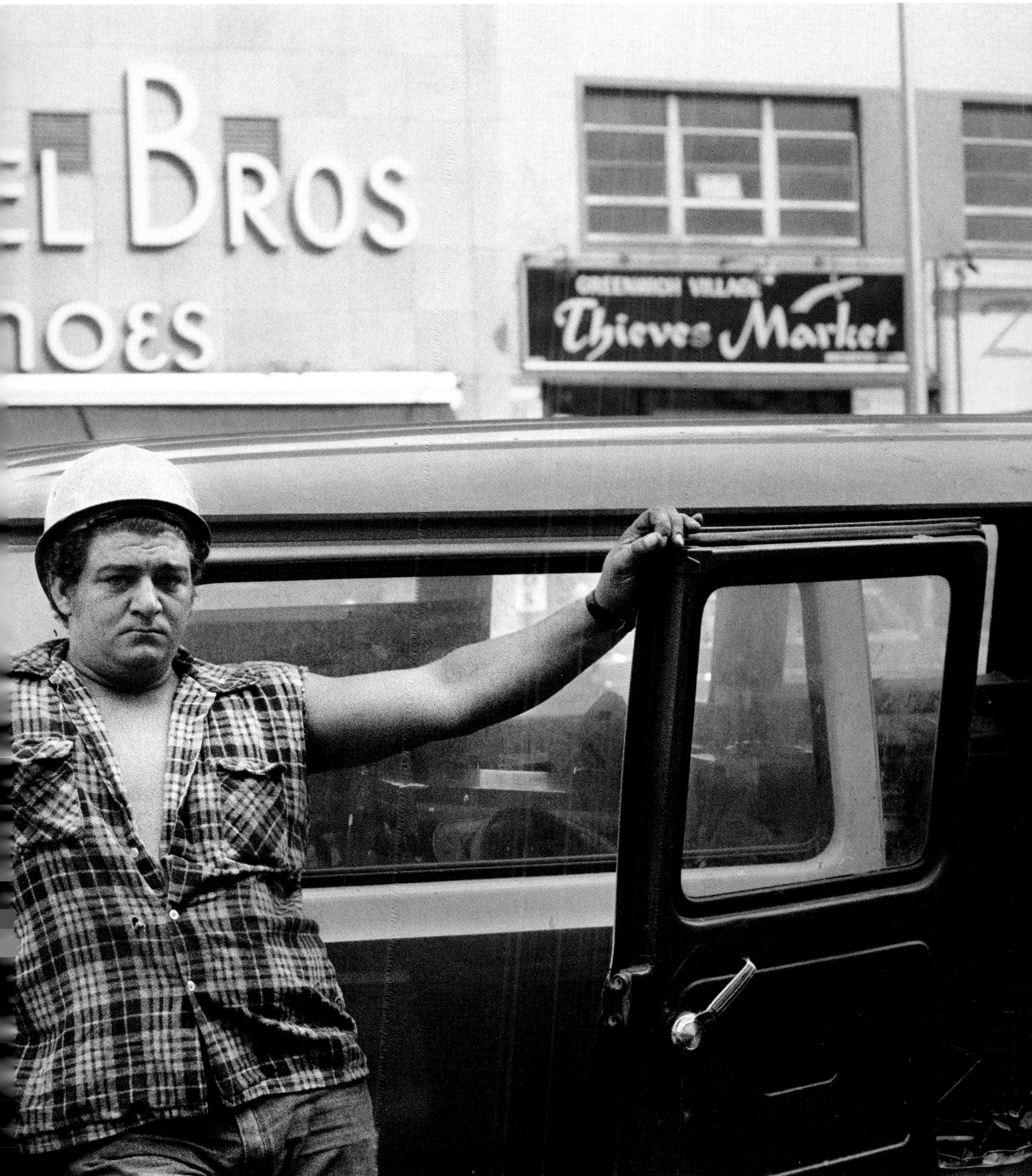
EL BROS
Thieves Market

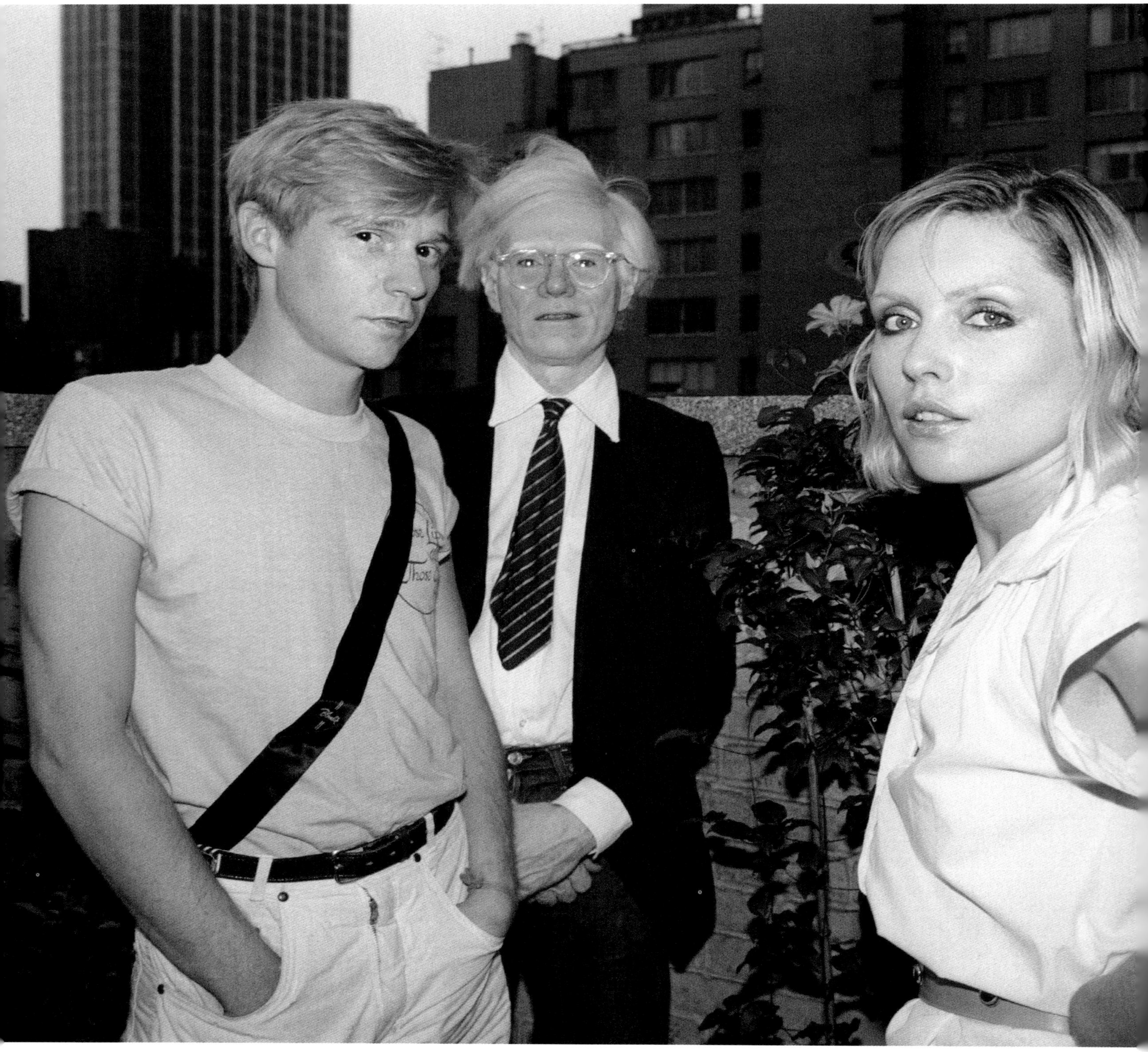

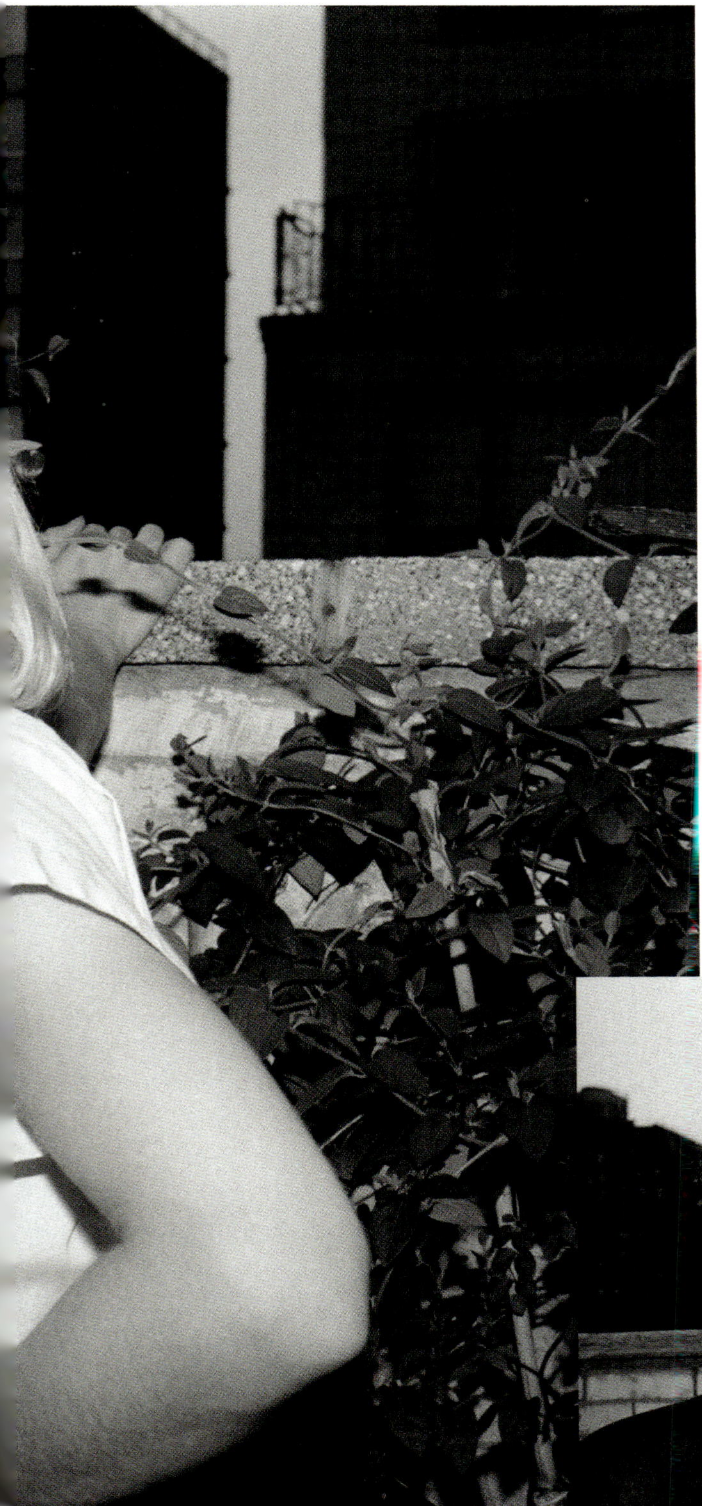

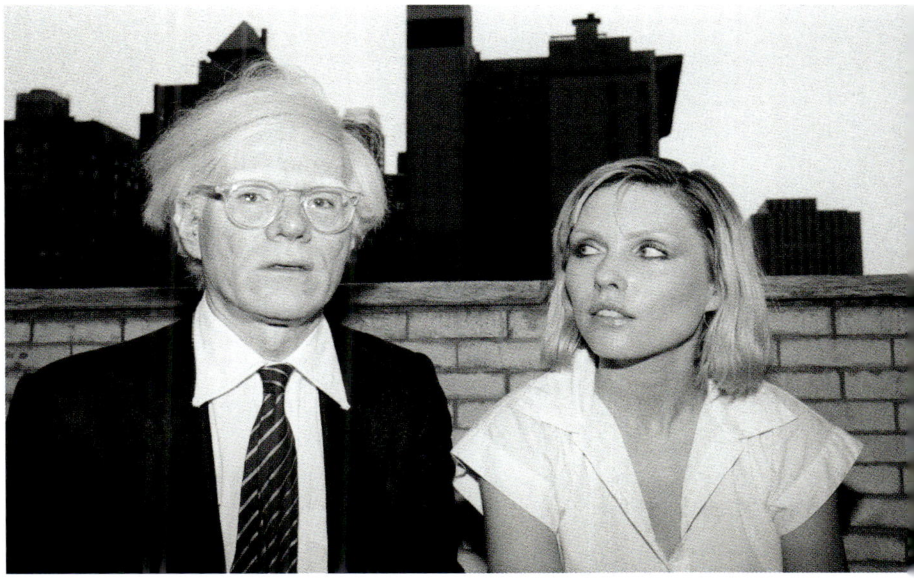

Dennis Christopher, Andy Warhol, and Debbie on the terrace of our 58th Street apartment.

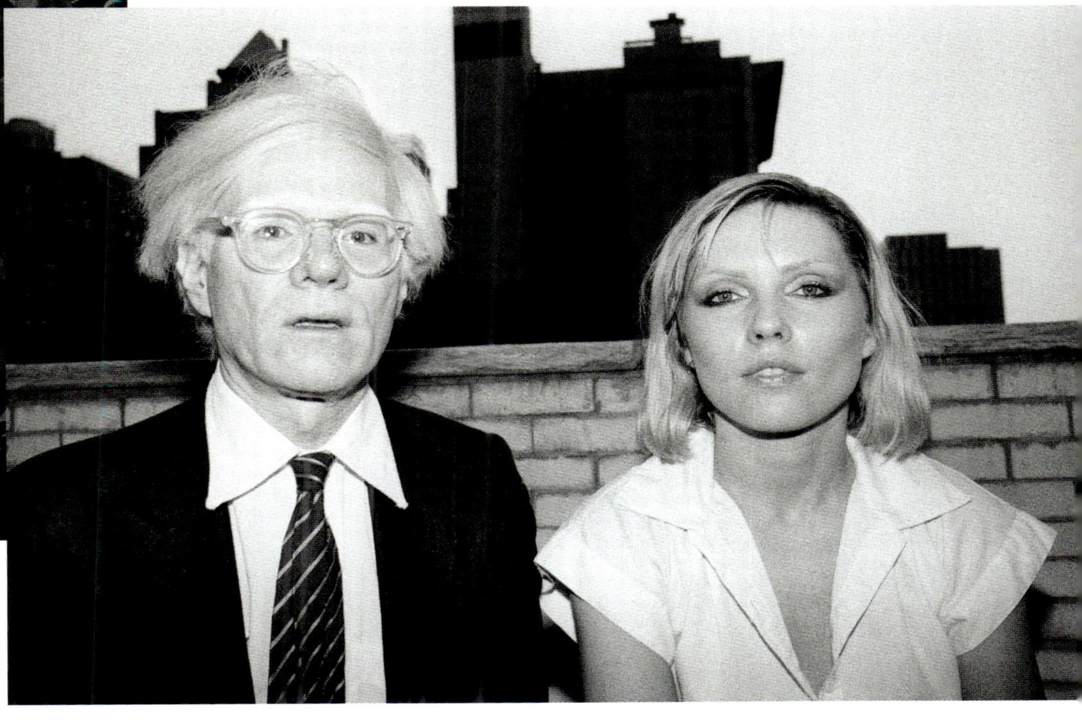

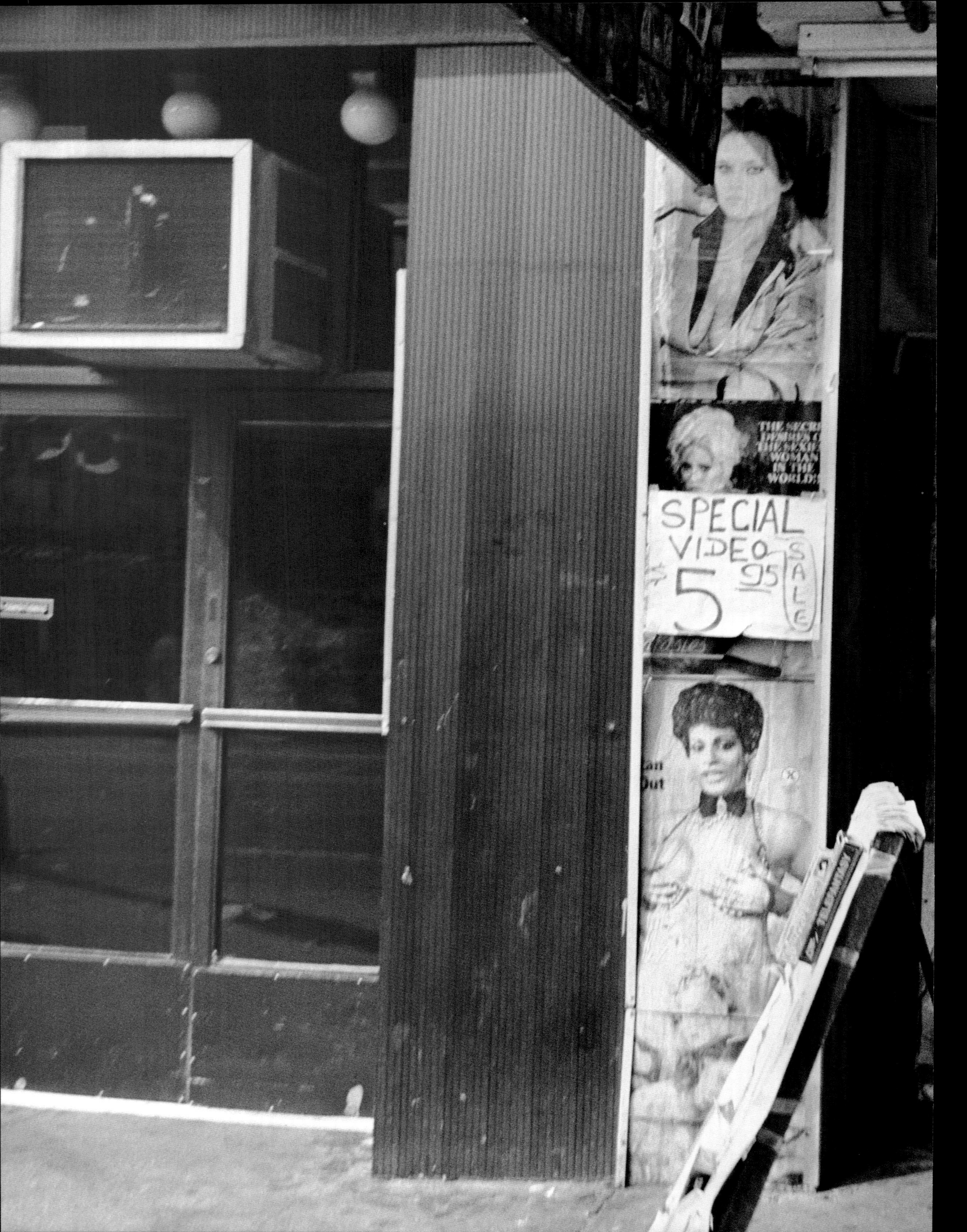
SPECIAL
VIDEO
$5 95
SALE

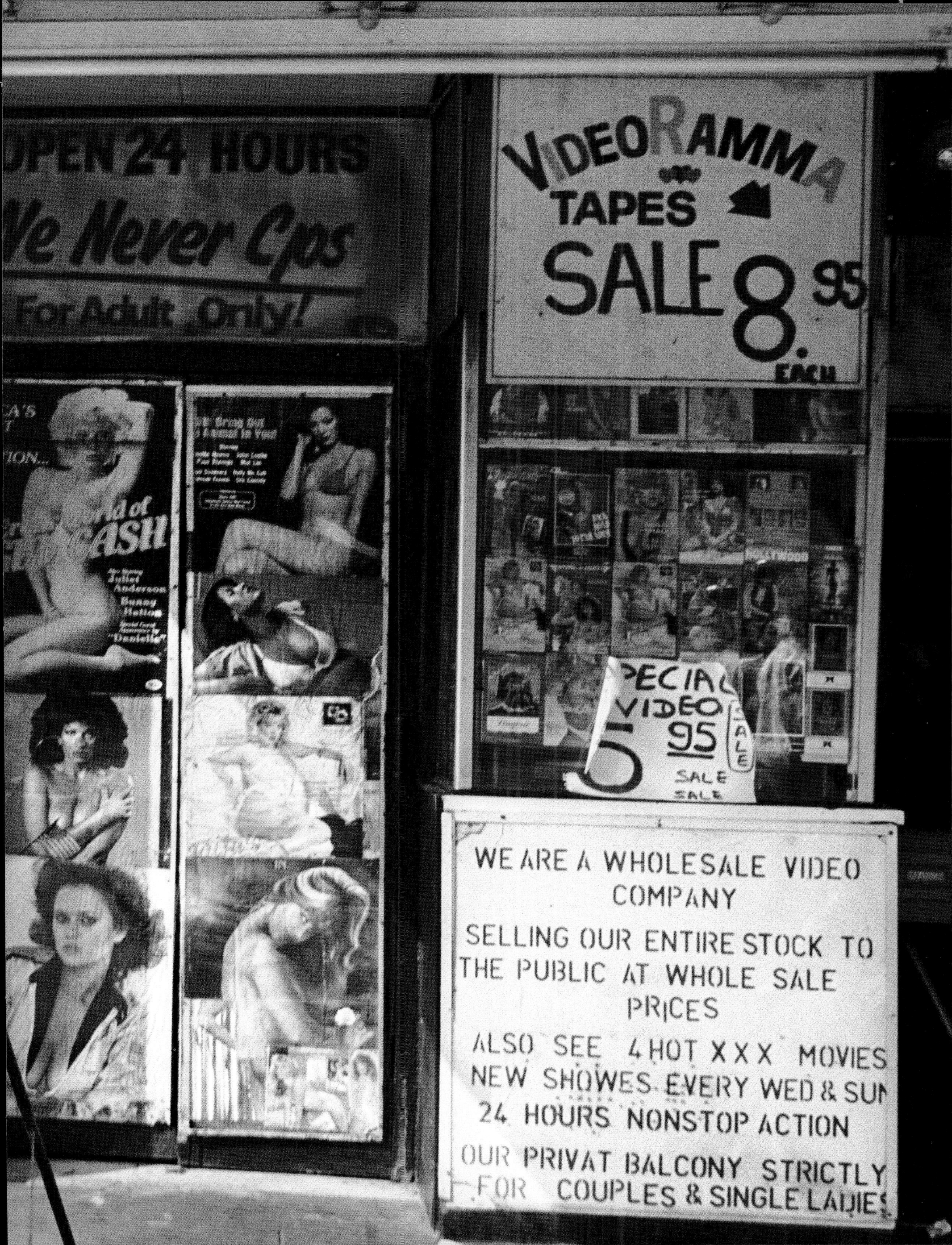
OPEN 24 HOURS
We Never Clos
For Adult Only!
VIDEORAMMA
TAPES
SALE 8.95
EACH
SPECIAL VIDEO
5.95
SALE
SALE
WE ARE A WHOLESALE VIDEO
COMPANY
SELLING OUR ENTIRE STOCK TO
THE PUBLIC AT WHOLE SALE
PRICES
ALSO SEE 4 HOT XXX MOVIES
NEW SHOWES EVERY WED & SUN
24 HOURS NONSTOP ACTION
OUR PRIVAT BALCONY STRICTLY
FOR COUPLES & SINGLE LADIES

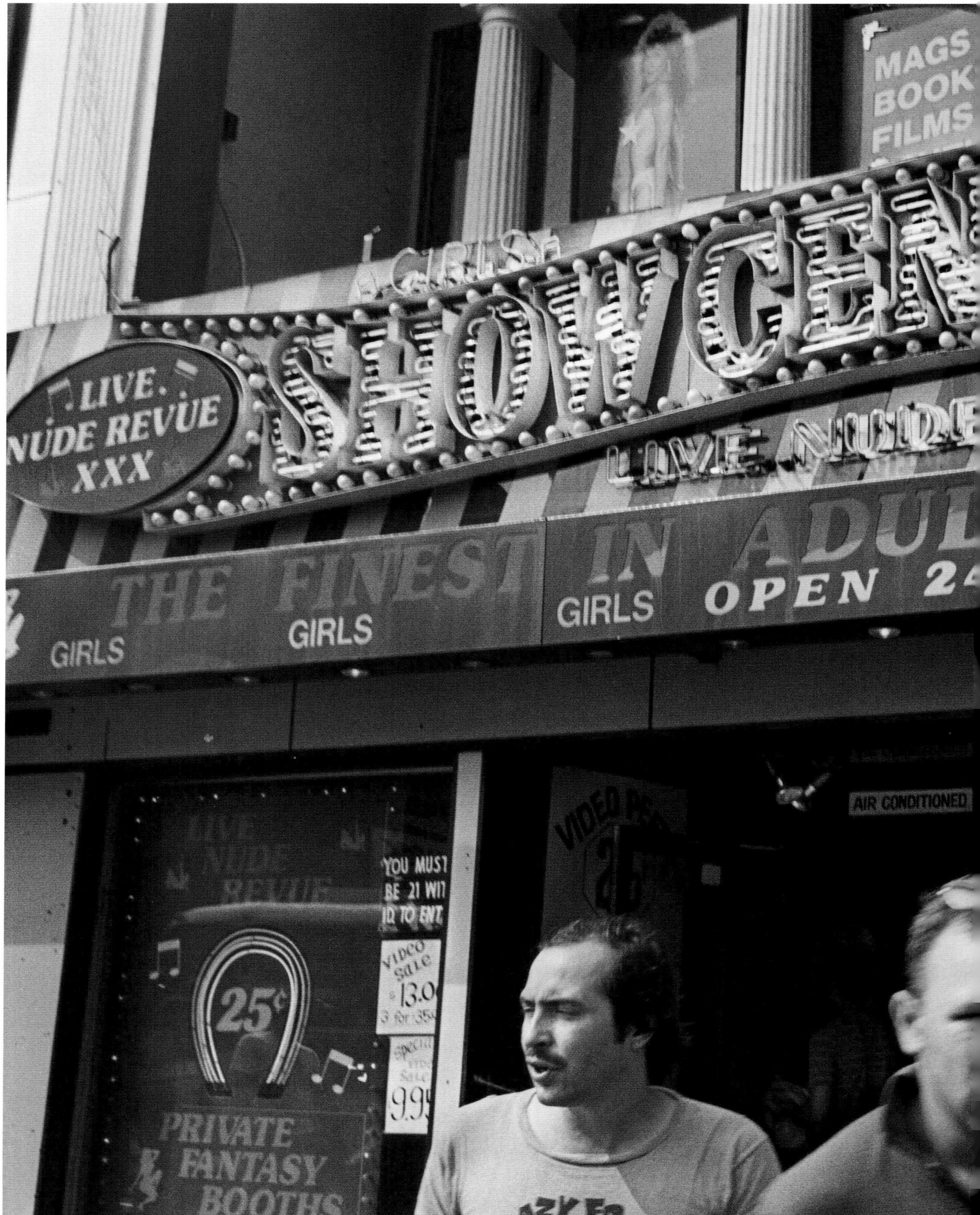
MAGS
FILMS
LIVE.
NUDE REVUE
XXX
THE FINEST IN
GIRLS
GIRLS
GIRLS
OPEN
AIR CONDITIONED
25¢
PRIVATE
FANTASY
BOOTHS

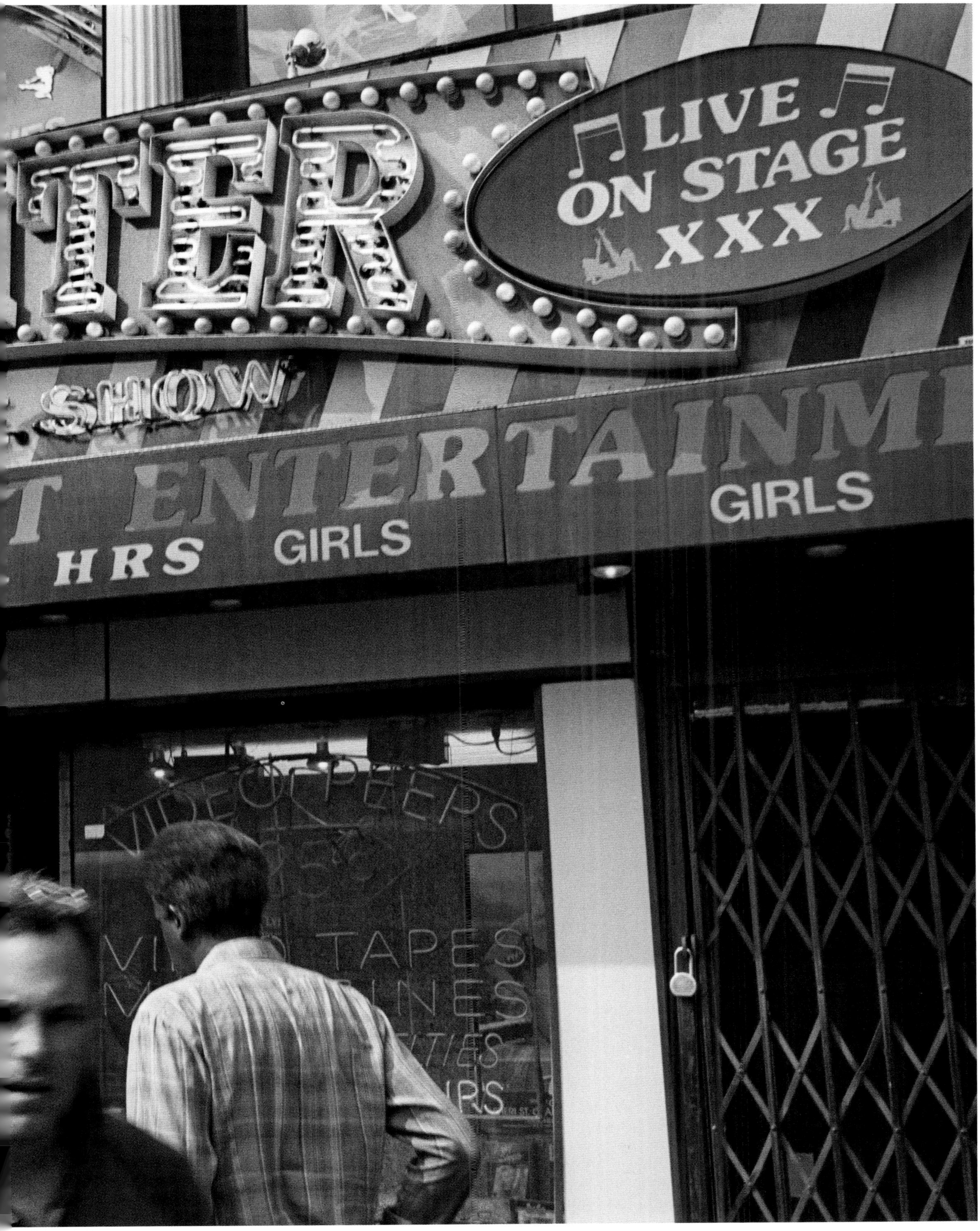
TER
LIVE
ON STAGE
XXX
SHOW
T ENTERTAINM
HRS GIRLS
GIRLS

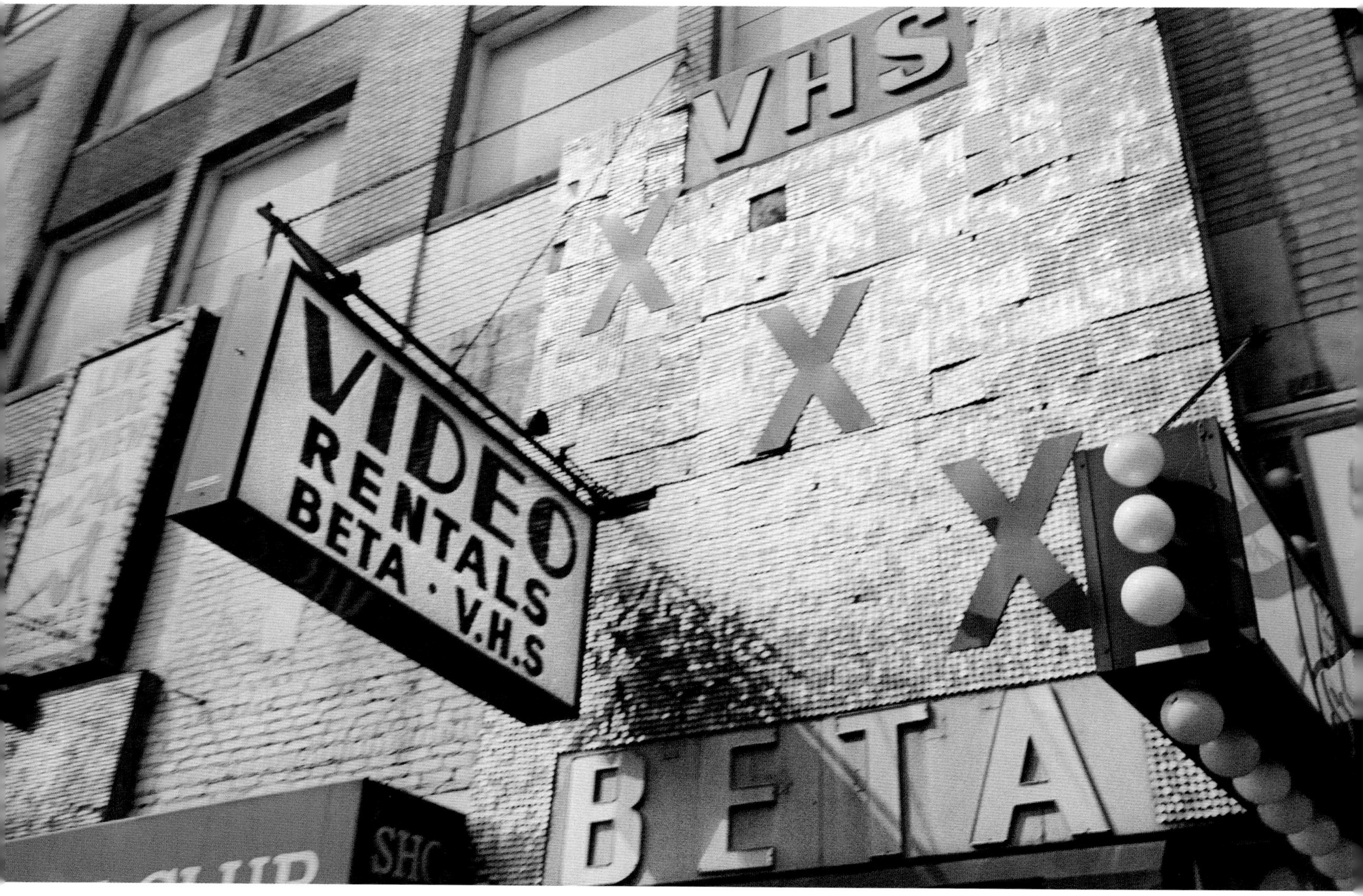

42nd Street and Times Square, mid-1980s.

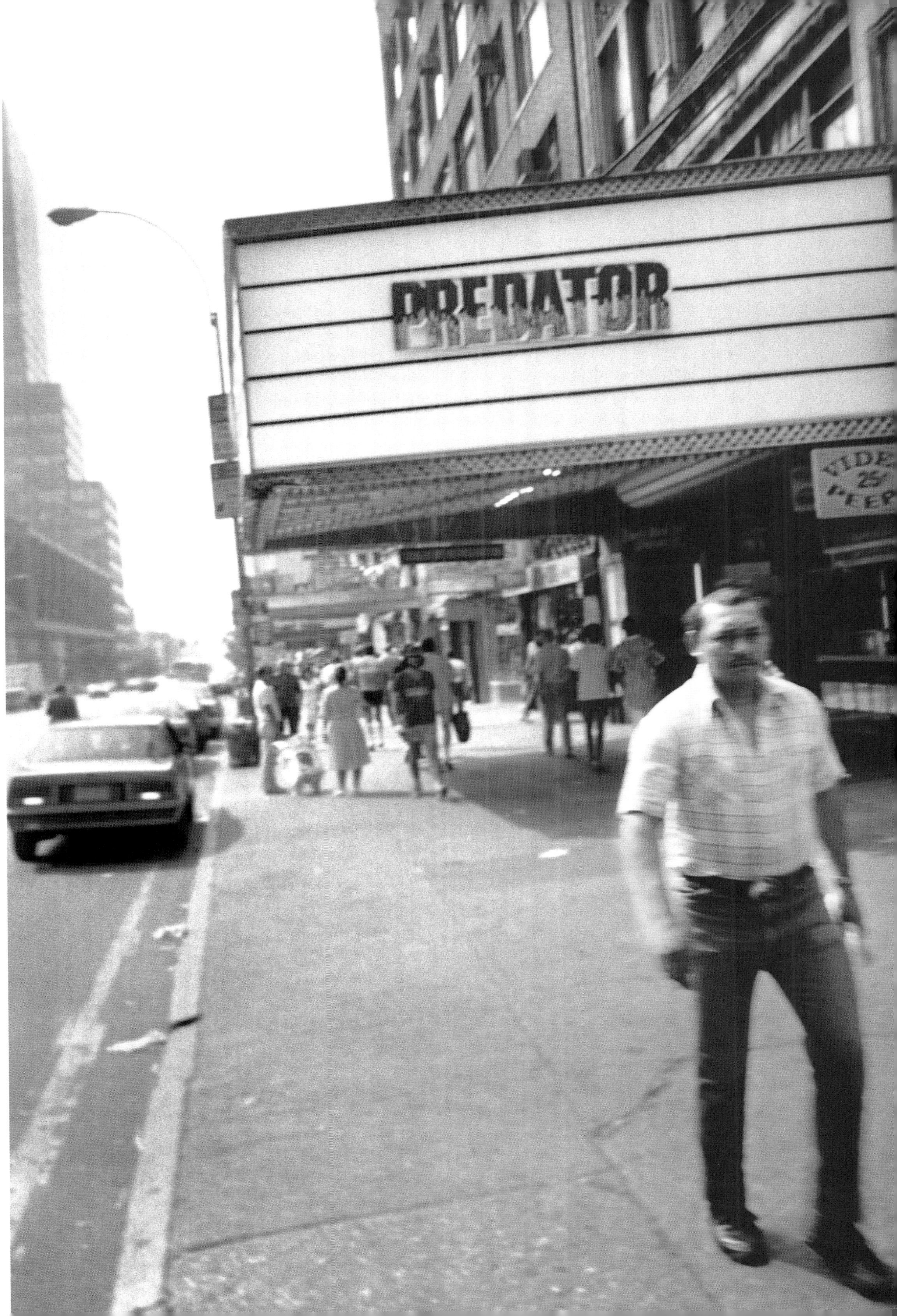
PREDATOR

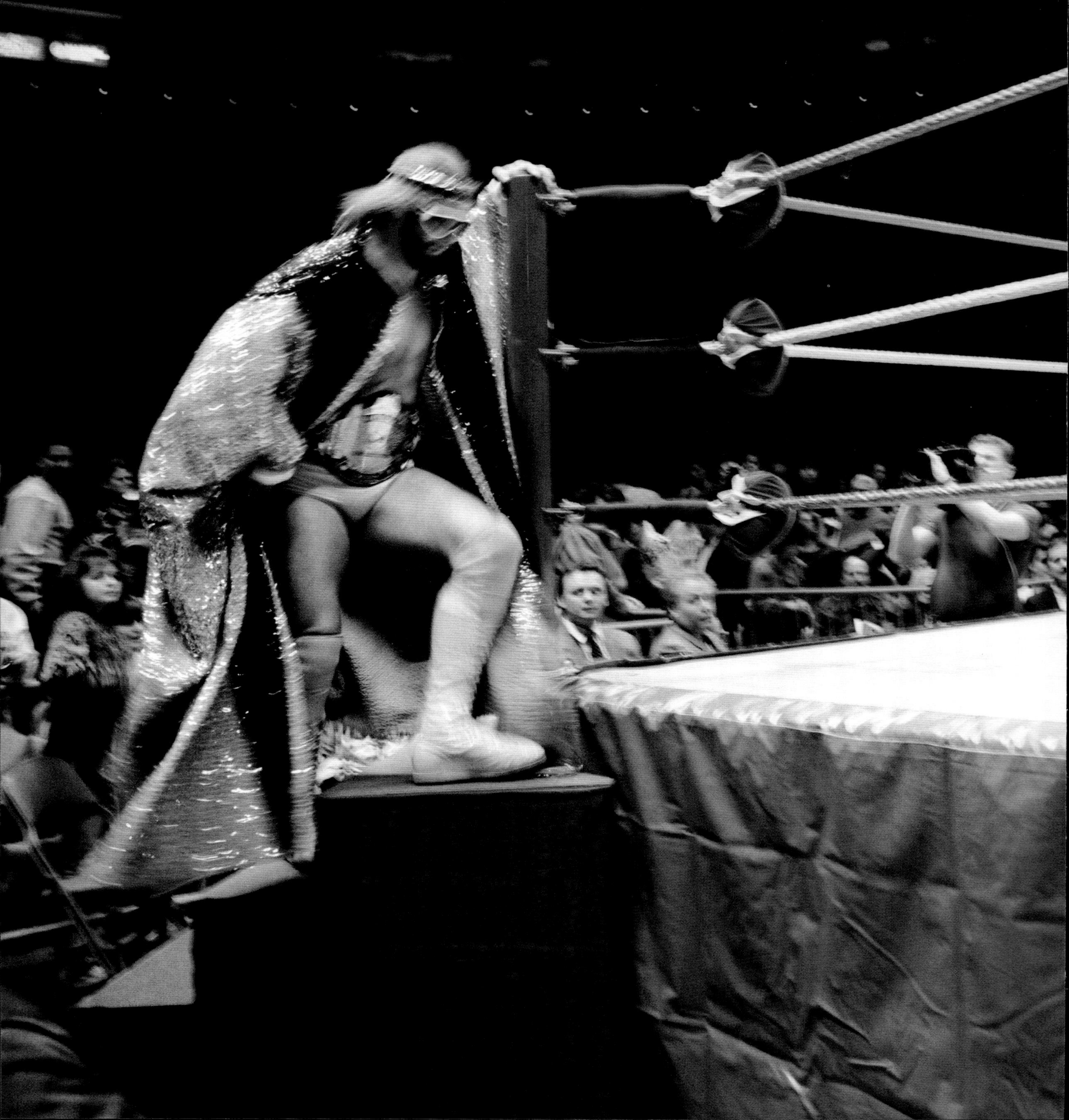

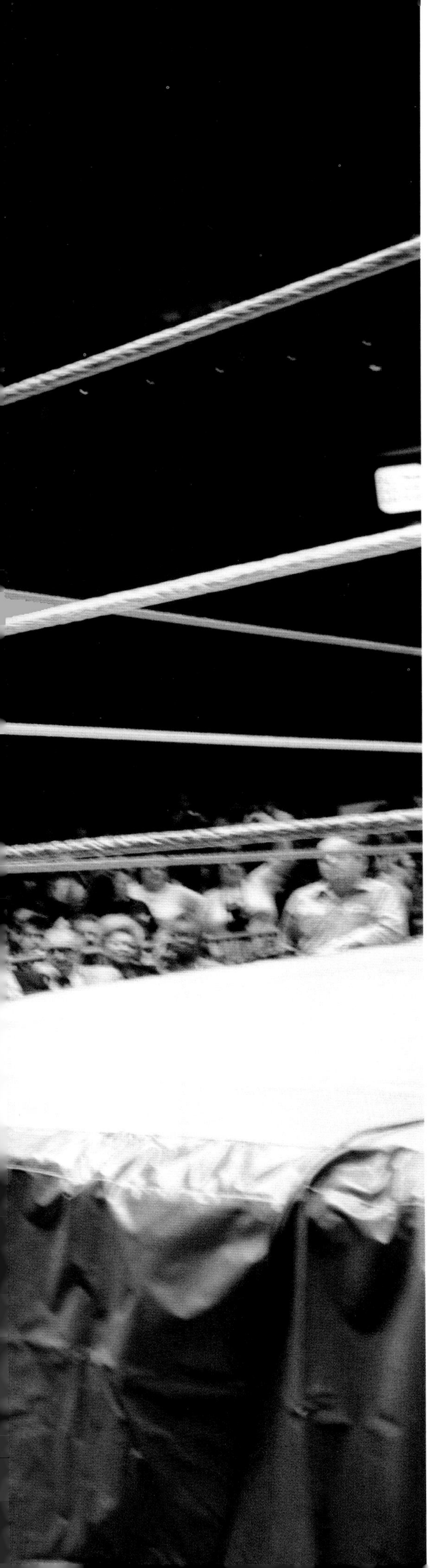

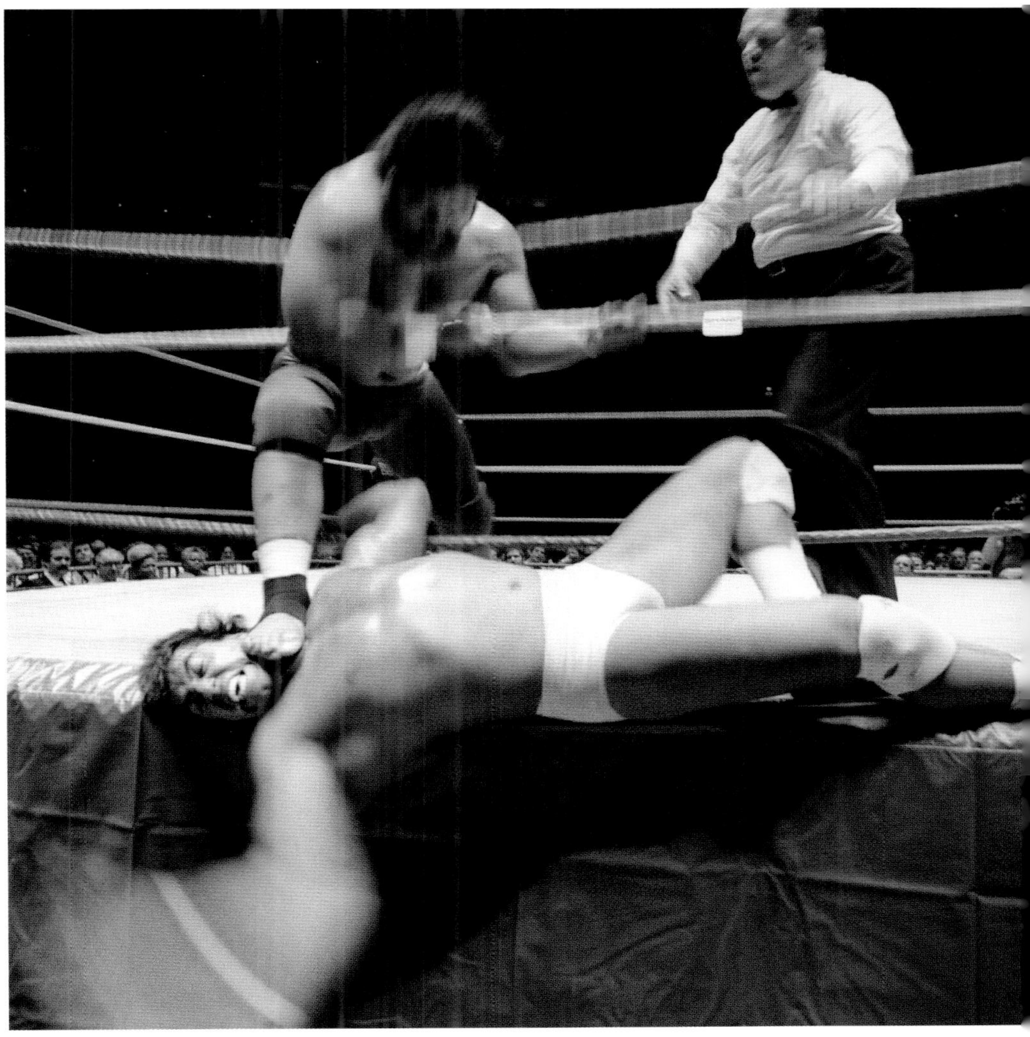

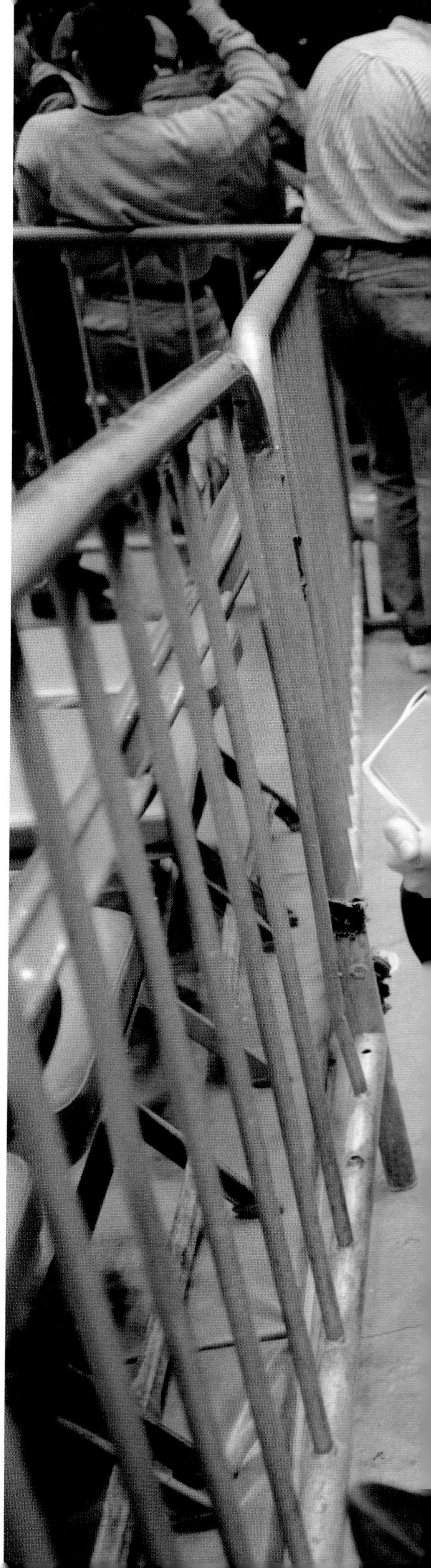

I was always a wrestling fan. Macho Man Randy Savage enters the squared circle at Madison Square Garden; Haku steps on the neck of Rick Martel; Jim Thirlwell and Lydia Lunch ringside at the match.

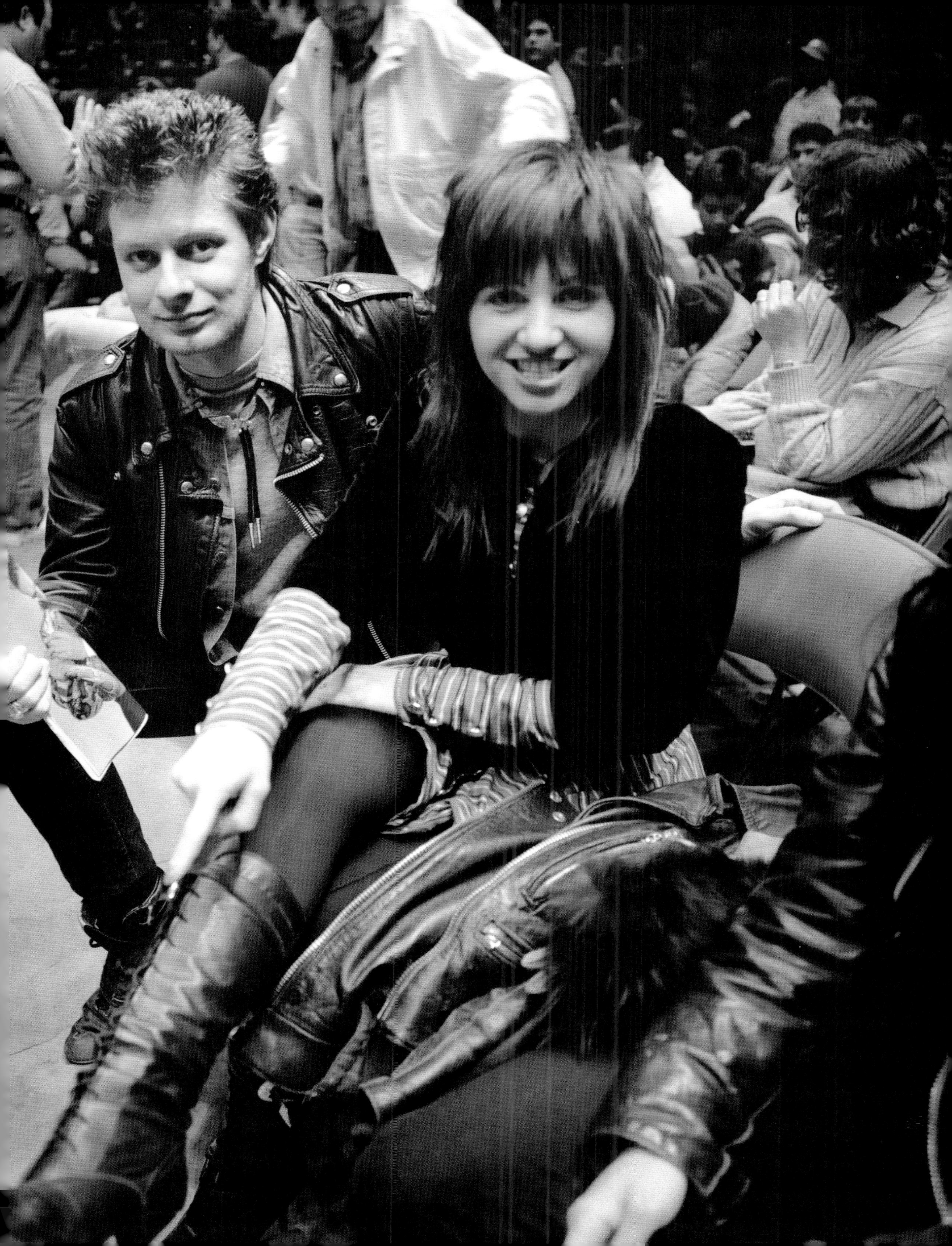

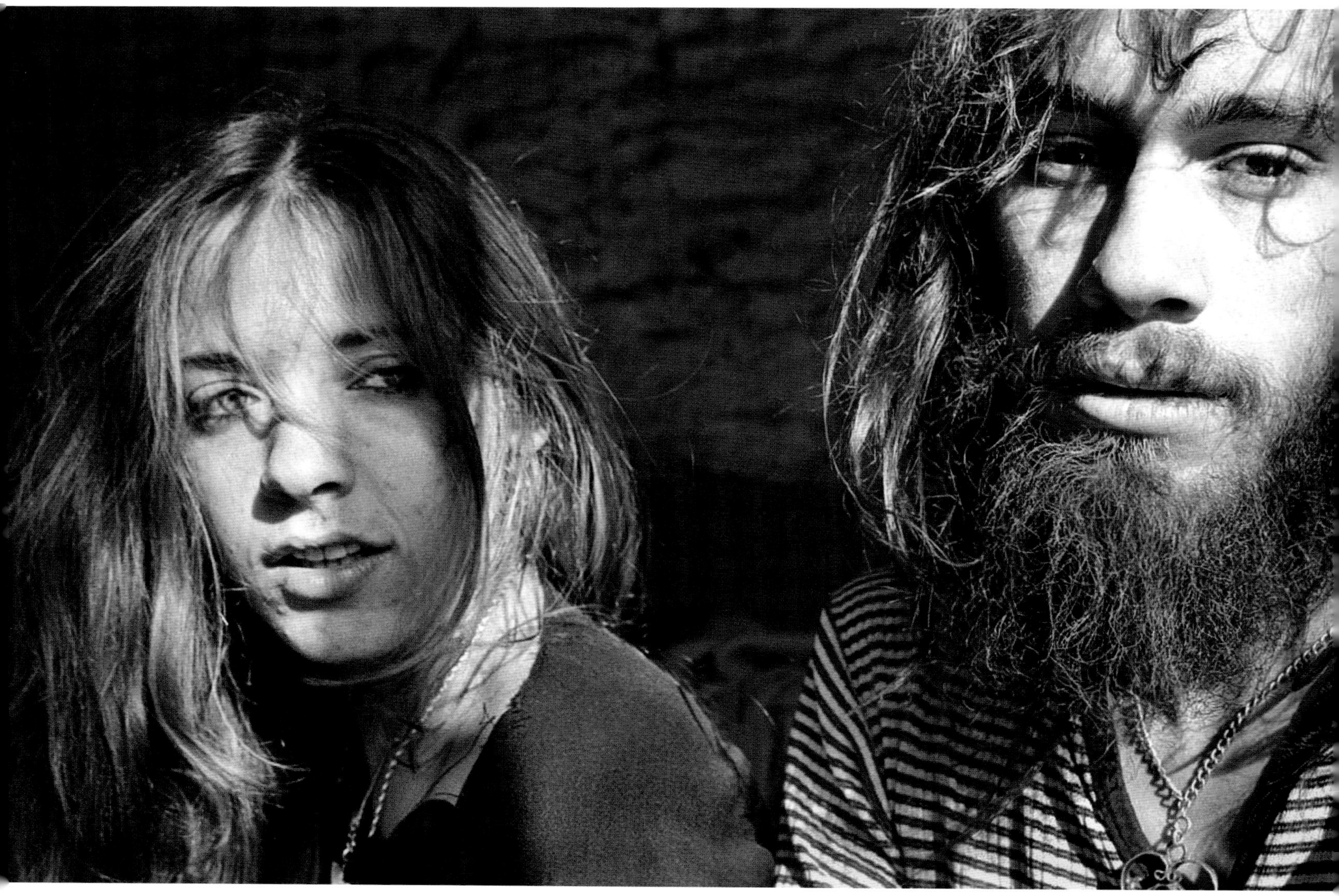

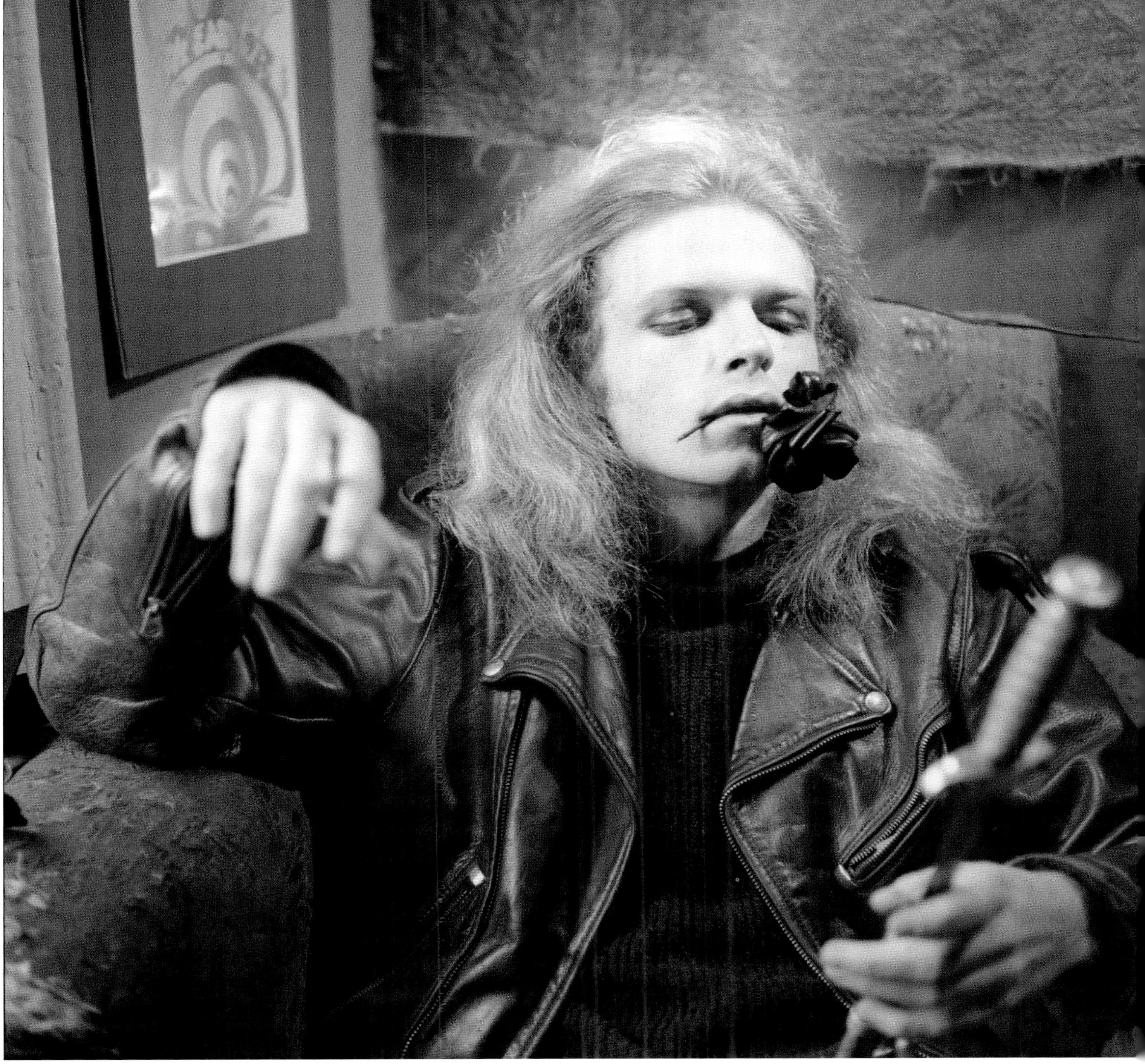

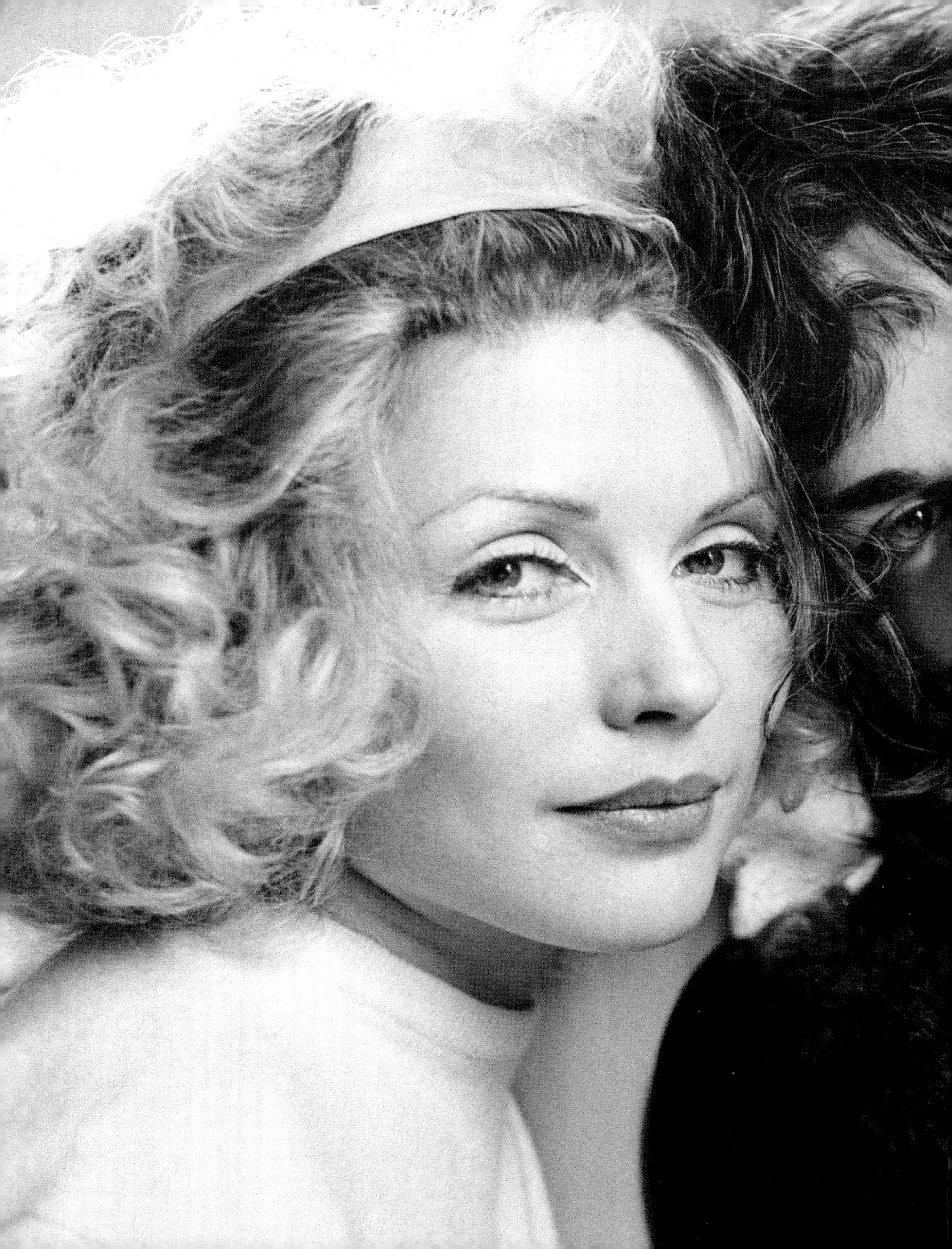

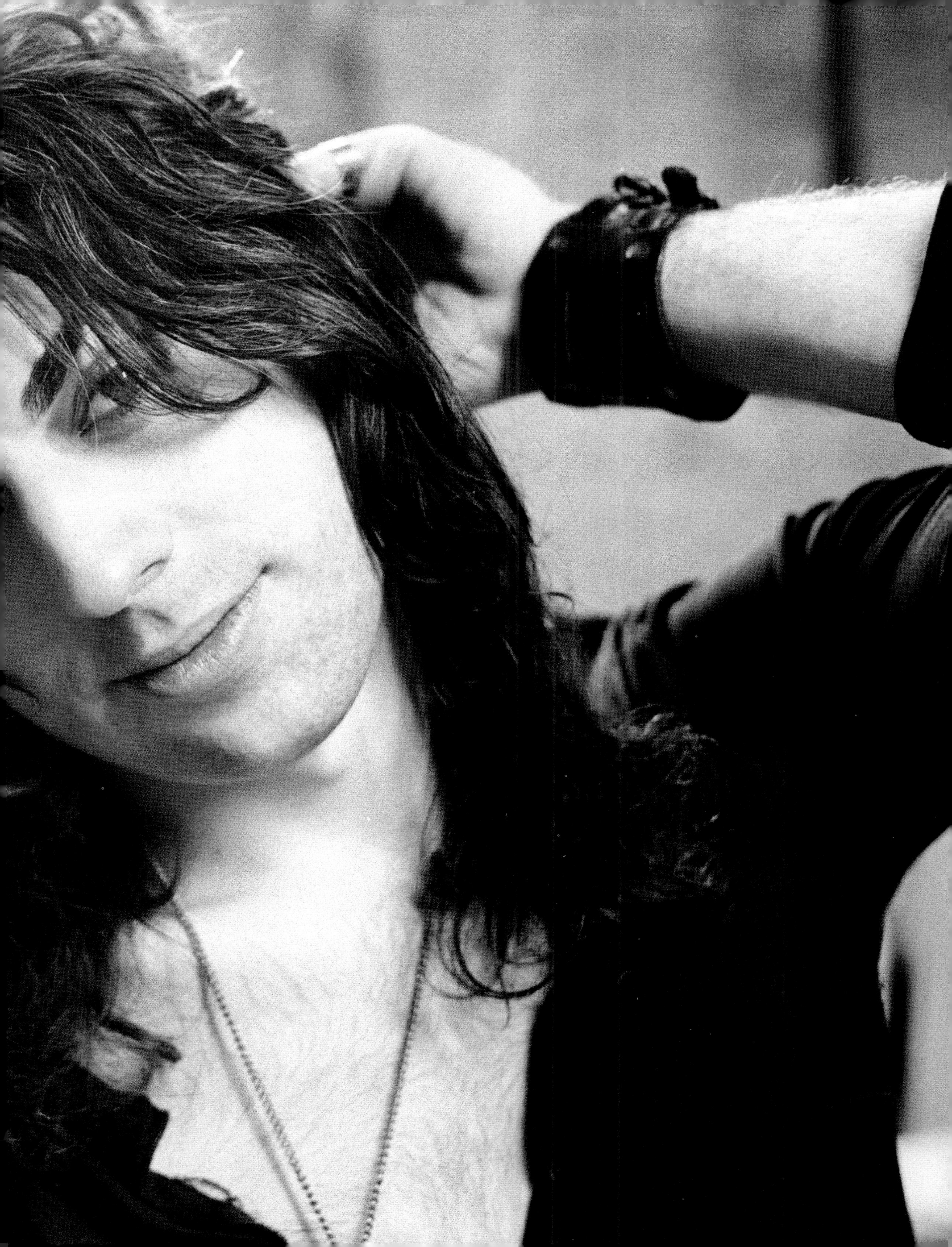

Debbie in her *Creem* T-shirt.

PREVIOUS PAGES:
Debbie and me, early 1974. Another shot by a guest with my camera; this person was good, I look human.

PAGE 156:
Sweetbryar and Robin Ludwig. I grew up with Robin in Brooklyn. He was a freak's freak. While my friends and I would be harassed for our long hair and style, Robin was so exceptionally strange that he was left alone. I remember an incident in junior high school—it was Robin's birthday and he took it upon himself to distribute daffodils to girls on the bus. The bus was populated by various juvenile delinquent gangster types (this was around 1965, 1966), but his actions were so alien that he was ignored instead of murdered.

PAGE 157:
Benton Quinn was our 'landlord' on the Bowery. Benton was a great downtown character. He'd taken over the lease of this three-story loft above a liquor store from Anne Wehrer, who had been Iggy's girlfriend. When Debbie and I were between living spaces he invited us to stay there, and it was there that most of the early Blondie music was formed and rehearsed.

PAGES 164–69:
Iggy on the Idiot tour, 1977; Debbie with Meatloaf; Debbie with Bowie on the Idiot tour, 1977; and Debbie with Ray Davies, 1978.

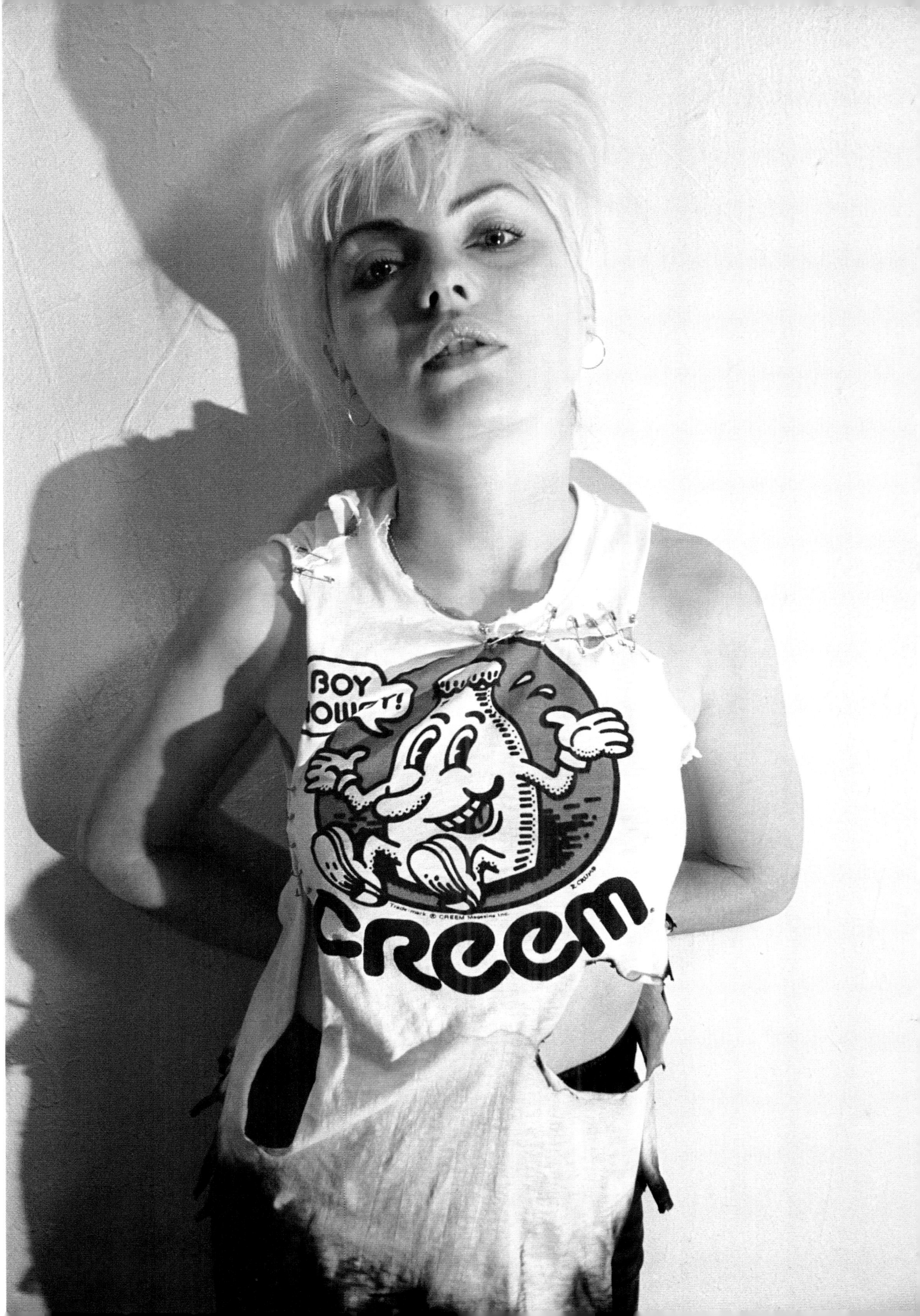
BOY
CREEM

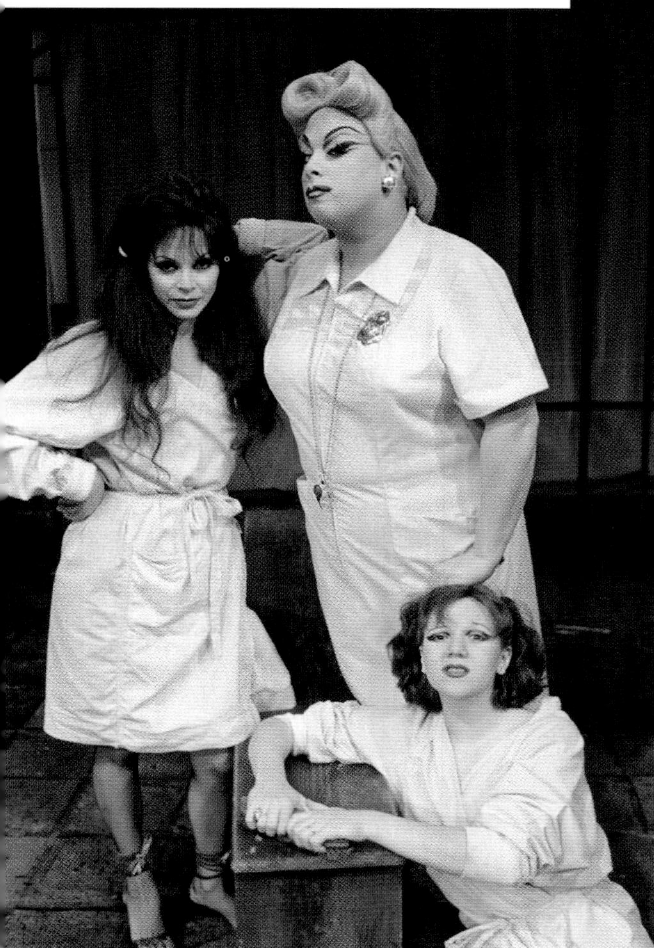

Fanne Foxe, Divine, and Lisa Jane Persky during the second production of Tom Eyen's *Women Behind Bars* in 1976, at the Truck and Warehouse Theatre, Lower East Side.

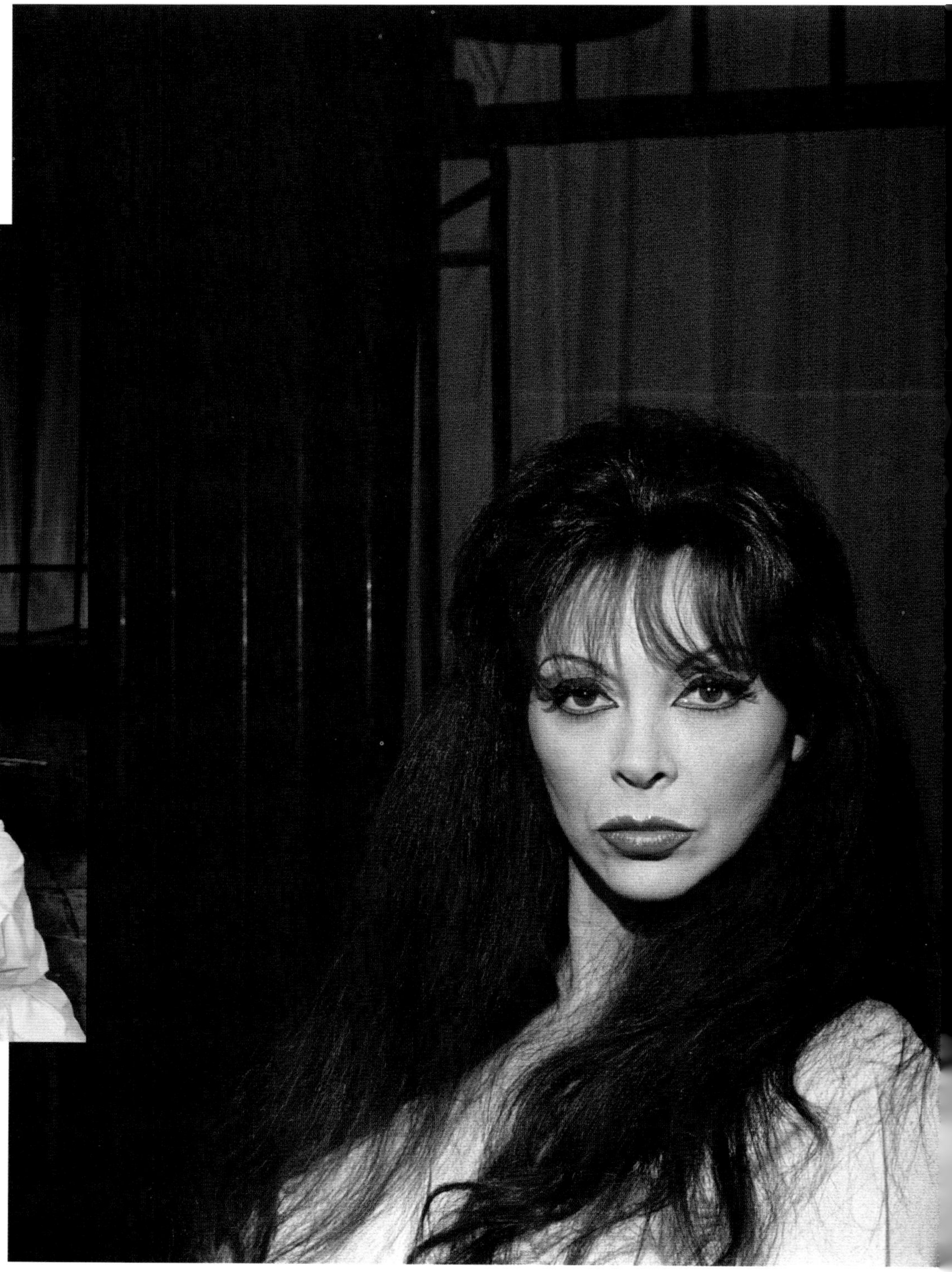

When I was thirteen, in 1963, I was turned on by pictures coming out of the UK related to the Profumo Affair. John Profumo was the Secretary of State for War in the conservative government of Harold Macmillan. He had a fling with Christine Keeler, a nineteen-year-old model, and soon the tabloids were filled with sexy pictures of her that I couldn't avoid. The era of the modern political sex scandal had arrived.

Wilbur Mills was an American congressman and Chairman of the House Committee on Ways and Means from 1958 to 1974. He was often referred to as "the most powerful man in Washington" and was even considered as a Democratic presidential candidate in 1972.

On October 9, 1974, Mills, who was tanked, was stopped in his car by the police. He had apparently been having some sort of drunken altercation

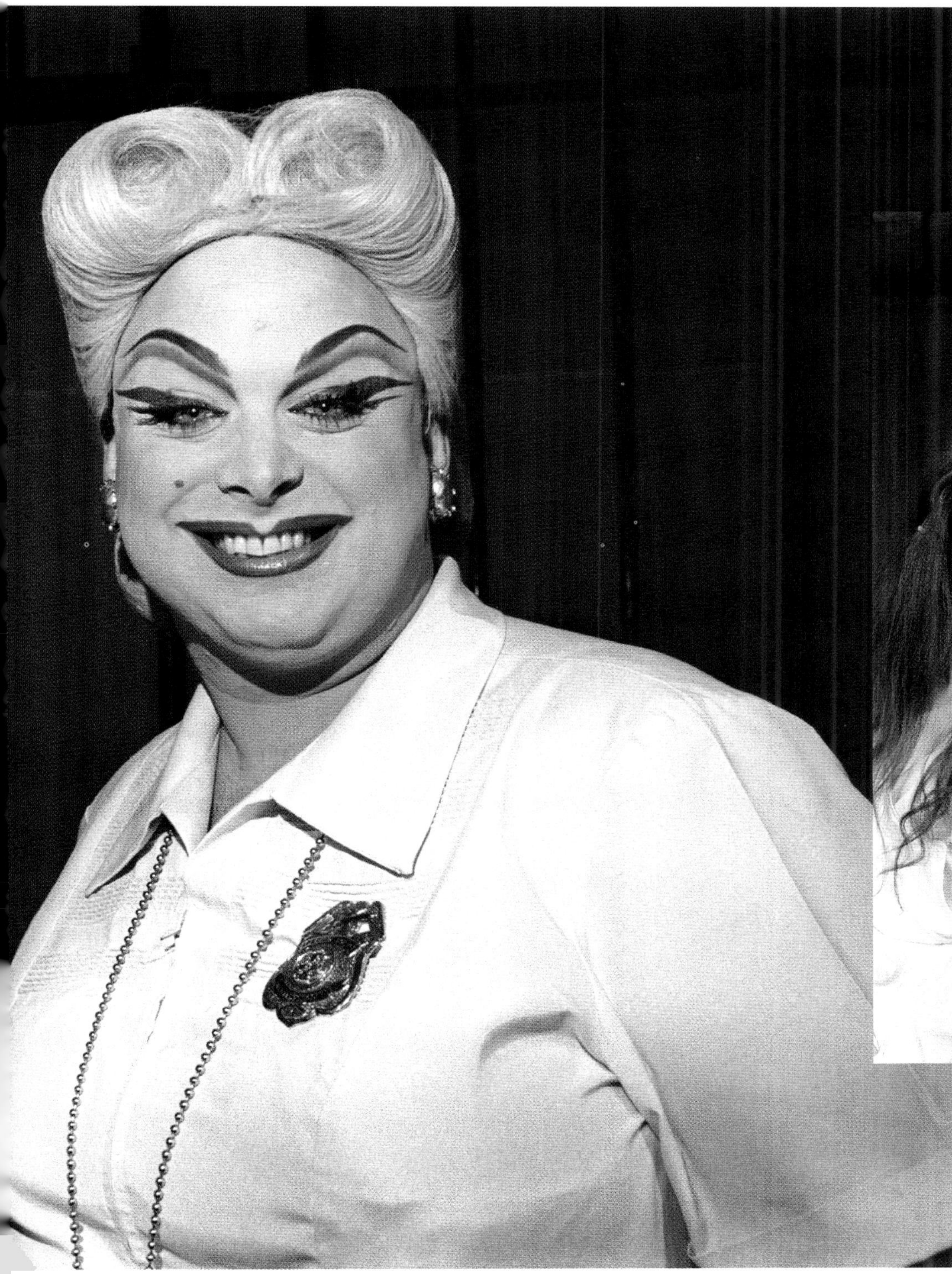

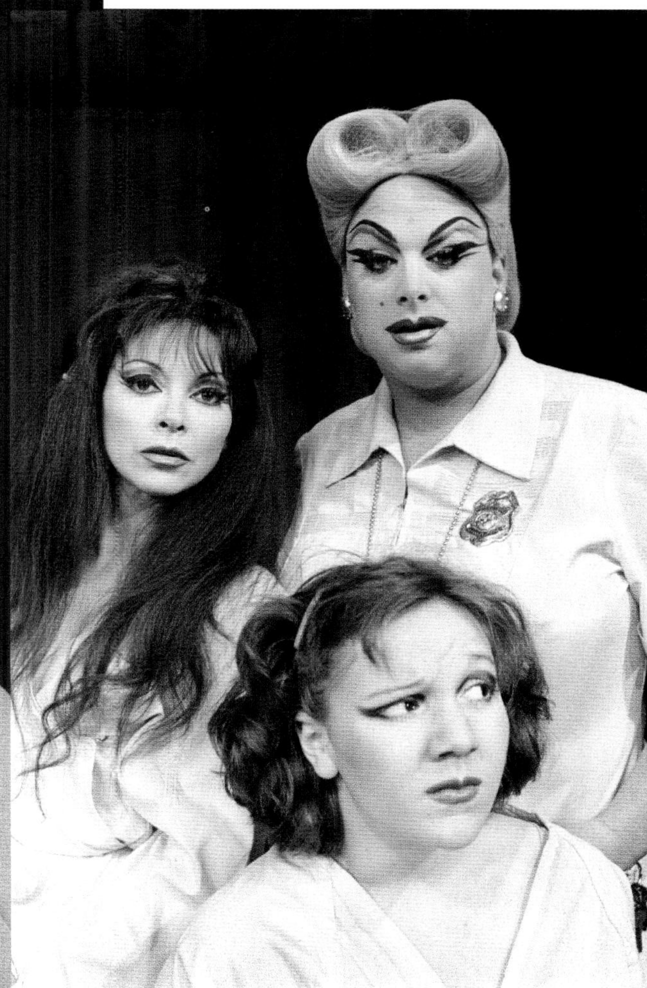

with Fanne Foxe, an exotic dancer. When police approached the car, Fanne ran out of the car and jumped into a nearby river. She was taken to a local mental hospital for observation. Mills was still re-elected to congress in November in spite of the large scandal fallout, and later that same month—apparently just to complete a cycle of self-destruction—he appeared with Foxe's husband onstage at a strip joint in Boston and then held a drunken press conference from her dressing room. Soon after, he quit the Ways and Means Committee and went into AA and rehab.

Fanne appearing in *Women Behind Bars* couldn't have been more appropriate.

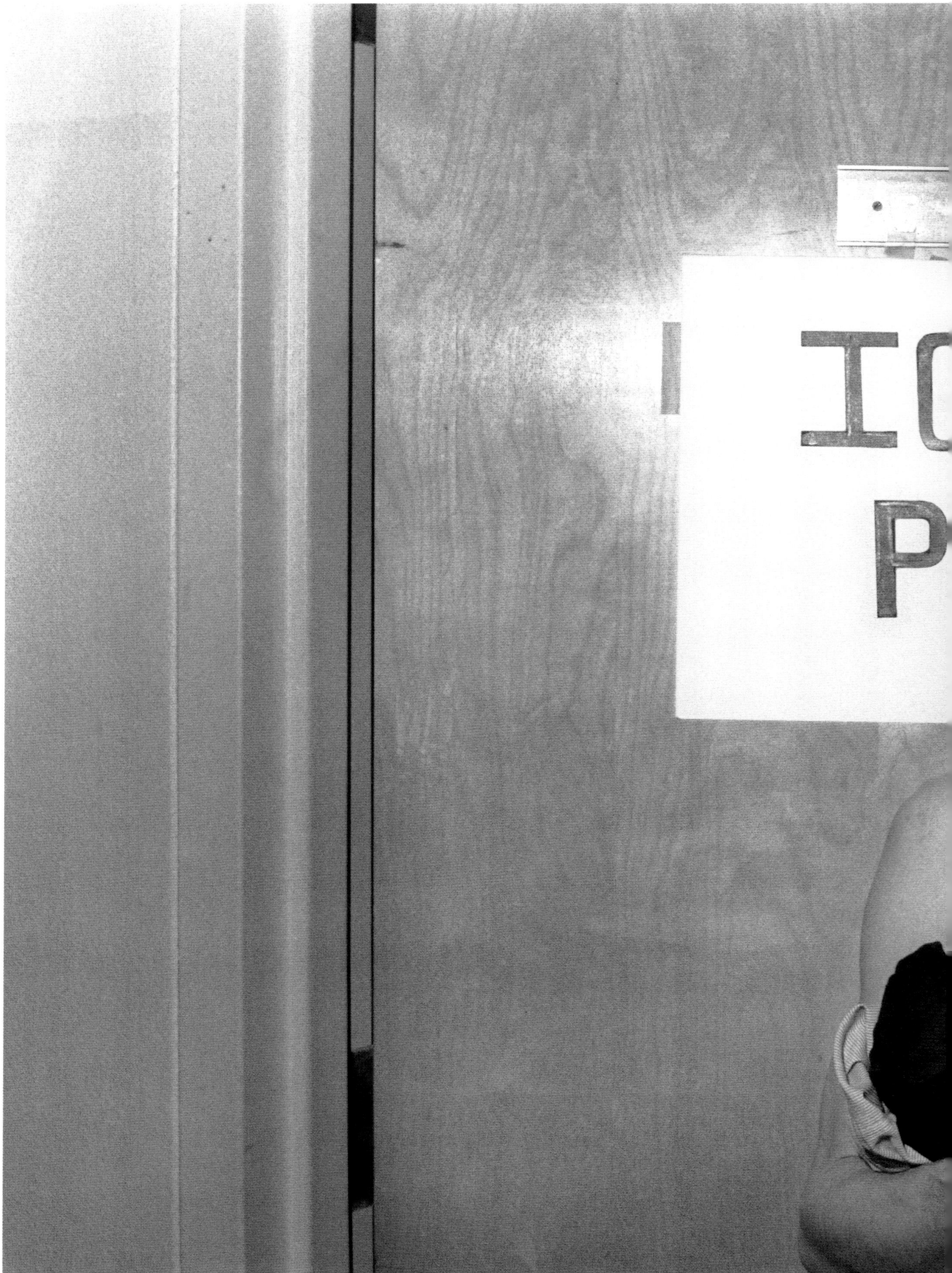

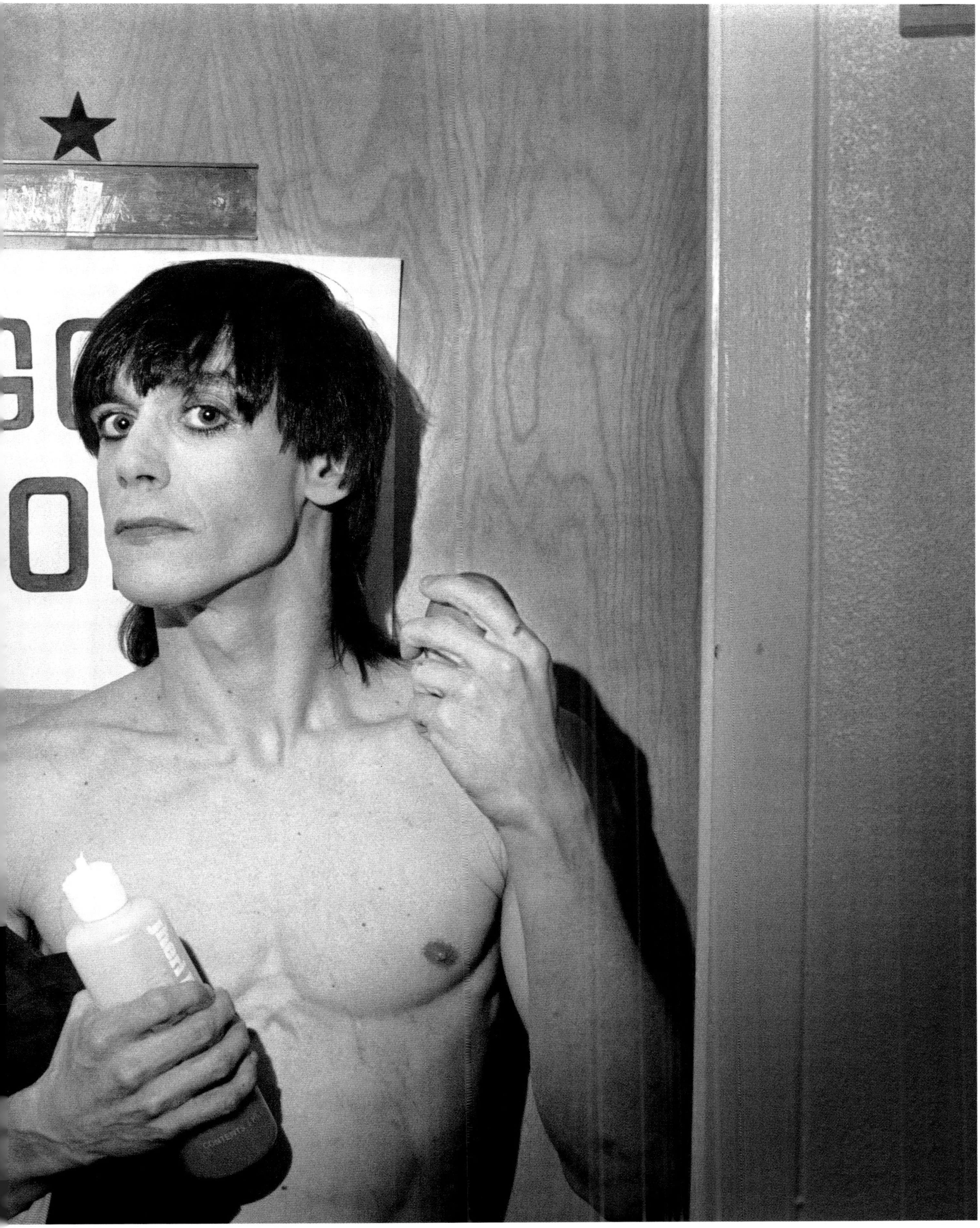

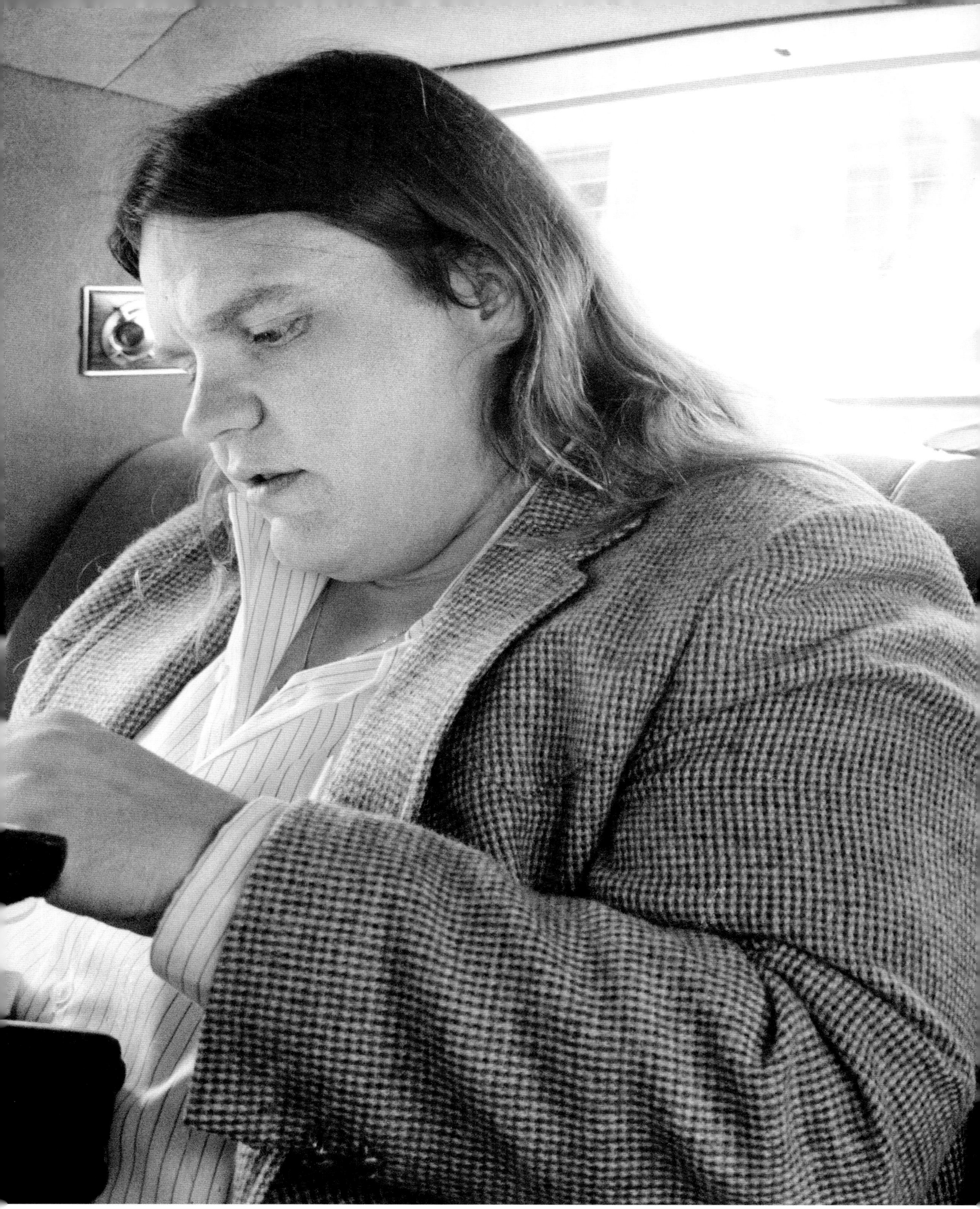

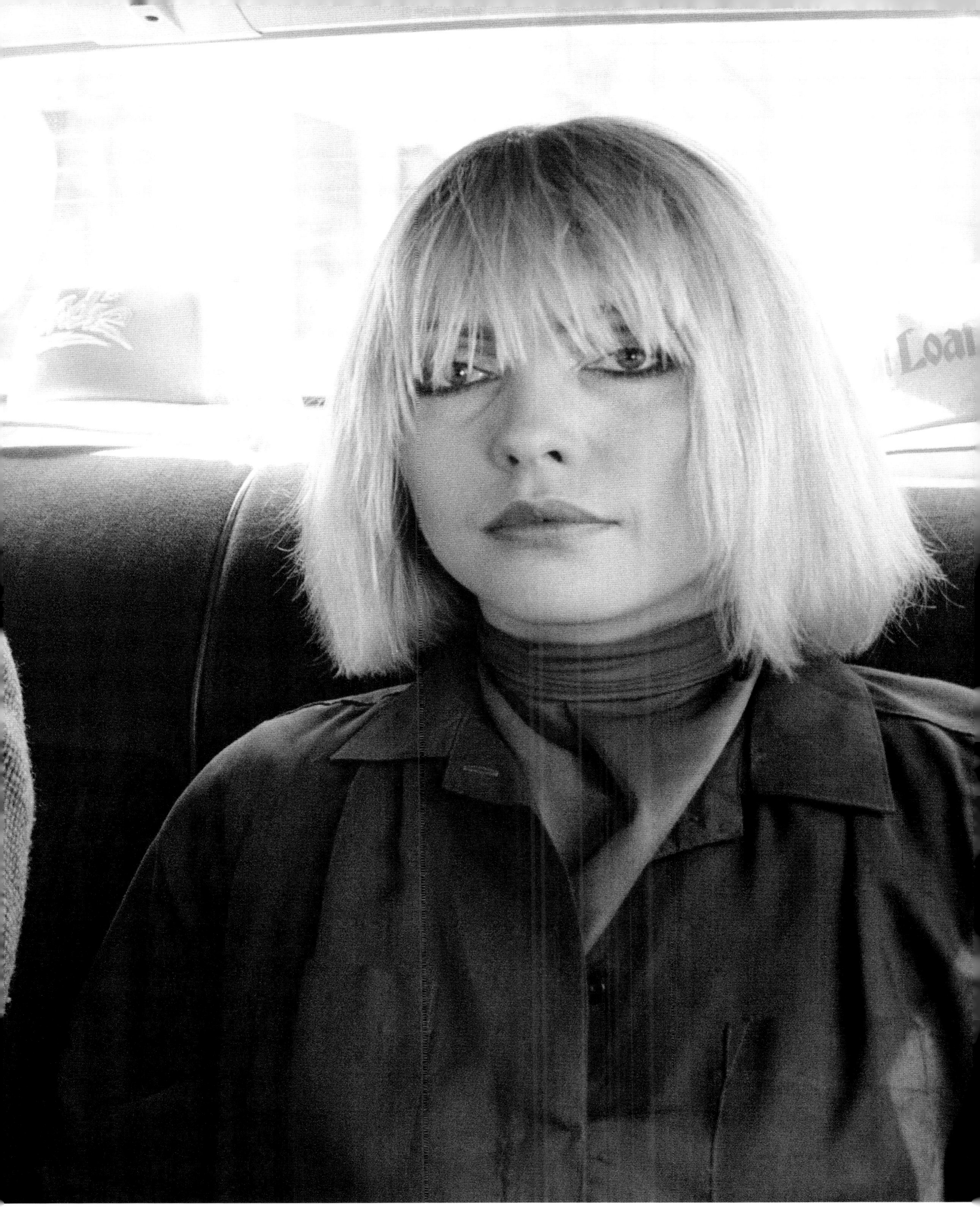

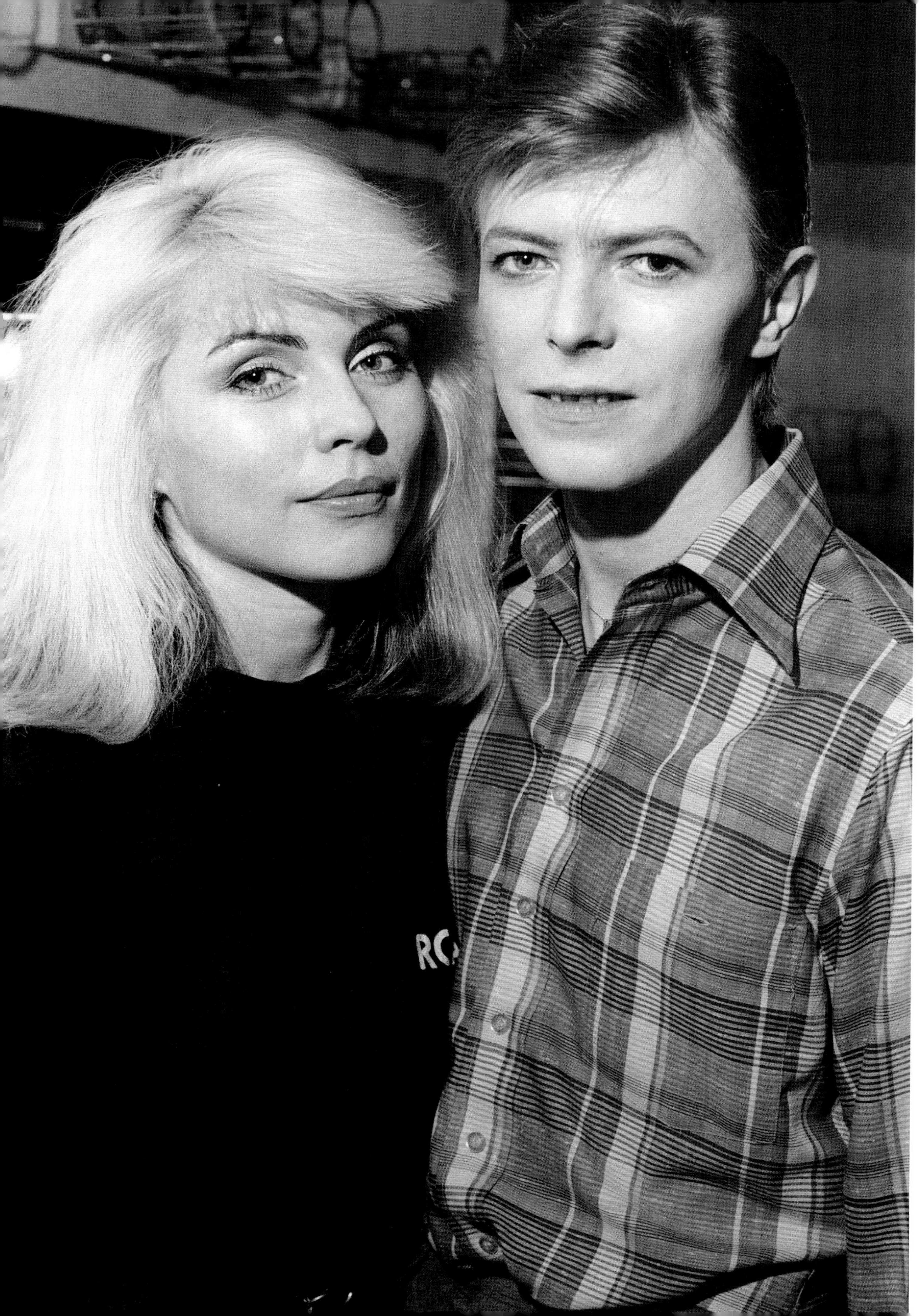

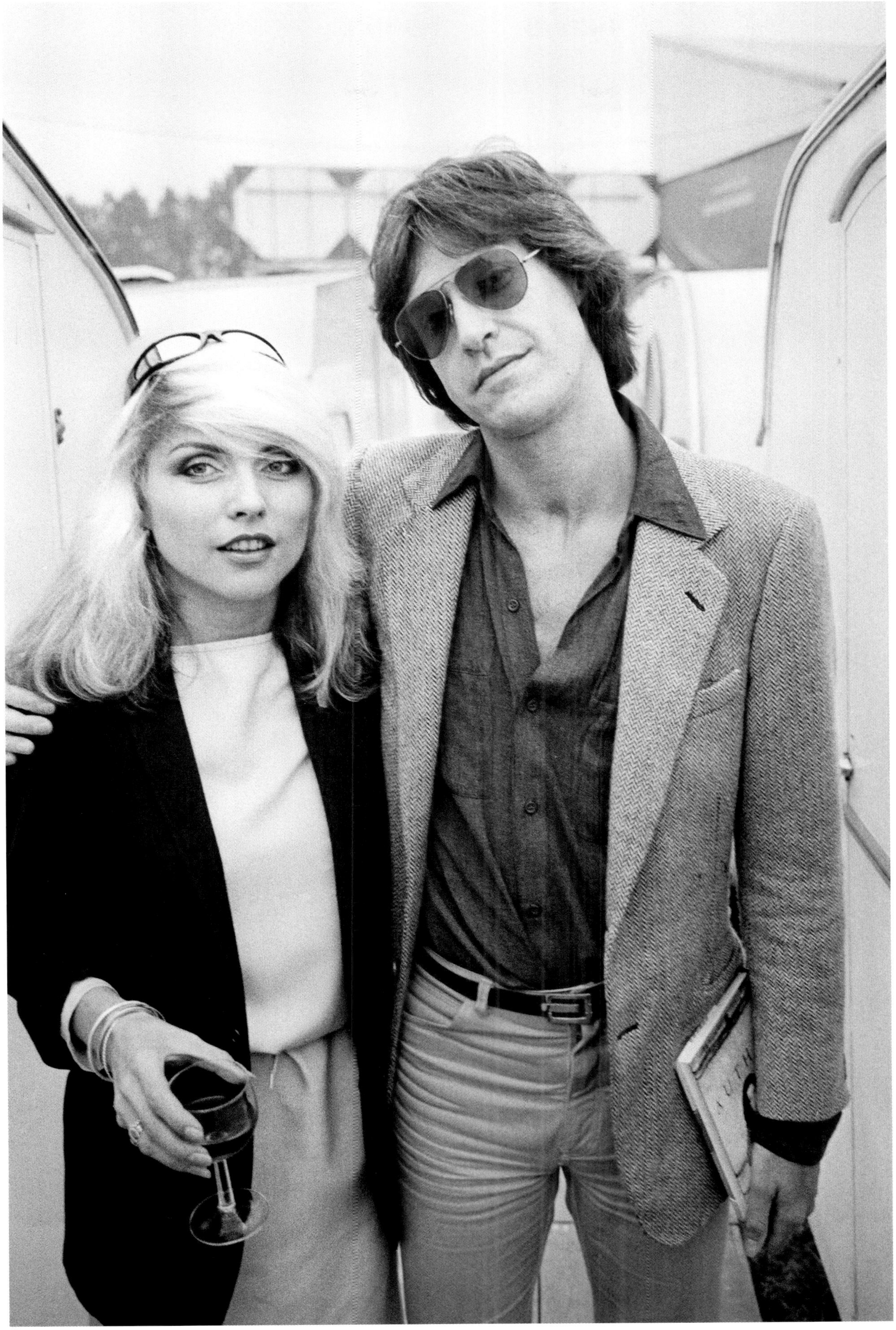

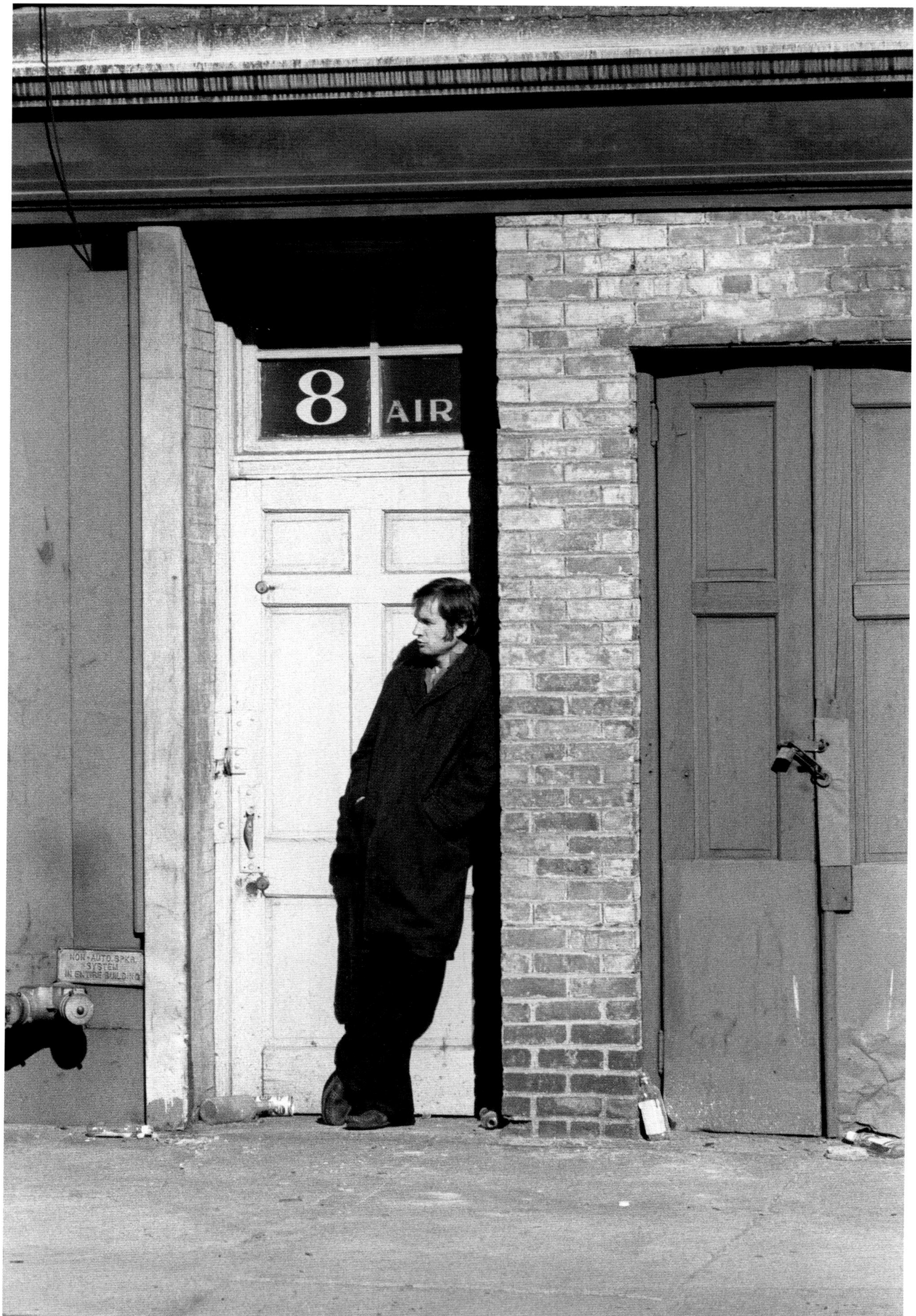
8 AIR
NON-AUTO SPKR SYSTEM IN ENTIRE BUILDING

THE OFFICE

I used to pass these guys whose office I think was on 23rd Street. I was glad then that I wasn't anywhere near this type of reality. The 'normal' world was all around, maybe a little more separated from the freak universe than it is now. I've never had a normal job. I painted a bathroom once for one of my art school teachers, but he said I did a shitty job and had to touch it up himself. Another time my buddy applied for a help wanted situation he found on a flyer on a bulletin board at the School of Visual Arts (this was where I'd see flyers for the New York Dolls a little later). The job, which I ended up helping with, involved helping an older woman, a sculptor, organize her huge loft that was full of raw materials prior to her moving

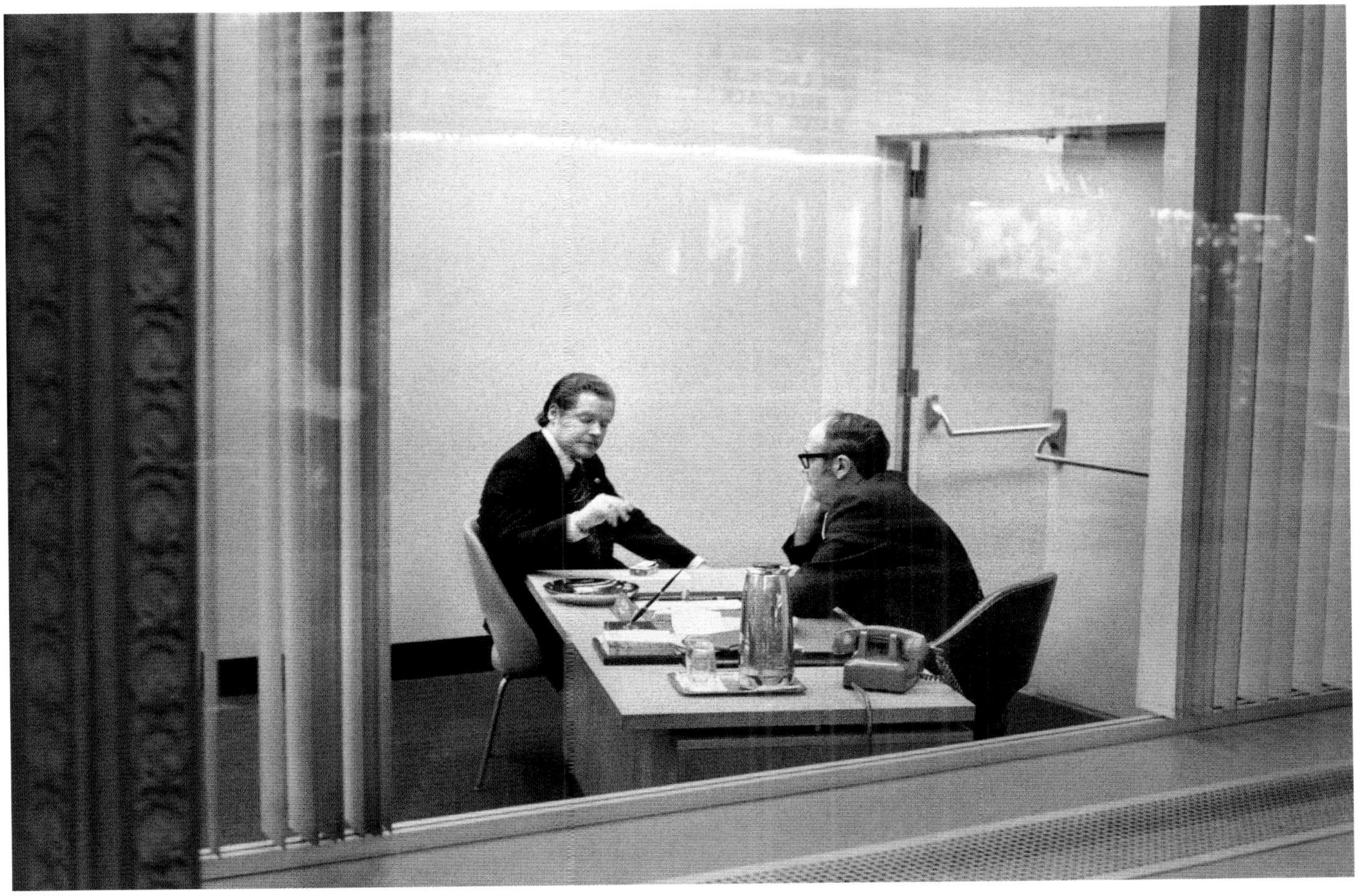

The 'AIR' sign stands for 'artist in residence.' The city would allow working artists to live in commercially zoned spaces. The program is long gone.

somewhere else. The gigantic space was filled with Louise Nevelson–like constructions and endless rows of shelves filled with metal and wood elements. I wish I knew this person's name; I may have heard it once in the few days my friend and I were struggling with this stuff. It was brutal. She must have been in this location for twenty or more years, and her collection of material of course bordered on obsessive hoarding. Pretty quickly I saw that my buddy just wanted to share his suffering and have a little company during his employ with this lady. We would leave exhausted and dirty from what seemed to be pointless Kafkaesque dragging of old barrels of iron rods and such from one spot to another. At the end of an afternoon of toil, we would be handed about twenty bucks. I wanted to murder my friend and forget the whole thing, but we were both too polite and wound up working there for several days before giving up. Maybe that qualifies as a 'normal' job—I don't know.

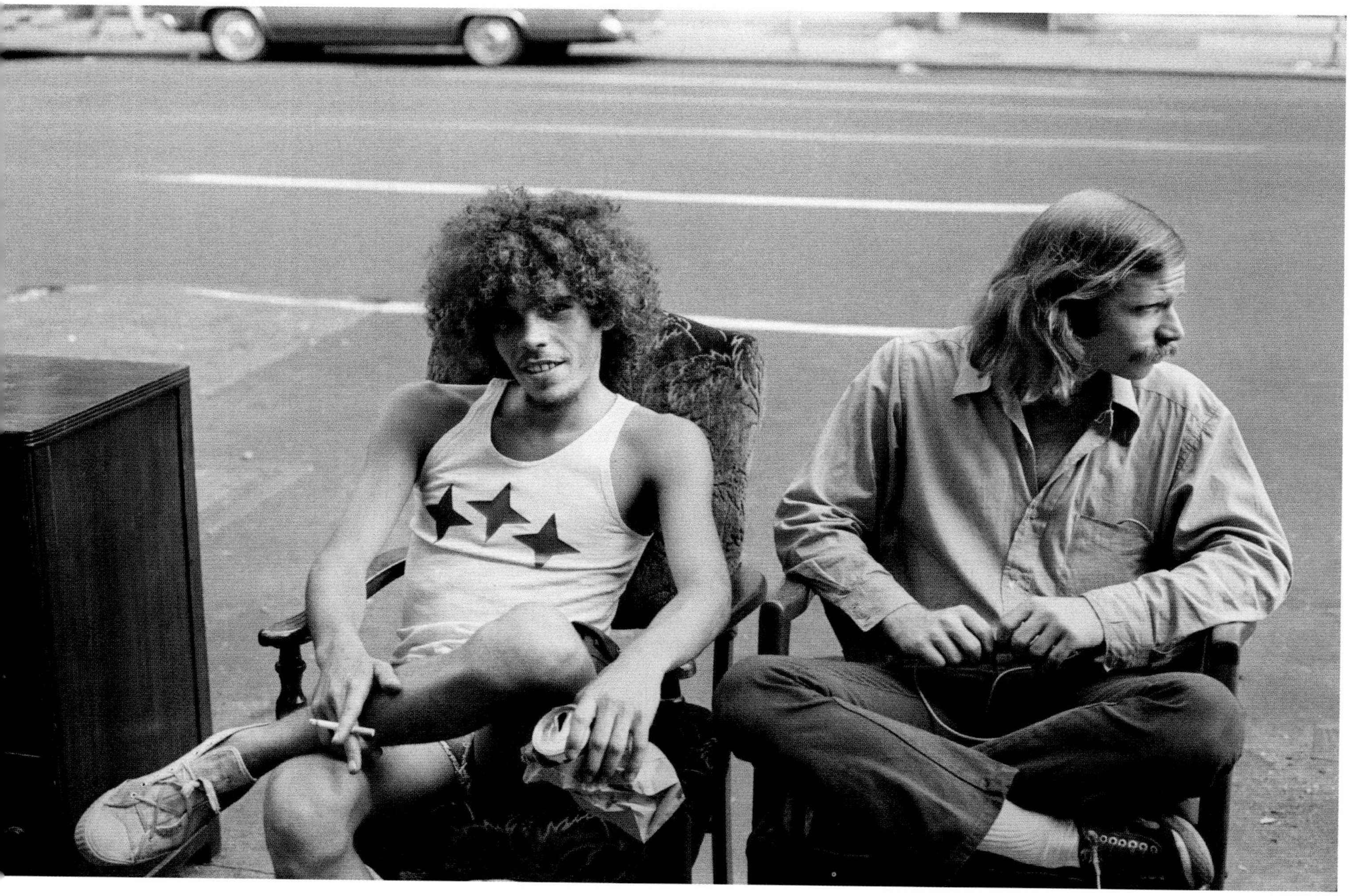

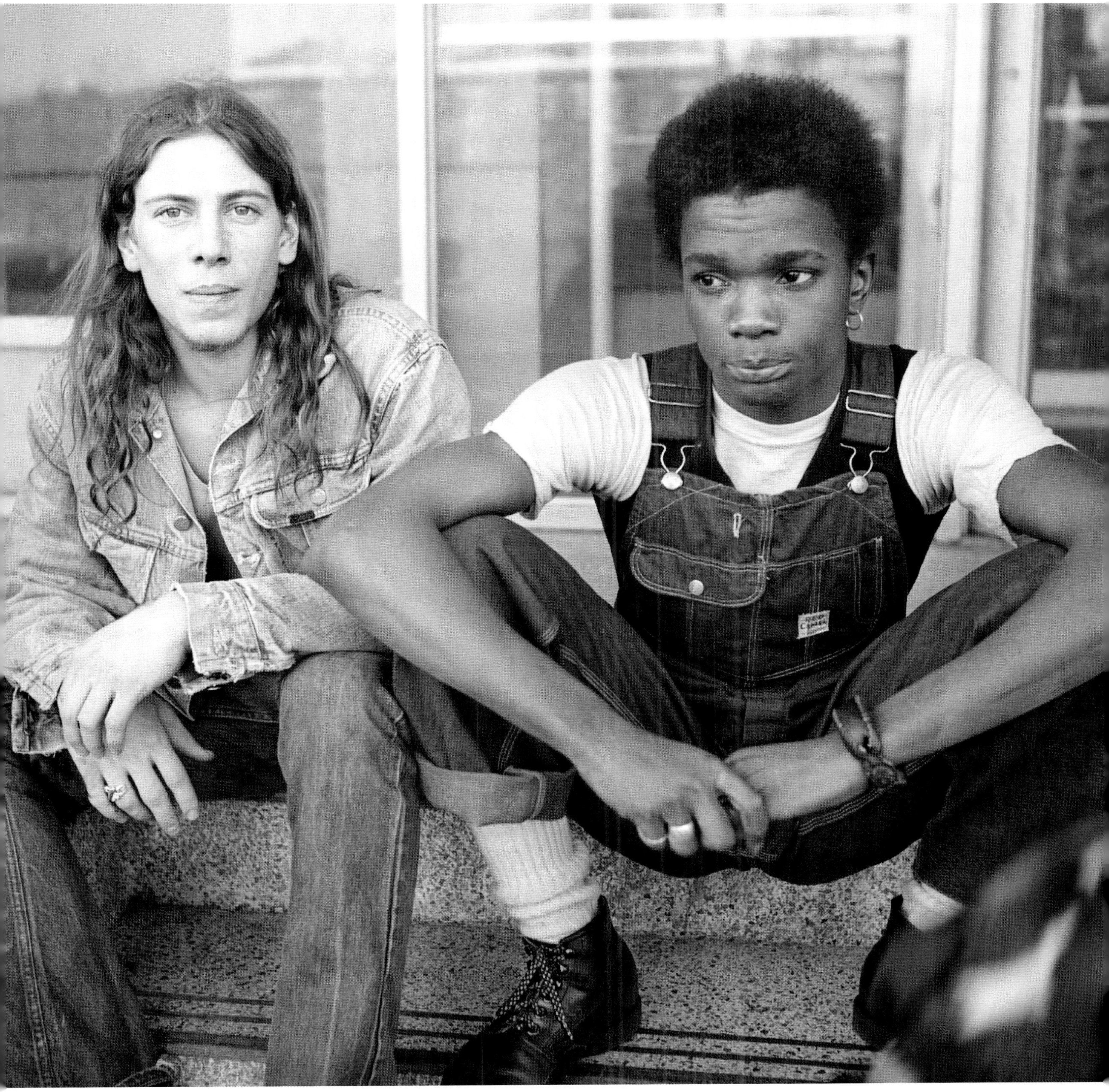

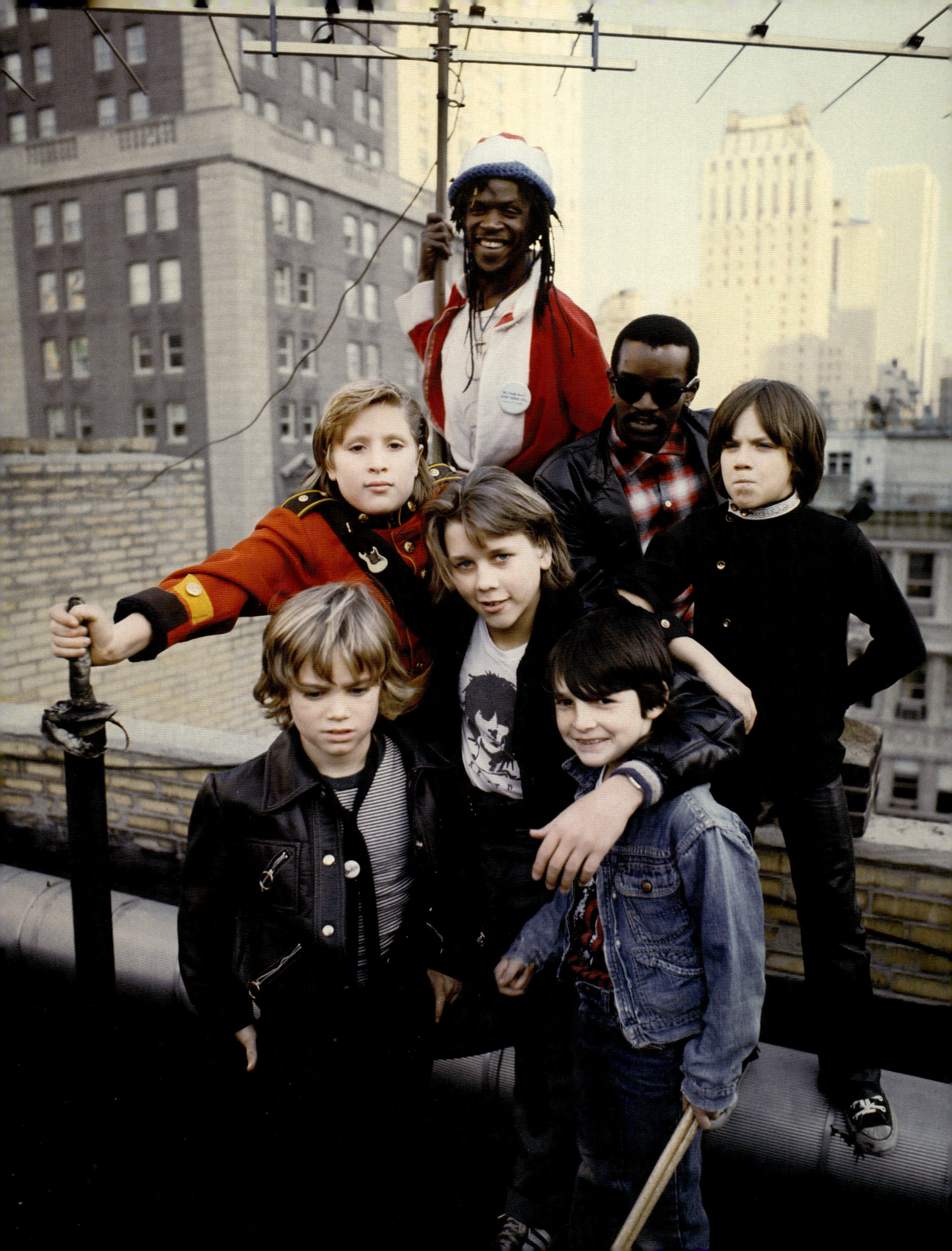

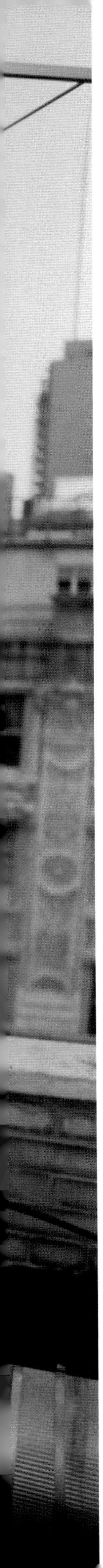

Snuky Tate, Fab 5 Freddy, and kid punk band the Brattles, 1981. The Brattles opened for the Clash at their New York City show at Bonds on Times Square.

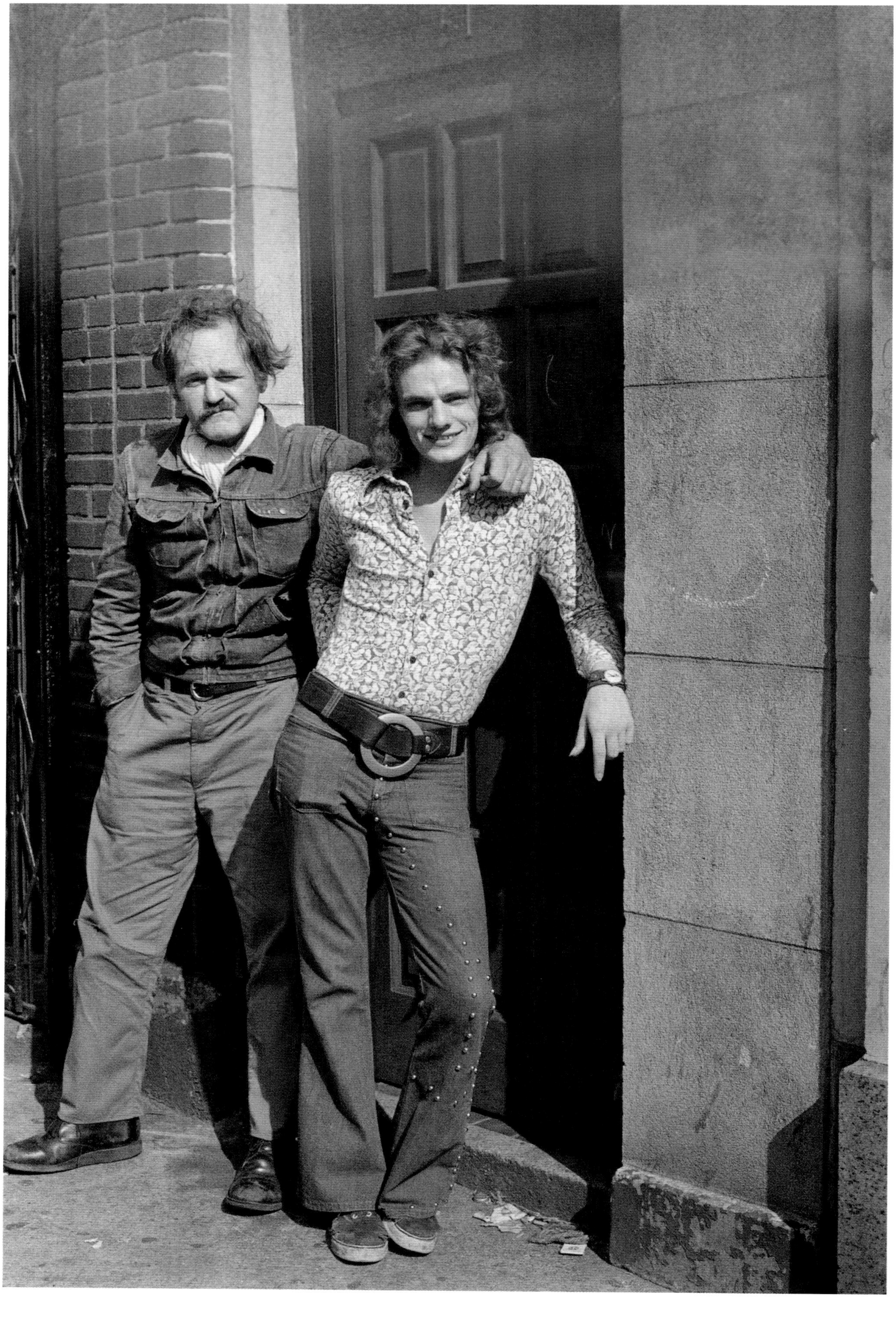

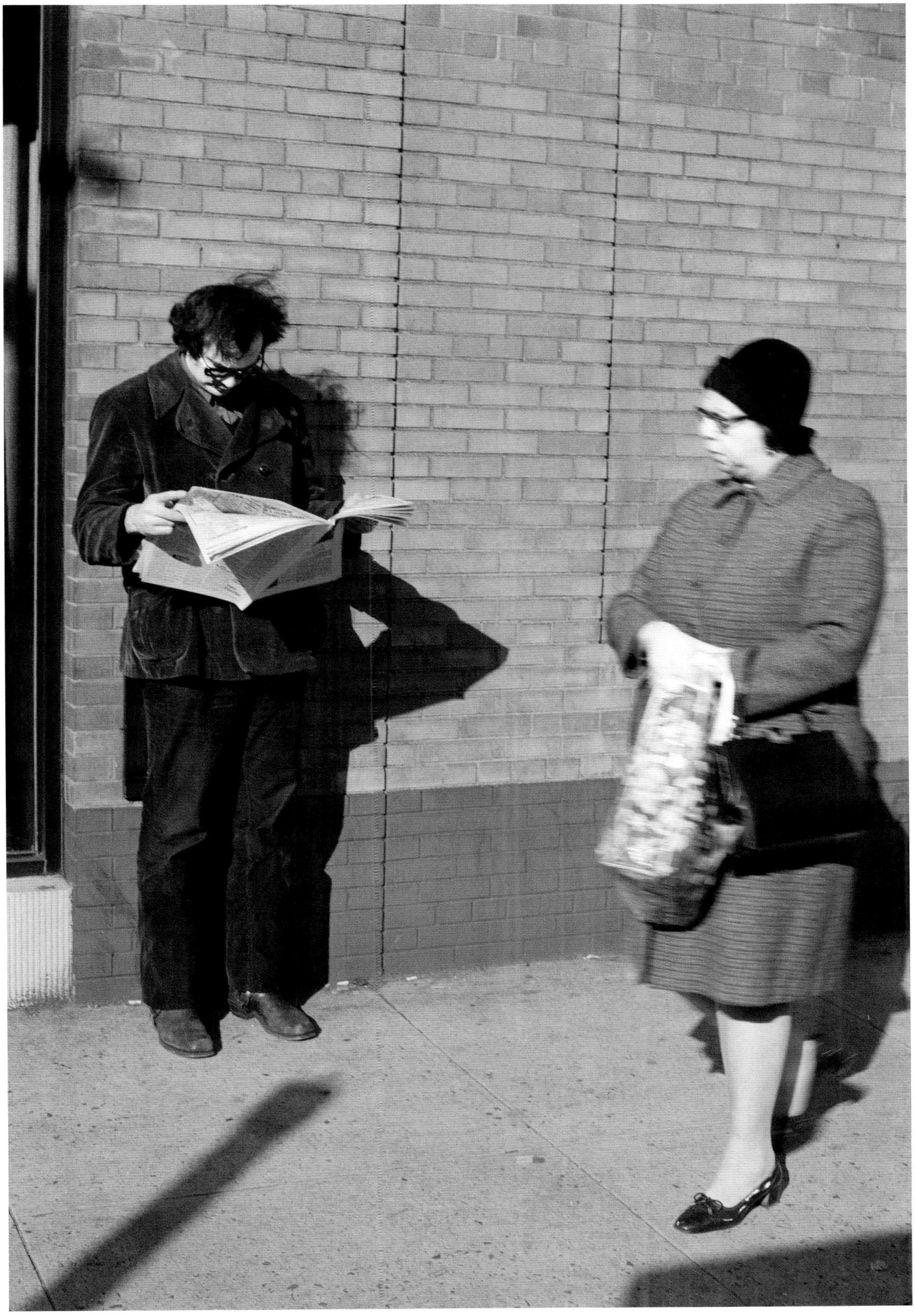

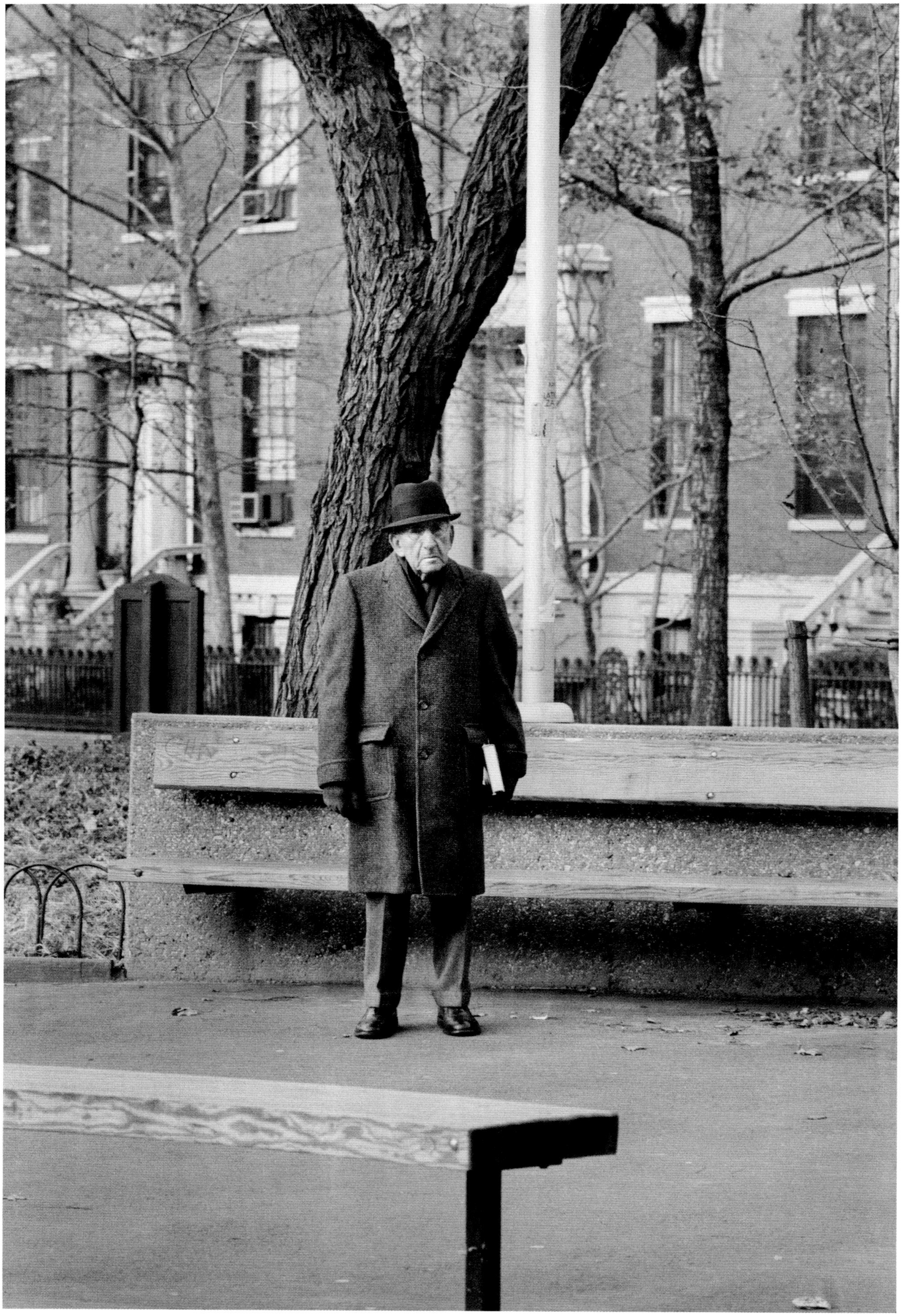

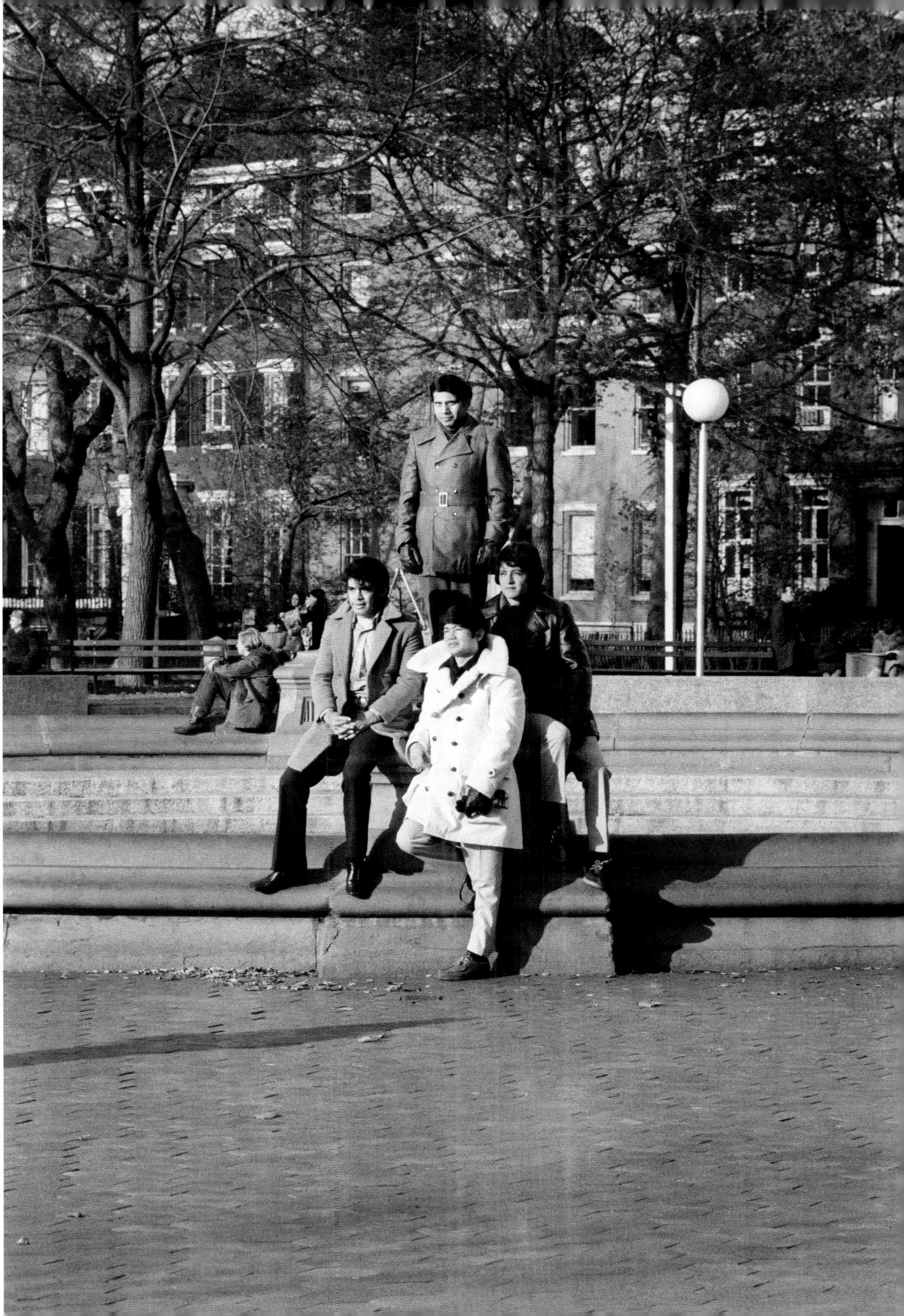

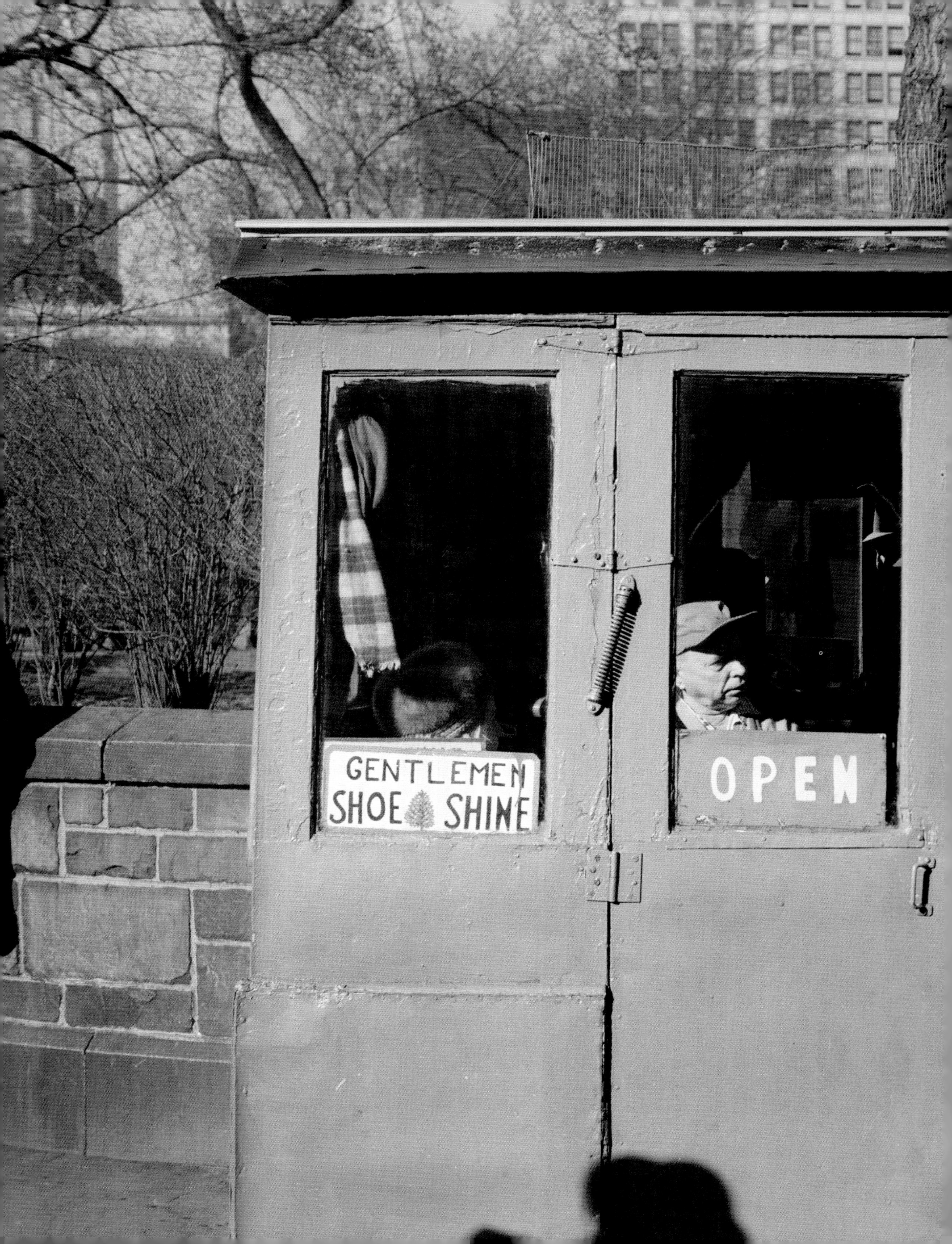
GENTLEMEN
SHOE SHINE
OPEN

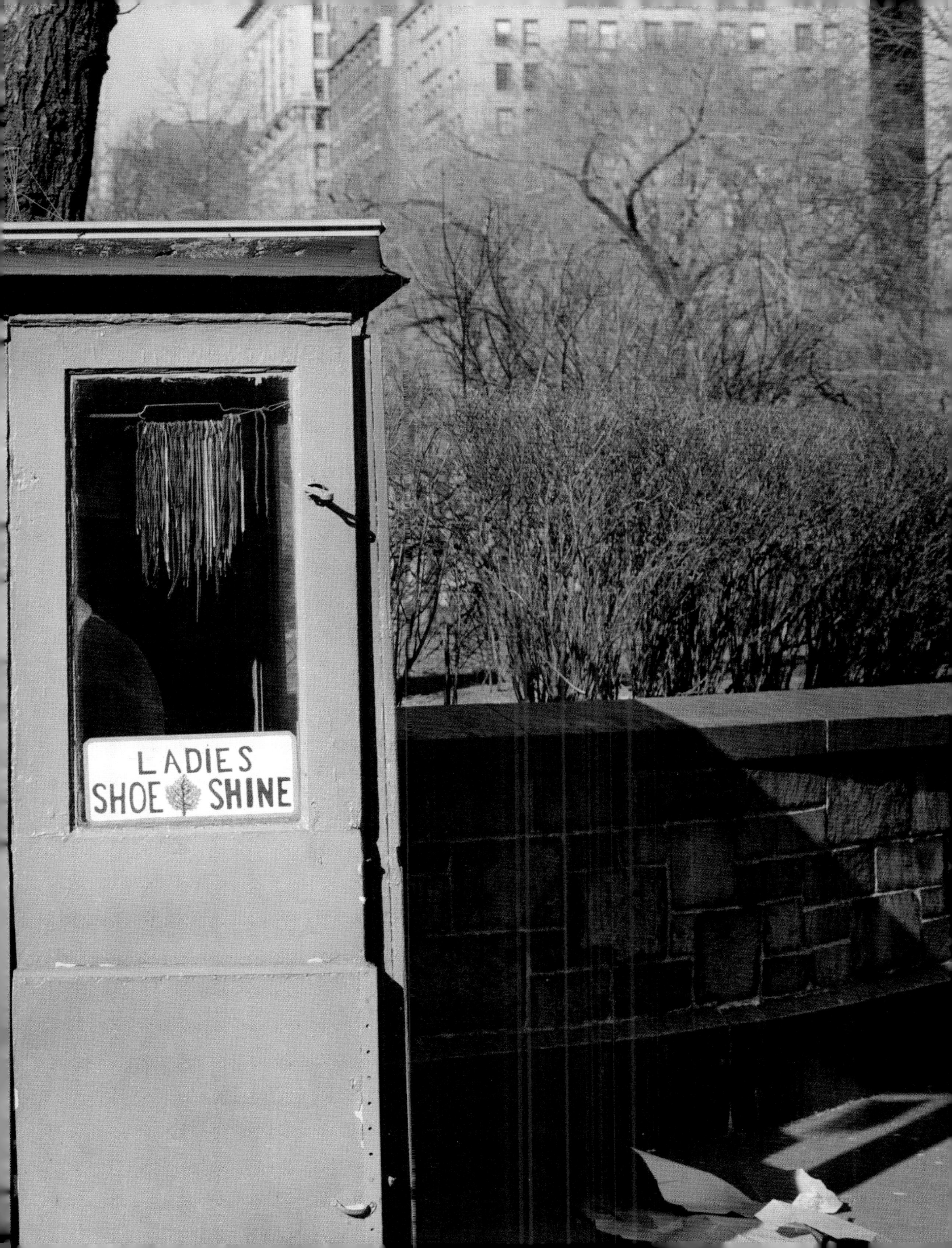
LADIES
SHOE SHINE

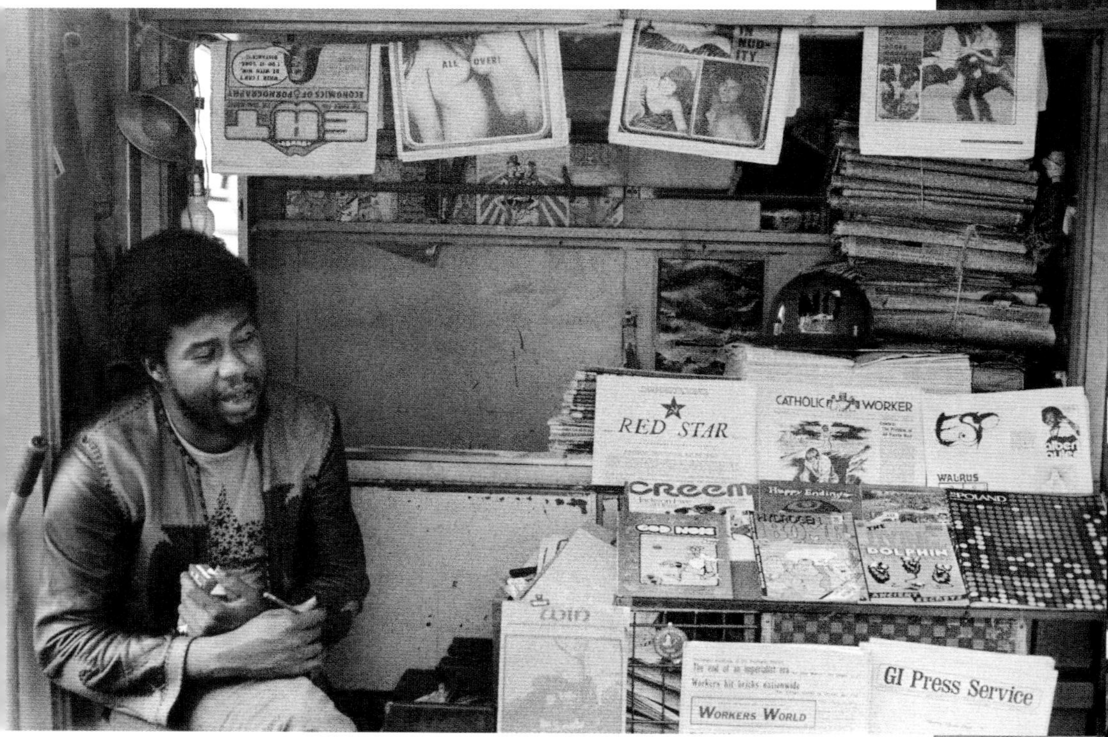

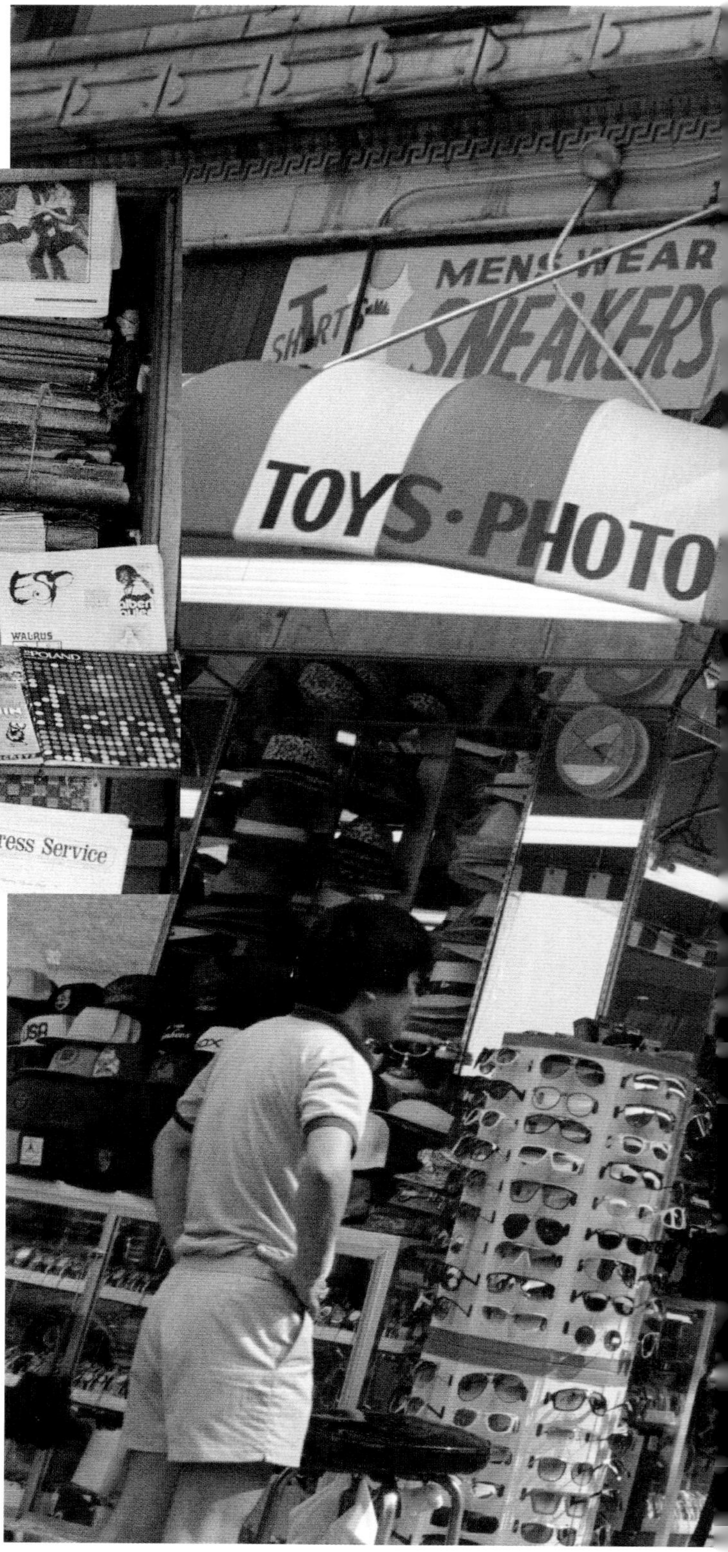

Dude in his radical leftist news stand, 1971–72, downtown. *The Catholic Worker* is still being published. I once found a few copies of *The Masses* on the street; John Reed really was a great writer.

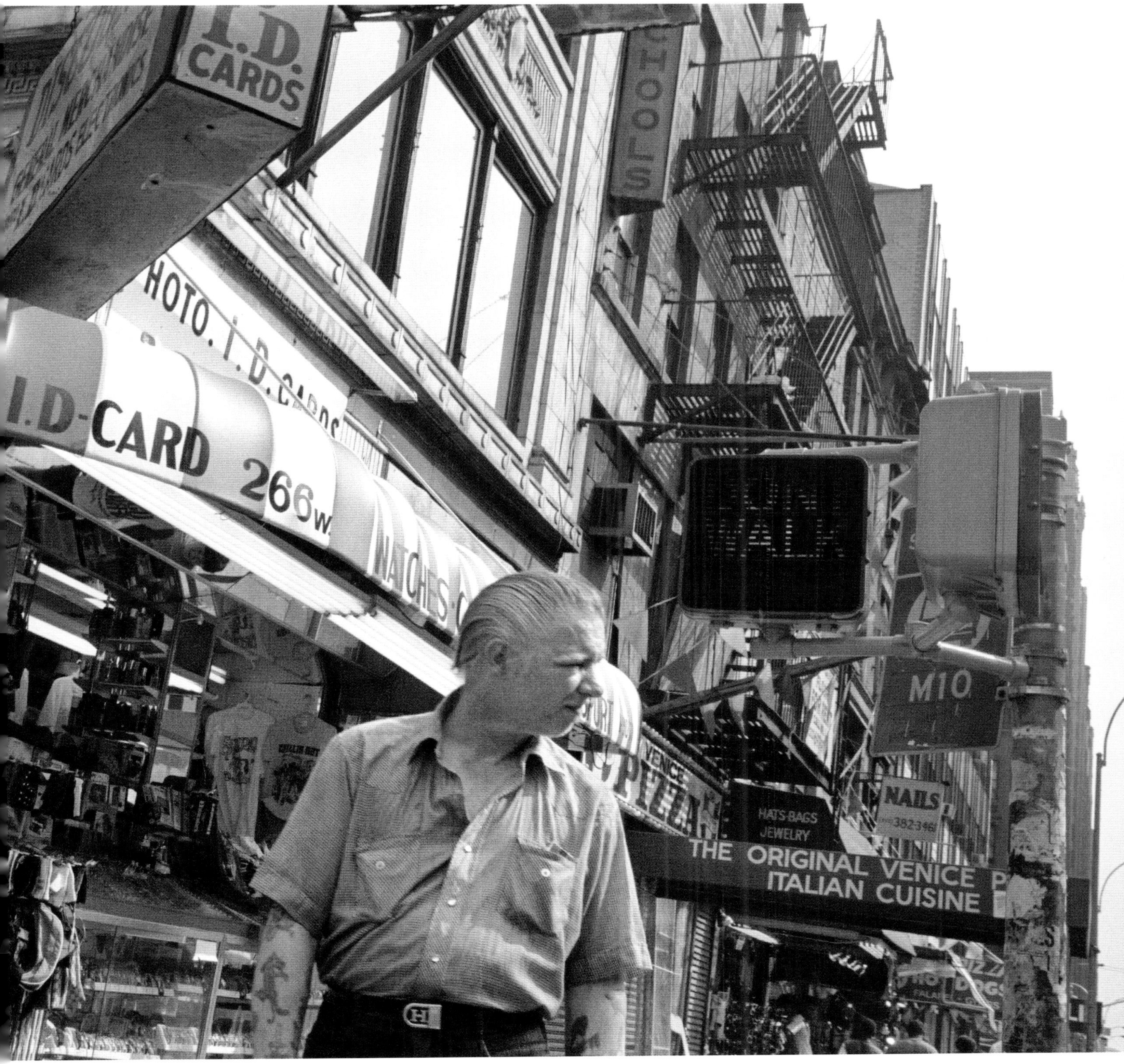
I.D.
CARDS
CHOOLS
HOTO. I.D.
I.D-CARD 266W
WATCHES
WALK
M10
VENICE
PIZZA
HATS·BAGS
JEWELRY
NAILS
382-3461
THE ORIGINAL VENICE P
ITALIAN CUISINE

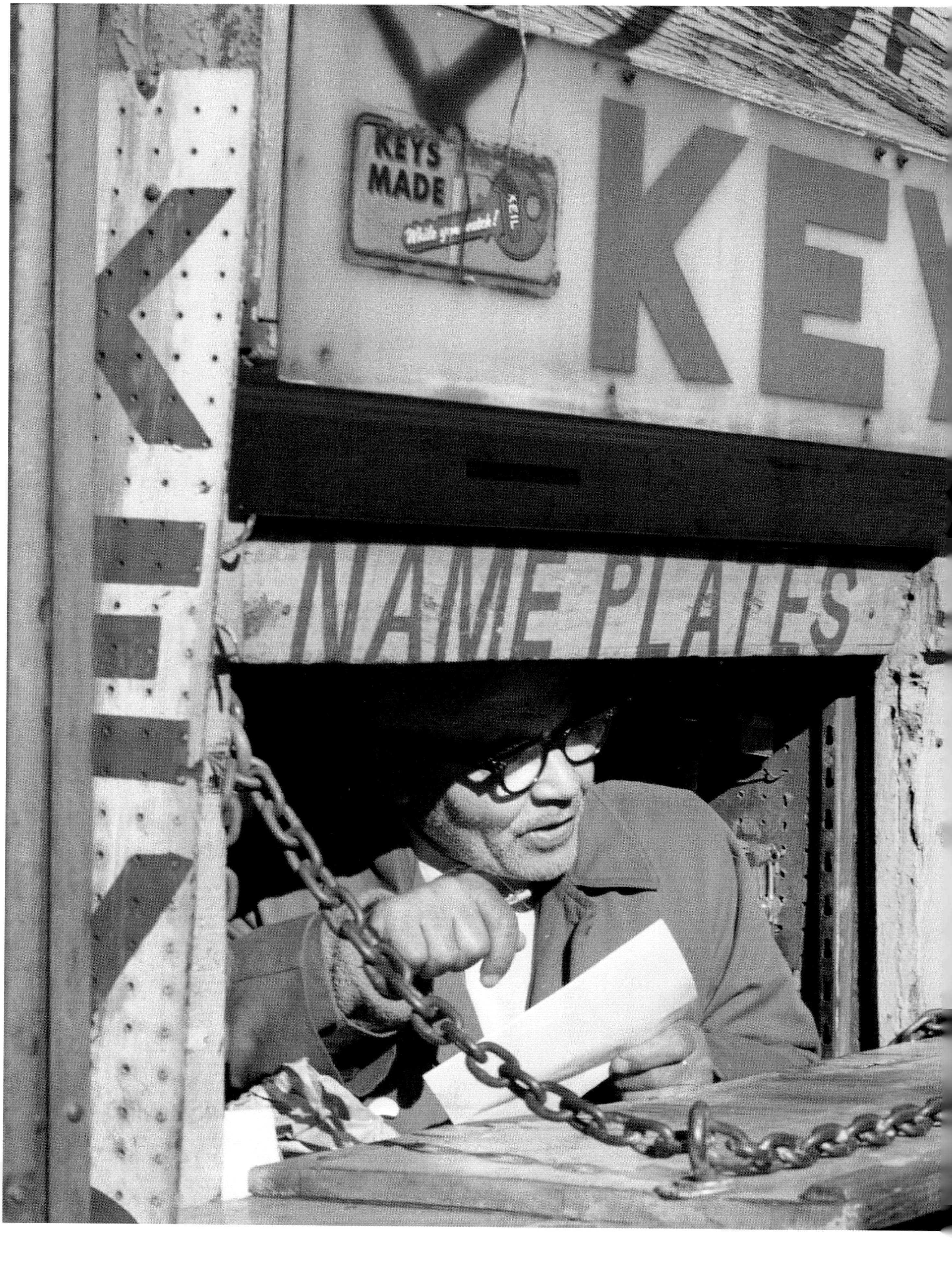
KEYS
MADE
While you watch!
KEIL
NAME PLATES

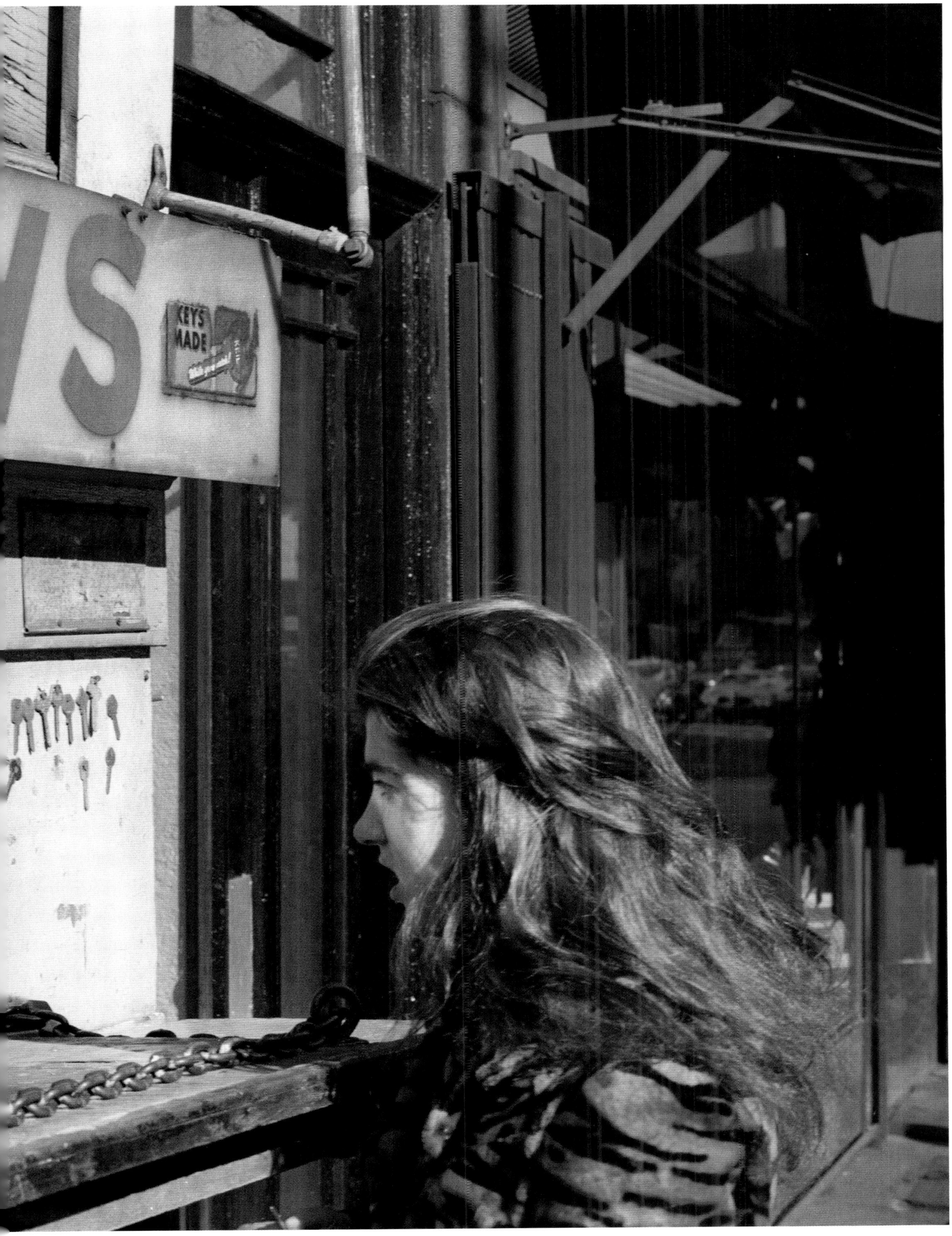
KEYS
MADE

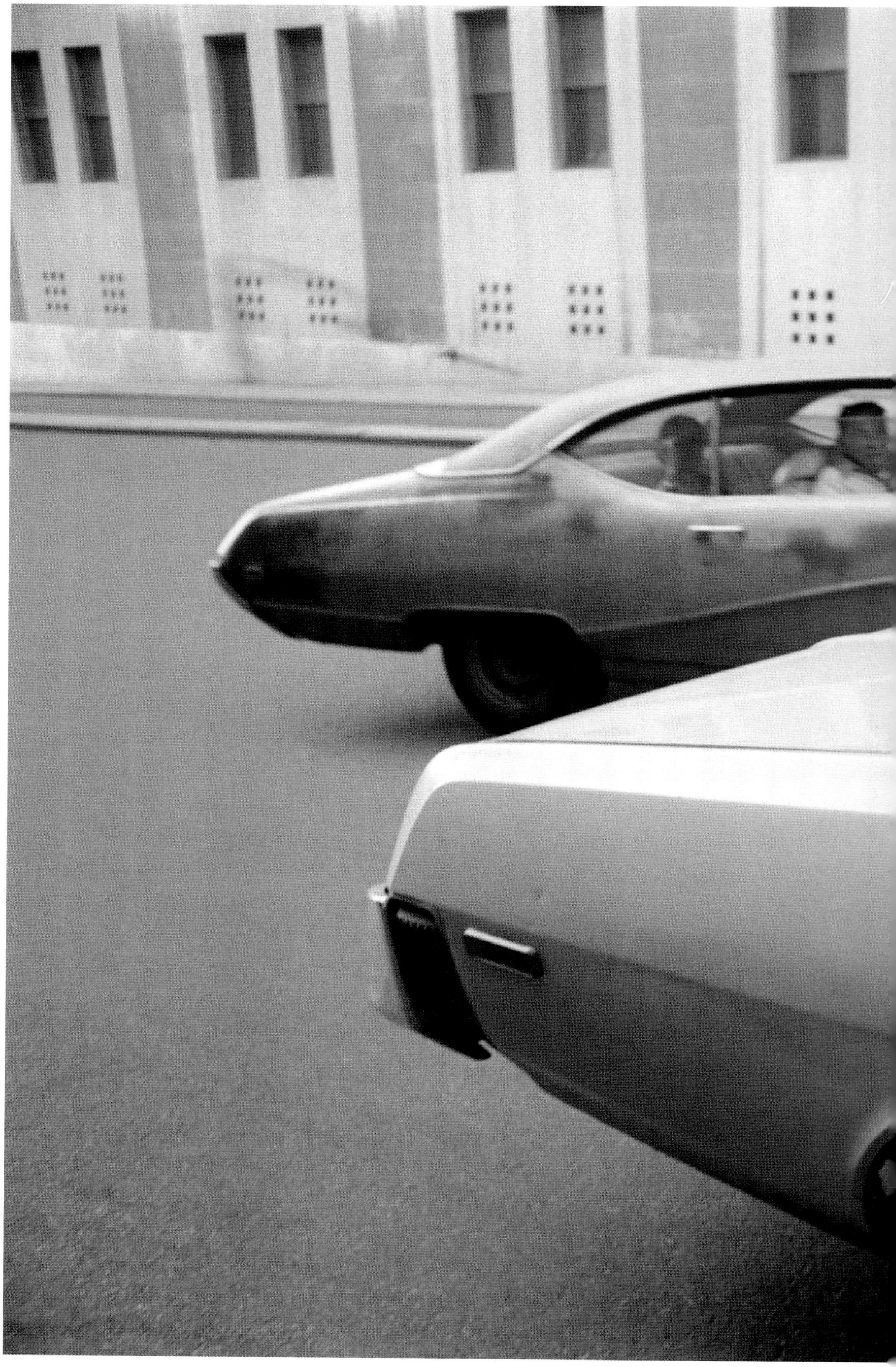

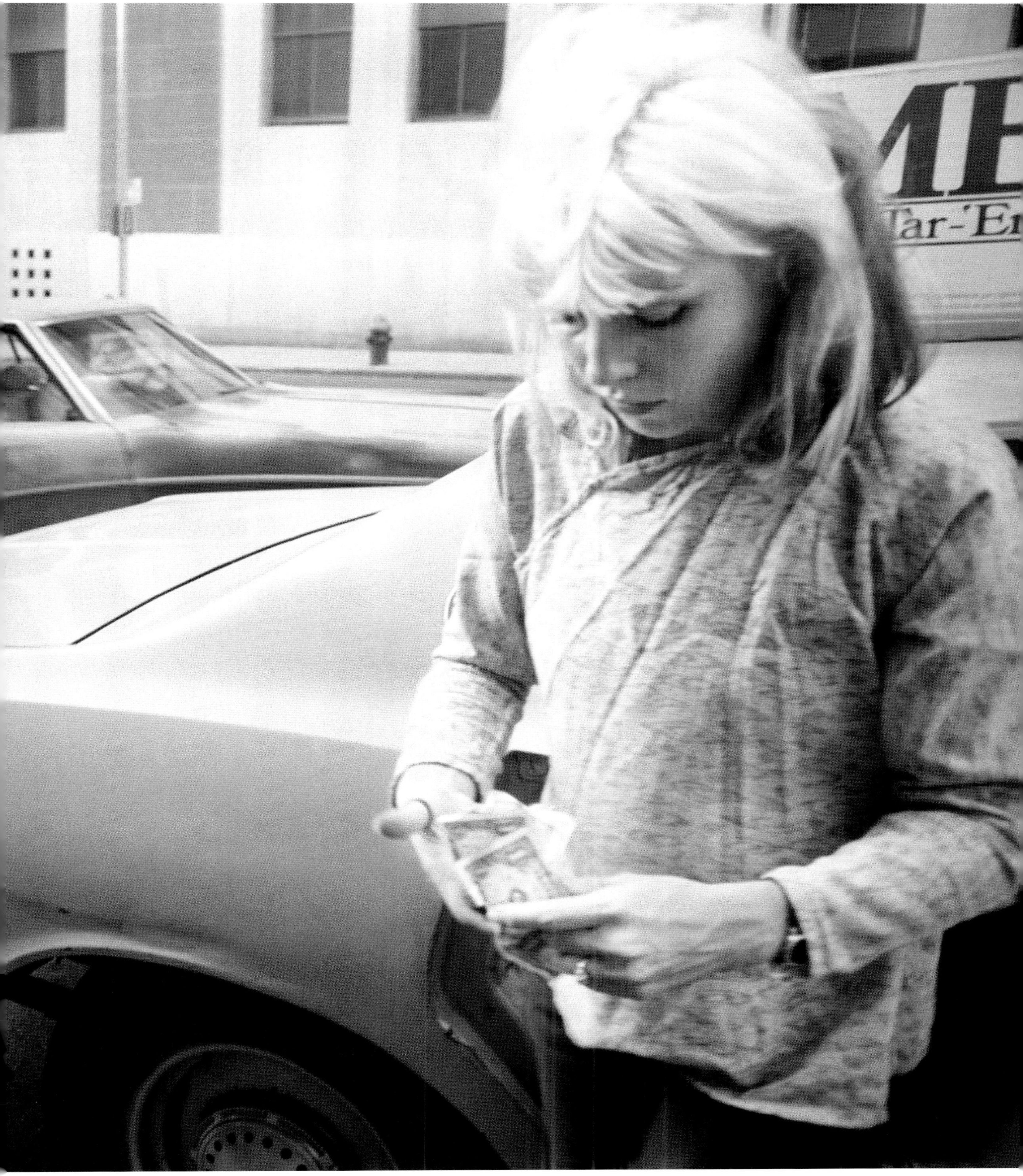

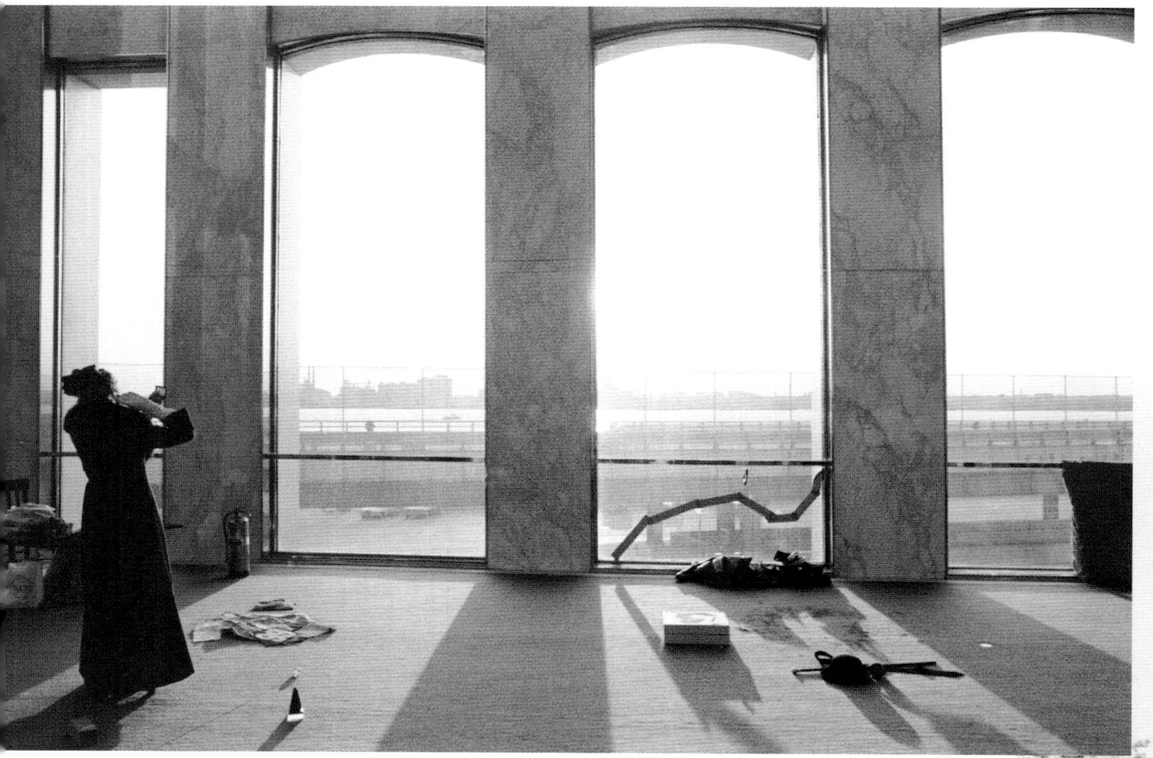

Facing West toward the river, a view of the old elevated West Side Highway.

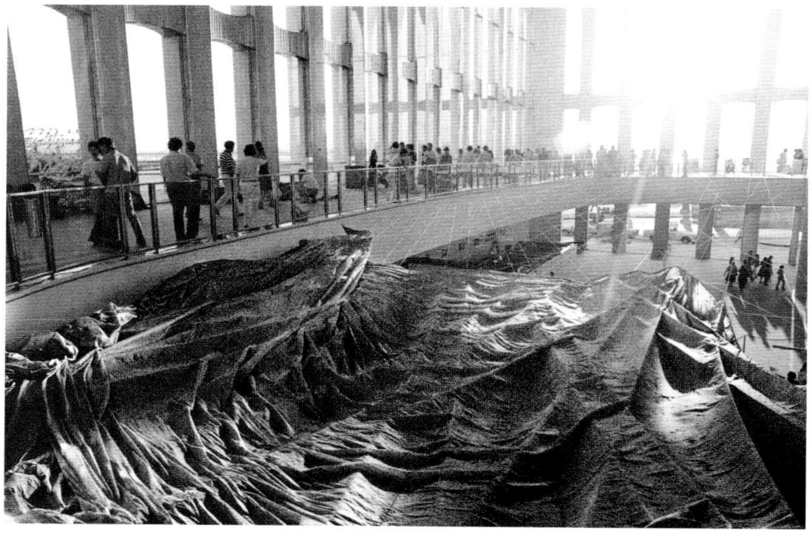

Art in the World Trade Center, maybe 1974–75. I'm pretty sure this was the south tower.

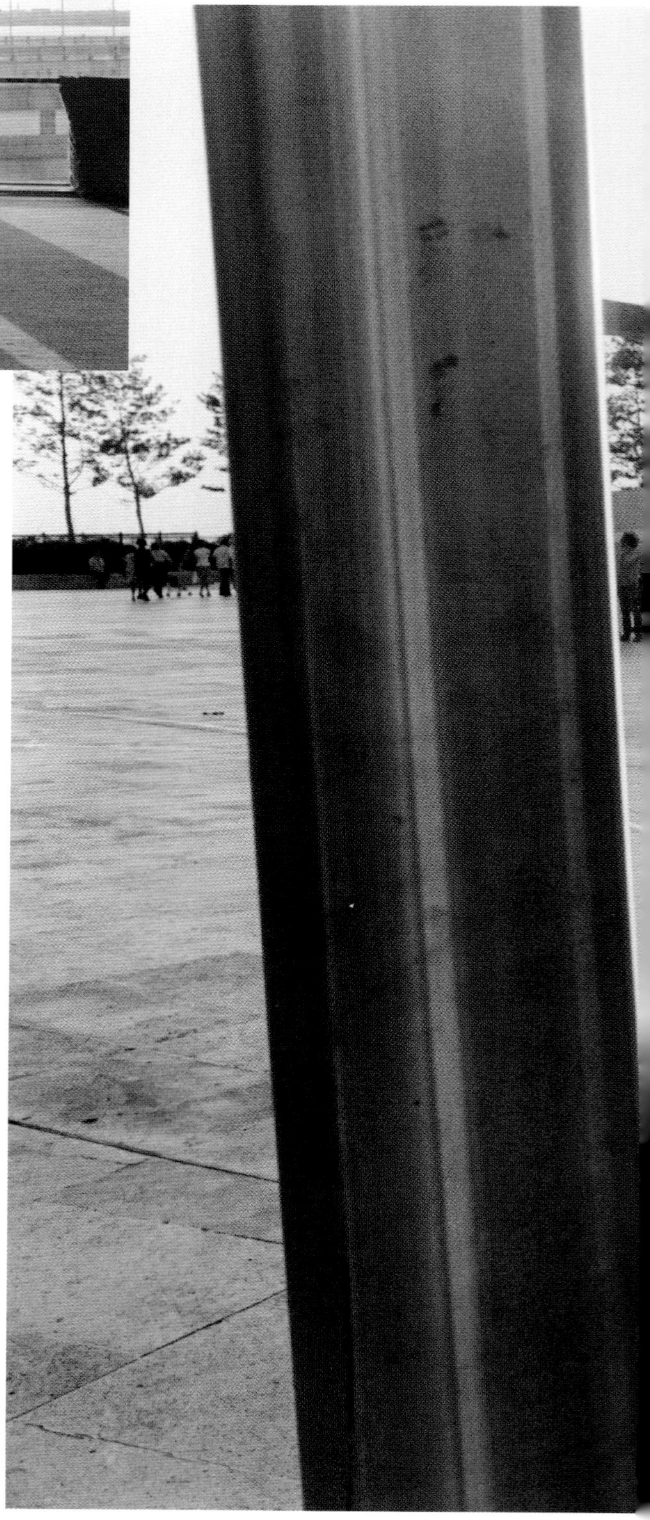

A day trip to the World Trade Center. Some sort of happening/art event was going on.

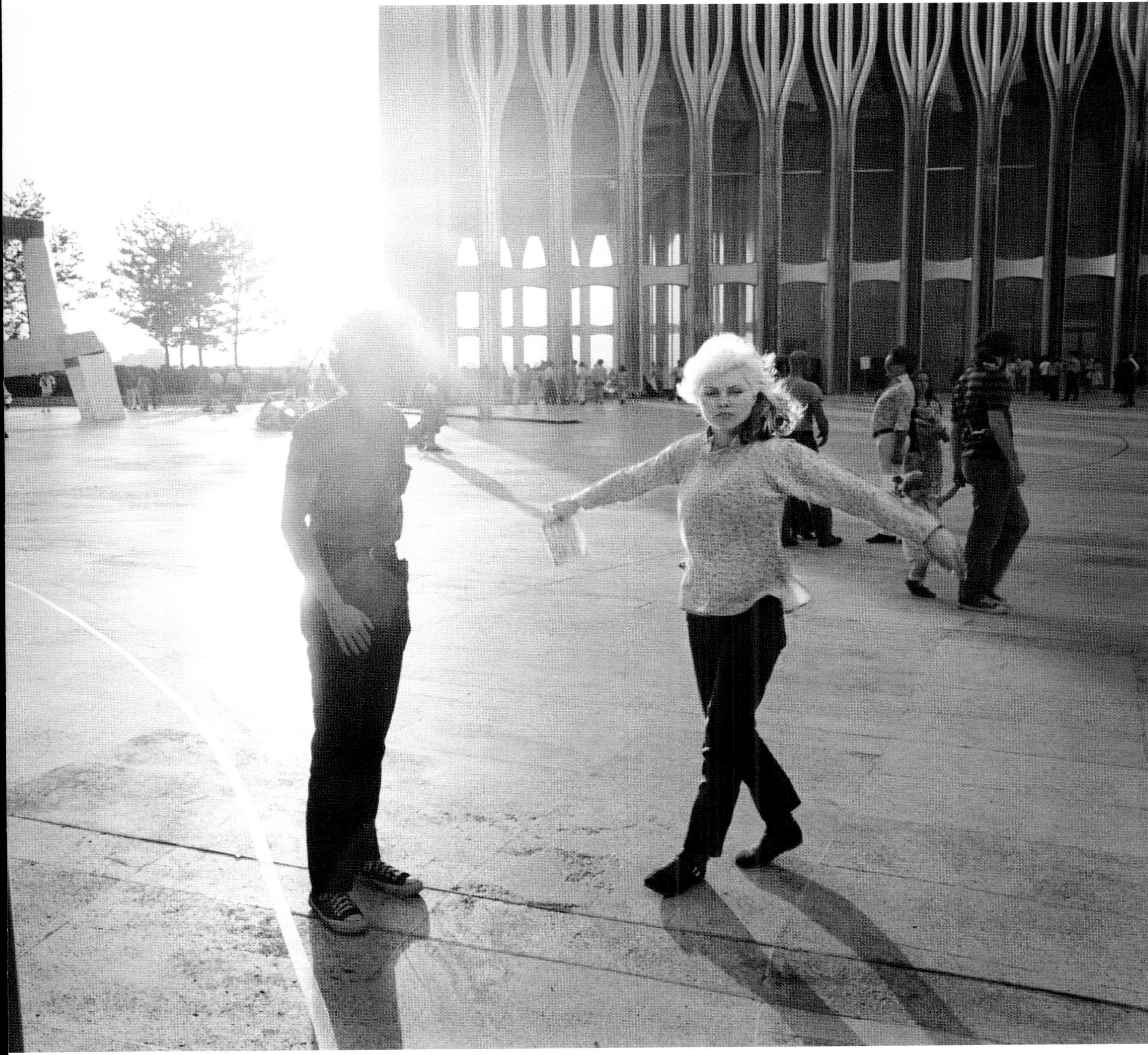

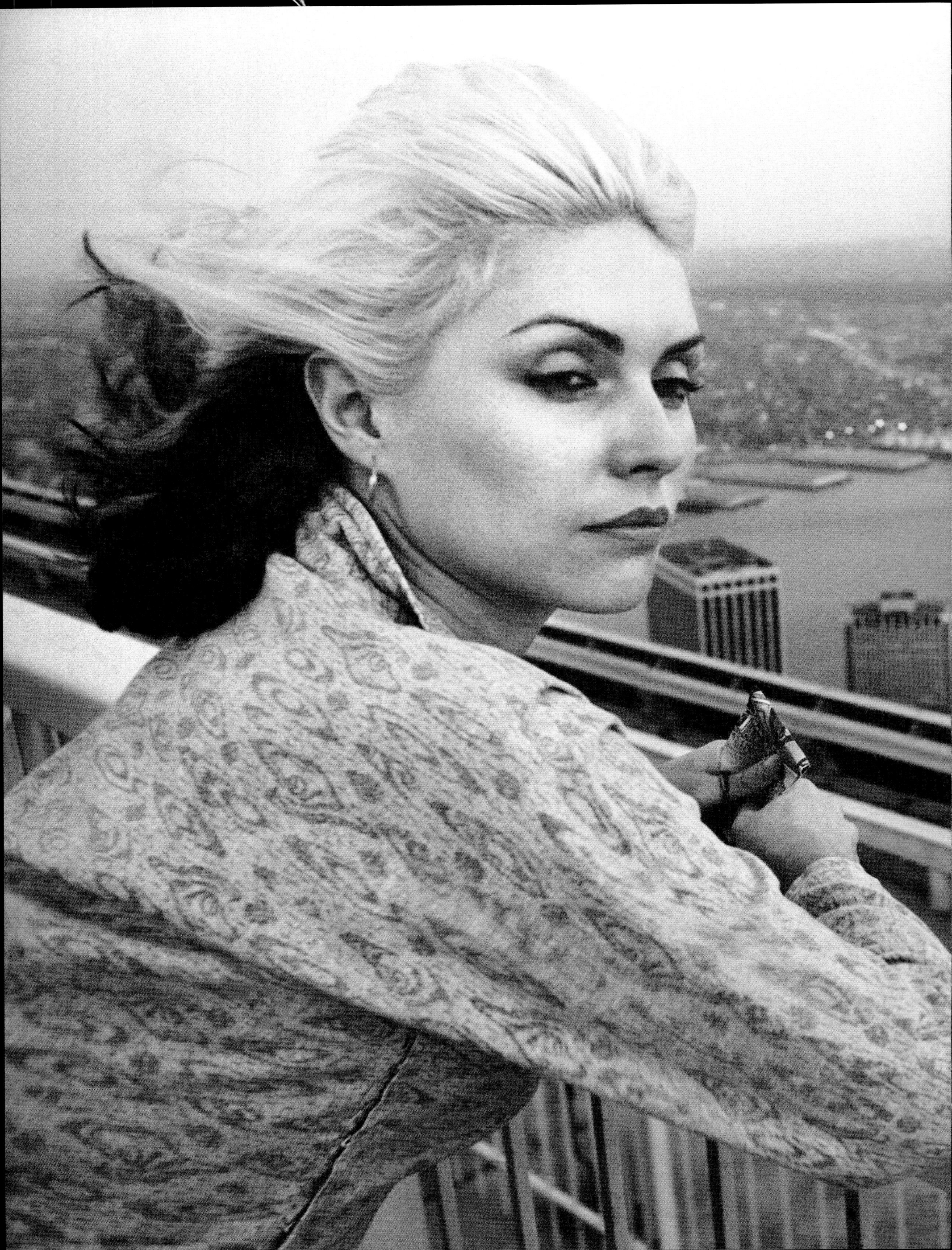

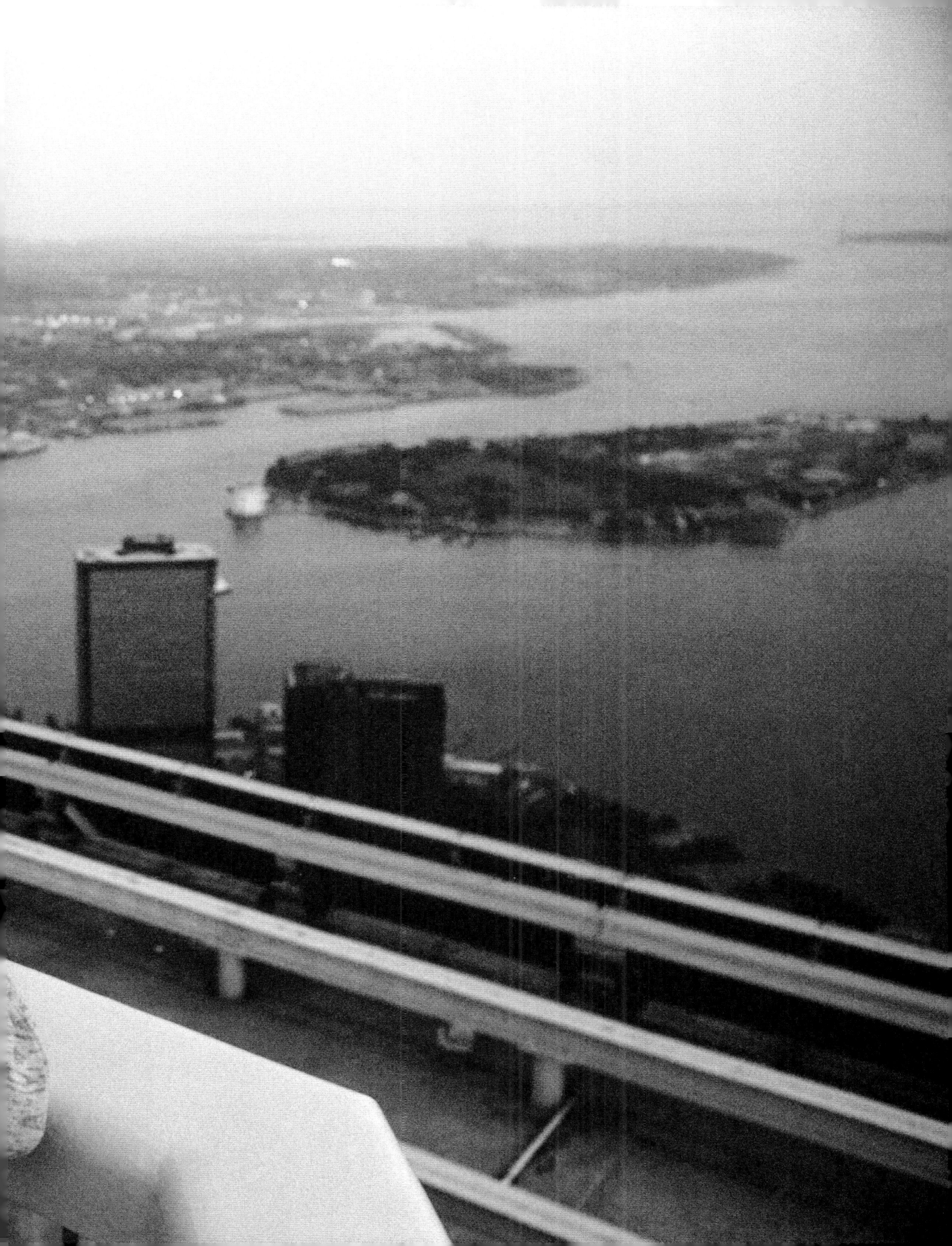

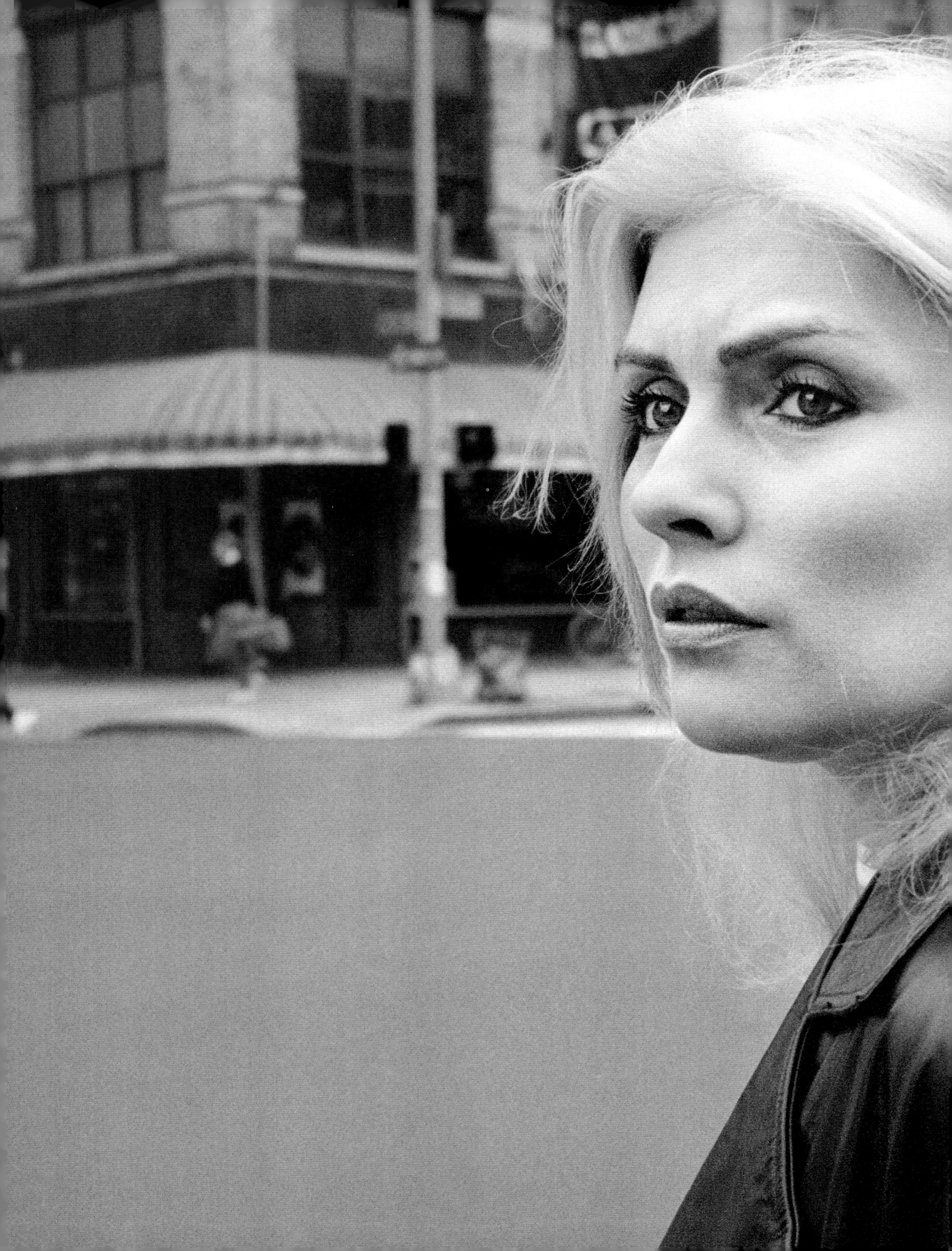

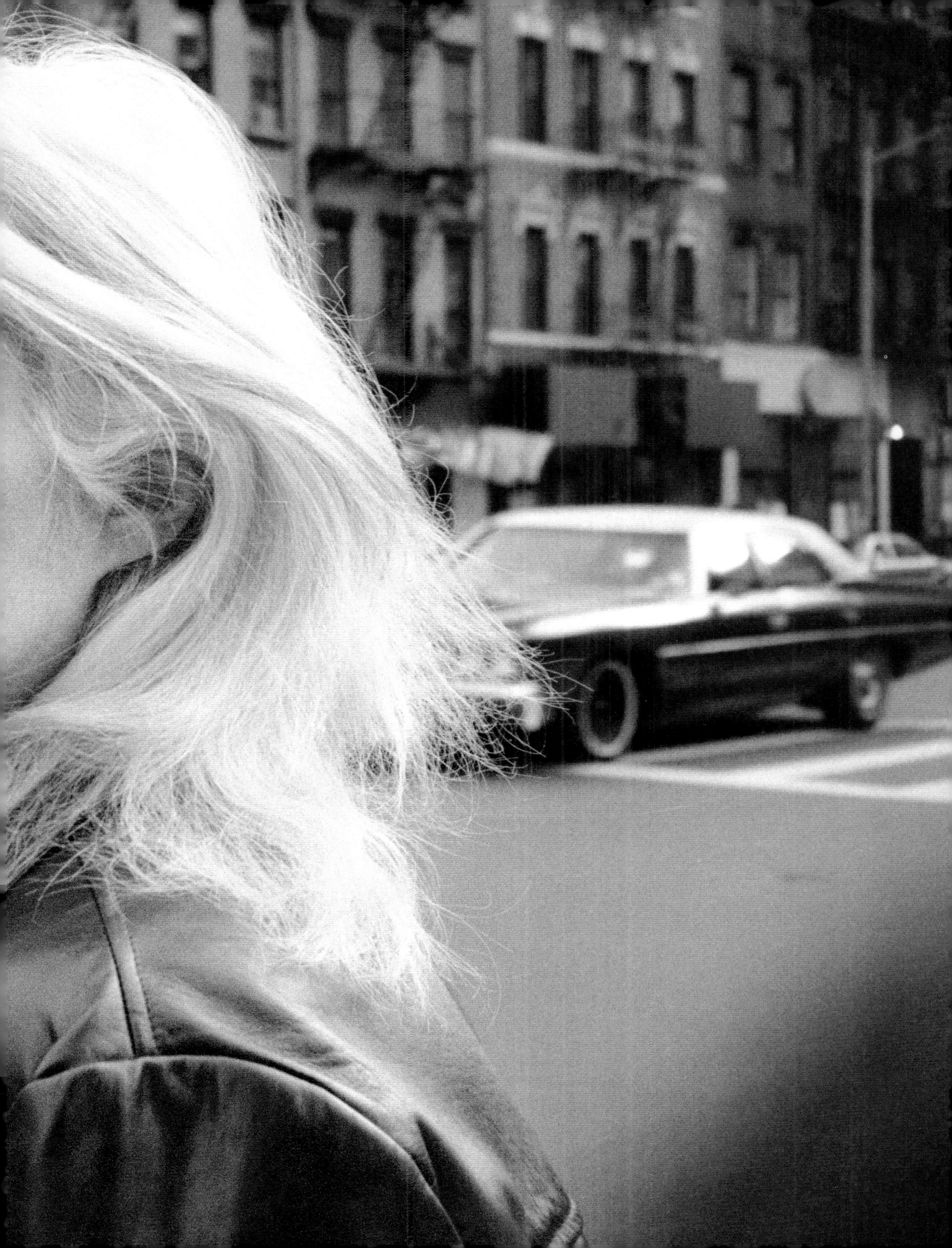

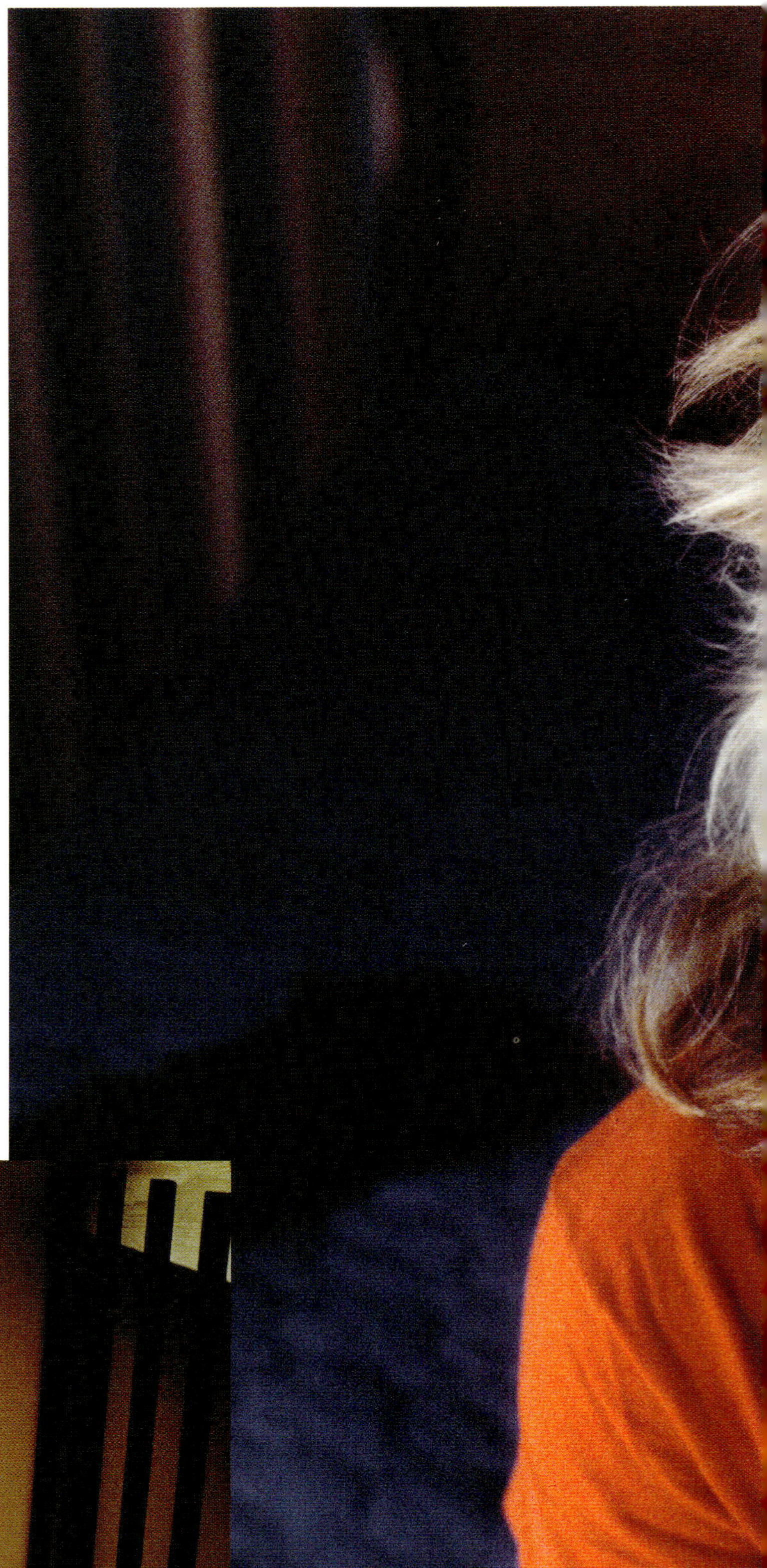

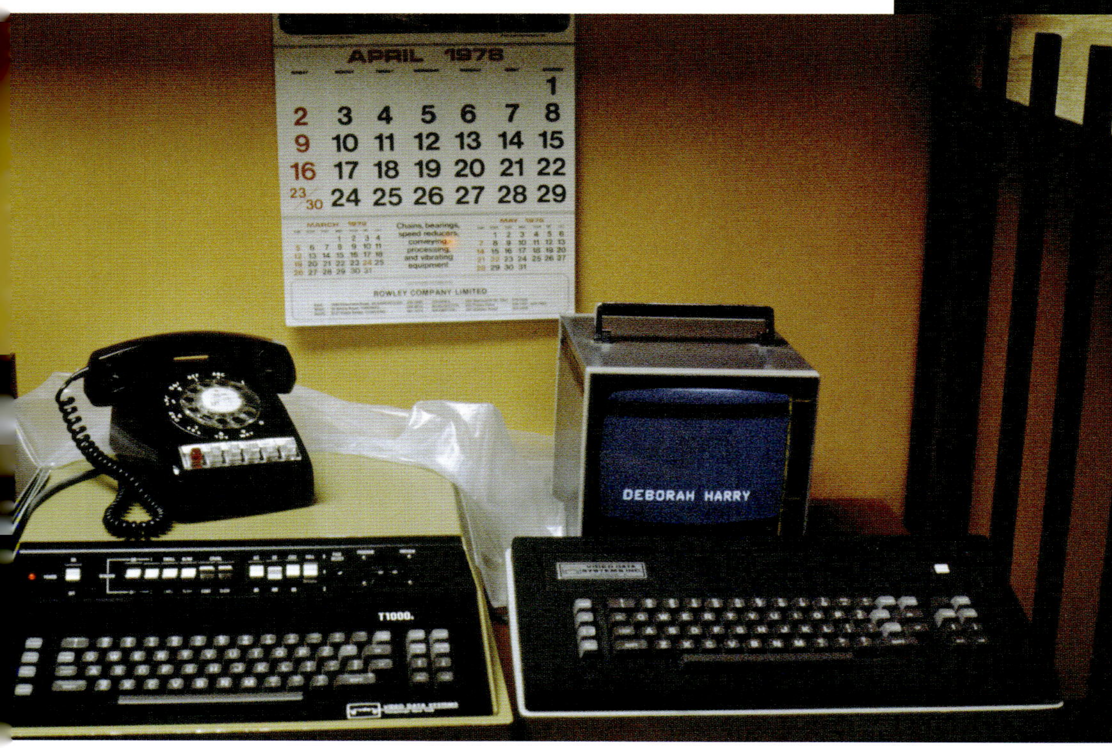
APRIL 1978
Chains, bearings, speed reducers, conveying, processing and vibrating equipment
ROWLEY COMPANY LIMITED
DEBORAH HARRY
T1000.

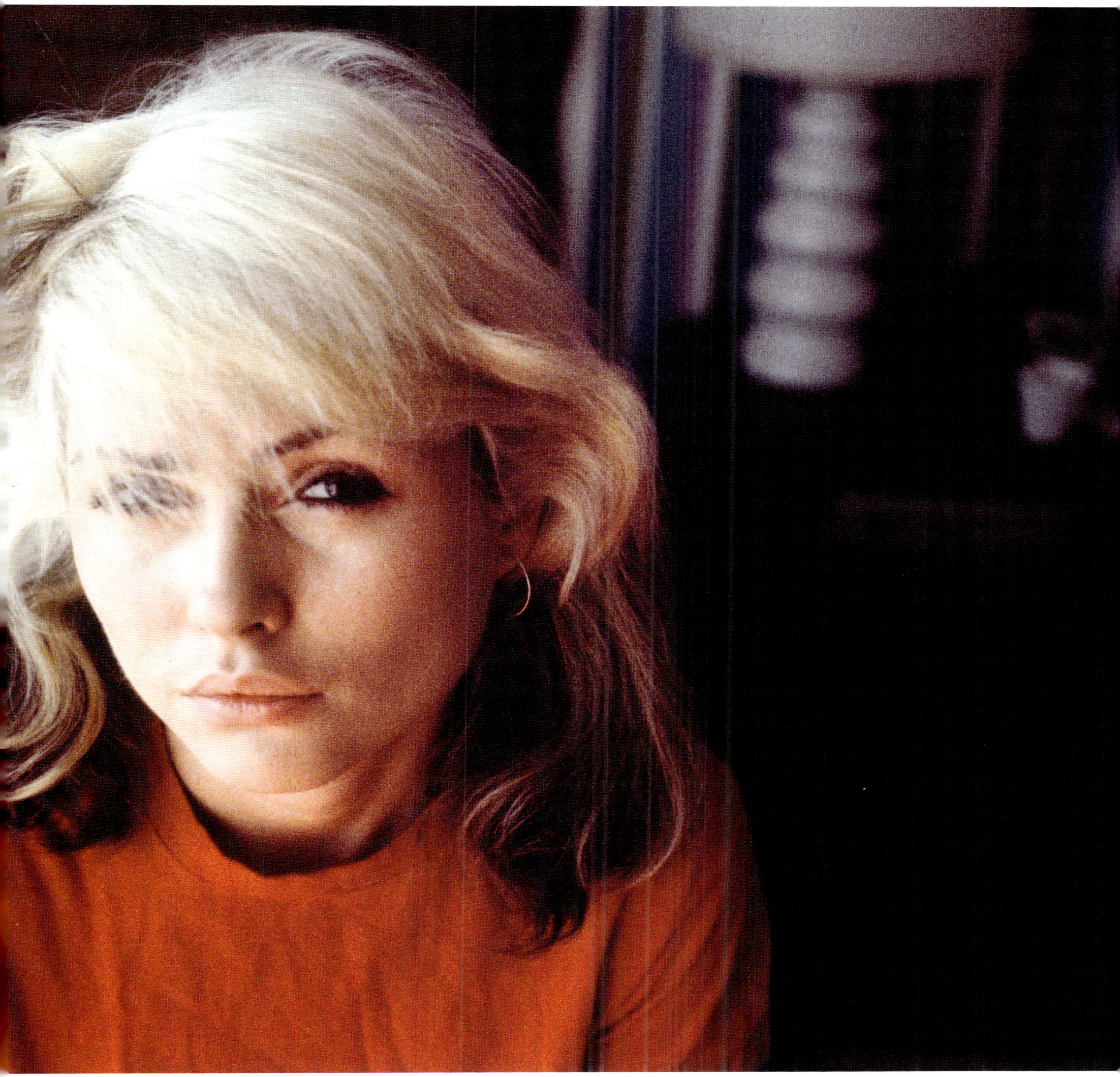

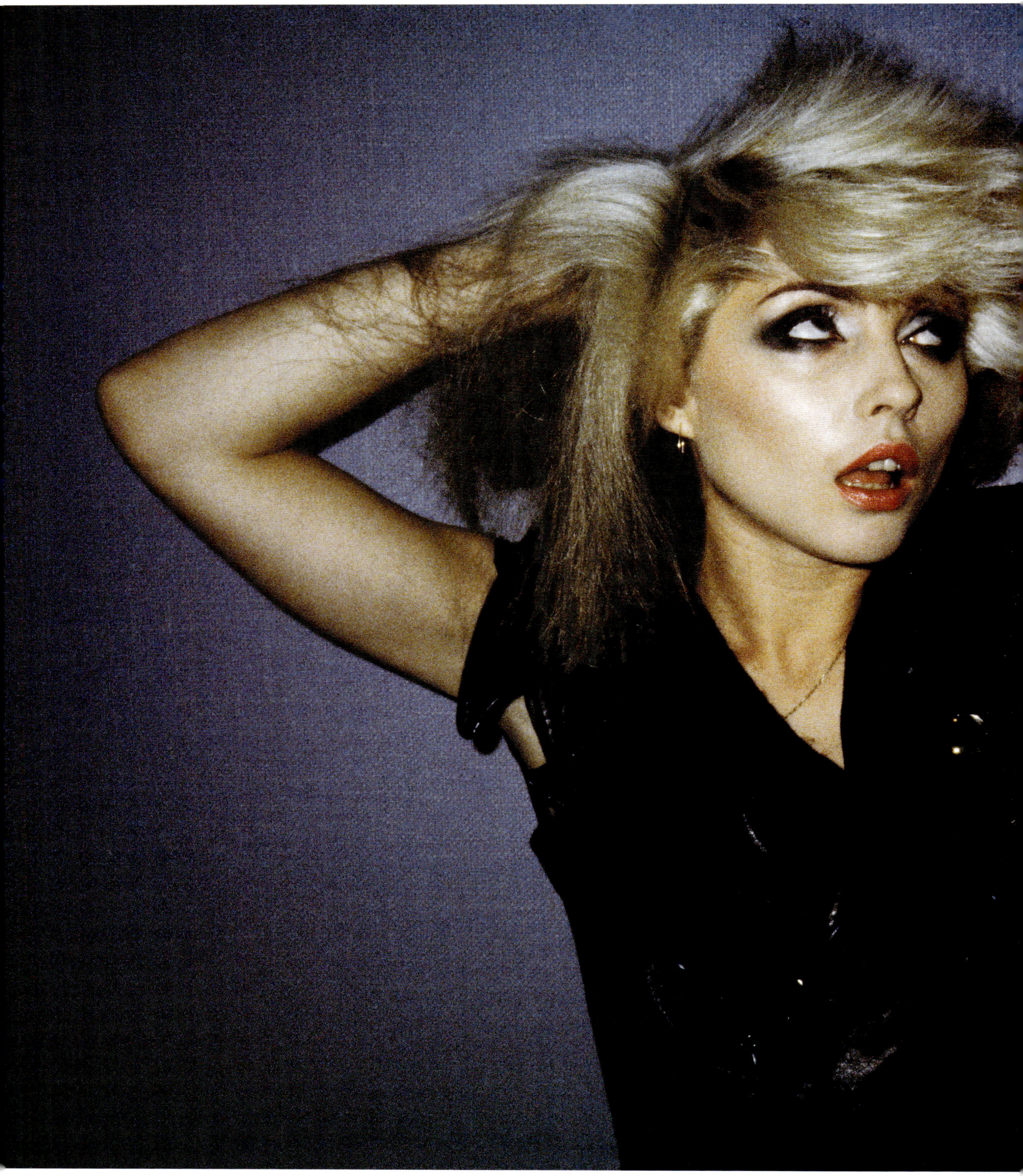

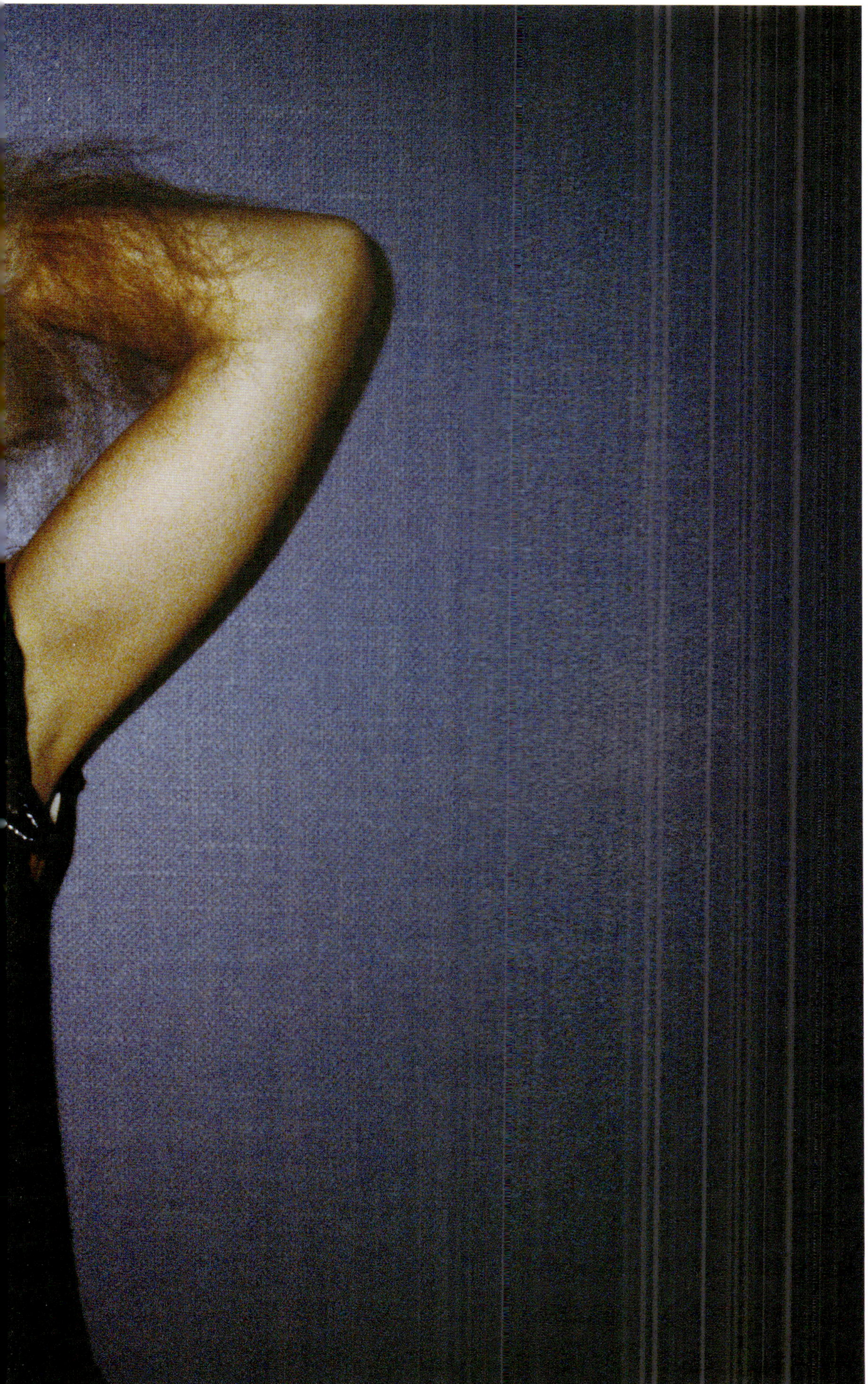

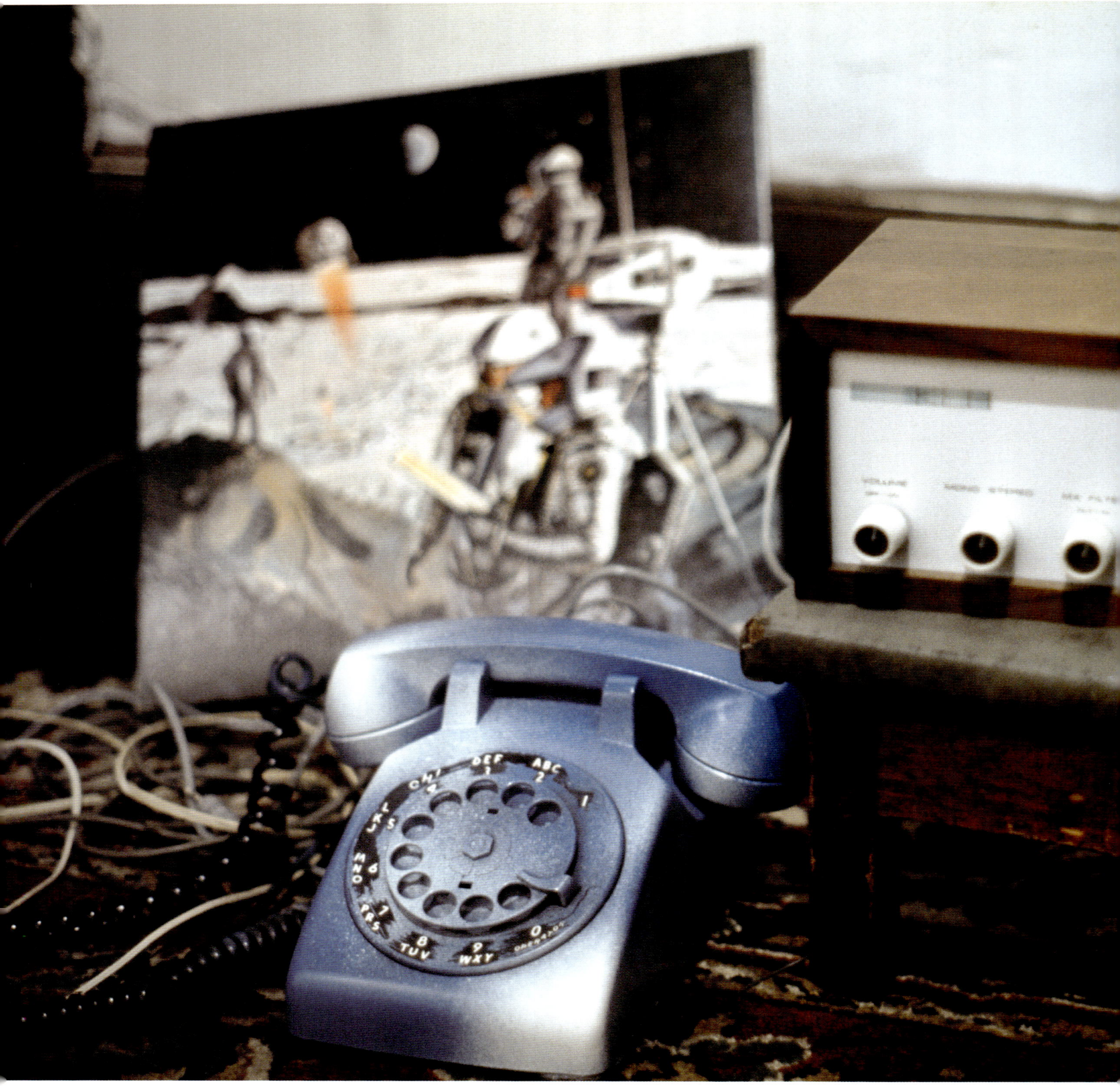
ABC
DEF
TUV
WXY
VOLUME
MONO STEREO

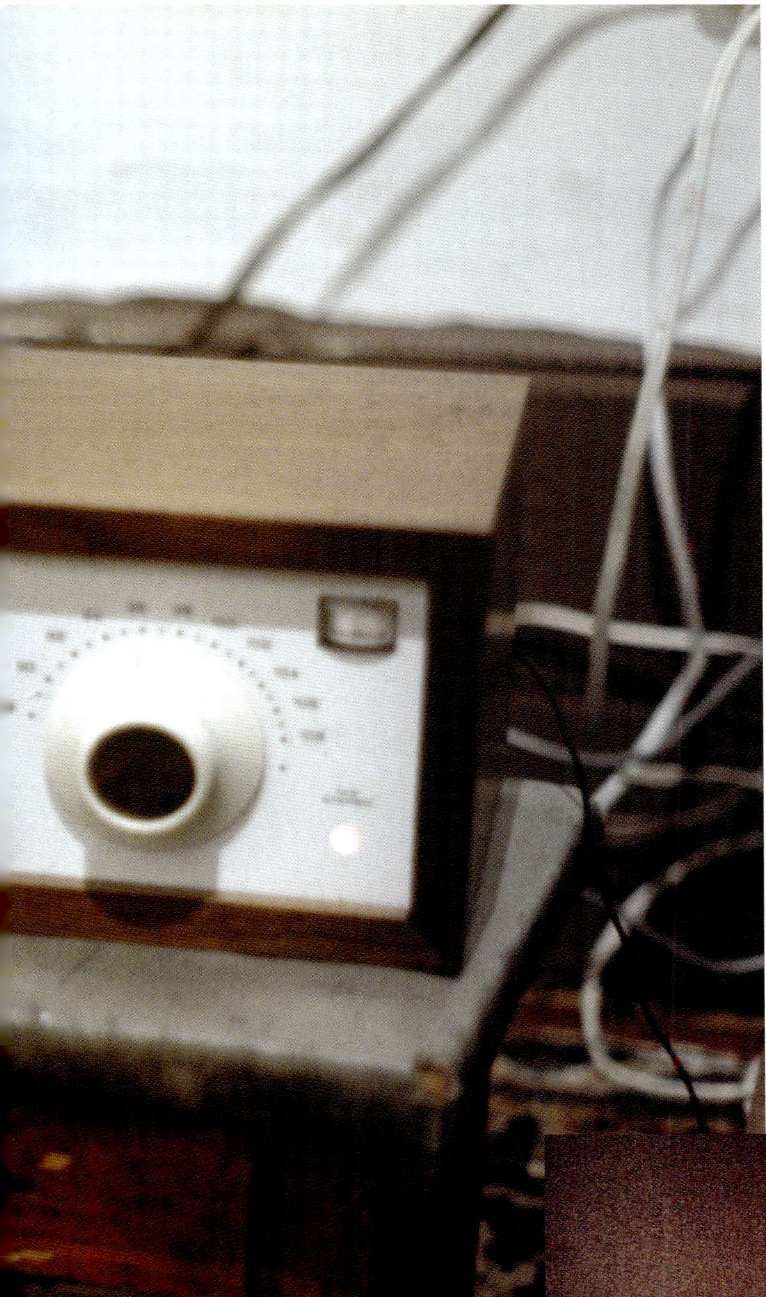

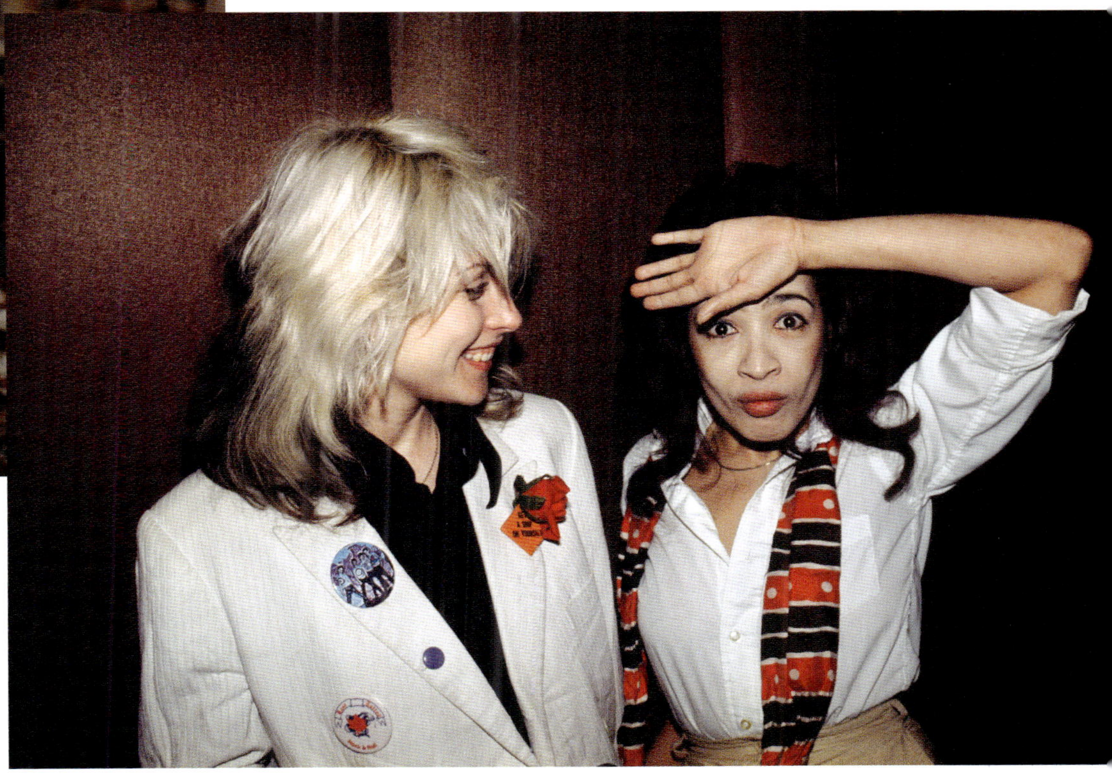

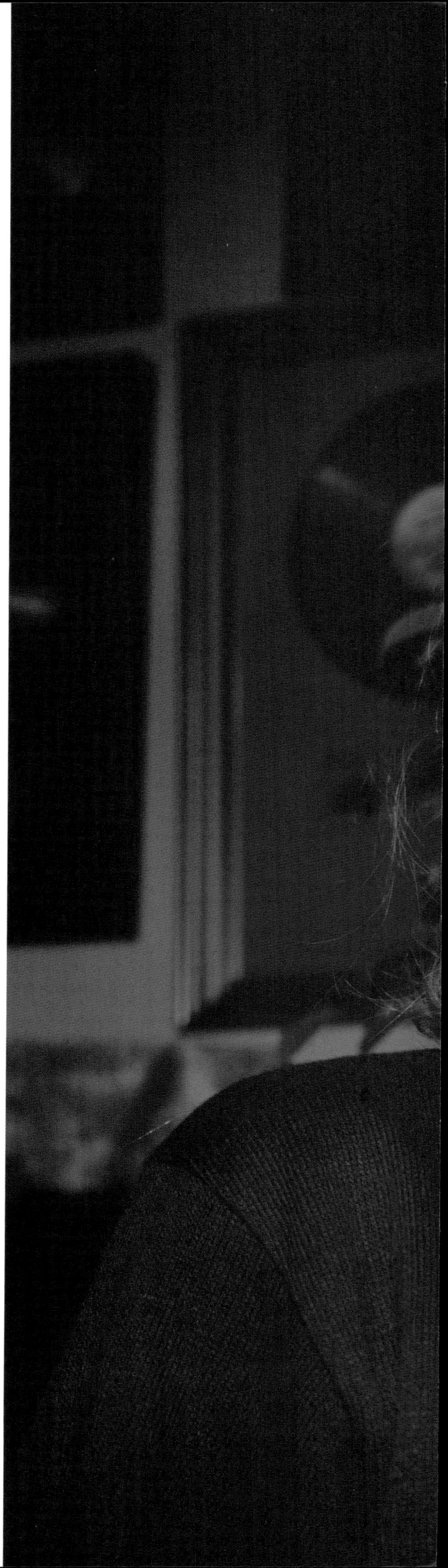

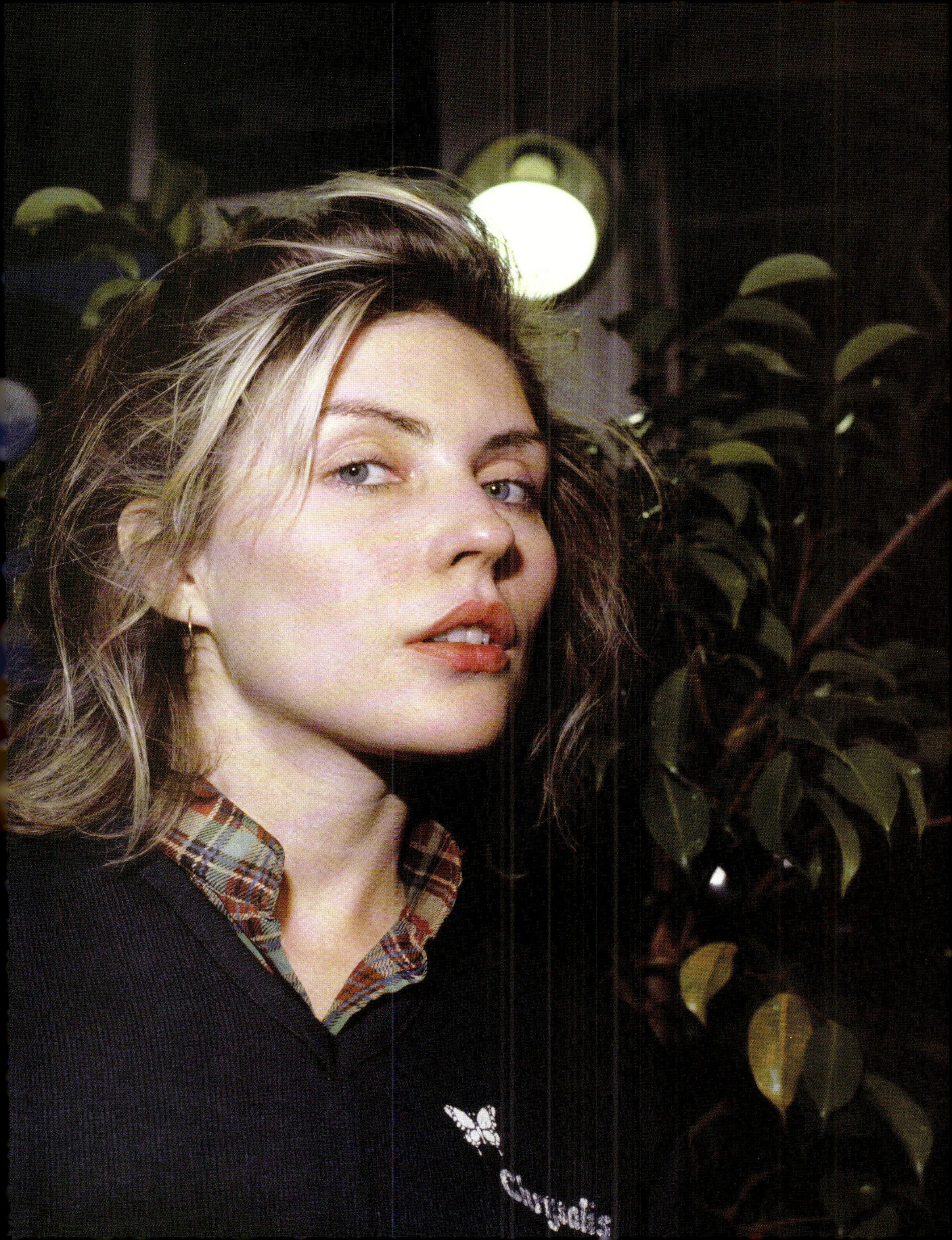
Chrysalis

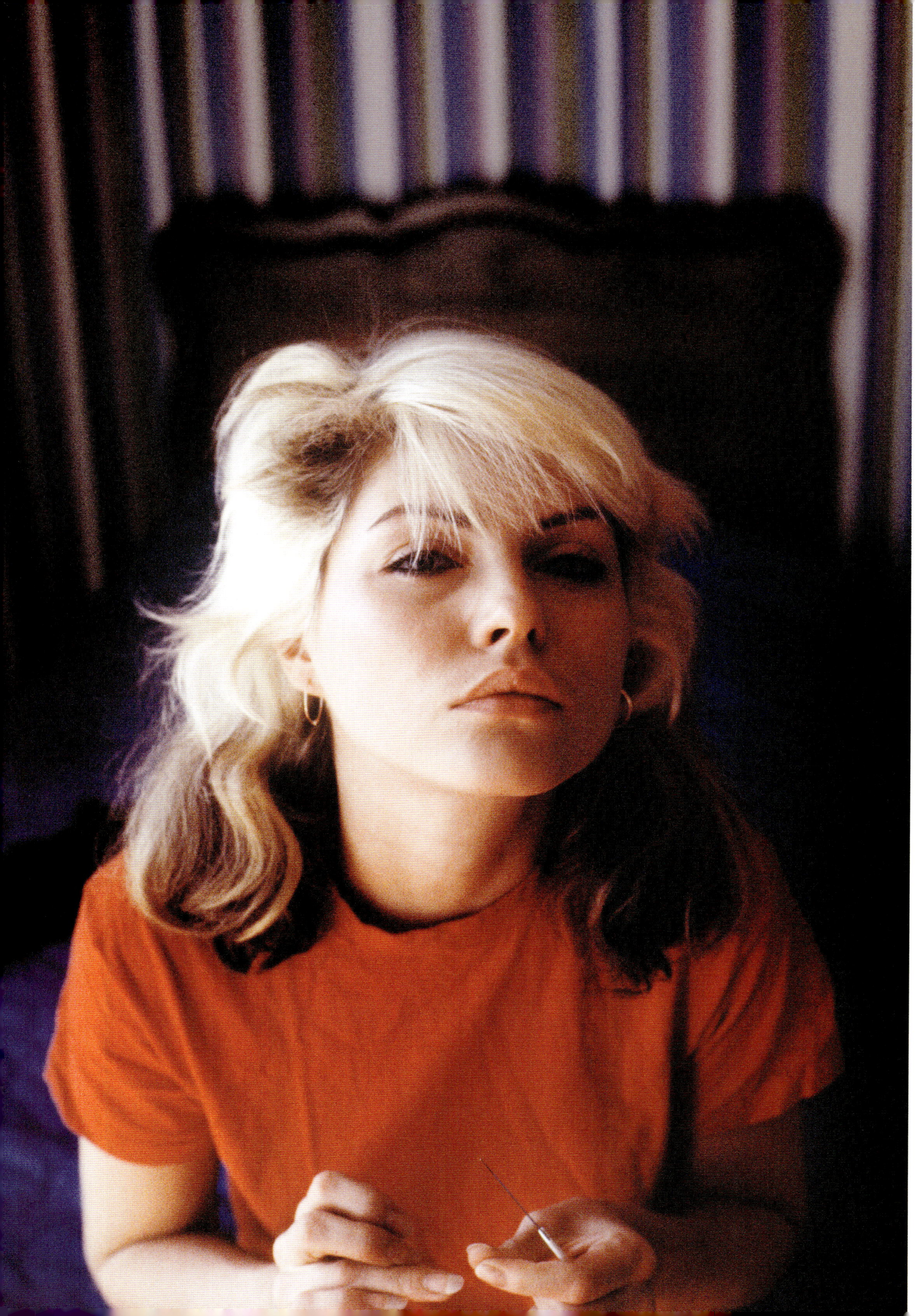

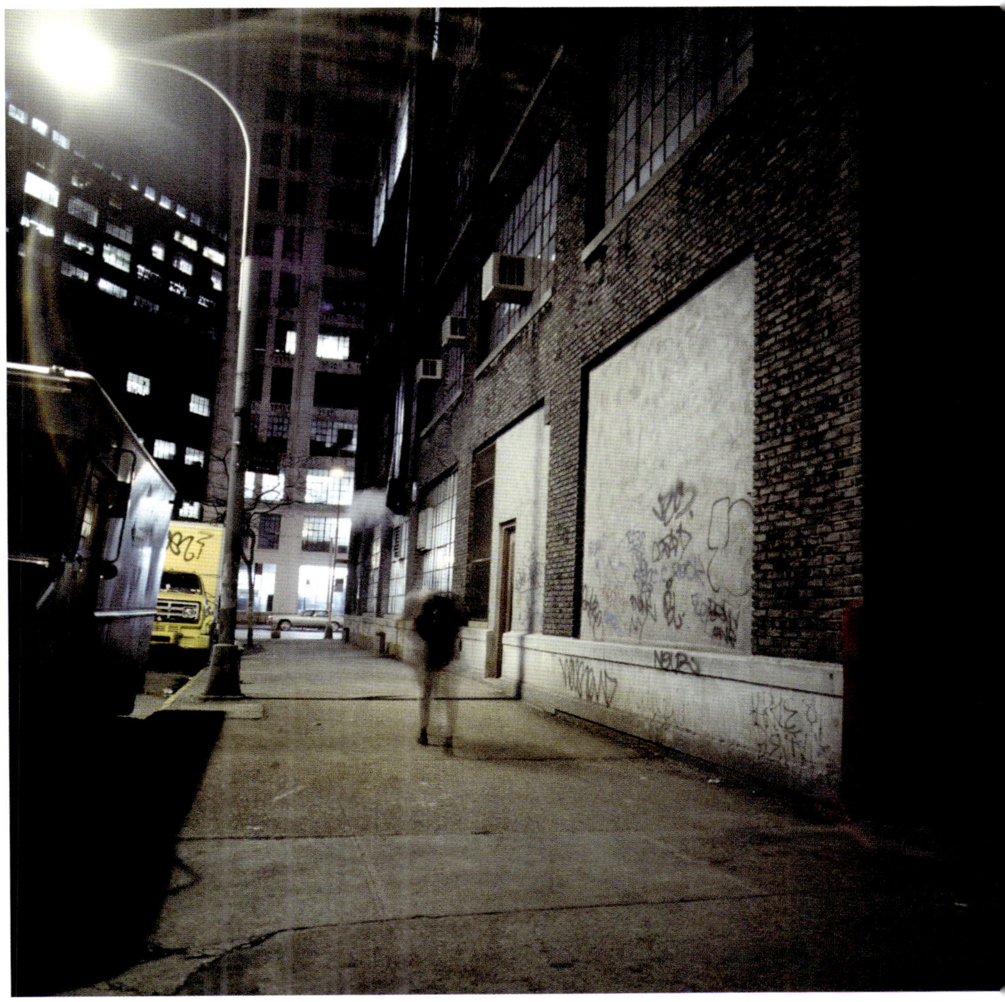

Tribeca at night.

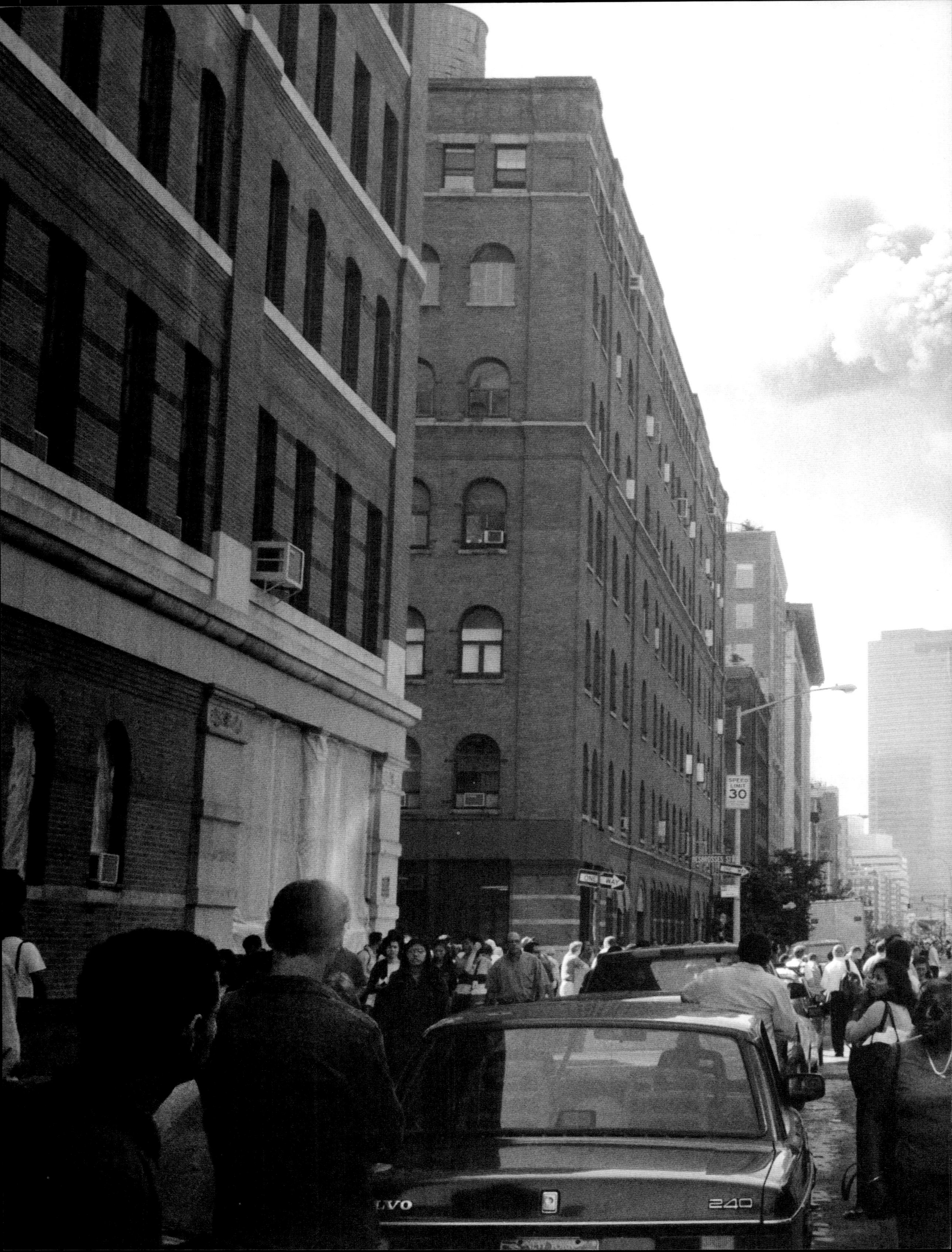
SPEED LIMIT
30
ONE WAY
240

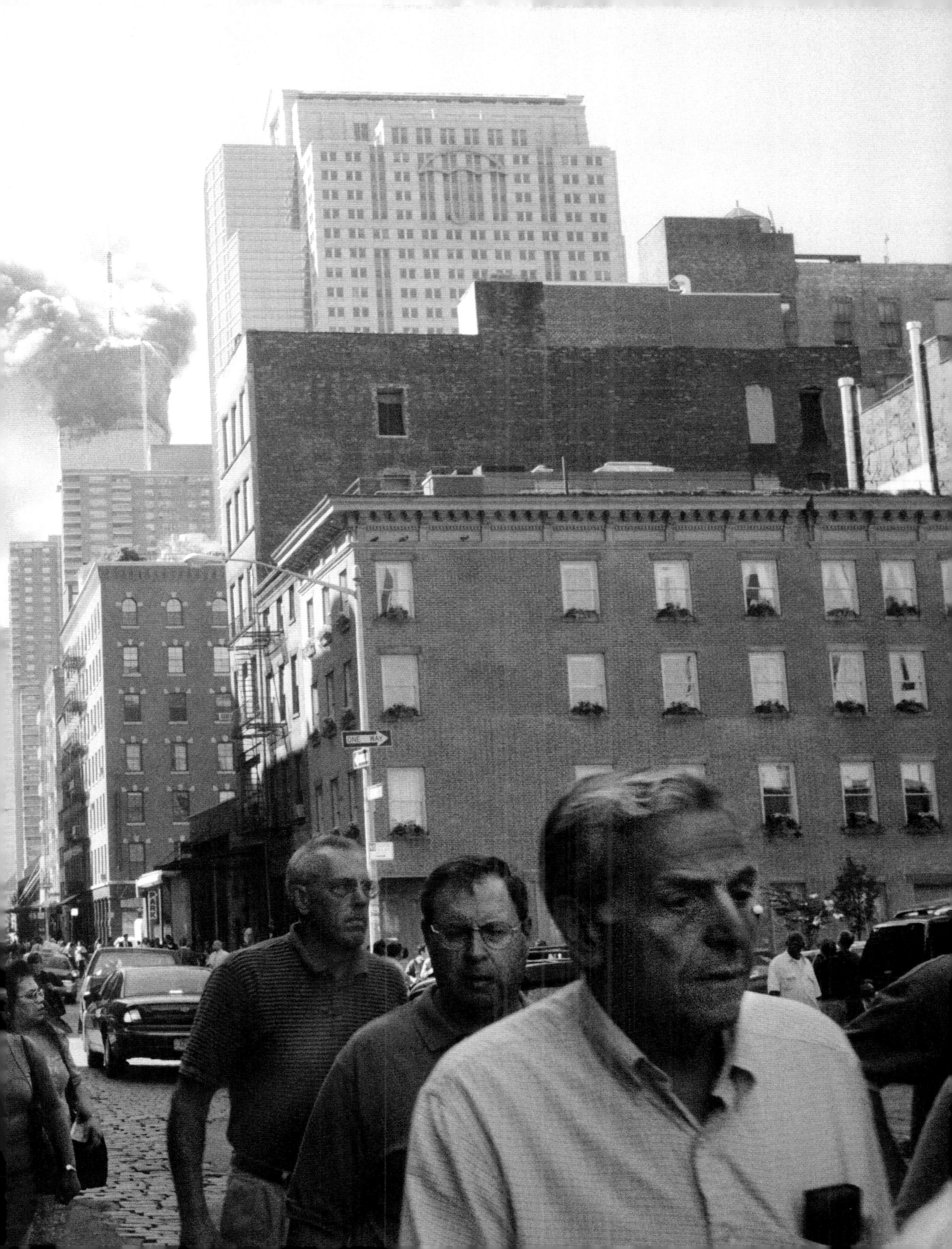
ONE WAY

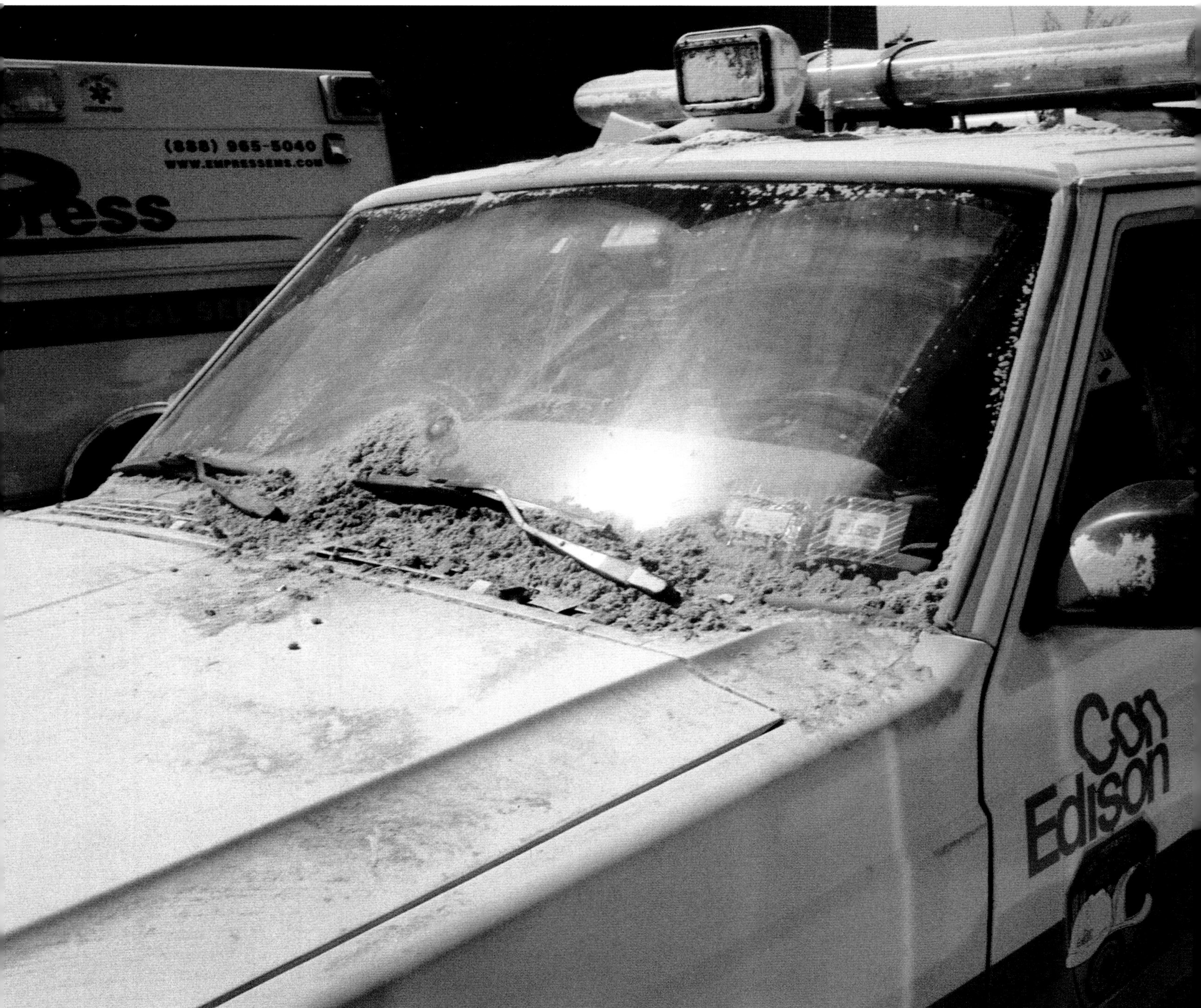
(888) 965-5040
WWW.EMPRESSEMS.COM
Con Edison

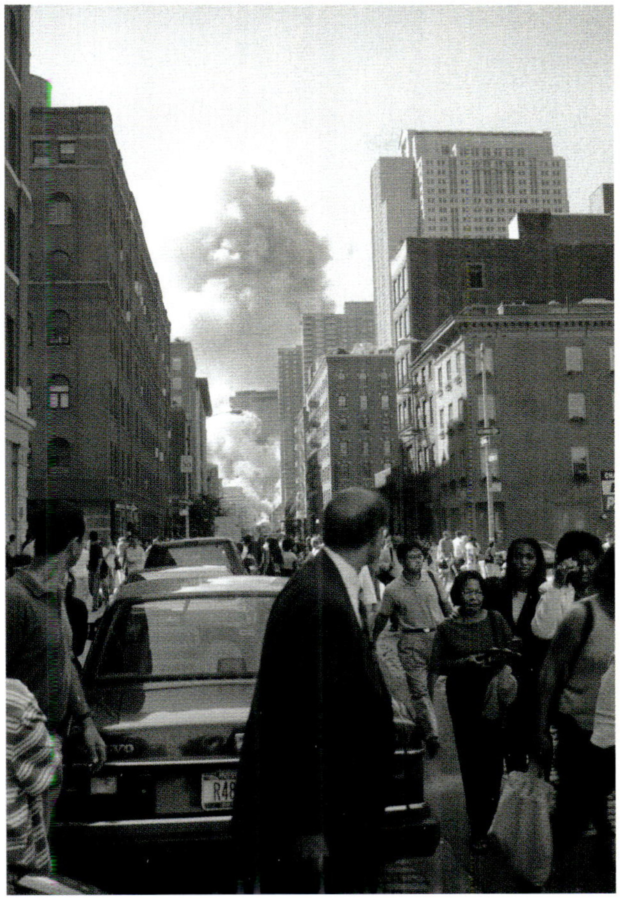

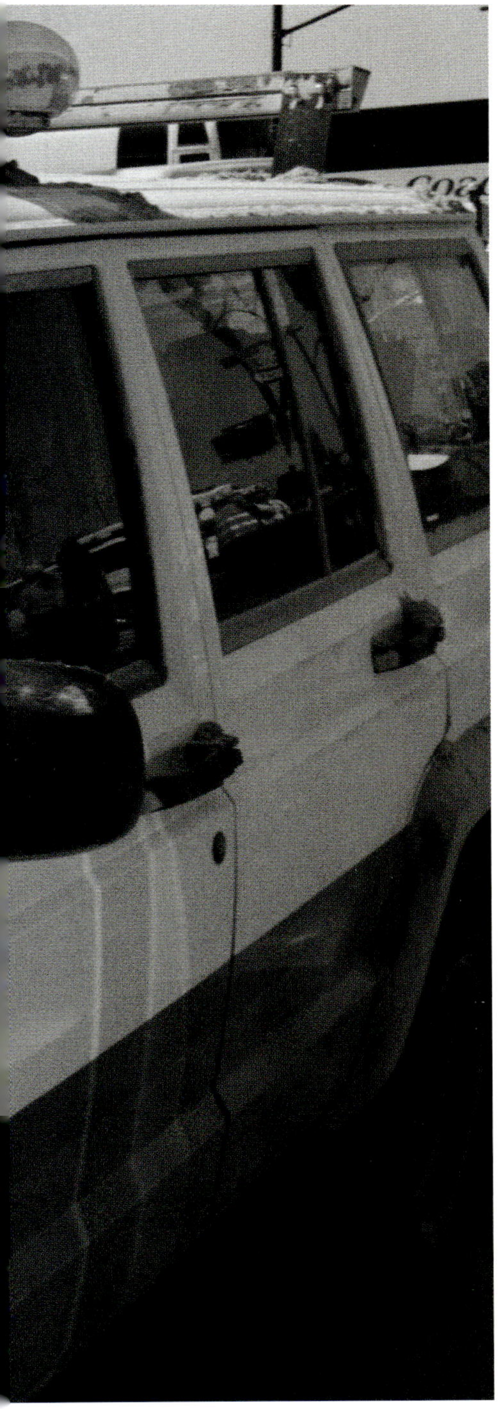

AFTERWORD

Barbara and I got married in 1999 and moved into my loft on Greenwich Street in Tribeca. In September 2001, we had just returned from our second trip to Burning Man. We'd been back for about five days. Barbara had this big old dog and I had just come back from walking him around the block in the morning. There was always the sound of planes, but I heard a really loud airplane engine followed by a muffled boom. Within a few minutes the phone started ringing. "Turn on the TV!" We went out to the street and saw the huge hole in the north tower. The whole event was unreal and surreal. It was a beautiful, cloudless day in the city. We shot some video. The second plane hit the south tower. We went uptown to Debbie's apartment. On the streets were groups of people standing around cars, with their doors open and radios on with the news. Debbie's power had gone out. She had a kitten somebody had given her. We walked back downtown, passing Saint Vincent Hospital, where there was a line around the block made up of people wanting to donate blood. By the time we got back to the block the towers had been replaced by a huge dust cloud.

Before the attacks, lots of weird stuff happened around where I lived on Greenwich Street. For a couple of days several blocks had been shut to traffic, and guys in hazmat suits had swarmed around doing some sort of drill or reenactment. I heard reports from people in the neighborhood of flashlights shone into skylights on top floors, police activity on roofs. So the press setting up tents and the National Guard making us show ID to get home didn't seem particularly odd. The first weekend after the attack saw a weirdly party like atmosphere all along Canal Street. Tourists came in droves and there were street vendors selling '9/11' T-shirts and refreshments. The pile of debris from the World Trade Center stood smoking for weeks at the end of Greenwich Street.

There was about a year of very communal feelings, of togetherness, in the city afterward. And then, as if a switch was pulled, New York City began its ascent (or descent) to becoming the almost final form of a vast corporate world center.

I still like it in New York City. I tried living away in the country for a bunch of years. We came back to the city. Back in the 1960s and 1970s, I had no idea that I'd come to miss the decay and the danger.

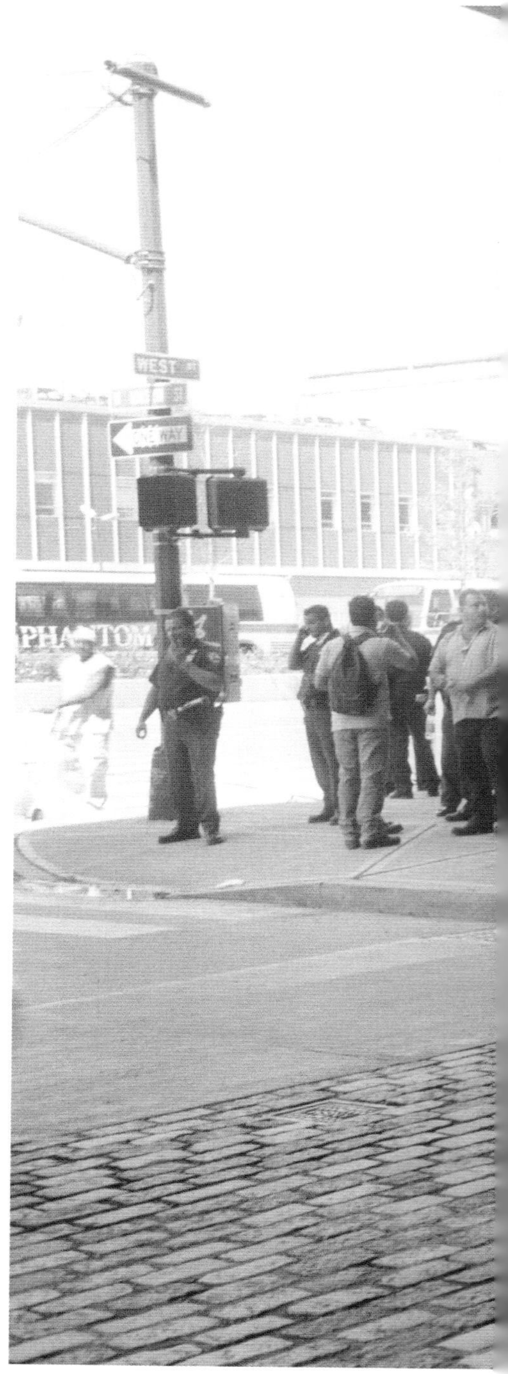

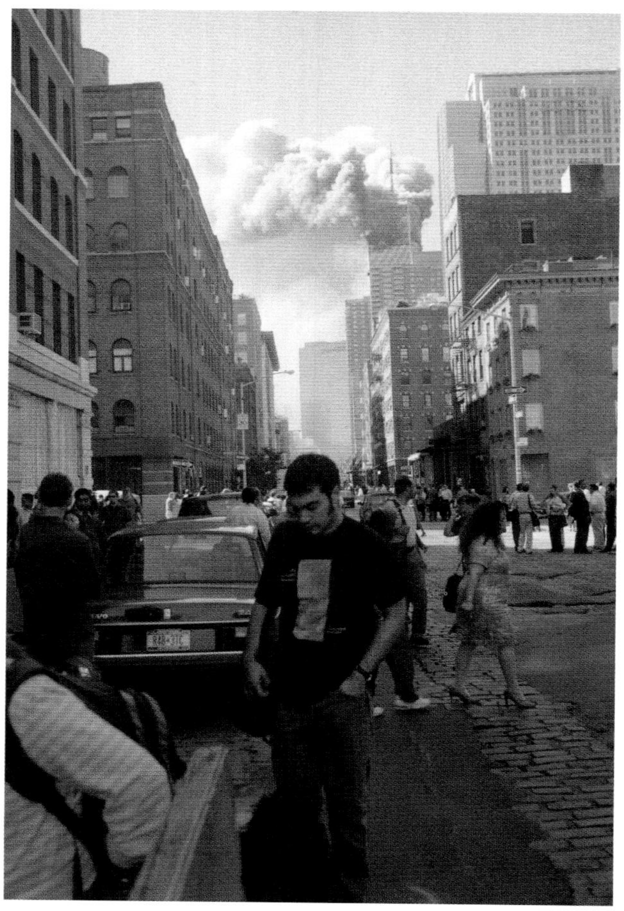

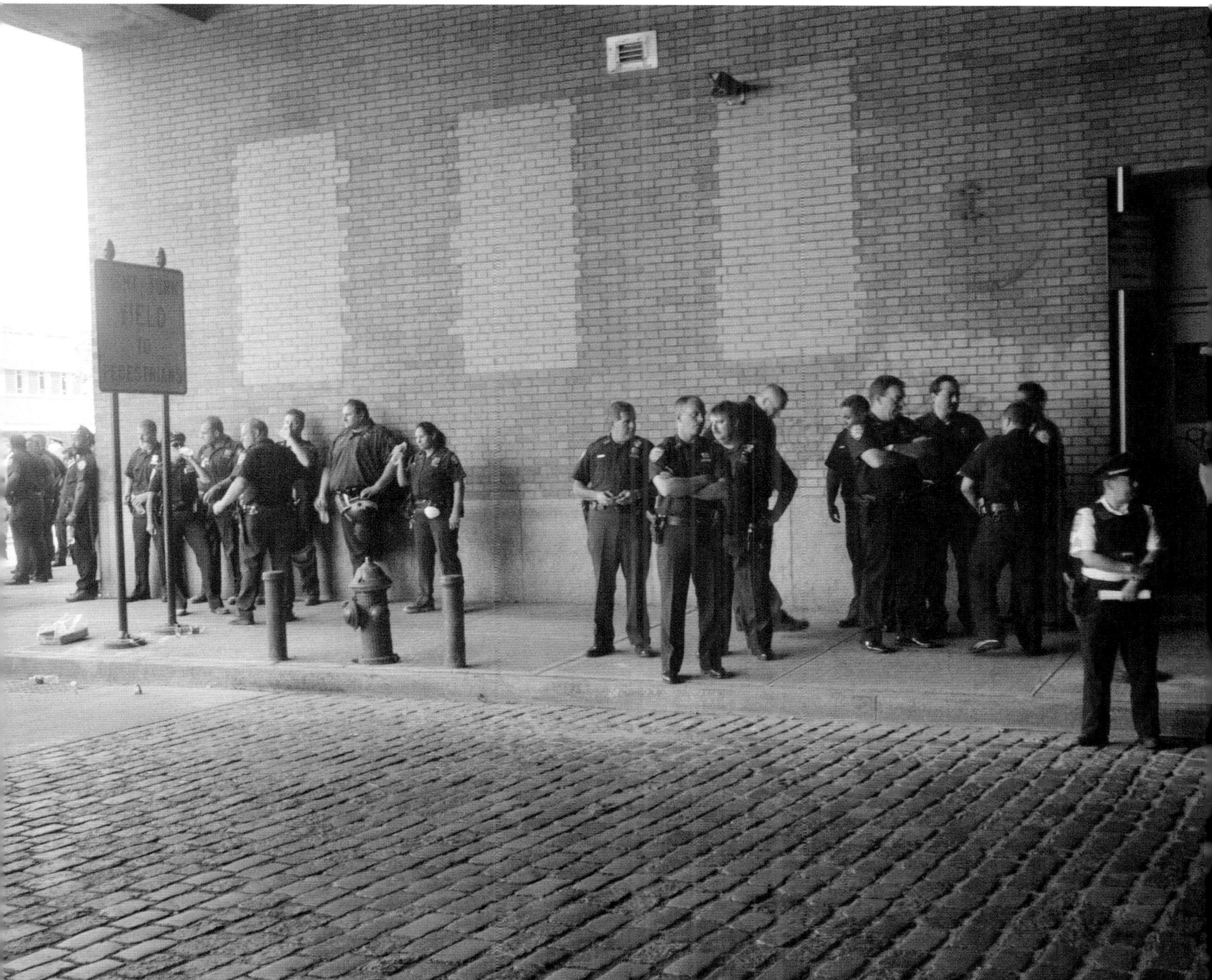

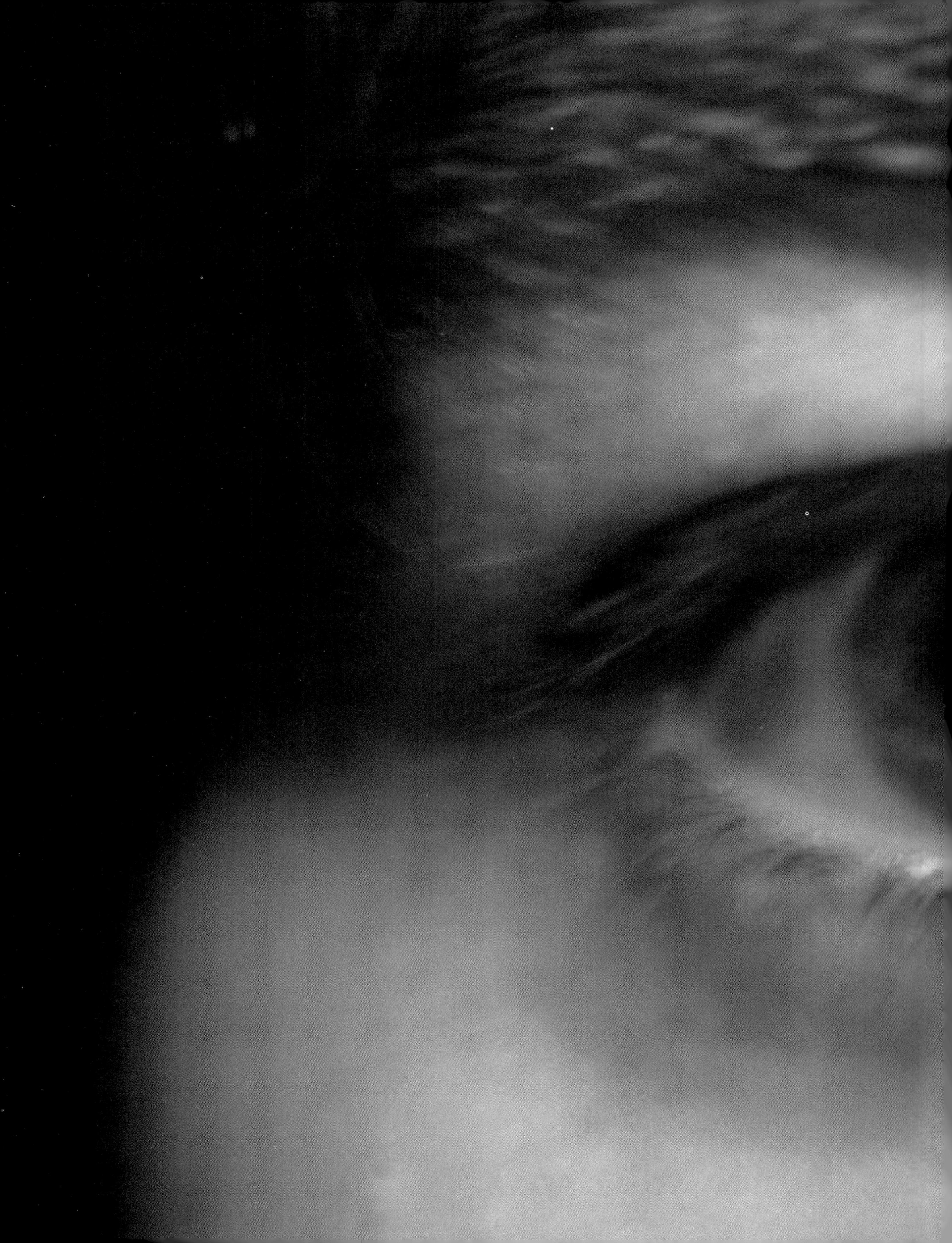

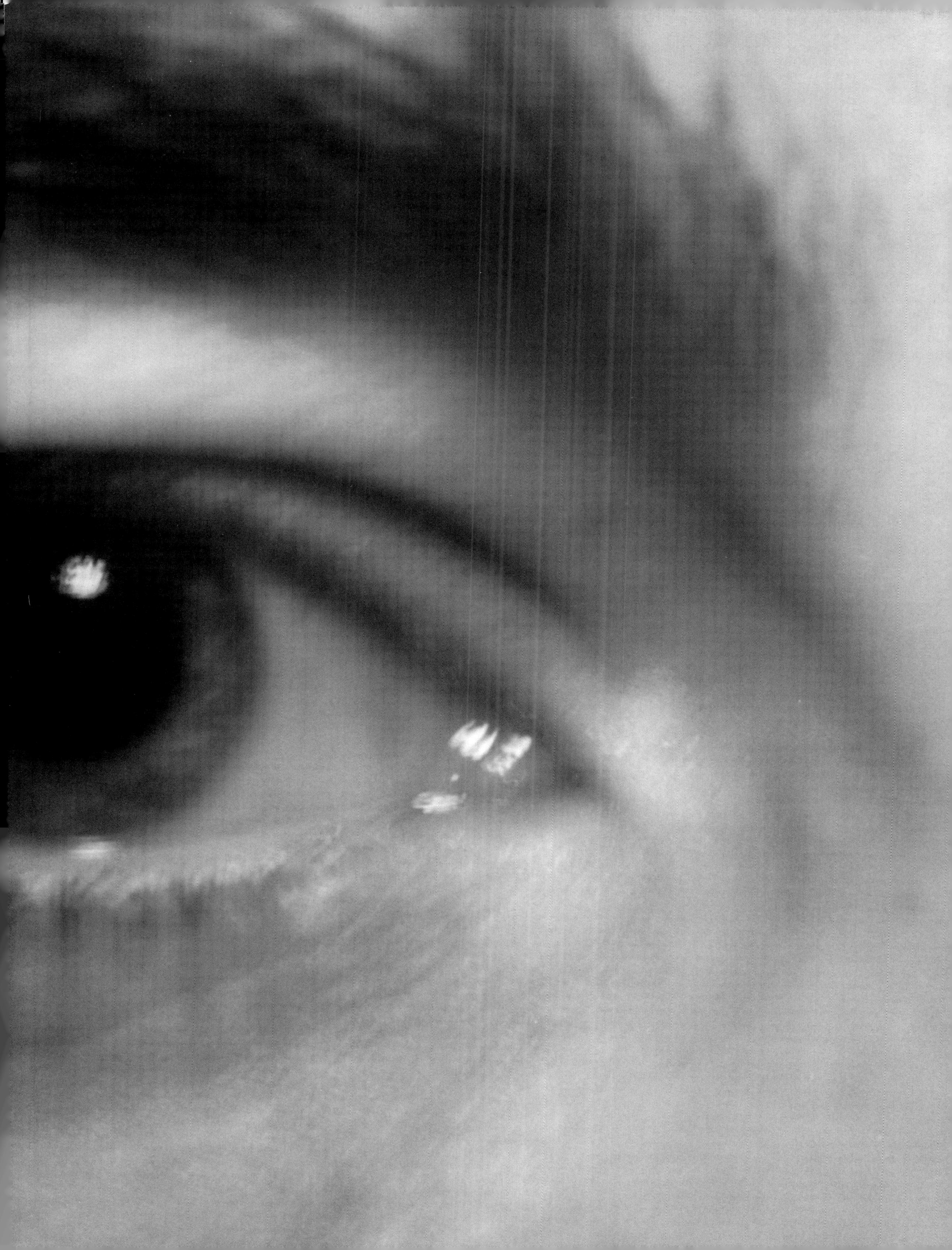

ACKNOWLEDGMENTS

Jacob Lehman and Tommy Manzi, for their help with the whole project
Debbie, for always supporting
China Miéville, for graciously letting me purloin the title of his novel

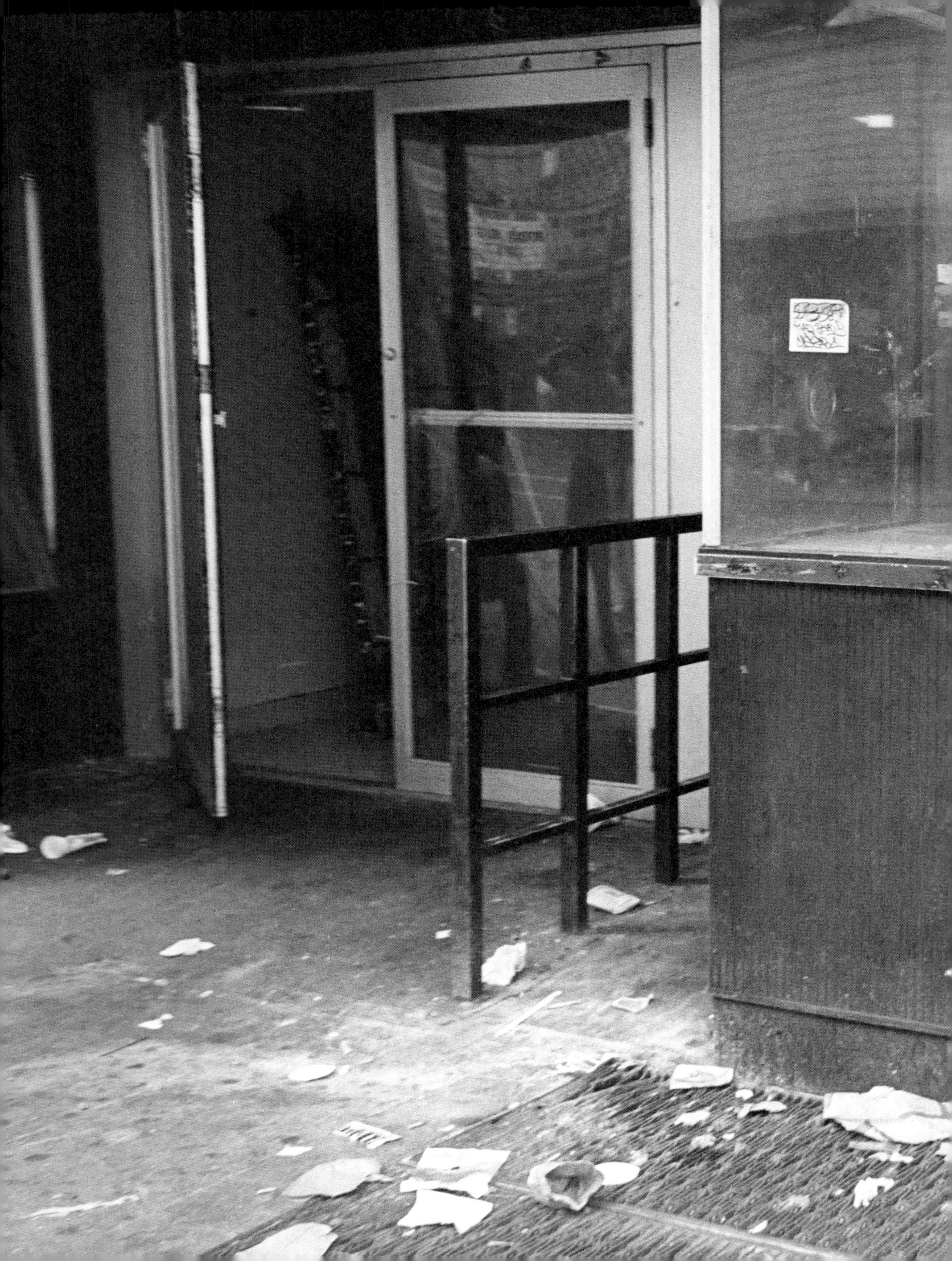